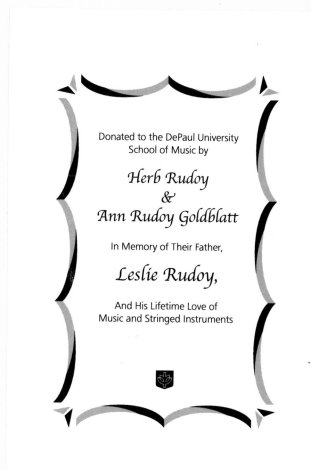

Donated to the DePaul University
School of Music by

Herb Rudoy
&
Ann Rudoy Goldblatt

In Memory of Their Father,

Leslie Rudoy,

And His Lifetime Love of
Music and Stringed Instruments

Paganini

THE GENOESE

VOLUME ONE

Paganini

THE GENOESE

By G. I. C. de Courcy

VOLUME ONE

NORMAN : UNIVERSITY OF OKLAHOMA PRESS

The publication of this work has been aided by a grant from
THE FORD FOUNDATION

Library of Congress Catalog Card Number: 57-5953

To the memory of

MY MOTHER

PREFACE

Before we can hope to see clearly into the mystery of this man's art, we shall have to remove from our imagination all the preconceived notions that have been placed there by a couple of generations of gossips. —JEFFREY PULVER.

THE STORY of Niccolò Paganini's career has been told so often in the past hundred years that there would now seem to be very little left for anyone to say. Yet a critical glance at the material will show that the saga started in his lifetime and since reinforced by time and tradition has never, despite its obvious inconsistencies and exaggerations, been tested in the fires of scholarly research, even in his native land. One was content to accept the legend and hesitated to embark on a voyage of exploration that might end in disillusionment. In consequence, the chronicle of his life, as it has come down to us, is so filled with faulty inferences, undocumented assertions, downright inventions, obscure anecdotes and travelers' tales that no single version can be accepted as authoritative. Even his personal correspondence has been often misinterpreted through ignorance or preconceived opinions founded, in the majority of cases, on hypotheses or the flimsiest of evidence.

Until the appearance of Professor Arturo Codignola's monumental work *Paganini Intimo,* wherein he edited 287 letters from the period 1817–40 (that is, from Paganini's middle years up to his death), it was extremely difficult to arrive at a clear picture of his nonprofessional life. But with the publication of this large collection, now expanded by numerous other hitherto unpublished letters extending back to 1813—one of the turning points of his career —it has been possible to fill in practically all the gaps and shatter many of the familiar myths. For in the effort to scrape the legend clean of its romantic accretions and remove serious misconceptions many of the old favorites had perforce to go, not only those launched by rivals or idol-worshipers, but even many deliberately propagated by himself.

In carrying out this task I have not attempted to appraise Paganini's influence on the world of music, preferring to leave this to the competence of the musical historian since it is impossible to assess his place in the history of violin playing and at the same time present a full-scale narrative of his life, which contained so much that was unfortunate, depressing, even tragic, so much frequently disassociated from his gifts or from the freaks and oddities of his private conduct, to which many of his afflictions have been attributed as the punishment of an avenging god. For this reason I have chosen a strictly biographical approach, hoping that by ridding his life story of spurious romantic elements, it would be easier to arrive at an understanding of his temperament, the causes of his deep-grained melancholy, his ever-increasing sadness, the depression and gloom that were attendant on his life and indisputably contributed to the widespread misconception of his character and actions. Needless to say, the leading incidents—the salient points of his career—have been restricted to those supported by contemporary documents or the testimony of recognized authorities. No important assertion has been made without careful documentation, no hypothesis advanced but what seems to be rooted in incontrovertible fact.

Whilst the possession of such amazing gifts, together with his meteor-like course through Europe at the meridian of his life as a "virtuoso in excelsis," undeniably contained the stuff of romance, he dissipated so many of his best years by frittering away his talents that his career, viewed as a whole, was by no means so romantic as that of Liszt, who shares virtuoso honors with him. It was neither so consistently glamorous, nor was it so continuously progressive, so purposively upward striving. Although his phenomenal technique was the product of independent thought and not the fruit of the long and thorough curriculum of a school, once he had attained the desired technical proficiency, the hitherto unprecedented peak, he rested there. There was the inevitable ripening of the emotional, the spiritual, the self-critical that comes with the experience of life. But there were no longer any of those exciting forays into fresh fields that lead to new discoveries, to the opening of wider territories, to the broadening of the artistic point of view. His youthful passion for experiment was over; life—artistic as well as personal—settled into a fixed pattern, and long stretches of it, frequently dominated by a sort of inner laziness (like many persons of great natural gifts he was constitutionally indolent), were un-equivocally arid and humdrum—a fact that becomes increasingly apparent as the story unrolls, but one that has always been over-looked, part through hero-worshiping portraiture—the natural in-clination of his countrymen to eulogize him—and part through the absence of any information regarding his friendships, his associates, and patrons in the early formative years.

His temperamental disequilibrium at times cannot be charged entirely to his ill-health; a good part of it was the product of the age to which he was born, while his sins were also those of the sensual male of his period and often far less scarlet than those of his denigrators—all excused and abundantly pardoned by his patience and courage vis-à-vis his long physical Calvary and the relentless persecution to which, outside Italy, he was constantly exposed. For even though he was primarily the architect of the illnesses that ended his career, he possessed, and to a supreme degree, the saintly capacity for resignation, which was Fate's form of compensation. Had he enjoyed the abundant health of his colleague Rossini, or had his boyhood and adolescence been passed, like that of Liszt, in the cultivated and competitive world of Paris, he might have been a composer in the greater creative sense. But as one reads of the numerous odds against him, of the milieu into which he drifted during his years of vagabondage, it is easy to understand how his first major work, the Twenty-four Capricci, remained his finest creative achievement. For from 1809 onward his compositions all carried the same pennon. From that time there was manifestly no great interest in the intricate craft of the composer. When urged to write, it was obviously to add new interest to his programs, to fol-low the pattern of past successes, or from the practical angle *pro-durre dei capitale,* one of the increasing engrossments of his life. Thus we find no transition in his style, no wandering from the early creative paths that material success had fully justified.

Although the mere accumulation of biographical material ordi-narily contributes very little to a portrait, in Paganini's case it has the very opposite effect, since the conventional conception was a largely spurious one, like the vast and shocking allegations laid to him. Hence, by linking together hitherto disconnected details, by reconciling traditional interpretations with the latest research, by amplifying the portrait of the man, accounting for his time, one gains a picture radically different from the familiar legend, and sees behind the glittering façade a tragic human fate, a man inwardly at war with destiny; which makes it possible to study his music in the atmosphere of the background from which he sprang, and to set off his human frailties against his outstandingly fine qualities so that in the end he emerges from this process of demythicization infinitely more inspiring than the gravely distorted figure associated with his legend. Needless to say, knowledge of his life and movements after he left Italy in 1828 is much more complete and reliable than is the information concerning his earlier years. Like Jean Anouilh's *L'Homme sans bagages,* he had "successfully forgotten his past" and was adamant in his refusal to reinvoke it. Yet, notwithstanding, sufficient details have now been brought to light to draw up a chronology that, despite some patches of arid territory, still outlines the years of early manhood close enough to follow through this period the general course of his career.

The present task could never have been carried to its present conclusion without the help of scores of willing coadjutors, each of whom deserves special commendation for helping to unravel some particularly persistent knot. My deepest gratitude is due the following people for their invaluable assistance in carrying out such research: Dr. Hayes, of the National Library of Ireland, and John Bebbington, of the Belfast Library, whose heroic sacrifice of time and labor enabled me to put Ireland on the Paganini map; the Mitchell Library, Glasgow; Count Antonio Saffi, London; Paul Lefranc, Valenciennes, for clarifying a long-established misconception; the Municipal Archives, Nice; Dr. Rasp, Hessian Landesbibliothek, Darmstadt; Dr. Erich Müller von Asow and Margarethe Wiemer, Berlin, for their tireless efforts in assembling much valuable material; the Municipal Library, Strasbourg; Christian Nebehay Company and the Gesellschaft der Musikfreunde, Vienna; Robert Muelher, for his expert research in various Vienna archives; Dr. Herbert Stubenrauch, Mannheim; Dr. Richard Mönnig, of Inter Nationes, Bonn; Christiane Engelbrecht, Marburg;

Dr. Wolfgang Schmieder, of the Frankfort Library, for clarifying several ambiguities in the Paganini epic; Dr. Günter Henle and staff, Duisburg and Munich; Arturo Codignola and Menotti Lungonelli, Genoa; Dr. Gugliermo Tixi, for permitting publication of the rare Germi portrait; Professor Pietro Berri, Rapallo; Dr. Nicola Scafati, Naples, for her expert and painstaking research in the Municipal Archives; Professor Silvio Rutteri, Dr. Guido Devescovi and the Biblioteca Civica, Trieste; Biblioteca Nazionale, Turin; Biblioteca Labronica, Leghorn; Dr. Jan Kraspecenak, for invaluable assistance in translating the Polish material placed at my disposition by the Cultural Attaché of the Polish Embassy, Washington, D. C.; Henry Werro, of Berne, for permitting publication of his Patten portrait, and Dr. Gertrude Adolf Altenburg, of Milan, for the portrait of Helene von Dobeneck.

I am also indebted to the Royal Academy of Music, the Public Records Office, and St. Bartholomew's Hospital, London; Clifford Musgrave, Brighton; Professor Newman and Jean Allen, Reid School of Music, Edinburgh; American Library, Paris; Mme Renée Masson and Georges Migot, of the Paris Conservatoire; Jean Délannoy, Amiens; Landesbibliothek, Duesseldorf; the late Professor Gézà Revesz, of the University of Amsterdam; Saechsische Landesbibliothek, Dresden; Wissenschaftliche Oeffentliche Bibliothek, Berlin; Mme Renata Puteani, the State Archives, and Professor Novack (Albertina), Vienna; Niedersaechsische Landesbibliothek, Hanover; Biblioteca Comunale Ariostia, Ferrara; Biblioteca Nazionale and State Archives, Florence; Biblioteca, Forli; Biblioteca Musicale S. Cecilia, Rome; Count Emilio Nasalli-Rocca, Piacenza; Professor Juan Manen, Barcelona; G. B. Boero, Genoa; the Cultural Attaché of the Polish Embassy, Washington, D. C.; State Archives, Venice; Carnegie Library, Pittsburgh; Dorothea Turner, Auckland, New Zealand; and Mr. A. Rizo-Rangabé, of London.

I am most grateful to the following public libraries: Reading, Dundee, Durham, Aberdeen, Ayr, Bath, Barrow-in-Furness, Berwick upon Tweed, Birmingham, Bradford, Canterbury, Carlisle, Cheltenham, Buxton, Exeter, Macclesfield, Gloucester, Liverpool (Phyllis Drey), Leamington, Leeds, York, Bodleian Library, Oxford; Norwich, Rouen, Boulogne sur Mer; Brussels, Evreux, Douai,

Marseilles, Havre, Lille, Karlsruhe, Cologne, Marburg, Gotha, Dessau, Aschaffenburg, Braunschweig Halle, State Archives in Bremen and Hamburg, Celle, Coburg, Elberfeld, Bad Ems, Erfurt, State Archives in Mainz, Leipzig, Rimini, Palermo, Parma, Bologna, Imola; and to the staffs of the music division of the Library of Congress, the New York Public Library, and Harvard Library.

In addition to the above, many others have contributed some helpful suggestion or valuable hint that has led to unexpected information, and to these also—far too numerous to mention—my sincerest acknowledgments are due. Finally, I would like to associate the work with Mr. Max Pfeffer, of New York, to whom it indirectly owes its inception.

Geraldine de Courcy

New York
March 17, 1957

CONTENTS OF VOLUME I

ILLUSTRATIONS IN VOLUME I

PART ONE

Prime

E fatto singolar da l'altra gente.—PETRARCH

NICCOLÒ PAGANINI passed his boyhood and youth in one of the most turbulent periods of modern history, as well as one of the richest in great personalities. According to the accounts that have come down to us, he would seem to have been indifferent to the political and social turmoils and passions of his epoch, absorbed solely and entirely in his art. But in reality this was far from true. Leaving out of consideration that a man cannot live wholly detached from his times, we are obliged to confess that very few figures are so expressive of their age as the Ligurian artist. One must only take care not to be led astray by appearances, which to the superficial observer reveal very few inner dichotomies. Let him look behind the mask and he will see that all the specious imperturbability cloaked a life agitated by the most violent contrasts—the index of a spirit not only exuberantly rich but emotional to an exceptional degree.

Humble and proud; ingenuous and sarcastic; prodigal and avaricious; pliant and obtuse; broad-minded and believing; callous and sensitive; meticulously precise and impenitently disorderly; the prototype, in short, of the man whom Machiavelli described as a *sacco di contradizzioni*. Extraordinary vices and *virtù*, which in such a strange temperament and in the high noon of Romanticism were nothing other than the expression of a potent vitality in the rough, concealed in a reserved character—so typical of the Ligurian race—which revealed itself only in violent spurts, making him one of the most complex personalities in our modern history.

—ARTURO CODIGNOLA.

I. CHILDHOOD AND ANCESTRY 1782–1795

Wir sprechen von unseren Herzen, unseren Plänen, als wären sie unser, und es ist doch eine fremde Gewalt, die uns herumwirft, und ins Grab legt, wie es ihr gefällt, und von der wir nicht wissen, von wannen sie kommt, noch wohin sie geht. —HÖLDERLIN.

RISING ON THE LOWER HILLS of the Ligurian Alps like a great amphitheatre suspended between the violent blue of sea and sky, Genoa, with its crescent coast line and encircling hills, has been known for centuries as the Paradise of Italy. Here in a scene of matchless beauty, the astute, intrepid Genoese—despite Dante's blistering arraignment—had steered their course with honor through some two hundred years of little wars and had even enjoyed a few decades of comparative tranquillity till, as the eighteenth century was closing in, imperialistic neighbors to the west and east swept over their garlanded coasts and turned them for a time into the battlefield of Europe, which was to leave an ineradicable mark on all those born, or who came to manhood, under the restless, conflicting influences of the "new Charlemagne."

On a Sunday night—October 27, 1782—before these fateful events were yet plotted in the stars, a male child was born to two humble Genoese, Antonio and Teresa Paganini, in the sign of the Scorpion.[1] And early next day—lest things go ill—the frail, velvet-eyed baby was borne to his christening in the Church of S. Croce e del SS. Salvatore nearby, where, in the sacrament of holy baptism, his godparents, Nicolao Caruta and his spouse Columba Maria Ferramolla,[2] safely enrolled him in the ranks of the Church Militant with the name of Niccolò.[3]

[1] The heavens at the moment of Paganini's birth bore the following aspect: Sun: Scorpio 4° 12″; Moon: Cancer 12° 21″; Saturn: Sagittarius 27° 28″; Jupiter: Sagittarius 26° 30″; Mars: Libra 12° 20″; Mercury: Scorpio 27° 37″; Uranus: Cancer 7° 3″; Neptune: Libra 8° 7″; Pluto: Aquarius 6° 5″; Moon's Node: Aries 5° 31″. I am indebted to Mr. Martin Harvey, of São Paulo, Brazil, for this interesting data.

[2] Paganini's baptismal certificate (No. 225, p. 213 of the parish register for 1782), with other records were destroyed by Allied action during World War II. Facsimile reproduced in Conestabile-Mompellio, p. 32.

[3] Paganini sometimes signed his name Niccolò, again Nicolò, and even Nicola, all according to his mood.

3

Had anyone suspected the historical importance of this little routine ceremony and had ventured to cast the horoscope of this tiny human pilgrim, they might have plausibly foretold the Scorpionic urge towards sensuality that later worked such havoc in his life. For to those with knowledge of these mysterious influences in the lives of men the heavens charted for career as well as destiny a pattern of contraries: genius offset by lifelong martyrdom; fame bestowed and domestic happiness withheld; material wealth paired with emotional frustration; the will to conquer obstacles, the courage to endure. The fairy and the wicked godmother were both present at this christening, the Caesarian largess of the one ever counterbalanced by the unregenerate leaven of the other.

As it was evidently the Genoese custom to christen children three days after birth—a procedure followed with the rest of the Paganini brood—this ceremony a few hours after birth would suggest that there must have been grave fears that the child's earthly hours were numbered. Indeed, there would seem to have been such haste to save this fluttering little soul from the limbo of unbaptized babies that his parents had no time to decide upon a name but quickly chose that of his godfather—surely a justifiable conjecture since, so far as can be learned, there was no precedent in the Paganini family for the choice of "Niccolò."

Paganini has frequently been accused of fraudulence, of deliberately misleading the world regarding his birth date, but considering all the circumstances he may never have known exactly when he was born, except that he arrived on the vigil of a saint's day, a point that his pious mother would not have failed to emphasize. To Peter Lichtenthal he said that he "was born on the eve of St. Simeon's Day (*sic*), 1784."[4] Schottky, writing for a German public unaccustomed to the religious designation, evidently consulted a church calendar and, finding that "St. Simeon's Day" fell in February, supplied the more explicit date.[5] It is not likely that Paganini furnished this information, else he would have given it to Lichtenthal; so to this extent at least he should not be held accountable

4 *"Nato a Genova nella notte di S. Simeone del 1784."* Peter Lichtenthal (1780–1853) was a Hungarian composer and musicologist, who settled in Milan in 1810.

5 *"Ich wurde im Februar 1784 zu Genua geboren."* The "18th" was added later by a more knowledgeable biographer. Here, the "17th" would, of course, have been more correct.

4

for an error that simple inductive reasoning attributes to the faulty orthography of Lichtenthal or the original German compositor.[6]

As for the year, in later life, like all Don Juans, he was a little sensitive about his age and, like all artists, prone to deduct a year or two when publicity demanded it, though, since in Latin countries name days take precedence over birthdays, the latter may never have been fixed in his memory during childhood by the usual family celebrations.[7] In 1809 the census of the parish of San Frediano in Lucca gave his age as "circa twenty-five," showing that even at that early date he had already settled on 1784 (which would account for Gervasoni's date); yet a decade later, when he required his baptismal certificate, he informed his lawyer that he "was born round 1780 or thereabouts."[8] Which reveals that by then he knew that he was older than he claimed to be. However, whatever his motive for selecting this particular year, his hagiography at any rate was scrupulously correct since he invariably stated that he "was born on the eve of a saint's day," the Feast of *St. Simon* and St. Jude, one of the Church's major holy days, falling on October 28. As can be plainly seen, here the real culprit was indubitably some printer's wayward imp![9]

ii

In the beginning, the family seems to have been a little unsettled, and moved—according to the parish register—at least three times within as many years. In 1780 they resided in the Vico Dighieri, in 1781, in the Vico Citadella, and from 1782 onward, in a three-roomed dwelling on the seventh story of the "Casa di Picassino"[10]

6 Lichtenthal's autobiographical sketch appeared some months previous to Schottky's work.

7 Paganini was even ignorant of the birth date of his son. When required to furnish this information, he had to refer his lawyer to Achilles' sponsor in Palermo, who "was the only person who could say" when he was born.

8 He was still of this opinion in 1830. He wrote Germi at that time that he "prayed that his mother would be spared him for another 50 years."

9 The following is a contemporary parallel: In 1878 a Dr. Tagliapietra published a series of articles in the Trieste paper *L'Arte,* which he entitled "Memories of a Contemporary." As subtitle of the first installment, he quoted the "Memoirs of J. C. Zobe of Weimar," meaning, of course, Johann Christian *Lobe.* These articles are quoted in all recent Italian biographical works and the information contained therein attributed to "Zobe"!

10 Whether at that time an apartment on the top floor indicated exclusiveness and a large bank roll, or the exact reverse, is not known.

(from the owner Tomaso Picasso), located at 1359 Vico delle Fosse del Colle, now 38 Passo di Gattamora, one of the narrow lanes in the old quarter of the city lying on the slopes of the hill of Sant'-Andrea,[11] on which rises the Cathedral of San Lorenzo.

These old alleys, or *carrughi,* as they are locally known, constituted in the Middle Ages the main arteries of the city, many of them so narrow that in the settling processes of time some of the buildings have so far tilted from the perpendicular that from the upper stories one can almost grasp hands across the street—an *"immense labyrinthe en pierre* [in de Maupassant's description], *percé de corridors, pareils à des souterrains, entre des murailles si hautes que l'on voit à peine le ciel";* though in Paganini's day, no doubt, the quarter was probably less congested, less squalid, more comfortably middle class. While the modern city is now rapidly encroaching on these older sections, with their swarms of children, cats, and chattering crowds, the slender stone house in which Niccolò was born, situated at the foot of a steep *scalita* not far from the Columbus House in the Vico Dritto Ponticello, is still standing, with very likely the same paving stones before the door on which he, his sisters, and his brother Carlo romped when they were children.

The façade, like that of the two adjoining buildings, is of a pale pink color, perhaps constructed of that baked earth employed in Italy from very early times as building material (particularly for frontages of houses), which weathers into a light rose color known as baked rose attar. To set it still more apart from its prosaic neighbors, the former owner, after the death in 1783 of some member of the family, adorned the house front with a little Madonna set in a framework of stucco fruit and flowers and flanked by three memorial tablets that promise "two hundred days indulgence" to all who pause before the shrine "to recite a litany."[12] Eleven decades later, in October, 1892, the city fathers added another tablet, this time to a reputedly unregenerate sinner.[13] Asking no prayers in rich ecclesiastical Latin, this one reminds the passer-by—in the vernacular—that "in this humble spot, Niccolò Paganini, insuper-

---

11 Known in Genoese as the *Cheullia.* The Passa di Gattamora is near the ancient Porta Soprana.

12 Over the door is the invocation: *I.H.S. Salutem ex inimicis nostris.*

able master of the divine art of music, was born to adorn Genoa and delight the world." And the claim is not too high. Although it took his native city fifty years to offer this belated tribute to his memory, the gesture has been consecrated by the host of pilgrims the tablet has since attracted to this spot—each and all perhaps more capable than preceding generations of appreciating what Paganini really meant to the development of music, and of seeing his character and work in their true historical perspective.

iii

Strange to say, none of his biographers ever attempted to trace his pedigree. Indeed, even he seems to have evinced no curiosity about his ancestors. It was simply taken for granted that he sprang from humble origins and it seemed well to leave things as they were, since an obscure lineage added another dash of romance to the saga. Schottky, with characteristic German thoroughness, apparently tried to draw him out by calling attention to an epitaph in the Church of St. Anne in Capua (mentioned in Keysler's "Travels through Germany, France and Italy") which commemorated the attainments of a distinguished namesake; but Paganini, "who was able to contribute very little information regarding his progenitors," was equally ignorant with respect to this eminent rhetorician, though he frankly doubted whether he was in any way related to him.

On the centenary of his death, in 1940 the National Paganini Committee finally awoke to the importance and interest of the question and requested G. B. Boero, who had performed a similar office for the Mazzini and Drago families, to undertake the necessary research—a tremendous task in view of the great frequency of the name and the absence of any tangible clues. Boero does not reveal the surely interesting steps that led him to the little hill town of Carro, in eastern Liguria, where a number of Paganinis had

---

13   *Alta ventura sortita ad umile luogo*
          In questa casa
    Il giorno XXVII di Ottobre dell'anno MDCCLXXXII
    A decoro di Genova, a delizia del mondo
        Niccolò Paganini.
    Nella divina arte dei suoni insuperato maestro.
          —Anton Giulio Barrili (1836–1908).

their family roots, but it was here that he at last found the missing link that enabled him to trace Niccolò's ancestry back at least to the commencement of the eighteenth century.

The little hamlet, which then belonged to the province of Genoa (at present, to La Spezia), is situated about eighteen miles to the northeast of Sestri Levante and even now has a population of only fifteen hundred, so that it will be sought in vain on any map. In the old fourteenth-century church the parochial records stretch back almost uninterruptedly to 1600, the recurrence of the same names over and over again indicating a sturdy race rooted deep in this little spot of earth through all the vicissitudes of the Renaissance and succeeding centuries. Among them the Paganinis were especially numerous, all no doubt originally stemming from a common ancestor, though frequent intermarriage, the passage of time, indifference, and the preoccupations of existence contrived as usual to loosen the ties so that it is now impossible to trace a connection between the several branches. Of simple peasant stock, they formed "part and parcel of that gray and passive subsoil of humanity whence great orchids" like Niccolò Paganini "draw their substance." But he was by no means the first to bring honor to the name. Although no Carro Paganini seems to have been a musician by vocation, there were still many who pursued an intellectual occupation and showed a high degree of learning and attainment,[14] several having risen to prominent and influential positions in the church. From one of the branches sprang Paganini's paternal grandfather, Giovanni Battista Paganini (b. 1720), the fourth of five children, who at some unrecorded date, probably in very early manhood, left Carro and settled in Genoa, where on April 29, 1745, he married Maria Angela Teresa Gambaro, a native of Montesignano in the province of Genoa and took up his residence in the Vico dei Parmigiani, as shown by the records of the parish of San Stefano for 1746. Two sons were born of this marriage: Giovanni Francesco Maria (b. 1750), who evidently did not survive his child-

[14] One Carro Paganini was Protonotary Apostolic and Canon of the Church of San Donato in Genoa. Another (Lorenzo) was the first rector of the Church of San Lorenzo in Carro, where he was succeeded by Giovanni Paganini. The last parish priest of that name in Carro was Orazio Paganini, who served in this capacity from 1794 to 1819, while another priest, Giovanni Batti Paganini (likewise from Carro), was known for his extensive charities.

hood since his name does not appear in the parish register for 1761, and Paganini's father, Francesco Antonio Maria (b. 1754), both of whom were baptized in the Church of San Stefano, where their parents were married. After his mother's death in 1791 it fell to Antonio, as only surviving son, to care for his aged father, who from that time on till his death in 1799, at the ripe old age of seventy-nine, lived with his son's family. On April 25, 1777, Antonio, then a young man of twenty-three, married Teresa (b. 1760), the daughter of Giovanni Bocciardo of Genoa, in the Church of Nuestra Signora della Grazie, and six children were born to them, one regularly every two years:

> Carlo (Jan. 21, 1778–October 15, 1830)
> Biagio (May 21, 1780–April 28, 1781)
> Niccolò (October 27, 1782–May 27, 1840)
> Angela (May 31, 1781–February 13, 1786)
> Nicoletta (August 10, 1786–?)
> Domenica (1788–?)[15]

We possess no information about the maternal side of the family beyond the fact that Teresa had at least two brothers, Paolo and Antonio, and if her husband spoke the truth in his will (which was questioned later) she brought him "a dowry of 2,200 lire," a not inconsiderable sum in those days. We also know that she was very pious, loved music—"a musical amateur," as her son phrased it— and could not write, a fairly usual circumstance for a woman of her station in a country and an age with an uncommonly high percentage of illiteracy.[16]

In after years Paganini was ashamed of this little maternal blemish, but from all accounts Teresa was far from being an exception, even in the highest circles.[17] When Napoleon's sister, Elise Baciocchi, began the reorganization of the cultural life of Lucca, one of the first things she did was to open schools for young women of

---

[15] Although both parents were still young at the time of Domenica's birth (Antonio 35, Teresa 28), she remained the baby of the family.

[16] At the time of the plebiscite in Lucca in 1805, out of 29,164 voters, more than half were unable to write. (Fleuriot de Langle, *Elisa, Soeur de Napoléon I*, 41.)

[17] The education of women in those days was entrusted solely to the Religious, so that it was not rare to find some marrying into the most noble families, yet still not knowing how to write.

noble or aristocratic birth, "very few of whom were able to write." And when the French occupied Genoa in 1800, one of the many obstacles towards a rapid and efficient reorganization of the government was the fact that only a very small percentage of the officials required for military, fiscal, and administrative posts could write, as testified by numerous French diplomatic documents of the period. Literacy was certainly not widespread, so that Antonio's proficiency in this respect, as shown by a document dating from 1803 giving him power of attorney "to institute certain legal suits and claims" for the wealthy Rebizzo family, compares favorably with the endowments of the candidates for civic and governmental positions, who unquestionably ranked higher in the social scale than he.[18]

In his first autobiographical sketch, which is no doubt the more accurate of the two since the second is filtered through Schottky's elaborate and allusive literary style, Paganini spoke of both parents as "musical amateurs," which would indicate that his mother also sang or played some instrument. For he would hardly have so described her had she been merely fond of music. Further, she must have approved of music as a means of livelihood since from her son's testimony she was able to invoke divine assistance to promote her ambitions for her baby Niccolò.[19] "Nevertheless [wrote Codignola] undue importance should not be attributed to the fact that music was cultivated by at least three members of the family, even though it should not be entirely ignored. For a person only moderately conversant with the history of Genoa knows that at the close of the eighteenth century the city was signalized by a vigorous flowering of musicians and that music played a very important role in the life of the community."[20] Hence, a family in which the talent manifested itself slipped easily and automatically into the groove.[21]

Whatever the real extent of Teresa's musical capacities or intellectual deficiencies, she was a very devoted mother, sacrificing her-

18 Arturo Codignola, *Paganini intimo*, 26; Dossier 612, document in the State Archives, Genoa.

19 In the Lichtenthal sketch, Paganini said that "the Saviour" appeared to his mother in a dream. In the Schottky version, it was "her guardian angel."

20 Codignola, *op. cit.*, 10.

21 In *La Musica a Genova* (Genova, 1951), Remo Giazotto writes that from 1584 to 1700 the city fathers would call on the city's instrumentalists to furnish the music for the great religious festivals. Music was an important factor in the life of the city.

self completely to her children and their interests, a quality that in Niccolò's case at least was fully appreciated and repaid with a tender love and solicitude that ended only with her life. In turn she never failed him in affection and in 1822–23, when he needed care, encouragement, and a perhaps restraining hand, she left her comfortable home in Genoa and the familiar objects of her daily life to follow him to Milan and Pavia, where she remained for seven months in the far less agreeable surroundings of the modest inns and lodginghouses that he patronized by predilection. She could never have had an easy existence, particularly in the early years of marriage—living on the top story of the house, trudging up and down six flights in the black well of the stairs, bearing, nursing, rearing, and losing children in cramped quarters when material conveniences and hygienic conditions were in a very primitive stage, quite apart from the restrictions and limitations imposed by the unsettled state of the country. After Antonio's death, things fortunately improved since Niccolò, now "rich and independent," did all he could to make her "happy and contented," giving her a regular income adequate for her needs and an "apartment for herself with all modern comforts and conveniences."

iv

There has always been considerable conjecture regarding Antonio's occupation, owing to Paganini's hazy statements on the subject. He told Schottky that his father was a "not very prosperous tradesman," but in the municipal records and census prior to 1785, according to Codignola, he was listed as a *ligaballe,* that is, a workman on the docks in the Porto Franco who packed the bales for shipment on merchant vessels. Perhaps his own father had a ship's chandlery and Antonio took over the business when the old man grew too old to work, operating it along with his other duties on the dock as long as it was feasible,[22] since in those days, "due partly to a fossilized system of guilds and fraternities, every working man was forced by law to follow the occupation of his father and grandfather before him."[23] "The steward or butcher [wrote Carlo Tiva-

[22] Conestabile wrote that Antonio was a "ship's broker" (Conestabile-Mompellio. p. 33), probably a conjecture.
[23] Archibald Colquhoun, *Manzoni and his Times,* 4.

roni] who tried to make his children study would have been guilty
of a crime against society."[24] At the end of 1794 the long-threatened
British blockade of the port of Genoa finally went into effect, and
the following April (1795) the French invaded the territory of the
Republic and for two years occupied practically half of Liguria.
Thus, caught between two warring forces, Genoa went with the
French, with the result that in June, 1797, Napoleon decreed the
end of the aristocratic government and organized a new one on the
democratic French pattern. These military operations, added to
the continuing blockade and the general unrest throughout the
entire territory, naturally brought maritime commerce to a standstill,[25] so that Antonio, whether longshoreman or ship's chandler,
had, by force of circumstances, to seek other means of livelihood.
This undoubtedly accounts for the fact that in 1798 the parish register described him as a "player," and the Napoleonic census, as a
teneur d'amandolines,[26] indicating that he was now pursuing
music professionally and selling mandolins. He then seems to have
followed this double occupation till after the siege of 1800, when
like numerous other workmen on the docks he presumably transferred his activities to Leghorn, only returning to Genoa when
conditions became more settled and maritime commerce there was
again resumed.

v

There does not seem to have been any very strong bond of affection
between Antonio and his gifted son, a circumstance that history—
again solely on Paganini's testimony—has attributed to Antonio's
severity. But beyond Schottky's free rendering of Paganini's alleged statements on the subject, we know nothing of the actual
relationship between the two since no early letters have survived
and Paganini, with this one exception, was always silent on the
subject. His attitude would seem to have been for the most part
frigidly dutiful, his heart turning more to his mother since he was
evidently a pale and fragile child and she very likely coddled him
for fear of losing him. In the Lichtenthal sketch he did not men-

24 Tivaroni, *L'Italie prima della rivoluzione francese,* quoted by Colquhoun.
25 See Calvini, *Il Porto di Genova* (Genoa, 1953).
26 Codignola, *op. cit.,* 25.

12

tion his father's harshness, but ten months later, after four months in Vienna, he told Schottky that as a child he "had his violin in his hand from morn till night. . . . It would be hard indeed to conceive of a stricter father; if he didn't think I was industrious enough, he compelled me to redouble my efforts by making me go without food so that I had to endure a great deal physically."[27]

Codignola questions the truth of these assertions and attributes them to Paganini's romantic urge to create a dramatic effect. It is, of course, not at all implausible that here, with his innate mimicry, he was playing the sedulous ape to Beethoven and deliberately fabricating a picture of his childhood that in the eyes of later generations would place him in the company of his idol. For he was extraordinarily receptive to suggestions, even his most quoted mots being all derivative and easily traceable to their original sources. We know from his own words and contemporary testimony that, like Berlioz, he too "put Beethoven at the summit of his musical Olympus."[28] Hardly a day passed, we are told, that he "did not play some work of Beethoven's," while the programs of all his important concerts—particularly his first appearances abroad, on which so much depended—almost invariably opened with a Beethoven work, as though he were invoking the spirit of his great colleague. In Vienna a year after Beethoven's death, he must have had many opportunities of discussing him with former associates and of hearing that his "father had been a pitiless tyrant, the boy a victim and a slave . . . compelled to unremitted application through fear, or the actual infliction, of punishment for neglect on the part of his harsh and unjust parent, his father keeping him at his studies with inflexible severity."[29]

With the exception of his statements quoted by Lichtenthal and Schottky, Paganini never alluded to his father in any communication that has come down to us. Even before Antonio's death, his

27 Schottky, *op. cit.*, 250.

28 Jacques Barzun, *Berlioz and the Romantic Century*, I, 152.

29 Compare Beethoven's "music became my first youthful pursuit in my fourth year" and Paganini's "I was enthusiastic about my instrument and studied it unceasingly." Thayer wrote: "Johann van Beethoven's main object was the earliest and greatest development of his son's musical genius so as to make it a marketable commodity. . . . Urged forward by his father's severity, by his tender love for his mother, and by the awakening of his own tastes, the development of his skill and talents was rapid." A. W. Thayer, *Life of Beethoven*, I, 58–59.

13

letters to different members of the family contained no affectionate messages, no inquiries about him, no evidence of any filial bond. Nor did his father's death seem to touch him personally. With his meditative cast of mind, did his thoughts never dwell with the person who had recognized his gifts and spared no effort to develop them? It would seem not. The history of music contains a long scroll of those who during childhood and adolescence had to contend with parental or material barriers to fight their way through to the foothills of Parnassus, so Niccolò's case in this respect was not unique. But, unlike practically all the others, he left us in later years no words of gratitude, no evidence of a sense of deep indebtedness. Antonio's "severity" had obviously left an ineradicable scar.

Given his natural reticence in all matters touching his personal feelings, the silence in itself is not surprising. But the fact that after going to Vienna he suddenly abandoned it in order to proclaim his wrongs and to stress and publish to the world his father's despotism and the tyrannical control to which he was subjected as a child makes one suspect that this unusual frankness was not entirely ingenuous. On the other hand, Antonio undoubtedly had a strong streak of peasant acquisitiveness and a laudable desire to better his position, which made him, like Beethoven's father, view his son's extraordinary talents "as a marketable commodity," as a stepping-stone to wealth more rapid and less risky than the gaming table. So, faced by two such powerful passions, it is not improbable that Paganini's picture of him as a *tiranno in casa* was fundamentally correct and that he was only brought to share this unpalatable memory with the world on hearing Beethoven's similar circumstances so openly discussed.

From Antonio's point of view he was the gifted one on whom the pride and hopes of the entire family were focused, the one who was to bring them the wealth that would satisfy their modest ideas of ease and allow them to indulge in those dreams of luxury that dwell in every human breast however restricted in their scope "by personal and inherited experience." Yet beyond this primary motive for Antonio's harshness it was quite usual in those days for Italian parents to hold their sons in leading strings till long after they had reached maturity. As Iris Origo wrote of Leopardi, a contemporary of Paganini's, the poet "was nearly twenty-one and had not only never left home alone, but had never possessed any money. His father had fed, clothed and educated him. . . . He was a *figlio di famiglia* and this implied that while the head of the family was still alive his sons must turn to him for all they might need. Even nowadays in some provincial families of the South this way of treating a grown-up son would not be odd."[30]

Since one of Paganini's most signal characteristics was his love of freedom, any restraint must have seemed to him far worse than imprisonment. The born nonconformist, all through life he fled from any kind of fetters, whether imposed by his parents, his masters, tradition, his profession, or a prospective wife, for to him "liberty was the best of all things." So, smarting under a yoke that he was powerless to throw off, he placed the whole responsibility for his frustration and unhappiness on his father and never really forgave him in his heart. While it was foreign to his nature to nurse rancor or vindictiveness, this wound still evidently went so deep that he was unable to forget it, his resentment being heightened by a fundamental lack of sympathy between the two.

Apart from this, Antonio was probably the normal father who unexpectedly finds himself the mentor and ward of a young prodigy. He obviously made every sacrifice to further Niccolò's musical education; had him taught by the best masters he could find and watched over him even to the point of deserting his family for several months at a critical period to accompany him to Parma. Of course, he may have failed to provide the affection and intuitive sympathy the lad's sensitive soul required and he may have held him in leash for a period longer than is natural; but other things aside, this too may not have been entirely unmotivated, for children on the shores of the Mediterranean reach adolescence early, and the supercharge of passion that later gave Niccolò's actions an explosive and incalculable quality must already have been clearly evident in childhood, or at any rate as soon as he began to express himself in music.

Codignola makes the point that Niccolò was his father's favorite, basing his theory on the fact that on his death, Antonio left the family in Niccolò's charge rather than in that of Carlo, the first born, as is usual in such cases. Yet this is hardly a criterion. In 1817,

[30] Iris Origo, *Leopardi*, 74.

Niccolò was the only active money-maker in the family and any father of two sons, one of whom was a failure from the worldly point of view and the other an equally brilliant success, would surely select the one considered as the firmest support of the family, even if there was no sympathy between them. Whatever Antonio's guiding impulse, Paganini carried out the charge generously, faithfully, and cheerfully to the day of his death, retaining a deep-rooted attachment to his family and a sense of duty to his kin, not only supporting his mother and his sisters with their shiftless husbands, but educating their children, caring for his widowed sister-in-law, and liberally helping the offspring of his mother's brothers, with whom he seems to have had small intimacy and less sympathy.

As for Antonio, he also might have nursed a secret ambition to be a musician rather than a tradesman, and the ship's chandlery may have been only an expedient which he relinquished without regret when the mechanism of fate forced him to change his occupation. Like the fathers of Liszt and Hugo Wolf, he may have looked on his son's gifts as the flowering of a personal ambition; and Teresa's vision of the heavenly messenger who left with her the promise that her curly-headed baby boy with his precocious gift of music would someday be a great violinist may also have been only a wish fulfillment, the sublimation of a common disappointment over Antonio's and her own inability to develop and give full expression to the music within them.

Paganini tells us that his father gave him his first lessons when he "was five and a half," in 1789–90 according to his reckoning, teaching him first the mandolin and two years later exchanging it for a little violin.[31] Antonio was probably teaching Carlo, a lad of eleven

[31] The mandolin and little violin used by Paganini as a boy were exhibited at the Turin Exposition in 1898, and in Cremona in 1937. (cf. *Revista Musicale Italiana*, Vol. IV [1898].) On May 15, 1933, the luthier Gaetano Sgarabotto identified the violin as a Hieronymus Amati of about 1672, though at the Paganini Exhibition in Genoa in 1953 it was listed as a Gasparo da Salo. The instrument is now in the possession of Paolo Paganini in Milan. The present location of the mandolin is not indicated. The fact that the violin has been certified as the work of one of Italy's great luthiers would indicate that Antonio's various business ventures, or the lottery, were more successful than his son imagined. At all events, Niccolò was not dependent on the generosity of "some itinerant rag-picker." (Theodore Valensi, *Niccolò Paganini*, 11, n. 3.) Achilles gave his father's guitar to Berlioz and it is now in the museum of the Paris Conservatoire, along with a *"violon muet"* that allegedly also belonged to Paganini, though the claim seems to be of dubious authenticity. Two more such in-

at the time, and baby Niccolò's manifest interest in the proceedings showed that he was the more highly gifted of the two, whereupon Antonio allowed him to share the lessons of his brother. In those days the Paganini apartment consisted of three small rooms occupied by three adults and four little children, so that the undisturbed quiet and solitude of a schoolroom were impossible, to say nothing of the turbulent atmosphere of the great world outside and Niccolò's frail constitution, all of which combined to make it difficult to follow Antonio's rigid daily routine. Paganini never spoke of his brother's musical instruction but he too must have had more advanced tuition than Antonio's rudimentary lessons, since he was able to make music his profession. His father, reported Niccolò, "was not without talent,"[32] though it was by no means equal to his love of music; yet his knowledge must have gone a little deeper than an ability to strum a mandolin since he was quick to recognize his younger son's definition of bent and to realize that this delicate and hypersensitive child was streaked with genius. Further, if Niccolò "wrote a sonata under his father's supervision," Antonio must also have known something about compositional technique, even if, in his famous son's opinion, his musical capacities by no means matched his passion for the art.

Paganini told Schottky that one of his father's coincident activities was playing the lottery and that he spent a good part of his time trying to work out winning combinations—an expenditure of effort that seems to have been as futile in Antonio's case as in that of others who stake their fortunes on the hazard table.[33] Yet though he spoke of gambling as his father's "principal passion," there was no note of censure in the comment. He was merely explaining how Antonio came to be at home so much and left the boys so little liberty; for gambling as a "passion" was then not one of the seven deadly sins. It was part of the pattern of the age, so it is by no means odd that Niccolò in time likewise fell a victim to its

struments exist for which the same claim is made: one in the possession of the Paganini heirs at Milan, the other the property of Henry Werro, Berne, Switzerland. It seems unlikely that Paganini ever possessed such an instrument. None is listed with his instruments either before or immediately after his death. It was obviously a tempting claim to make and after his death could naturally never be proved to be an imposture.

32 Schottky, *op. cit.*, 250.
33 *Ibid.*, 250.

fascination and admittedly sacrificed a hecatomb of hours to the gods of gambling.[34] Accustomed from early childhood to his father's preoccupation with various games of chance and then thrown later into a society that thought of little else, it would have been strange indeed if he had not ventured to exhibit his own prowess at the gaming table, particularly in the arid intervals between his transient love affairs. That he had sufficient will power to jettison the inclination before it settled into habit, when the shock of an impending catastrophe brought him to his senses, shows a force of character unusual at his age, and was not unlike the experience of Richard Wagner, who had similar inclinations in his callow years.

vi

All biographers have stressed his deficient education, meaning by this that there is no record of his ever having gone to school,[35] and leaving us to infer that he picked up the primary matters of reading, writing, and arithmetic in some mysterious way. But with Antonio's intractability in pursuing his aims, is it not reasonable to suppose that to give his sons a groundwork in the indispensable elementary subjects was as much a part of his plan as the rudiments of music?[36] Although one assumes that he himself had sufficient education to teach the boys the fundamentals, had these advantages been denied to him, he would all the more have desired them for his sons, particularly if he foresaw for them a professional musical career. At all events, if Niccolò "wrote a sonata before he was ten," he must by then have learned to read and write and only his father could have taught him, since to send the lads to a parochial school would have placed too heavy a burden on Antonio's now uncertain budget. Besides, it seems to have been the custom, even many years later, for parents in their walk of life to teach their children, as shown by the violent reaction of Paganini's brother-in-law when he

[34] "The Court which Princess Elise held for some years at Florence did nothing for the Tuscans except to introduce the dissipation of French habits and spoil the proverbial purity of the language by accustoming the upper classes to the use of French." (Carlo Botta, *History of Italy during the Consulate and Empire*.)

[35] Liszt also had little education as a boy.

[36] In the Paganini family, musical talent evidently went with the male sex since the compulsory musical training did not extend to the two girls.

offered to send his nieces to a convent school, the inference being that only illiterate parents sent their children to a public school. And Antonio may have had the same quality of peasant pride.

Wherever Niccolò picked up his education, the other children must have enjoyed similar advantages, since they all could read and write.[37] If later he outdistanced them in worldly polish, poise, and general knowledge, it was because with his high sense of social values and his sensitive response to traditions of honor and conduct (for libertine though he was there is no evidence that he ever deliberately defied public opinion), he always gravitated to the gently bred, the intellectually cultivated. Moreover, from his early twenties the lot fell unto him in patrician circles, in the ambience of the wealthy, the noble, the intellectual; hence, apt to his opportunities and with his inordinate ambition and lively sense of his own immortality—for this was always very present in his mind—it could not have been difficult for him to acquire the outward marks of general culture that enabled him to hold his own in any company, particularly since he so readily responded to the influence of others. Unlike Liszt, whose father's family was originally of noble origin, he seems never to have been embittered by the social prejudices of his day but unprotestingly accepted the breach between the Bohemian and the aristocrat. At least one gains this impression since in later years when his achievements and his personality protected him from "the insolence of the great," he too took pains, as we are told, to "have no contact with the herd." Meanwhile, in his youth these circles had much to give him and he was quite willing to be, in Liszt's words, *"un musicien aux gages des grands seigneurs, patronisé et salarié par eux à l'égal d'un jongleur."* Pliable and impressionable, and with a strong imitative streak, probably no gesture, no inflection of the voice was ever lost on him. In a drawing room, we are told, he always spoke in a low voice, which he had quickly noted was the hallmark of good breeding, while his manner was reserved and always punctiliously correct. As a striking illustration of this quality of mimicry we have Schottky's testimony that when he once asked him to autograph a picture for him, Niccolò first suggested several quotations from Dante and Tasso, then,

[37] The letters of Paganini's sisters were written by a public letter writer, but they signed their names.

pondering for a moment, burst out with: *"Bisogna forte sentire per far sentire,"* which has now been generally adopted as his motto.[38] Original with him? By no means! He was merely translating verbatim Carl Philipp Emanuel Bach's *Indem ein Musikus nicht anders rühren kann, er sey dann selbst gerührt,* which obviously some friend in Vienna had recently quoted to him.

However, the mere fact that he always laid great weight on education is enough to indicate that in his own youth he had had little opportunity of enjoying its unlimited advantages. "I also love and honor the sciences [he told Schottky] and have studied them a little; but certainly not so deeply that I can speak of learnedness in the way you Germans can. In such things, I'm only a helpless novice, but my present association with learned men gives me the greatest possible pleasure. Heaven apparently did not wish me to enjoy this privilege in my early youth."[39] Here he no doubt felt the same as Liszt, who wrote his son in middle life: *"On a beau faire et travailler plus tard, il manque un certain fonds, aisé à mobiliser et à faire valoir, à ceux qui n'ont pas passé les echelons réguliers des études de collège."*

He was always keenly aware of his deficiencies and since he was in no position to remedy them, he turned to those who could. His correspondence contains many such requests, especially when he had to write to someone socially above him. In fact one of his notebooks contains a list of graceful phrases for rounding off his letters, though this was surely not so urgent, since his natural gallantry never deserted him when he required an effusive phrase or rhetorical flourish to convey a compliment. His spelling and syntax may have been faulty, but this of course argues no lack of formal education; for not every one who has been to school is a master of orthography.[40] The important point was that he sensed the divergence between the requirements of formal social intercourse and his own scanty education (as Codignola says, his license with gram-

---

[38] Schottky, *op. cit.,* 283; C. P. E. Bach, *Versuch über die wahre Art das Clavier zu spielen,* 91.

[39] Schottky, *op. cit.,* 327.

[40] Pulver's statement that "none of his friends ever saw him read a book" is without foundation. (Jeffrey Pulver, *Paganini, the Romantic Virtuoso,* 25.) His conversation (on reliable testimony) was frequently sprinkled with classical allusions, Latin phrases, etc. Several of his letters also contain references to books that he had read.

mar may have been more the result of haste and carelessness than actual ignorance) and, being aware of the weak point in his armor, he preferred to rely on those with a little firmer background.

Although apt to learn he seems to have had little gift for languages, except French, which he apparently spoke with moderate fluency. During his childhood and adolescence, continental Italy was in the French orbit, particularly Sardinia, Piedmont, and Tuscany, which were administered as French occupied territory and where use of the French language was maintained in both civil and military administration. So, since Genoa had also early succumbed to the intoxicating doctrines of revolution and "was French in everything but name," even tradesmen and lesser gentry must have been forced to learn the language if they wished to do any business with the conqueror. Niccolò, therefore, probably picked it up as a boy or acquired it while at the court of Lucca by the simple process of daily exposure to it. [Boucher de Perthes wrote from Genoa (*Sous dix rois,* I, 208, 422): "Vous aurez peine à croire qu'à Gênes on ne parle que peu ou point l'italian . . . on parle genois ou bien français."]

vii

We know nothing of his childhood, his playmates, his daily environment, except that he passed his boyhood in a period of revolutionary crisis, that the family lived in the crowded artisan quarter, and the home life—dominated by a harsh parent—was not altogether prosperous or happy. As both parents were deeply religious, he presumably made his first Communion at an early age, observed in the prescribed manner all the religious festivals,[41] regularly confessed his boyish peccadilloes, and on Sundays and greater holy days accompanied his parents to Mass, since in after years he recalled that "the tones of the organ affected him so violently that he trembled all over and burst into a flood of tears"— conclusive evidence of a nervous system hypersensitive to noise, which, united to a delicate physique, was unable to withstand the triple shock of a strong spiritual, emotional, sensuous experience.

---

41 Such festivals were so numerous that certain foreign writers were prone to attribute to this fact the "prevalence of idleness, mendicancy, shiftlessness, etc. among the lower classes."

Throughout his infancy and perhaps even all through childhood his hold on life must have been precarious. For we are told that at the age of four (1786) he was critically ill with measles, a disease that undoubtedly caused the death of his baby sister Angela, which occurred at this time. There was a severe measles epidemic in northern Italy that year,[42] so in an age when neither preventive nor curative medicine was yet developed, when infectious complaints were numerous and the importance of environmental hygiene was not yet recognized,[43] the likelihood of contagion during such a severe and widespread epidemic, in such a household and under such cramped living conditions, with inadequate ventilation, needs no underlining, quite apart from the fact that Teresa was then expecting another child and was therefore hampered in caring for two little invalids (one four years of age, the other two). Niccolò must have still been convalescent when the new baby arrived in August since she was christened Nicoletta, probably to perpetuate the name should they lose him after all. In referring to this first serious illness, he told Dr. Bennati that he lay in a coma for twelve hours and that his parents had already given him up for dead when someone noticed a slight movement that revealed in the nick of time that catalepsy and not death had laid its hand on the frail child.[44] Then at the age of seven he came down with a severe case of scarlet fever, another disease that is usually benign with children of that age, yet with him this, too, took an unusually virulent form and from then on to the day of his death he never enjoyed really robust health, a condition that he unquestionably aggravated through an early lack of self-control and temperance in satisfying the imperious demands of his highly erotic temperament. Nevertheless, the mere fact that such a delicate child survived in an age when such epidemics were frequent and infant mortality was excessively high betokened a huge reserve of physical strength and nervous vitality.

Tibaldi-Chiesa and Renée de Saussine have reproduced in their

[42] Walter R. Bett, ed., *History and Conquest of Common Diseases* (Norman, Okla., 1954), 40.

[43] In those years the political and social conditions in Italy did not conduce to progress in medicine corresponding to that in countries politically free and more flourishing economically.

[44] Liszt, when a child, had a similar experience. (Guy de Pourtales, *Franz Liszt*, 18.)

biographies a portrait head of a lad whom they erroneously identify as Niccolò at about 1795. Had they examined this lithograph
with care they would have found in the lower right-hand corner
the signature of G. Isola and the date 1835,[45] showing that it is a
portrait of Achilles painted in Genoa at the same time as Isola's
portrait of Paganini now in the Municipal Museum in Genoa. Although Paganini once said that Achilles "was the very image of
him," this was clearly wishful thinking since Achilles seems to have
resembled his mother far more than his father. The Isola portrait
therefore cannot be taken as in any way suggestive of Niccolò at a
similar age. As a matter of fact, we have no way of knowing what
he looked like as a boy or even which side of the family he took
after, though very likely he, too, looked more like his mother, with
parchment-like skin, curly locks, and two eyes "like black rosary
beads that did not shine, but glinted." To his Ligurian birth he
undoubtedly owed his commercial instincts, his long view of the
main chance, and his modest demands as regards the amenities of
life; to Antonio, his music, parsimony, and obstinacy; and to
Teresa, his slender build, his cast of features, and his imagination.
As a child his several youthful maladies and close application to
study in sunless, airless rooms, with the economic restrictions following in the wake of war, must have made him appear even more
delicate than he was. Yet his pronounced emaciation in his young
manhood must have been traceable rather to his manner of life and
a constitutional tendency to tuberculosis[46] than to any lack of
proper nourishment when a child.[47] Of course, long hours spent in
practice while he was growing could not help but have some effect
on his physique, which—as in the case of athletes or specialized
workmen—gradually adapted itself to the demands made upon it
as part of the protective mechanism given by Nature to both plants
and animals. Hence, some of the peculiarities in which his technical gifts were rooted may easily have resulted from overconcentra-

45 G. Isola (1808–93), a distinguished portrait painter of the epoch.

46 Professor Pietro Berri expressed the opinion that Paganini had a distinct pre-
disposition to tuberculosis. (*Il Calvario di Paganini.*)

47 There is no reason to believe that Paganini, when a boy, was a "neglected little
ragamuffin." The family were not paupers, and since Niccolò represented his father's
pledge for the future, it is hardly likely that he was *"toujours en guenilles."* (Renée
de Saussine, *Paganini le magicien*, 26.)

tion on the technical side of his art for many hours a day in the early years when bones and muscles were passing through the formative stage.

Money may have been scarce at times in the Paganini household, particularly between 1793 and 1800; but one gathers that Antonio, notwithstanding the lottery and the general feeling of insecurity and instability, was by no means shiftless, that he had the astute business head of all Genoese, that he provided for his family, and that either he or his father had put by enough to purchase a house and a little plot of ground in the Polcevera Valley[48] where the family spent their summers and which served as a safe harbor during the siege of 1800 and the recurring cholera epidemics. Although the scale of life in the Passa di Gattamora was undoubtedly primitive, we have no reason to assume that the children were ever the victims of real privation unless imposed for disciplinary measures, and if so, such punishment could never have been frequent since one receives the impression that Carlo and Niccolò were never such mischievous little madcaps as Rossini. Perhaps the only time they were given to rebellion was when the call of spring was in the air and the happy shouts and laughter of little playmates in the street below wafted upward to the seventh story and truant thoughts wandered from chromatic scales, tiny hands itched to toss a ball, and restless legs to make a dash for freedom—moments when both longed to be carefree, happy, boisterous little boys for a golden hour or two. But these moments, too, must also have been infrequent, for it was Niccolò's tremendous capacity for toil, his eagerness to learn, and his quick apprehension that awakened Antonio to the fact that there was genuine metal in this ore. So when he weighed its financial potentialities with the uncertainties of the lottery and the instrument trade, he lost no time in bringing Niccolò's childhood to an end.

"The most beautiful and fortunate age of man [wrote Leopardi] is tormented to such a degree with a thousand anxieties, fears, and labors of education and instruction that a grown-up man, even in the midst of all the unhappiness caused by the disillusionment and tedium of life, and the deadening of the imagination, would yet

---

[48] The four-storied house is still standing and is fairly inaccessible even now, being a full hour from the nearest village.

not accept to return to childhood, if he had again to suffer what he suffered then."[49] It may therefore be for this reason, rather than for any deliberate harshness on Antonio's part, that he lived in his son's recollection; for the dwarfing of childhood leaves a permanent wound and in this case very likely put that seal on Paganini's lips that later contributed so greatly to his loneliness and the abiding sorrowfulness of his life.

[49] Origo, *op. cit.,* 22.

II. THE STUDENT 1791–1795

Tristo e quel discepolo che non avanza il suo maestro.
—LEONARDO DA VINCI.

AFTER WORKING WITH Niccolò for two years, Antonio realized that the time had come, if his son's gifts were to be turned to good account, to place him in the hands of a trained, experienced musician who could give him the final virtuoso touch. In casting about for a suitable mentor, his choice, Gervasoni tells us, fell on a certain Giovanni Servetto (or Cervetto, as the name is sometimes given), a violinist in the theatre orchestra—no doubt, in Antonio's eyes, the best person to initiate Niccolò into actual theatre routine, which probably then represented the height of his ambition.[1] Indeed, given Antonio's background and utilitarian point of view, one suspects that this choice was prompted solely by motives of expediency; in other words, that he looked to Servetto to use his backstairs influence to secure Niccolò a paying post, for in those days it was not at all unusual for talented lads under fourteen years of age to find employment in theatre orchestras.[2] All things considered, it is extremely doubtful if Antonio ever aimed much higher for his sons since there were then in Italy no glamorous instrumentalists earning fabulous sums as roving virtuosos who might have aroused his cupidity. Practically all the great names associated, within the compass of the century, with Italy's golden age of the violin had by this time disappeared: Corelli in 1713, Vivaldi in 1743, Veracini in 1750, Geminiani in 1762, Somis in 1763, Locatelli in 1764, and Tartini in 1770. True, Lolli was in Sicily, Nardini in Florence, and Pugnani in Turin, but they were now old men, so it is hardly likely that Antonio had ever heard them at the apex of their careers; in fact, even Pugnani's fame does not seem to have crossed the Ligurian Alps, else Niccolò might have been sent

[1] Gervasoni is the original authority for this statement.
[2] Practically all Paganini's contemporaries began their careers in theatre orchestras, and usually in their early adolescence.

to Turin rather than to Parma, which was far less convenient for him.[3]

Unfortunately, we know nothing more about Servetto, who in all likelihood was a modest local talent whose musical career, like that of Paganini's brother Carlo, was passed in subordinate positions—a plodding, thoroughgoing craftsman whose gifts were not sensational enough to capture, or deserve, the attention of contemporaneous lexicographers. It is also very possible that in writing on hearsay and after the passage of twenty years, Gervasoni, or his informant, might have been mistaken in the name, particularly since in such cases Paganini's testimony (if Gervasoni ever questioned him) was also never quite reliable even when the association retained a sentimental interest for him. In itself, the detail is of very small importance, the essential point being that his father brought him, not to an eminent professor of the violin, but to a practical orchestral player, with the obvious intention of enabling him to assume as soon as possible his destined responsibilities and help support the family.

It probably did not take the precocious youngster very long to see that this particular pool was far too shallow for his heady plunges, which may explain his subsequent failure to give Servetto any credit—granting, of course, his fixed determination from the first to have the world believe that he was self-schooled, a statement he repeatedly made in later life, both directly and by innuendo. "Paganini cannot remember a time when he was ignorant of music [wrote Dr. Bennati]. From the very beginning he had an awareness of his future greatness, an unshakable faith in his own genius. His progress was so rapid that he would be hard put to it indeed to say how it all came about. There was an element of spontaneity about it that was beyond his comprehension. Each day he found himself a more consummate musician. It was as though his talent waxed and progressed entirely unawares. His genius developed without fatigue and without effort. Great attainments and great ideas sprang spontaneously from the inner flame that animated him."[4]

---

3 Pugnani died in 1798, Lolli in 1802, and Nardini in 1824.

4 Francesco Bennati, "Notice psychologique sur Niccolò Paganini," *Revue de Paris,* (May, 1831).

Except in one single instance—and even then with certain reservations—he was always singularly loath to record gratitude to his violin instructors and was equally reticent with respect to his musical experiences as a student: the awakening perception, stimulated by contact with the great masterworks of music, his reactions to their spiritual or inner beauty, his developing responsiveness to aesthetic media, the whole gradual unfoldment of his genius— these early years of preparation—were encompassed in an atmosphere of ambiguity, of secrecy. Later, in invoking some moments in the past, he recorded no formative influences except Gnecco and (if we can believe Fétis) Durand and Locatelli; for he wished to owe no debt to anyone. He must make the world believe that, as he assured Boucher de Perthes, he was "self-taught," self-made, and self-directed, that "great ideas sprang spontaneously from the inner flame that animated him."[5]

All very well, but nonetheless, one suspects that the humble Servetto was at least responsible for giving him his first foretaste of the lyrical theatre, which afterwards, throughout his life, had such a great attraction for him. As a regular member of the orchestra, even if not the violinist-leader, he could always obtain admission for his friends and probably more than once slipped the eager, perceptive lad into a musical performance.[6] Indeed, the surmise is plausible that it was he who enabled little Niccolò to hear Auguste Durand, whose playing made such a deep impression on him.[7] For up to the middle of the nineteenth century practically all concerts were given in the theatre and in Genoa the Polish violinist would have played only in the Teatro Sant'Agostino.[8] Certainly, Niccolò's parents, music lovers though they were, could not often have indulged in luxuries of this kind, so that if Niccolò heard any secular

[5] "Rapports de Boucher de Perthes avec Paganini," *Revue de musicologie* (August, 1928).

[6] When Paganini drew up his reorganization plan for the Parma orchestra in 1835, he stipulated (Article 19) that "no professor would be permitted to admit any person (either a member of his family or an outsider) to the orchestra during a performance, either at a Court function or in the Ducal Theatre."

[7] It has been impossible to verify the date of Durand's concert in Genoa since it was unnecessary at that time to obtain a license from the police, as was the case later.

[8] The Teatro Sant'Agostino, inaugurated in 1702, was the most important in the city before the inauguration of the Carlo Felice. It took its name from the nearby church. See Boucher de Perthes, *Sous dix rois*, I, 208.

music during his boyhood years, it could only have been through the kindness of musicians like Servetto and Gnecco or some of his father's customers and cronies who were connected in some way with the theatre.

Before going to Servetto, Niccolò, following in the footsteps of his famous forerunners, had already begun to experiment with composition so that he could write his own sonatas, caprices, and concertos.[9] But in this field Servetto was, of course, no guide; he was merely an executant musician and must have realized that he was not the proper person to direct a budding talent of such extraordinary promise, whereupon he turned Niccolò over to his young colleague Francesco Gnecco,[10] who had recently achieved a flattering success with his first lyrical work, *Madama Auretta e Masullo ossia il Contratempo,* which was produced at the Teatro Sant'-Agostino in May, 1792, probably round the time that Niccolò went to him. He had studied with Giovanni Mariani (1737–95) and Giacomo Costa,[11] and according to Chladni,[12] who knew him well, was an extremely versatile musician who played a number of stringed and wind instruments with more than average ability besides writing at least twenty-six operas and numerous works in other genres. He was thus able to open up to Niccolò's imagination still uncharted territory, teaching him the resources of the various instruments, the combination of the different groups, and scoring in general, which provided an excellent groundwork for his future studies with Paer. Later, Paganini only spoke of him in general terms to the effect that he "often saw him" and that he "had some influence on his musical training," leaving one with the impression that the influence was more in the nature of advice than in any systematic teaching. All the same, any association with a musician of Gnecco's capabilities after Antonio's limited musical scholarship would have thrown open a new world to this intrepid young experimenter, even though Fétis thought little of his creative talent and

9 Schottky, *op. cit.,* 251.

10 Francesco Gnecco (1769–1810). Some authorities give his birth date as 1764.

11 There is little information available regarding Costa beyond the fact that he was born in Genoa in 1761 and taught Paganini, Giovanni Serra, Gnecco, and Camillo Sivori.

12 Ernst Chladni (1756–1827), well-known acoustician, hailed as the "father of modern acoustics."

dismissed his style as *"lache et incorrect."* We may also safely assume that it was either Gnecco or Costa who presented Niccolò to Marquis Gian Carlo di Negro (1769–1857),[13] a young Genoese aristocrat of Gnecco's age who was an enthusiastic patron of the arts and who, according to a well-established but unconfirmed tradition, helped Niccolò in a material way. When he returned to Genoa toward the end of 1792 upon the completion of his schooling in Modena and a two years' tour of Italy, circumstances brought him into the orbit of the Roman poet and extemporizer Francesco Gianni, whose revolutionary sympathies had recently made him *persona non grata* in his native city.[14] Finding in the francophile Genoa of that day a more congenial atmosphere, Gianni, through the active championship of Marchioness Anna Brignole, soon had many friends and furtherers there in aristocratic circles, among them Di Negro's uncle and guardian, Andrea di Negro, who, to protect the poet from the various restrictions and annoyances to which he was being subjected by the police at the behest of Rome, had taken him into his home as a member of his family. In this way Gian Carlo, who also nursed poetic aspirations, came under Gianni's immediate influence and it is presumed that while profiting from the latter's literary guidance he absorbed at the same time some of his liberal political opinions, which made it easier for a member of the proletariat like Niccolò to break through the feudal traditions and enlist the active backing of a young aristocrat of Di Negro's cast.[15] Unfortunately, even under Gianni's inspiration, Gian Carlo's own artistic ambitions were never fully realized, though in later years his *villetta* became the rendezvous of the most eminent minds in Italy. As Manzoni said of him: "Di Negro is a man whom one

[13] Colonel Maxwell Montgomery wrote a friend from Genoa in 1815: "This evening I paid a visit to Mme de Staël and found her surrounded by savants, the only one of whom I knew personally was my friend Giancarlo di Negro, who stood high among the circle that surrounded the celebrated lady. Gian was upwards of six feet and a half in length. He was very fond of a little theatrical display and throwing himself into attitude would favor us with long recitations from Tasso."

[14] Francesco Gianni (1759–1822) settled in Genoa about 1795. In 1800 he went to Paris, where Napoleon gave him the title of *Improvisateur impérial* and an annual salary of 6,000 francs.

[15] When Paganini first knew Di Negro, he resided in the Via Lomellino, but in 1802 he purchased the *villetta* belonging to Ippolito Durazzo and later filled house and grounds with marble busts of famous men, among others: Paganini (1835), Columbus (1837), and Canova (1842). Umberto Monti, *Giancarlo di Negro*.

should like, at whose table one should eat, and whose verses one should not read."

It was in this milieu that Niccolò no doubt received his introduction to cultivated society and when he said that "after his return from Parma he played at various social affairs," we may be sure that he was referring to the soirees and fetes given by Di Negro and his aristocratic friends, who through him had become interested in this picturesque little prodigy with the strangely magnetic personality and the "stars sparkling between his lashes." Here the sensitive, impressionable lad learned to take his maiden social steps under the guidance of a master who by precept and example, by encouraging his art and generally broadening his mind, helped him to acquire polite, well-bred manners and the necessary poise so that in later years he never betrayed by incorrect behavior or by language his otherwise faulty education. Niccolò never spoke of having received any financial assistance from Di Negro; in fact, so far as can be learned, he never mentioned him at all, though this omission may have been owing to his native pride and independence. "The cynics [wrote Ernest Newman] assure us that charity leaves a secret resentment in the breast of the recipient." So perhaps this is the explanation, for though fidelity was not included among Niccolò's sundry virtues, he always showed himself extremely grateful even for small favors. Furthermore, unlike so many geniuses, he never expected others to provide him with the means to live and so far as we know never borrowed money, never sponged on his friends, never failed to pay his way. Thus, he may have been unwilling to admit that there had ever been a time when he required material assistance or had accepted it without immediately "repaying it in kind." That he seems to have felt no sense of indebtedness towards Di Negro is indirectly indicated by the fact that he never dedicated any works to him, though two duets for violin and guitar (a Minuetto in A Major and a Sonata Concertata) were dedicated to Emilia di Negro, probably a cousin, who on December 28, 1804, married the son of the Polish general, Jean Henri Dombrowski (1755–1818), commander of the Polish Legion during Napoleon's Italian campaign.[16]

We do not know how long he remained with Gnecco, but the

16 It has been impossible to learn whether Emiglia di Negro was a niece or a cousin.

31

latter must have been equally quick to see that this lad, so inventive and so revolutionary in his ideas, was moulded of a little different clay than the luxuriant crop of prodigies that periodically captured the attention of the public. At all events, while possibly still continuing to advise him in his compositional work, Gnecco passed him on to Costa, "Genoa's leading violinist" and reputedly a very able teacher, who soon had him playing in the different churches, sometimes as often as "three times a week." As he grew more proficient and had satisfactorily mastered a Pleyel concerto, he not only played regularly at the cathedral[17] but also on special occasions in other churches when new works by high ecclesiastical dignitaries were to be performed.[18] The earliest records of these "engagements" are contained in three notices in the Genoa *Avvisi* between May, 1794 and May, 1795, which is probably the period he spent with Costa, though he gave Schottky to understand that he worked with him only six months, receiving on an average one lesson a week.

May 31, 1794. On Monday, May 26, in the Church of S. Filippo Neri, the Grand Mass of the Rev. Giacomo Cepollina, Canon Preposito, was celebrated with the accompaniment of select instrumental and vocal music. During this ceremony a melodious concerto was performed by a very talented boy of eleven, Signor Niccolò Paganini, pupil of the celebrated Signor Giacomo Costa, professor of the violin, which aroused universal admiration.

December 6, 1794. On the Festival of San Eligio on December 1, in the Church of Nostra Signora della Vigna, Signor Niccolò Paganini, at the tender age of twelve, played a melodious concerto with the greatest dexterity and mastery. He repeated it on the following Monday (December 8) at eight o'clock in the evening, in the Oratorio of S. Filippo Neri.

May 26, 1795. At the Patronal Festival in the Church of S. Filippo Neri, the Grand Mass of the Rev. Monsignore Luigi Antonio Schiaffino, Vicar General of the Diocese and Canon Magiscola, was performed with select vocal and instrumental music. A very talented lad of twelve, Signor Niccolò Paganini, pupil of the celebrated Signor Giacomo

17 Paganini's chronology is here incorrect. He told Lichtenthal that he went to Costa after his first performance in the church, i.e., after May, 1794; whereas, he told Schottky that he went to him after his debut concert (1795). Both dates are manifestly incorrect.

18 The sacristan at the cathedral still points out the place where Paganini stood to play his solo numbers—unquestionably pure surmise.

Costa, professor of the violin, played a melodious concerto, which evoked universal admiration.[19]

At that time, music in the churches was not restricted to the liturgy, but the sacred and the secular were regularly intermingled, permitting the insertion of elaborate instrumental numbers even during the celebration of the Mass.[20] At the church in Padua, for instance, so Dr. Burney tells us, the "orchestra on common days consisted of four organs, eight violins, four violas, four violoncellos, four double basses, and four wind instruments with sixteen voices (of whom eight were castrati), some of more than local fame. In the church at Turin there is commonly a symphony played every morning, between eleven and twelve o'clock by the king's band, which is divided into three orchestras, and placed in three different galleries, and though far separated from each other the performers know their business so well that there is no want of a person to beat time, as in the opera and Concert Spirituel at Paris. The king, the royal family, and the whole city seem very constant in their attendance at Mass, and on common days all their devotion is silently performed at the Messa Bassa, during the symphony. On festivals, Signor Pugnani plays a solo, or the Besozzis a duet, and sometimes motets are performed with voices. The organ is in the gallery which faces the king and in this stands the principal first violin."[21]

"I think back with pleasure on the painstaking interest of good old Costa [Paganini told Schottky], to whom, however, I was no great delight since his principles often seemed unnatural to me, and I showed no inclination to adopt his bowing."[22] With his extraordinary technical precocity, his exploring spirit, and his imperative need for working things out in his own way, which ran so counter to the canons, one can readily believe that he often proved a thorn in the flesh for his tradition-bound instructor. Trained in the classical Italian tradition, with fidelity to yesterday, Costa could

19 It will be noted that these notices give Paganini's age correctly, showing that in 1794 and 1795 his parents did not try to make him any younger than he was.

20 Mario Pedemonte wrote that in many manuscripts of the concertos performed at church services the first violin part is missing. The soloist presumably took it home for study and then failed to return it so that no one could copy the embellishments and variations introduced by the soloist to display his technique.

21 Charles Burney, *The Present State of Music in France and Italy*, 120 f.

22 Schottky, *op. cit.*, 253.

only view his fantastic notions and boundless audacity, his rank, unweeded pyrotechnics, as entirely wanting in taste. For Costa was then a comparatively young man, without the vision of an older pedagogue, which made him less elastic in his loyalties. A fervent disciple of his masters, he refused to be warped out of his orbit by innovations foreign to his classical concepts, with the result that he and this young fiddling magician must have frequently come to grips.

To increase the psychological difficulties between master and pupil, either the latter part of 1794 or in 1795—at any rate while still in Costa's hands—Niccolò had an experience that, as he put it (if we can accept Fétis' reportage after twenty years!), "revealed to him the secret of everything one could do on the violin," in short, that "he owed his talent to the light that came to him when he heard Auguste Frédéric Durand play."

This Franco-Polish violinist, of whom we shall hear more later, was born in Warsaw round 1770, the son of a French émigré who was a musician at the court of Prince Oginski at Slonim. After learning the fundamentals of violin playing from his father, Auguste Frédéric was sent by Prince Oginski to Viotti in Paris but, like Niccolò, in preference to adopting the classical style of his master, he followed the bent of his own talent and gave his attention solely to the execution of brilliant technical tours de force, which created a tremendous sensation not only because of his natural gifts, which were of an exceptional order, but through the originality of his ideas. After three years with Viotti, he was appointed violinist-leader at the Brussels Opera and about four years later, according to early Viennese sources, he resigned the position and set out in 1794 on a tour of Germany and Italy, which must have been when Niccolò first heard him.

One can easily understand the impact of such feats of execution on a boy already addicted to similar experiments. Indeed, he allegedly told Fétis that Durand was one of the seeds that fertilized his genius and that "many of his most brilliant and popular effects were derived to a considerable extent" from this fantastic artist. (Here again his imitative trait was coming into play.) If so, he must, as he told Schottky, have had an opportunity of hearing him more than once, or even of making his acquaintance, since a lad of twelve or thirteen, no matter how great his musical capacities, could not in one single hearing carry away more than a general impression of such pyrotechnical feats. At such an early age, even superficial imitation would have been impossible, as shown by the futile attempts of Paganini's own contemporaries—all trained, experienced, and gifted artists—to imitate his tours de force, even after hearing them many times and listening with the utmost concentration.[23]

Three or four years later Durand, who took the name Duranowski after his marriage, discarded the violin for the musket and, joining General Dumbrowski's Polish Legion in Italy, became aide-de-camp to one of the generals till round 1800, when, for some grave misdemeanor, he was arrested at Milan and sent to prison, after which he had to quit the service. When he was released (presumably in 1805 in the amnesty previous to Napoleon's coronation) he resumed his musical career, at this time playing in a number of places in northern Italy.[24] From then on he seems to have led a roving life, moving continually from one place to another and finally settling in Strasbourg, where on June 7, 1827, he was appointed director of the theatre orchestra, though he evidently was too restless to hold the post for long. The full development of his talent appears to have been impeded all through life by his irregular habits and it was said of him that he was often without an instrument and had to play any violin that came to hand.[25] "But bad as it generally was [wrote Prince Oginski], he always enchanted his public with his playing. If he had been able to settle down and give his entire attention to the development of his talent, he would have been one of the most outstanding violinists of his era. His technical facility was prodigious and he invented a multitude of technical tricks and devices that no one but himself could play. His tone was full and rich, and his bowing irresistible,

23 Among Paganini's contemporaries were Giornovicchi (d. 1804); Puppo, who was active in Lucca and Florence from 1811–27; Ghebart, first violin at the Teatro Regio in Turin and later with Pietrini Zamboni at the Teatro Carcano in Milan; Felice Radicati, a pupil of Pugnani's, in Bologna; and Giovanni Polledro (1781–1853), another Pugnani pupil famed for his full tone and classical style.

24 Durand was concertizing in Italy again in 1805, when Paganini may also have heard him, although by this time he was already well started on his way.

25 See Spohr, *Selbstbiographie* I, 247 ff. for an account of Durand's irresponsibility.

while his playing exhibited an inexhaustible variety of effects."[26] Thus it can easily be seen how he and Paganini later may have become confused in the public mind. With so many characteristics and qualities in common, the twelve years difference in age was a relatively small matter.

If Costa found it difficult to hold young Niccolò on leash, the feat—after hearing Durand—must have been impossible. Pedantry was then more than ever irksome to him, though an experienced instructor like Costa could not have been blind to the fact that here something more was involved than parrot-like imitation of the technical artificialities and more obvious aspects of Durand's performance. The latter had provided Niccolò with a set of vivid impressions that he at once set about duplicating in his own way, much of it undoubtedly boyish floundering—an attempt to play with the tools of the giants—yet, even so, Costa should have recognized that his experiments were fundamentally individual and if developed sagely must lead to an enormous enrichment of the violin.

By 1795 he had made such astounding progress that his father was urged to place him in the hands of some distinguished master who would open the golden wings of this upward-striving young figure and not hold him down to a narrow set of values, yet at the same time teach him that the classical ideals of his great forerunners imposed "selection, differentiation between the precious and the base, between what was right and wrong aesthetically"; in other words, the art of "distinguishing, rejecting, refining." Since the grain was finer here, the metal purer, the surface could be more easily defaced. Hence, to avoid stagnation or a diversion of his gifts he should be entrusted to a wise, experienced artist capable of taking in hand this "nursling of immortality" and curing him of any adolescent whimsies that threatened to mar or arrest the perfect unfoldment of his gifts. Such a man, they felt, was Maestro Alessandro Rolla, violinist-leader of the Royal Orchestra of Parma.

ii

Niccolò had now arrived at a corner in his career, a turning point

26 Michel Kleofas Oginski, *Lettres sur la musique à un ami à Florence* (1828), quoted by Fétis in *Biographie universelle*, III, 87.

that presented certain problems of a practical nature, for to study with Rolla meant leaving home, and since it was out of the question to send a lad of thirteen alone to a distant town, especially when the country was so unsettled, his father must accompany him. This naturally demanded ready money not only for Antonio and Niccolò in Parma but for the family in Genoa—two adults and three children—who also had to be looked after during this first stage of Antonio's great investment. The mere fact that he was in a position to leave his family argues a degree of economic independence that is slightly at variance with the "impoverished circumstances" that Paganini's biographers associate with his humble station in life, that is, unless funds were forthcoming from other sources, an offer that the canny peasant strain in Paganini *père* would not have declined, even if unnecessary. Some interested patron must also have suggested the benefit concert as an advisable preliminary—an undocumented surmise but one backed by simple logic since Antonio, on his own initiative and responsibility, would hardly have risked such an ambitious undertaking at that season of the year unless he had the backing of wealthy patrons who were in a position to defray the requisite expenses if the public response did not come up to expectations.

As we shall see from Paganini's later negotiations, an artist—if not engaged by the impresario to play the "intermezzo concert,"[27] for which he usually received a stipulated percentage of the receipts—rented the theatre and assumed all financial risks himself, including the fees of the orchestra and assisting artists. Since the benefit took place during the torrid heat of summer, the theatre may have been closed. At any rate, there could have been no regular performance on that day since July 31 fell on a Friday. Therefore, gambler though he was, Antonio was surely in no position to assume such a responsibility unless he was positive of covering expenses; so it is a reasonable conjecture that Di Negro guaranteed the outlay and thus played the role of Niccolò's Maecenas at this important stage in his career.

On July 25 the following notice appeared in the Genoa *Avvisi:*

[27] In Italy most of Paganini's concerts took place between the two numbers of a double bill.

There will be a concert in the Teatro di Sant'Agostino next Friday, July 31. It will be given by Niccolò Paganini of Genoa, a boy already known in his *paese* for his skill as a violinist.[28] Having decided to go to Parma to perfect himself in his profession under the guidance of the renowned Professor Rolla, and not being in a position to defray the many necessary expenses, he has conceived this plan to give him courage to ask his fellow citizens to contribute towards his project, hereby inviting them to be present at this event which he hopes will prove enjoyable.

We have no information regarding this historic occurrence other than this announcement and Paganini's two widely divergent accounts of it. We do not know, for instance, whether he was accompanied by a piano or an orchestra, who his assisting artists were, how he acquitted himself, or how much money remained for the Parma venture after the deduction of expenses. His activities in the churches during the preceding year had brought his name before the public and he had already received several friendly notices, yet still the "début"—and in such an ambitious setting—seems to have aroused no journalistic curiosity (at least careful research has failed to bring to light any critical reviews), which is all the more regrettable since from his own confused accounts it is impossible to know whether he played at one or two concerts in the theatre before he went to Parma.

To Lichtenthal he said: "At eleven and a half [i.e., 1795, as he was then computing his age] I gave a big concert in the Teatro Sant'Agostino, at which Bertinotti sang." A year later Schottky quoted him as saying: "In my ninth year [1793] I soon found an opportunity of playing in the big theatre. Marchesi had arrived in Genoa. This Marchesi, who was then associated with the excellent singer Albertinotti *(sic)*[29] asked my father to allow me to play at his benefit, in return for which he would sing at mine, which I was planning to give shortly. Both took place."[30] In the Lichtenthal version, the year is correct but Schottky, paraphrasing a conversation probably weeks or months after it had taken place, makes him

28 The Italians at this time always referred to their native city as their *paese* (country). As Metternich said, "Italy was merely a geographical idea."

29 Teresa Bertinotti (1776–1854), a celebrated dramatic singer of that day, a pupil of La Barbiera of Naples. Paganini undoubtedly said, "La Bertinotti," and the German printer inadvertently reversed the first two letters; in other words, Paganini has again been blamed for a simple typographical error!

30 Schottky, *op. cit.*, 253.

nine instead of thirteen. It seems also extremely doubtful, for very cogent reasons, that Marchesi sang at the "début." On the whole, of the two versions of his autobiography, Lichtenthal's is indubitably more correct since he took it down directly at Paganini's dictation, while Schottky, who by nature was inclined to embellishment, was tapping his recollections of conversations that occurred on various occasions and at a time when Paganini was vitally interested in giving his listeners, and above all his official biographer, the impression that even as a lad he associated with the eminent and had received extraordinary recognition from the greatest artists in his native country.[31]

After a brilliant career in his own country Marchesi went abroad in 1781 and at the conclusion of a European tour settled in London, where he remained till the outbreak of the French Revolution.[32] Returning then to Italy, he entered the service of the King of Sardinia and, as his personal contribution towards the war, renounced his salary for six years (1792–98).[33] So it is very difficult to believe that a concert of such a feted singer during just these critical years when his patriotic action was universally acclaimed would have passed without any comment in the press or would not have been preceded by the customary announcements.

"His singing [wrote Dr. Burney] was not only elegant and refined to an uncommon degree, but often grand and full of dignity"; yet despite his gifts and his tremendous popularity he still found it necessary to dramatize himself. "He insisted on making his first entry [Lord Derwent tells us], whatever the opera might be, on a ramp in full panoply of war—plumed helmet, sword, shield, and lance, and announced by a fanfare, after which he would launch out on one of his favorite airs, chosen from some other opera." With this unconcealed bent for histrionics, which was implicit in his character, he surely would have been the last person in the world to have appeared in any concert or on any opera stage without seeing that he got his full meed of publicity before and after-

[31] The fact that Paganini played his variations on *La Carmagnole* at his debut makes Schottky's date demonstrably incorrect since the great popularity of this song dated first from 1794.

[32] Luigi Marchesi (1755–1829), one of the last of the famous male soprani.

[33] Giulio Roberti, *La cappella regia de Torino*, 42. According to Pietro Zaguri, Marchesi was engaged at the Fenice Theatre in Venice from 1791 to 1798.

wards; and it is equally improbable that with such a tremendous drawing card as "the great Marchesi," Paganini's *Avvisi* notice would have failed to stress this fact as a further bait for the music-loving Genoese. Moreover—and the point is important—the great opera stars only gave a "benefit concert" after a prolonged engagement and it is hardly likely that a singer of Marchesi's fame was appearing at the Teatro Sant'Agostino at that season of the year. In later life Paganini was a great admirer of this type of singing and frequently spoke of Crescentini and Velluti (two famous *castrati* of that period), so that his complete silence on Marchesi, beyond this one casual remark, makes the statement all the more suspicious.[34]

On the other hand, it is clear that he must have had some assisting artist since it was not customary for an instrumentalist to appear alone, though, unless a singer of Marchesi's or Bertinotti's eminence came forward voluntarily and offered his services, it seems unlikely that Antonio, or Niccolò's patrons, would have aimed higher than some member of the local ensemble—almost a fixed principle with Paganini in his later professional career. For in those days of political unrest and uncertainty of the morrow no one would have risked jeopardizing the financial success of an enterprise upon which so much depended by assuming such a heavy expense (especially in midsummer when the wealthy members of society, as Paganini's letters so frequently attest, were residing in the country) except as an inducement to the public.[35] And then the fact would manifestly have been given due prominence in the press.

As to the program, his first number was probably one of the Pleyel or Viotti concertos that he had studied with Costa, and the second his Carmagnole Variations, which he seems to have dropped from his repertory after he went to Lucca. At that time Genoa was "a radical hot bed" so strongly in sympathy with the ideals of the French Revolution as to be "French in everything but name," so that Niccolò's uninhibited treatment of this popular revolutionary version of *Marlborough, s'en va t'en guerre* was undoubtedly a

[34] It is difficult for anyone today to form an idea of the charm exerted by this type of singing. See Prince de Beloselsky, *La musique en Italie* (The Hague, 1770), 38.

[35] In Turin the leading theatres were closed from 1793 to 1797 and again from 1800 to 1802, a condition that presumably existed in many other cities.

smash hit.[36] Perhaps he chose the tune because everybody was singing it, or the selection may have been dictated by Antonio's political sympathies since Niccolò's later reputation as a "radical" and "flaming patriot" would indicate that the Paganinis were then one with the proletariat. Be that as it may, the success of this maiden composition, which evidently manifested that inclination to extemporize that later caught the attention of every public, contributed greatly to his self-reliance and the conviction that despite his unconventional procedure he had chosen the right course, which he would unswervingly hold to in the future. "As a child of the people who had grown up among the voices of an animated quarter of the city [wrote Tibaldi-Chiesa] he transferred this atmosphere to his music. The themes he felt germinating within him, that overflowed from his soul and were liberated from the strings of his violin, were spiritually akin to the simple flowing melodies of the Italian soul. Like these they were pure, natural, mellifluous, effervescent, capable of being engraved immediately and indelibly on the memories of all who heard them."[37]

iii

Early in September, when the heat was over, Antonio and Niccolò (on Conestabile's statement, accompanied by Di Negro) then set out for Parma, taking the longer southern route via Florence, where they called on the violinist and composer Salvatore Tinti, perhaps at Costa's suggestion.[38] Florence was then a five-day journey from Genoa, if they did not go by water to Leghorn, but one assumes that this long detour was unavoidable since the highways north of Genoa, especially between Tortosa, Piazenza, and Parma (as attested by numerous contemporaneous writers), were temporarily inaccessible for vehicles of any sort, thus making it practically impossible to approach Parma from the north. Henri Beyle also wrote of the great perils of travel in that section of the country, of the peasant bands pillaging everywhere, of mountain roads infested with bandits, of the cutthroat revolutionaries ambushed in the wretched country inns and posting stations. So it may be that a

[36] According to Belgrano, "Genoa received everything French with open arms."

[37] Maria Tibaldi-Chiesa, *Paganini. La vita e l'opera,* 19.

[38] Conestabile allegedly obtained his information from Di Negro, but the latter was then over eighty, so he may no longer have remembered dates and details.

wealthy aristocrat like Di Negro found it safer to follow the beaten trade routes along the coast and in the center of the country.[39]

Although Parma still enjoyed the title of "the Athens of Italy," the court was not so brilliant as under the regency of Du Tillot since the priest-ridden sovereign, Duke Ferdinand, spent most of his time in Colerno, where, "surrounded by monks," he lived an almost monastic life "given over to the minutest practices of religion" while his consort, Duchess Maria Amalia resided in Sala— an arrangement that amounted to virtual retirement after Parma fell to the French in 1796 and the Duke was divested of his sovereignty in everything but name.[40] Music and the arts, however, were cultivated as ardently as ever, the city's reputation as a musical center being second only to Milan. Alessandro Rolla,[41] the goal of Niccolò's journey and later leading violin instructor at the conservatory of which Ferdinand Paer was then director,[42] had been called to the court of Parma in 1782, first as solo viola and chamber virtuoso and then as violinist-leader of the orchestra, a post for which his long routine in the theatre, especially in Vienna, most eminently fitted him. Indeed, this may have been the principal reason for sending Niccolò to him since there were few violinist-leaders of his rank in Italy at that time who had had the equivalent of his theatrical experience at the Italian Opera in Vienna. If we concede that this was the height of Antonio's ambition for his son, he had been wisely advised to place him in the hands of Alessandro Rolla.

Niccolò tells us that upon arrival at their destination he and his father presented themselves at Rolla's door only to be told to their dismay that the Maestro was ill in bed and unable to receive them. However, nothing daunted, Antonio produced his letters of intro-

[39] There were three routes open to them: the northern, via Tortona, Piacenza, and Parma, where the roads were inaccessible in certain districts; the southern, along the coast via Pisa or by water to Leghorn; and a road across the Ligurian Alps via Sarzana and Nunziata, which was then rough and dangerous.

[40] From October, 1802, the French were in complete command.

[41] Alessandro Rolla (1757–1841),·when very young, went to the Italian Opera in Vienna, where he remained till about 1791. He was a pupil of Renzi and Conti.

[42] Federico Mompellio, in his annotated edition of Conestabile's biography, states (p. 72) that the Parma Conservatory did not then exist and attributes this erroneous statement to Conestabile. But the latter took it from Schottky, who here was quoting Paganini.

duction and while awaiting the Maestro's decision suddenly espied a violin and manuscript lying on a table, whereupon he motioned to Niccolò to seize this providential opportunity and capture the Maestro's interest by assault. "The ill composer was immediately interested [he said] and inquired who was playing in this way. He couldn't believe that it was only a little boy. However, when he had convinced himself that this was so, he exclaimed: 'I too can teach you nothing! For goodness' sake, go to Paer. Here you'd only be wasting your time!' "[43]

From this advice one gathers that Rolla must have heard more than the extemporized performance of his own work that Niccolò "had played at sight." When he had recovered from his first surprise, he probably put the lad through his modest repertory, including not only the Carmagnole Variations but the sonata and perhaps some other *ouvrettes* with which he was endeavoring to exercise his groping creative gift, since what he heard immediately convinced him that as far as technique was concerned this youngster was already a virtuoso. What he now needed was an experienced teacher of composition who would woo and develop an inventive and melodic gift of astonishing maturity.

Ferdinand Paer, a native of Parma, of German origin, was, till Rossini's conquest of the field, one of the leading representatives of the Italian operatic school, an admirable craftsman with an authentic lyrical gift.[44] Just at that time he was engaged in writing his opera *L'Intrige Amoroso*, commissioned by Duke Ferdinand for the forthcoming carnival, so for the moment he had no time to take a personal interest in Costa's little pupil, though, like Rolla, he was so impressed with the lad's creative gifts that in order to lose no time he sent him to his own teacher, Gasparo Ghiretti, second

[43] Fétis quotes this incident in all three of his biographical articles, but erroneously attributes it to a "Viennese paper," indicating that he had not read his Schottky very carefully.

[44] Paer's first opera to be given in Vienna was *Camilla—Il Sotterano*, the first performance taking place at the Kaertnerstrasse Theater on February 23, 1799. This shows that he must have gone to Vienna in 1798, since the opera was written there. Granting Paganini's unreliability with respect to dates, it is still difficult to reconcile this information with his alleged movements. If we accept his statement that his "parting with Paer" took place ten months after his arrival in Parma, it must have been because of his own return to Genoa. If Paganini "returned to him often," it could only have been during Paer's occasional visits to Italy.

cellist of the royal orchestra.[45] It was probably through the latter's influence that Niccolò was enabled "to give a concert in the Royal Theatre" and had the privilege of playing before the sovereigns in Colerno and Sala, for in those days such favors were not accorded indiscriminately and often depended more on influence than on skill. As soon as Paer's opera was completed, he then sent for Niccolò and taught him personally as long as he remained in Parma.

Paer [he said] referred me to his own teacher, the old but very experienced Neapolitan conductor Ghiretti, who now took me systematically in hand and for six months gave me three lessons a week in counterpoint. Under his direction I composed, as an exercise, twenty-four fugues for four hands, without any instrument—just with ink, pen, and paper. I made great progress because I myself was interested and Paer himself soon became so interested in me that he grew very fond of me and absolutely insisted that I come to him twice a day to work with him. After about four months he told me to write a *duetto,* which he then looked over, saying with a pleased smile that he could find in it no violations of pure form. Shortly after this he left for Vienna to write an opera. We parted for a long time. Yet later I often returned with pleasure to this great master and am happy to call myself his grateful pupil.[46]

In the Lichtenthal sketch Paganini said that he had brought a letter of introduction to Paer but left the impression that he had studied only with Ghiretti, an omission on his part that has led to deplorable misunderstandings. Although Fétis had published a French translation of the Lichtenthal article in his *Revue Musicale* (probably submitted by Anders), when he came to write his article on Paganini for Volume VII of his *Biographie Universelle,* he quoted the above account from Schottky but cut out all references to Paer, adding on his own authority that Paganini had never studied with him "because Paer was then in Germany." Here no more glaring illustration of Fétis' unreliability is required since in his biographical notice on Paer in the same volume he correctly states that Paer's first Viennese production took place in 1798, in other words, three years later. Codignola, accepting Fétis unquestioningly, ignores Schottky and quotes only Lichtenthal, with the

45 Gasparo Ghiretti (1747–97) was appointed to the ducal orchestra in Parma in 1774. Paganini does not mention his death—another indication that Paganini was not in Parma in 1797.

46 Schottky, *op. cit.,* 254.

comment that "early biographers, incorrectly interpreting this passage *("raccomandato alla corte, a Rolla ed al maestro Paer")*, assert that Paganini had lessons also with Paer, a statement that Conestabile showed was incorrect." Conestabile, who otherwise leaned heavily on Schottky, also disregarded the latter's autobiographical sketch (p. 249) and held to Lichtenthal's Italian article—no doubt because of an inadequate knowledge of German—adding in a footnote: "I don't say that Paganini really studied with Paer because I have no information to that effect." Such errors are astonishing, and all the more so since a couple of Paganini's letters to Paer have survived (to one of which Codignola himself refers on page 650 of his work) in which he signed himself Paer's "devoted pupil," a fact that Fétis also should have known since Paganini in Paris made no secret of the old relationship. At all events, as will be seen, it was not "the early [German] biographers" who "incorrectly interpreted the aforesaid passage," since they had all obviously read their Schottky very carefully as well as a letter of the latter published in the German and English press in which he expressly quoted Paganini's statement: "I received my musical training from Paer."

As for Rolla, Paganini never personally claimed to have studied with him, the only basis for the statement being Gervasoni's unauthenticated assertion. Fétis wrote that "Gervasoni knew Paganini as a child in Parma," but this was a mere conjecture on his part since there is no documentary evidence to prove it, nor is there anything in Gervasoni's brief article that would justify such an assumption. Perhaps in the intimate circle of the court musicians—a little world unto itself—the two were often thrown together and, being interested in this extraordinary talent, Rolla tried to divert him from the various tours de force that were then preponderately engaging his attention and that as yet he still could only imperfectly execute. Furthermore, since neither Rolla nor his son Antonio ever spoke of Niccolò as a "Rolla pupil"—in those days the most powerful publicity for any violin instructor—it is probable that the teacher-pupil relationship was purely an informal one based more on friendship and mutual regard and an absorbing interest shared in common, a master endeavoring by precept and example to keep a young explorer from wandering too far afield.

But with Paer, and no doubt also with Ghiretti, Niccolò's musical vocabulary was enriched by a new word—style. He now had to
learn to set down his rippling fantasies and "uninhibited fireworks" in phrases that would not "violate pure form," to mold on
classical precedents his innovations, technical, interpretative, expressive. Just when and where Locatelli's *Arte de nuova modulazione* fell into his hands and ignited his fantasy in a new world
of ideas it is impossible to determine, but it must have followed
rather than have preceded his contact with Durand. Fétis (p. 76)
gives the impression that Paganini told him that he came on this
work by accident and "that it opened up to him a world of new
ideas and devices that had never had the merited success owing to
their excessive difficulty." Although one hesitates to quote Fétis as
an authority, and attribution also has its dangers even when fortified by evidence, intuition still traces the inspiration for the
Twenty-four Capricci to the Locatelli work.[47] Somewhere, sometime, during this early experimental stage, Locatelli's shadow must
have crossed his path, though, too, he may also have heard Lolli,
who had returned to Italy about this time and "was astonishing
audiences everywhere by the ease with which he played the most
difficult double stops, octaves, tenths, trills in thirds, sixths, harmonics, etc."—all things that were in Niccolò's field of vision at
this time.[48] Since it is not likely that such strict classicists as Rolla,
Ghiretti, and Paer would have referred their pupil to such heretical models, he must have tumbled on them by himself; for it was
by taking over certain of Locatelli's ideas, in particular, and by reviving certain effects, added to some discoveries of his own, that he
eventually achieved the style that characterized his talent and made
possible technical and expressive effects that had been beyond the
reach of all his forerunners. Since Locatelli's ideas were still ad-
judged impracticable, Niccolò, in trying to carry the problem
further towards its complete solution, proved the link in the his-

[47] Similar technical devices can be found in the following *capricci*:

Paganini	Locatelli
1	7
2	4
9	2
14	8

[48] Charles Burney, *A General History of Music*, II, 1020.

torical chain—the creative tool that unlocked the technical secret. To trace Locatelli's influence it is only necessary to compare the *Capricci Enigmatici* in his *Arte di nuova modulazione* with Paganini's *Capricci*. For example, Locatelli's seventh caprice opens with an arpeggiated movement identical in tonality and note values to Paganini's first caprice (groups of eight thirty-second notes in E Major); the harmonic treatment is also similar (four notes ascending and four descending), while the march rhythm of Locatelli's twentieth caprice is found again in Paganini's fourteenth. The middle section of the twenty-fifth (where the four-note chords alternate with rapid descending scales) also has points of resemblance, more in stylistic treatment than in actual reminiscence, with the opening of the Andante of Paganini's eighteenth.

"Under Ghiretti's tutelage [he said] I composed a large number of instrumental works," and then spoke of playing "two of his concertos" in the Royal Theatre. As the first two concertos that have come down to us were written in the period 1811–26, he must either have destroyed all these early works as *juvenilia* or he was exaggerating for rhetorical effect since his programs for the next four or five years contained only his Carmagnole Variations, his embellishments to a Lodoïska Overture,[49] a Fandango Spagnuolo (probably inspired by Carlo Farinai's *Capriccio stravagante* [1627], which imitated the barking of dogs, caterwauling, fifes and drums, etc.) and concertos by Pleyel, Rode, Viotti, and Kreutzer, ornamented with embellishments or intercalated movements of his own, which no doubt led him to look upon them as his personal creations.[50]

iv

We do not know whether Antonio remained in Parma with him the entire time, or whether he went back and forth to Genoa. To have remained even ten months away from his family must have involved a very heavy expense and to have left Teresa alone in

---

[49] This was either the overture to Simon Mayr's opera of that name (1800) or to Kreutzer's (1791), which was produced the same year as Cherubini's. However, evidence seems to point to that of Simon Mayr, which was the most recent in date and was then very popular in Italy.

[50] Tibaldi-Chiesa (*op. cit.,* 23) states that he gave "two concerts in the theatre," but Paganini speaks of only one.

Genoa with three little children and her aged father-in-law when the whole country was rattling with musketry argues a degree of callousness and indifference towards his responsibilities that is a little hard to reconcile with our knowledge of Antonio's character.

Paganini told Dr. Bennati that he was gravely ill in Parma with pleuropneumonia, his life being "saved only by numerous bleedings and a protracted treatment of antiphlogistics"—the usual treatment at that time to reduce the inflammation in the chest which was then thought to be the cause. While one is inclined to question all these early dates, the fact itself is not improbable, owing to the many privations and the widespread penury resulting from the general unrest which made it difficult for the general masses to obtain the proper food, clothing, fuel, and other necessaries of life. Napoleon had launched his Italian campaign on March 20 (1796) and, after the surrender of the Piedmontese, had entered Milan on May 15, shortly thereafter occupying Lombardy, Piedmont, and Tuscany as well as a part of the Romagna, with troop movements all round, as far down as Foligno, which touched off numerous movements of revolt as a result of the heavy contributions levied, the marauding, the spoliations, and requisitions that followed in the wake of the military operations. Although the Duke of Parma had signed an armistice with Napoleon early in May, northern Italy was no longer the place for a delicate lad recovering from a serious illness, so as soon as he was able to make the journey he and Antonio no doubt returned to Genoa where, as he told Schottky, he then "remained for a long time." In fixing certain events in the early days of his career, Paganini's biographers have all been prone to overlook his environment, though it should be apparent to anyone familiar with the ways of conquering armies that under such conditions a sickly lad of thirteen would hardly be in a position to profit from Parma's musical advantages or even to exercise his talent sufficiently to support his father and himself.

Paganini's statement that he "remained in Genoa for a long time" is definite enough, and in view of the battles and troop movements then taking place he surely had no opportunity of traveling about the country, even had he so desired. For the time being he was lucratively occupied "playing at private affairs" and undoubtedly made enough, through the assistance of Di Negro and his

Niccolò Paganini

Unsigned portrait attributed to George Patten, London.

Courtesy of Henry Werro, Berne, Switzerland.

Luigi Germi

Courtesy of Guglielmo Tixi, Genoa.

friends, to support the family while waiting for Italy's fate to be decided. (Di Negro went to Paris and London in 1798 and remained abroad two years).

The only fairly certain date in all this period is that of an audition with Rudolphe Kreutzer, which allegedly took place at Di Negro's in the autumn of either 1796 or 1797.[51] The Genoa *Avvisi* of December 3, 1796, contained a notice to the effect that "on the occasion of the festivities organized in Genoa in honor of Mme Josephine de la Pagerie Bonaparte, wife of the Generalissimo of the French Armed Forces in Italy, a vocal and instrumental concert was given on November 27, at which the professor of violin, Signor Creutzez, received a great ovation,"[52] so that it has been generally assumed that on this occasion Di Negro entertained the French artist and asked Niccolò to play for him. However, Fétis stated, this time correctly, that Kreutzer toured Italy in the autumn of 1797, a fact attested by the following communication:

Dr. Domenico Giovannelli to Captain Giovanni Mariti, Leghorn, October 11, 1797.
On Monday evening, October 9, I went to hear the violinist Kreutzer at our theatre, where he gave a concert before a fair-sized audience. His manner of playing pleased me greatly and was said to be quite new. I stayed an hour and a half and then went home.[53]

On this *tournée* Kreutzer must have played in Genoa also and, if so, may have had more time at his disposal than during the hectic weeks of 1796. Thus it is possible that Niccolò's audition took place a year later than is ordinarily supposed. However, whenever the event occurred, one can easily imagine Kreutzer's interest as Di Negro put his talented young protégé through all his circus tricks. For at that time he, too, had a little prodigy among his pupils—young Charles Philippe Lafont, Niccolò's senior by one

51 Mompellio assumes that Paganini remained in Parma till November 1796. Codignola (*op. cit.,* 11) extends the period to two years and places the Kreutzer audition (p. 10) in 1793, quoting as authority Antonio Crocco, who, in his work *Elogio di Gian Carlo di Negro* (1861), states that Paganini played for Kreutzer in Di Negro's *villetta,* which, according to Monti (*op. cit.,* 75), was not acquired till 1802. Crocco therefore cannot be quoted as an impeccable authority. See Codignola, *op. cit.,* 10–11.

52 Kreutzer was often called *Kretsche* by the French, and in the London papers of 1844 he was referred to as *Greitzer.*

53 Now in the Biblioteca Labronica, Leghorn, Italy.

year. And as he compared the lads' capacities he must have told Niccolò of his little colleague at the Paris Conservatoire; which made such a lasting impression on him that twenty years later his curiosity was still keen enough to send him racing to Milan when word reached him that Lafont was playing there.

v

After the French conquest of Italy in 1796, Napoleon in the spring of 1797 put an end to the old Genoese Republic and forced the Genoese to adopt a democratic form of government on the pattern of the French, which was not unsympathetic to the body politic for whom the heady doctrines of the revolution and the equalitarian dogmatism of the French had, at first, a very strong appeal. Although the city "fell like ripe fruit into Napoleon's hands," the act of submission was accompanied by a lively little revolution carried out with true Latin emotionalism. On May 24 the Jacobins rose against the senate and demanded a change of constitution. Next day the populace, incited by the clergy, put down the democrats and saved the senate. Since Niccolò was described as an ardent Jacobin, he no doubt participated in the fray, during which the statue of Andrea Doria was overthrown, criminals liberated from the prisons, and the Book of Gold publicly burned. In the early summer, outbreaks of rebellion also took place in different parts of Piedmont, culminating in September in a general uprising of the peasants and mountaineers of the surrounding valleys, which finally had to be forcibly put down by the French troops.

When spinning his reminiscences to Schottky and no doubt deliberately painting a picture of his past as an *homme de bonnes fortunes* that would glorify his present and his future, Niccolò spoke of touring "northern Italy when he was about fourteen" (i.e., 1798, according to his calculation) and of "playing in Milan, Bologna, Florence, Pisa and Leghorn," which, as one can see, was practically impossible owing to the military operations. To Lichtenthal, in referring to this tour, he gave his age as seventeen (1801), which comes closer to the mark. But one should not hold these little discrepancies against him. In a life so erratic, so restless, and so disordered, it is no matter for surprise that in late middle life he could no longer accurately recall dates and places in that distant stage of his career when he was merely jumping through the hoop like *"le savant chien Munito"* when trainer Antonio cracked the parental whip.

Meanwhile, the military situation in Piedmont and Lombardy was steadily growing more acute, important battles between the French and the Austro-Russian forces taking place at several nodal points—in Tortona, in Novi, almost at the doors of Genoa, where the threat of famine was no longer only a bugaboo. For the ships laden with grain from France had to run the British blockade, so that their arrivals were so uncertain and irregular that the riotings at the rationing center in the city grew daily more tempestuous. Indeed, from the early summer of 1799 the *Gazzetta di Genova,* in spite of a brave effort to encourage the desperate populace, spoke continually of the *stato lagrimevole di incertezza, di inquietudine, e di miseria* of the people, and by September had to admit that the city was nominally in a state of siege.[54] The wealthy aristocrats and merchants, even the musicians, were all "emigrating" to safer zones, leaving behind only the unfortunate populace and those whose official duties prevented their departure. "I have no news from Genoa [wrote the Italian correspondent of the *Allgemeine Musikalische Zeitung* in November, 1799] because the timid Muses fled the city months ago; even the Ligurian fields are deserted. Tinti and Drey, our best composers, are now living in Venice and the other musicians have scattered to quieter provinces till times have settled down again."

In the midsummer of that year (1799) the city organized a national guard to maintain order and quell the rioting, drafting for this duty all males of seventeen and over, so it will readily be believed that, if not before, then surely when news of this intended measure got abroad, the Paganinis lost no time in "emigrating" to Antonio's property in Ramairone, in the Polcevera Valley, if for no other reason than to remove the two boys from this hazardous military duty. Once there Antonio and his sons then evidently devoted themselves "to agriculture," not only to supply the family's needs, but as a sure means of livelihood now that all the accustomed

[54] *Gazzetta di Genova,* No. 15 (September 21, 1799), 126.

avenues were cut off.[55] Finally, on December 29, to increase the disaster, the French closed the Free Port, including the 355 ware-houses in the area of the port, after which, as official records tell us, most of the workmen on the docks transferred their activities to Leghorn, where maritime commerce was still unaffected. This will therefore easily account for Niccolò's "long residence" there in 1800 since Antonio must have taken him with him. In fact, they may very well have been there during the long and bitter siege when Massena held the city against the Austrians.

Je ne me sens pas le courage de décrire ce que la garnison et la popula-tion de Gènes eurent à souffrir pendant les deux mois que dura ce siège mémorable [wrote General Marbot]. *La famine, la guerre, et un terri-ble typhus firent des ravages immenses! La garnison perdit 10,000 hommes sur 16,000, et l'on ramassait tous les jours dans les rues sept à huit cents cadavres d'habitants de tout âge, de tout sexe, et de toute condition qu'on portait derrière l'église de Carignan dans une énorme fosse remplie de chaux vive. Le nombre de ces victimes s'éleva à plus de trente mille, presque toutes mortes de faim!*

Since Niccolò never referred to the siege in any of his rambling conversations, he must have been far enough away to have known nothing of its horrors.

Although he linked together his interest in "agriculture and the guitar," thus tempting his biographers (with Fétis' aid) to indulge in the most romantic fancies, his interest in the guitar very likely dated from his return from Parma, when "he played more the dilettante than the virtuoso," and arose quite naturally from the circumstances of his environment. The Spanish or French classical guitar was then a very fashionable instrument and it may have in-terested his agile, inquiring mind to see what he could do with it, in the process of which he discovered that it was not only a "spur to creation" but an actual aid in composition and the working out of some of his most striking chord effects.

On my first visit [Schottky wrote] I saw a guitar lying on the bed and, since I had heard a great deal about his guitar playing, I asked if he

[55] Genoa's geographical situation, with the Ligurian Alps plunging straight into the Mediterranean, made it dependent on the neighboring provinces for all agricul-tural products except fruit and olives.

never played the instrument any more in public. "No," he replied, "I don't like it and look upon it merely as a thought conductor. I pick it up occasionally as a spur to creation or to work out some special harmony that I can't produce on the violin. Otherwise, it has no value in my eyes." He plays it admirably and executes very difficult chords and beautiful arpeggios. He also uses a special fingering of his own. He always works out the accompaniment of his concertos first of all on the guitar but with this exception he never uses an instrument for composing. He either sings or whistles.[56]

If any person was responsible at this time for turning his attention to this instrument, we may be sure that he had more cause for gratitude with respect to his music than for any emotional experiences that may have been associated with it since none of those that came to him, either early or late, were ever able to satisfy his inner craving for fulfillment. This he found only in his music, for as he once confessed in an expansive moment, "True affinity is a rare thing." Hence, if any anonymous charmer awakened his interest in this instrument he was undoubtedly more grateful to her for something much more satisfying to a person of his temperament than the memory of a few enchanted hours.[57]

In describing his movements and activities in these first post-Parma years, he spoke of arriving in "Leghorn again just at the time of the French Revolution," by which he meant the French occupation of the city in the early autumn of 1800. Here his use of the word "again" also intimates that he and his father were in Leghorn during the siege and returned to Genoa when they could get through to Ramairone, where the family was living during these difficult and anxious weeks. Articles have appeared from time to time stating that while in Leghorn on this second visit he played for Lady Emma Hamilton and her famous lover, Lord Nelson, the assertion being based on an episode in Manuel Komroff's romance, "The Magic Bow," which is, of course, the sheerest fiction. True, Nelson, accompanied by the Queen of Naples and Sir William and Lady Hamilton, arrived in Leghorn on the evening of June 14 and

---

56 Schottky, *op. cit.*, 270.

57 Carl Maria von Weber was also a guitarist in his younger years. Berlioz was another composer who played this instrument, the influence of which can be seen in his spacing of chords. Cf. W. D. Browne, "Modern Harmonic Tendencies," Musical Association *Proceedings*, 1914, p. 141; also, Barzun, *op. cit.*, 35.

remained there till July 11, when they left for England via the overland route,[58] so if Niccolò had happened to be in Leghorn at that time, Colonel Archibald MacNeill, the British consul, would no doubt have presented the brilliant youth to Lady Hamilton, who, wherever she might be, "gave musical soirees every evening," for which she engaged the most noted artists. On the other hand, if Niccolò had ever played for her, especially in the setting of a musicale attended by the Queen of Naples, we may be sure that he would not have failed, in later years, to publicize the fact, even as he recalled his meeting with the less prominent figure of Colonel MacNeill.[59]

On one of my concert tours I arrived in Leghorn again just at the time of the French Revolution with a letter of introduction to the British Consul, who received me very kindly, helped me to engage a hall and made sure that I would have a large audience. But Leghorn, like so many other towns, had its own private musical club (Società degli Esercizi Musicali), whose members felt slighted at my failing to call upon them and fixed it so that the regular orchestral players broke their word with me. The concert was to begin at eight o'clock, the hall was full and still no musicians had appeared. At length three or four second-rate individuals turned up, but I was of course obliged to alter my program. This fired my ambition and I exerted my utmost efforts to entertain the audience for nearly three hours with a youthfully virile performance. My endeavors were rewarded with loud applause and my hateful opponents were censored with equal vehemence, with the result that I had a capacity audience at my next concert, which took place in the theatre with full orchestral accompaniment. On this occasion my adversaries excused themselves by saying that they thought I was too young to do all the things I claimed.[60]

Antonio was presumably returning to his work on the Leghorn docks—Niccolò's music being temporarily a secondary issue— which would explain their "long residence" there without any special activities on Niccolò's part beyond the two concerts and a

[58] Lady Emma Hamilton (1765–1815), born Amy Lyon, was the mistress of Charles Greville (nephew of Sir William Hamilton) and Lord Nelson.

[59] Conestabile, with complete disregard of historical facts, placed this incident in 1808! According to information kindly furnished by the Public Record Office, London, the "Foreign Office Correspondence, Tuscany (F.O. 79) states that Col. Archibald McNeill, British Consul at Leghorn, was forced by the French to leave the city in October 1800. Thereafter there was no official British representative there till 1814, when Mr. Edward Watson became Acting Vice Consul."

[60] Schottky, *op. cit.*, 255.

"work for the bassoon" that he wrote at the request of a "Swedish amateur." With any serious initiative impeded by the unrest and turmoil of the period and the uncertainty of what each new day might bring, Niccolò must more than once, on idle days, have trekked with his companions over the twenty-five miles of the old post road that led to Lucca, which had a lure and enchantment of its own for one reared in the constant presence of the sea. It was like passing through a gate from the noise and sweltering sunlight of the market place into the shade and silence of a cloistered garden.

He does not tell us who introduced him to the British Consul, but one may safely surmise that it was Di Negro, who was also evidently responsible for the two engagements at the Modena Theatre in December. For he must have had many influential friendships there dating from his school days at the College of San Carlo. When referring to this tour, Niccolò did not mention Modena, which he may have forgotten in the meantime, though it seems more likely that he chose places whose names, like Florence and Bologna, would sound in Schottky's ears a more familiar note. Anyhow, the detail was unimportant after thirty years. Some things were better left unsaid, like his father's plebian duties on the Leghorn docks. Still unknown and with no personal influence behind him, he would have found it difficult to obtain engagements at the theatres in "Milan, Bologna and Florence," especially at a time when political factors also probably played a certain role. So he confined himself to smaller towns where he could rent a hall and give his own performance. This explains why there is no record of any of his early appearances, except the two concerts in Modena recorded in the theatre archives.[61] We can therefore confidently say, on the basis of this evidence, that in the period 1800–1801 his "professional activities," if one can call them such, were outside the theatre and on a very modest scale.

[61] Alessandro Gandini (*Cronistoria dei Teatri di Modena*) gives the following details on these concerts: Dec. 5, 1800: Teatro Rangoni: after the two-act comedy, *Il marito di quattro mogli,* the violinist Niccolò Paganini, seventeen years of age, gave an instrumental concert (his first appearance in Modena), when he presented the following program: Violin concerto by Rode. Lodoïska Symphony, embellished by Paganini with harmonics, La Carmagnole Variations, Concerto by Kreutzer. Dec. 21, 1800: Five symphonies performed by the orchestra. Two violin concertos by Paganini, Fandango Spagnuolo in which he imitated the songs of different birds. He was assisted at the latter concert by the singer Andrea Reggianini.

By now he was eighteen years of age and had as yet made no effort to break away to freedom, an effect very probably of his yielding disposition when in the presence of a stronger will; but the urge to independence lay just below the surface and Antonio must have noted with dismay that this eaglet that he had unaccountably hatched among his brood of ducklings was possessed of a disturbing fever of curiosity, not only in the sphere of his genius but as regards the spectacle of life. For the justifiable assurance and sense of inner energy that unfolded with each new success, modest though it was, now inspired him with the desire to free himself from the constraint of Antonio's tyrannical control—surely a normal ambition for a person of his age though one that did not happen to conform with the plans of his moneygrubbing parent, whose chief concern was to maintain at any cost his sinecure of croupier.

He always had an extremely clear vision when it came to his own interests, so it could not have taken long to draw comparisons between his family environment and that of the social circles to which his gifts now gave him access. He had first seen the world and made intimate acquaintance with the facts of life in the *carrughi* of Genoa and from there, without bridging interlude, had stepped into the salons of the aristocracy where he had had occasion to note the power and the glory of wealth, of rank, of worldly position, even of celebrity. By the turn of the century he had clearly seen enough to realize that he must be free to unwind his own clues, work out his own development; he must have room to work, time to think, the freedom to taste life in full rich drafts; in other words, he must cast off the drudgery, the control by others, and be at liberty to take the open road and determine his own destiny, for better or for worse. "My father's excessive severity [he told Schottky] now seemed more oppressive than ever as my talent developed and my knowledge increased. I should have liked to break away from him so that I could travel alone; but my harsh mentor never left my side."[62]

However, by the end of 1800, after his successes in Leghorn and Modena, he had already, within himself, made the great decision; so six months later when the opportunity arose he was prepared to

[62] Schottky, *op. cit.*, 254.

seize it. The dauntless spirit that later enabled him to surmount almost insuperable physical obstacles had at last risen to the surface and from then on nothing was ever again able to hold him prisoner against his will.

III. *LUCCA 1801–1805*

*Der eigene Wille sei der Herr des Menschen, die eigene Lust sein
einzig Gesetz, die eigene Kraft sein ganzes Eigentum, denn das
Heilige ist allein der freie Mensch und nichts Höheres ist denn Er.*
—RICHARD WAGNER.

*Many roads lead to Rome, but every artist must find his own. Only
that artist is a master who is able to express his own ideas in a language peculiarly his own.*—MAX LIEBERMANN.

BORN IN THE overpopulated alleys of proletarian Genoa, coming
to maturity in the tempestuous years when desperate humanity
was reduced to misery by war and the ravages of pestilence and
famine, passing months of servitude in Leghorn, in dingy surroundings with an endless vista of unlovely days to come, Niccolò,
from the moment of his arrival in Lucca, was evidently completely
captive, a pleasure no doubt heightened by the discovery of the
satisfying opportunities it offered a musician—opportunities of
listening, learning, playing, teaching, and earning his own way,
entirely free of parental leading strings. After his return to Genoa
in the early weeks of 1801 the memory of this enchanting spot
"dipped in a thicket of nightingales" must have occupied his every
waking thought, while even at night dreams probably came to
trouble him. For Lucca seems to have given him his first sense of
release, so it is not surprising that when once his ambition was
achieved he adopted it as his *seconda patria* (the phrase is his)[1] and
remained faithful to it for well over a decade.[2]

Protected from sharp winds on the landward horizon by the
bright blue Apennines, and the summer heat tempered by cool
breezes from the Gulf of Genoa, this compact little town, enclosed

[1] Codignola, *op. cit.*, 210.
[2] In his monograph, Fétis stated that Paganini "left Lucca after three years, never
to return." He seems to have continued to use Lucca as his base of operations till
1811–12, when he evidently transferred his "headquarters" to Parma. (*Notice biographique sur Niccolò Paganini*, 42.)

within the cincture of its ancient fortifications,[3] was "the very model of a small *pays de Cocaigne*" overflowing with everything that made "for ease, for plenty, for beauty, for interest, and good example";[4] a little terrestrial paradise for ears deafened by the noises of a busy seaport and nerves taut with the harsh realities of war. Thus the very thought of being free and self-supporting in such an atmosphere might well have turned an older and far wiser head.

Although relatively small (in 1805 the population all told numbered only thirty thousand), Lucca was the seat of an old and wealthy aristocracy who passed their urbane lives behind the severe façades of their sombre palaces, playing a preponderate role in the destiny of their city and taking special pride in the fame of their great religious festivals and their several music institutions to which a long tradition had given permanence.[5] Besides several theatres where lyrical drama and oratorio were fostered with great zeal, there was the old Cappella della Signoria, founded in 1372 by Charles IX;[6] three seminaries with music departments under the direction of eminent pedagogues;[7] two great musical dynasties, the Quilici and Puccini families; and last of all, of course, the annual festivities connected with the two great religious festivals—the Feast of San Croce, or Elevation of the Cross, on September 14,[8] and St. Martin's Day on November 11.

The first, which was the more important and solemn of the two, was dedicated to the veneration of the *Volto Santo,* or Sacred Countenance,[9] a cedarwood crucifix said by legend to have been carved by Nicodemus and miraculously transported, in the early Middle

---

[3] The walls of Lucca dated from 1504–1650.

[4] Henry James, *Italian Hours,* 450.

[5] When the French occupied Lucca for the first time on January 2, 1799, the army levied several millions from the aristocracy, then when they entered the city for the second time on January 9, 1800, the civilian commissioner (Angles) instituted a dictatorship till the aristocracy, who had collaborated with the Austrians, had paid the million francs damages exacted by Massena.

[6] In 1800 this orchestra consisted of five violins and violas, two oboes, one double bass, one cello, trumpets, trombones, hunting horn, cembalo, and four soloists. (See Lazzareschi, *Il soggiornò di Niccolo Paganini a Lucca,* p. 6, n. 2.)

[7] The Seminary of San Martino, founded in 1572; the Seminary of San Michele. dating from 1518; and the Seminary of San Giovanni, founded in 1599.

[8] See Eugenio Lazzareschi, *La Festa di Santa Croce a Lucca,* 4.

[9] In the cathedral the relic is kept in a little temple constructed in 1484 by Matteo Civitalli.

Ages, from the Holy Land to Tuscany, since which time Lucca had vied with Santiago de Compostela in Spanish Galicia as the goal of pilgrims, thousands yearly streaming to the Tuscan shrine, particularly for the autumn festival, which was celebrated with great music and "an extravagant expenditure of candles."

The ceremonies on the vigil of the feast consisted of a celebration of Solemn Vespers and the traditional *Luminaria,* or torchlight procession after sundown from the Cathedral to the Church of San Frediano and return, the marchers, each with a lighted taper, including all the highest civil, military, and ecclesiastical authorities, members of the different monastic orders, the various guilds and corporations, trumpeters and musicians from the neighboring towns, and the entire male citizenry of Lucca and surrounding hamlets between the ages of fourteen and sixty.

> *In Lucca for the autumn festival*
> *The streets are tulip gay . . .*

sang one entranced spectator, while to Heinrich Heine, gazing enraptured at the quivering light against the background of brocaded houses, with roofs, balconies, doorways, and latticed windows ablaze with candles and filled with women in their richest finery, it seemed "as though life were celebrating its nuptials with death, inviting youth and beauty to the feast." Next morning, at stroke of dawn, an opening salvo from the ramparts, accompanied by the pealing bells of all the monasteries, shrines, and churches,[10] summoned the Luccans to early Mass, after which they surged in crowds to the Piazzo Michele, where, amidst rows of market booths with jugglers, fortune tellers, mountebanks, and singing *ciechi,*[11] they gave themselves over until sunset to the carefree merrymaking of a popular Italian festival.

At the cathedral, the music, which for over a century had been under the direction of some member of the Puccini family,[12] represented one of the leading magnets of the festival. It was more in the nature of a gala concert in a religious setting than elaborate liturgical music during the time of divine service, so the privilege of per-

10 In 1805 there were seventeen convents and fifteen monasteries in Lucca.
11 Blind beggars.
12 Ancestors of Giacomo Puccini, composer of *La Bohème.*

forming at either Vespers or High Mass was greatly coveted by the most eminent artists in the country. However, as there were always many applicants and the number of players was limited, it was the custom to have the candidates perform before a selection board or jury, which then chose the soloists on the basis of their merits. Hence, to win out in such a competition was an honor in itself.[13]

As the November festival attracted fewer pilgrims, the music was less elaborate, yet, even so, musicians were ever ready to offer their services merely for the distinction of having taken part, irrespective of the honorarium. However, after the waves of France's revolution broke over Italy, war and civil discord (*"Il n'est pas de pays plus divisé sur terre,"* Saliceti wrote of Lucca) had combined to dim the ancient glory of both festivals, the authorities being forced to cut down more and more the sums allocated for the music, which naturally resulted in a falling off, both in the quality of the offerings and the eminence of the participating artists. Up to 1790 a sum of 500 scudi (roughly 2800 lire) had been annually appropriated for the San Croce music, but during the ensuing decade this sum had gradually dwindled to 200, so that the occasion now offered little inducement for outsiders, most of whom, during those lean and troublous years, could ill afford the journey. The ceremonies had therefore lost much of their attraction for visitors, which caused great dissatisfaction amongst the Luccans, who each year looked forward to the additional income arising from this brief but lucrative "tourist trade."

In the summer of 1800, after the French had instituted on July 8 a provisional democratic government, the latter, desiring to revive the former brilliance of these festivals and incidentally curry favor with the Luccans, increased the appropriation for the San Croce music to 400 scudi and sent out a circular letter to "all professors and teachers of music" in the leading cities, notifying them that "any virtuoso, singer, or instrumentalist was privileged to exercise his talents at the ceremonies in celebration of the Feast of San Croce to take place in Lucca at first and second Vespers and High Mass on September 13 and 14 (1800) respectively,[14] the only excep-

---

13 Gervasoni, *Nuovo Teoria di musica . . .*, 240. As far as can be learned, Paganini played at the festival for the last time in 1818.

14 *"Sperando che en tale maniera sia per passarne la notizia a tutti i Professori, che se resolveranno in avvenire di dar saggio del loro talento nella detta funzione."*

tions being "organists and conductors (of which there were enough in Lucca), flutists and performers on the *colascione* and other instruments unsuited for sacred concerts."[15] Otherwise, any candidates would be sure of "receiving proper recognition."

As already said, Niccolò and his father may have gone to Leghorn early in the summer and, if so, could hardly have avoided hearing of the competition and the financial and professional rewards attached to it. If, however, they were still in Genoa when the circular was issued, the information would have reached them all the more certainly since a copy was sent to the Reverend Antonio Mangiarotti of the cathedral and he would have passed it on at once to Niccolò's old master, who would surely have taken special pride in his gifted pupil winning out on such a coveted occasion. Be that as it may, it is difficult to believe that Niccolò failed to attend if he was in Leghorn and only twenty-six miles away. Perhaps he did and the unconventional nature of his "contribution" did not please the classical taste of the cathedral's eminent organist, or maybe his recent interest in "agriculture and the guitar" had taken a little toll of his virtuosity, or (which is even more likely) his political opinions were unpopular in Lucca, so that he did not win selection.[16] One can think of any number of things that might have stepped between him and his ambition; but it is almost inconceivable that he did not make a try for it, if not in September, then surely in November; and all the more so since, if he played in Modena on December 5, he must have been in or round Lucca on St. Martin's Day and have remained there long enough, either at this time or on some earlier occasion, to decide that this was where he wished to make his future home. It is clear that Antonio must also have had some more cogent reason for his reluctance to allow him to visit Lucca in 1801 than his own inability to accompany him, or even the possible expense of the long journey. He probably sensed with a father's intuition Lucca's great attraction for his son, or if Niccolò had really tried and failed in 1800, he may have felt that political considerations had governed the decision and therefore

15 The *colascione* was a European offshoot of the Arabian long lute.

16 His lifelong habit of preserving a strict silence on any passing defeat would explain his failure to refer in any way to the 1800 visit, if he had been unsuccessful.

looked upon another excursion under such conditions as a futile waste of time.

Codignola states (without, however, any supporting evidence) that the Lucca visit of 1801 was prompted by Niccolò's having learned that the post of first violin in the theatre orchestra was vacant[17]—a not implausible surmise in view of later developments. Yet if we concede the possibility of a rejection in 1800, the injury to his pride may also have moved him to try again the following year. At any rate, whether he was in Leghorn or in Genoa at the time,[18] or whatever may have been the actual impetus, there is no question that the festival of 1801 furnished him with the needed pretext for the fulfillment of his purpose, particularly since he had probably ascertained beforehand that this time his father, for some reason, could not go along.

If the orchestral position were the magnet, one can understand how the idea would appeal to him. In addition to its being a position that he had always ultimately envisaged, he would now be his own master, and in another town where, when the theatre was closed, he would have much free time for himself with numerous opportunities of adding to his income, not only in Leghorn, where he was now well acquainted, but at the near-by Baths of Lucca with their fashionable throngs.

Since his name has not yet come to light in any official Lucca records of 1802, it is easy to make small debating points; but where music was so generally cultivated and where there were several bands and theatres in the town, a clever young musician with the gift of improvisation and the command of two popular instruments, even if he had no fixed appointment, would never lack sufficient paying engagements to satisfy his modest needs. Moreover, that he must have spent these early years in close association with some lyrical theatre is clearly manifest from his later mastery of all phases of the work—a mastery that derives only from experience, and a far richer, fuller one than the occasional opera performances that he conducted during his three years of service at the Baciocchi

---

[17] Codignola, *op. cit.,* 12.

[18] Fétis, *op. cit.,* 86, attributes his statement that "Paganini was in Leghorn in 1801" to Gervasoni, but the latter does not mention it in his *Nuova Theoria.*

court. For it was undoubtedly a close connection with the theatre during the most impressionable period of youth that always made it so fascinating for him.[19]

Although the young man who would arrive in Lucca for the festival would be nineteen in another month and knew that he held his fortune in his fingers, he neither ventured to take French leave, as many youths in similar circumstances would have done, nor to undertake the enterprise alone. With characteristic pliancy he was perfectly willing to have his brother Carlo squire him if that were a condition; which may have seemed to Antonio a sufficiently sure pledge since Carlo was marrying Anna Bruzzo at the Church of San Tomaso in Genoa on September 26, so the two could hardly remain in Lucca longer than four days.[20]

The psychological consequences of such restraint on a temperament like Niccolò's were unquestionably incalculable. The suppression of his desires till he had reached adolescence without probably ever having had an object for his affections generated in him an inordinate inquisitiveness, so that after shaking off the distasteful parental fetters he tasted pleasure to the full before he knew real love, which made the latter sentiment, from then on, impossible for him, and may have contributed very largely to his lifelong aversion to marriage. However, it surely would be unjust to attribute his father's obstinacy solely to cupidity, to Italian customs, or even to selfish personal considerations. True, the journey threatened to remove Niccolò and possibly his brother from his sphere of influence, but an even more important consideration was that it would make him his own master in the vicinity of a large

[19] An interesting, hitherto unknown work that has just come to light—a sonata for solo violin, accompanied by two violins—is dedicated to *L'Intreccio o Balli delle Orsi* (The Entanglement, or the Ball of the Bears), which was evidently a play or operetta. The closing words, *"Finis, Laus Deo Patris,"* shows that it must date from the period 1802–1806 since the same phrase (in Paganini's Latin) is to be found on another work dating from this period. The work is dated September 24, but without a year. The last page contains the following note: "I'm not leaving you, though he's back. I hope some day you'll see things never before seen. You'll do what you have never yet done. Praise be to God the Father Almighty, Creator of heaven and earth. Praised be the name of Jesus and Maria. I'm feeling absolutely tiptop. I'm well physically and very flush." The Orsi were call-boys and occasional supernumeraries.

[20] Since Carlo was five years older than Niccolò and by this time was probably a good routine second violinist, he may have secured an appointment even before his brilliant brother.

seaport where liberty means most to one young and ardent in the pursuit of pleasure, and this just when a restrictive hand was necessary to keep within bounds even the normal disturbances of adolescence. Like any father, Antonio must fundamentally have had his sons' welfare at heart and was concerned about such possibilities, realizing that the Dionysiac element, in such a convulsive personality as Niccolò's, should it once come to white heat, could only end in promiscuity. Knowing also by his own work on and round the docks the numerous pitfalls awaiting a magnetic youth, he may have striven in his harsh, tyrannical way to step between his son and inevitable catastrophe. For "a person of Paganini's temperament [the words are Professor Berri's], a delicate and emaciated adolescent, precociously initiated by his comrades and the *carrughi* of his native city, was not dedicated to the mortification of his instincts." Further, that gay and dissolute age imposed no moral curbs; so Niccolò should not be harshly judged for early sensual excesses when temptation lay everywhere around him.[21] In any case, his escapades did not differ from those of other young blades of that day, once they drifted into a fast set. Beyle, who was in Italy in the early years of the century, spoke of the "inviting and easy manners of the women, openly flaunting their lovers like their arms and breasts in the modish Roman costumes that revealed all their physical charms." So with perpetual invitation before him, it required little persuasion on the part of boisterous companions to launch Niccolò, whose "sensuality [like Byron's] was diffuse and uncontrollable," on a raffish course, which later was to have such disastrous effects. "When one is young and has a great thirst, what does it matter where he quenches it?" wrote Beyle of this period of his life.[22] "However [reflects Professor Berri] one does not quaff the cup of pleasure with impunity! A vague, microscopic little creature resembling a grain of coffee and a slender filament fashioned like a corkscrew,[23] gliding with suggestive elegance and both so infinitesimal that not even Lazzaro Spallanzani could detect them with his famous microscope and thus never suspected their

21 In his monograph and the second edition of his dictionary, Fétis makes a libertine and gambler of Paganini at the early age of fifteen.

22 See Matthew Josephson, *Life of Henri Beyle*, 66 f., for a description of conditions at that time.

23 The *Treponema pallidum*, the causative organism of syphilis.

existence, joined together to Niccolò's detriment, and combining with the bacillus discovered by Robert Koch in 1882, condemned him to a premature and inglorious end after a lifetime of pain and suffering." With Niccolò, in the last analysis, the victory always lay with Destiny.

ii

Although his dates might be indefinite, his chronology confused, this time at least he was correct in placing his Lucca debut "four years before the coronation of Napoleon at Milan." One wonders how he came to link this first Lucca visit with the Emperor. Perhaps because he viewed the latter's coronation and the events connected with it as the real starting point of his career, "Going by the statutes, [he continued] everybody laughed at my big bow and heavy strings.[24] But after the concerto there was great applause, indeed so much that the other candidates didn't venture to play. At a big evening service in the church my concerto caused such a furore that all the monks rushed out, shouting to the people to be quiet."[25] Abbé Jacobo Chelini, a member of the cathedral orchestra at the time, has given us the following eyewitness account in his *Zibaldone Lucchese:*[26]

The morning of the festival [Sept. 14, 1801] the Government attended the solemn pontifical Mass celebrated by Archbishop Filippo Sardi, which because of the music was even more festive than it would have been. . . . It so happened that it fell to a certain Paganini to play—a Genoese Jacobin famed as a patriot and especially as a violinist.[27] The

[24] Upon being appointed to Turin in 1771, Pugnani demanded that the strings be *"montati di grosso, come se vuol dire, cioe armati di grosse cordi."* He always used much heavier strings than any of his contemporaries. Paganini may have heard him in Parma or at Di Negro's.

[25] This evidently occurred at Solemn Vespers, September 13, just before the Luminaria.

[26] A *zibaldone* is a collection of miscellaneous writings, memoirs, reports, anecdotes, etc. Chelini's account is found in Manuscript 93, pp. 507–508, State Archives, Lucca. The same account, with a few minor divergencies, is found in a duplicate copy of the Zibaldone, Manuscript 101, pp. 839–40.

[27] A Jacobin was an extreme radical in politics. The term originally was applied to the members of the French political club established in 1789 at Paris in the old convent of the Jacobins, who had vowed to maintain and propagate the principles of extreme democracy and absolute equality. Later on, the word became a nickname for any political reformer.

Government wished this excellent violinist to exhibit his musical ability but since the Motet at the Epistle and another concerto at the Offertory gave him no opportunity to play during the celebration of the Mass, the Minister of the Interior, Adriano Mencarelli, gave orders (contrary to all the regulations) that Paganini was to play a violin concerto at the conclusion of the Kyrie, and he was indiscreet enough to play one that took fully twenty-eight minutes. This professor certainly manifested an unusual and unprecedented ability and virtuosity. He imitated on his strings the songs of birds, the flute, trombone, and horn, and, though everyone admired his astounding bravura, when they heard such mimicry produced on a violin, it nevertheless aroused laughter even in church.[28] In short, he was a professor of great ability, but he lacked judgment and self-criticism. He was also able to play a whole concerto on one string. I have said that he lacked judgment and self-criticism because to imitate on the violin the songs of birds and the tones of other instruments certainly shows great ability but, being only mimicry, it is merely a youthful caprice and should be performed at a concert in a theatre, but not in a sacred edifice. However, the concerto received great applause, like all the music, the Jacobins leading the ovation. They said that such music had never before been heard at a San Croce celebration, and if anyone had dared to criticise it, they ran the risk of being arrested.

Niccolò no doubt received a handsome fee for this spectacular performance and seems to have played in other churches while awaiting a permanent appointment. With the democratic government now solidly behind him and particularly with such a potent advocate as the Minister of the Interior, who, to favor his young protégé, did not hesitate to rearrange the traditional ritual of a pontifical Mass, he knew it was only a question of time till he was properly taken care of and appointed to a position worthy of his skill.

Domenico Gemignani to Bartholomeo Quilici.
The first time Lucca ever heard Paganini was at a concert in the Cathedral on the Feast of San Croce, September 14, 1801. Paganini was then invited to play in the Church of the Capucines on the Feast of San Serafino on October 12, but this concert did not take place till December 8, the Feast of the Immaculate Conception, in the Church of Santa Maria. A few days later he played a concerto at the Residence and fol-

[28] These were the years when Paganini played to the gallery with his imitative effects of birds, animals, etc., which was then "the fashion."

lowing this was appointed first violin of the Republic. This information is taken from the documents compiled by the person who recorded the procedures of the republican government.

He probably received the requisite assurances while his brother Carlo was still in Lucca and therefore made him the bearer of his declaration of independence, sending his father word that he was throwing off the parental yoke and would in future be shifting for himself. Since for the next seven years Carlo's life seems to have been bound up with his, it is quite likely that he too received promise of appointment, which may have precipitated his marriage plans.

Nothing has been found, as yet, in either the state archives or the various parish registers that would throw light on Niccolò's activities after his appointment, but inductive reasoning tells us that the incident he related to Lichtenthal and Schottky regarding the valuable violin he received from M. Livron undoubtedly occurred in the autumn of 1802. Livron was a wealthy French merchant who was in business in Leghorn with a compatriot, M. Hamelin. In April, 1802, he and his partner received permission to construct at their own expense on property they had recently acquired outside the Porta San Marco a "Teatro nel Rivellino," despite the fact that several months earlier a certain Matteo Stefanini and twenty associates had been refused a permit to construct a theatre in the suburb Porta a Pisa (on the recommendation of the Accademia degli Avvalorati) because "people in the suburbs did not patronize the theatre and the people of Leghorn were not in a position to go to a theatre situated outside the city limits," nor was it deemed "politically prudent" to have large crowds congregate in a site in the country that "was not immediately accessible to the police."[29] The fact that such permission was granted the two Frenchmen a short time later therefore witnesses either to the power of their wealth, or their political influence—or both. As the inauguration of the new theatre presumably received appropriate publicity (Livron was a very liberal patron of the arts), Niccolò may have come over from Lucca to take part in the festivities and

29 Dossier 1362 (1802) and Dossier 79 (1st quarter, 1802), State Archives, Leghorn, Italy.

was invited by Livron to grace the opening performance; which would account for the gift of the violin. At all events, he received it while the Frenchmen were operating their theatre, that is, some-time between the late summer of 1802 and 1804.

He told Finck, editor of the *Allgemeine Musikalische Zeitung,* that he had resided in Lucca continually through all the changing governments;[30] so if one had the patience and the time to search through the old parish registers of Lucca's seventy-five churches, one would very likely run across his name, just as it was discovered in the parish register of San Frediano for 1809, at which time he was residing with Francesco and Anna Bucchianeri.[31] Anna, like her youngest sister Eleanora, followed the trade of dressmaker, while their father, Vincenzo Quilici (a postilion), was presumably a member of the Quilici clan whose nominal head was the Abbé Domenico Quilici.[32] A brother, Bartolomeo, was a captain of the grenadiers and another sister, Teresa, married to Salvatore Chicca,[33] was a hosier—humble members of the Lucca proletariat that formed Niccolò's new environment. It was to the *"ragazza Eleanora"*[34] that he dedicated his Op. 3, so that this work and his Op. 2, dedicated to Dellepiane, one of his Lucca pupils,[35] was ob-viously written between 1802 and 1809. As for Eleanora, she was evidently his first love (perhaps the magnet that drew him to Lucca!)—an experience that left him with tender memories that he always cherished; her girlish laughter, zest for fun, and some sweet, lovely quality in her devotion and surrender that was ever

---

[30] During the years 1799–1801, Lucca passed through several different political *étapes,* all of them brief and largely experimental. It finally emerged as a full-fledged republic on December 28, 1801, and retained this form of government till July, 1805. Paganini's original contract with the national orchestra must thus have dated from January, 1802.

[31] The Bucchianeri family "lived on the first floor of the first house opposite the church, one of the two forming the large *palazzo* opposite the lateral entrance of the church, now bearing the number eight."

[32] Domenico Quilici (b. 1757). Six other members of the family were well-known musicians.

[33] Salvatore Chicca may have been related to the Lucca violin maker of that name who, on September 14, 1811, sold an instrument to Prince Felix Baciocchi for fifteen louis, which was charged to the "music of the court."

[34] Born in 1791, she was nine years younger than Niccolò.

[35] Agostino Dellepiane was a friend of Paganini all his life. Professor Giovannetti, another Lucca pupil, was a member of the Cappella Palatina from 1780 to 1805, which is further proof of Paganini's activities in Lucca during the first years of the century.

present with him and that from thenceforth drew him so strongly to young girls barely on the threshold of womanhood—a mixture of gratitude and penitence, perhaps. Three times we find her name mentioned in his correspondence, the first on May 25, 1838, when he wrote to Germi from Paris: "I beg you to arrange again to have the sum of 300 lire sent from my account to Signora Eleanora Quilici in Pistoia"; on September 7, 1839, "We will speak again of Eleanora," and, most eloquent of all, she was the only person outside his immediate family who was remembered in his will. "I bequeath herewith to Eleanora Quilici of Lucca, sister of Anna Bucchianeri, an annual pension of 600 new lire during her lifetime." She apparently never married, and may have found it difficult in later years to get along, which would account for Paganini's gifts, though one suspects that he had always supported her. "The documents that have come to light to date [wrote Lazzareschi] do not reveal what stronger and more tenacious ties of memory bound him to this friend of his youth. And it is well that this is so, for it is quite in keeping with his legend to find the shadow of a human mystery in the chapter of his private life during his early youth in Lucca."[36] That his friend Lazzaro Rebizzo was aware of his ties with the Quilici family is apparent from his calling upon Bartolomeo and Teresa to furnish testimony regarding Paganini's early years in Lucca at the time of the ecclesiastical trial after his death.

Bartolomeo Quilici to Lazzaro Rebizzo.
There's no doubt that Paganini aroused universal admiration when, as a young man, he went to Lucca, where he obtained an engagement. . . . He was charitable towards the wretched and especially towards those of his own profession, as far as his means permitted. He was neither jealous nor envious, and though he himself was teaching, he respected the other professors, albeit they were far inferior to him. Sometimes he urged them very courteously and without any display of superiority, to adopt other methods. Although at that time there were few professors who were skilled musicians, he not only tolerated their ignorance, but he also never reprimanded them. He studied and played other stringed instruments besides the violin. In fact, he gave cello lessons to Signor Angelo Torre, to the latter's great advantage. He also took a friendly interest in Professor Francesco Bandettini (at that time first double bass of the Royal Orchestra) and persuaded him to change his method

[36] E. Lazzareschi, *op. cit.,* 18.

of playing the double bass, which Bandettini found very excellent. Professor Dellepiane and Professor Giovannetti were two good violin pupils of his; he wrote some music especially for them, with consummate mastery.

Teresa Quilici Chicca to Lazzaro Rebizzo.
In accordance with my brother's request, I will tell you something about Niccolò Paganini, the famous violinist, when he lived in Lucca. When I gave birth to a son in 1811 not long after my husband's death, I asked Signor Paganini to act as sponsor. Through great delicacy of feeling, he showed some reluctance at first, since the tenets of our religion require the sponsor to assume certain obligations towards the child. But then acceding to my request, he carried him to the sacred font and on that occasion, as is customary, wanted to give me a present, though at the time he was still in straightened circumstances. To the honor of Signor Paganini, I would only add that he was very charitable to his neighbors and gave alms to the poor and was a man of virtuous and exemplary conduct."[37]

Paganini's friends were no doubt related to Abbé Domenico Quilici, director of the Seminary of San Michele where he taught solfeggio, singing, harmony, counterpoint, and composition from 1785 till 1807, when Princess Elise secularized religious property in Lucca and Piombino. Gathering round him a few young men he then opened a private music school, which he ran at his own expense till it was taken over by the city a decade later. An eminent teacher with many pupils in important posts throughout the country, it was possibly under his direction or at least within his circle of influence that Niccolò worked out the finished versions of his Capricci and committed them to paper. Be that as it may, there can be no doubt that life in such an intensely musical atmosphere, making music, hearing music, living music in his own way and on his own terms must have borne rich fruit for such a nature.[38] For in this pleasant little world in which his life revolved, with all its undeniable temptations,[39] even if no events of consequence oc-

---

[37] Teresa, writing after thirty years, erred in the date of her son's birth. The child, christened Nicolò Stefano, was born in 1810, as attested by the parish register of the Church of S. Paolino. The certificate indicates that Paganini was not present at the ceremony but was represented by the priest, Fr. Michele Salvoni.

[38] Codignola, *op. cit.*, 13.

[39] Serristori wrote Angiolini: "I don't know if you know the Baths of Lucca, but there is a tremendous crowd. The luxury is *sans égal*. Gambling goes on continuously."

curred he must still have been under some more powerful artistic stimulus, some greater spur to endeavor than the "dilettante" activities he pursued in the ambit of the wealthy Genoese with whom Di Negro's patronage brought him into contact. Or even for that matter in quiet Ramairone, where, particularly in the agitated years between 1797–1800, his home environment, the total lack of order in the Paganini household, must have made the conception and working out of such creations well-nigh impossible, even had he been guaranteed the uninterrupted repose to put them down on paper.

On the whole it is very difficult to date exactly many of his early compositions, or trace their first performance. With other composers a study and comparison of the stylistic features of compositions written at different stages of their career often makes it possible to date a work approximately; but with Paganini no epochs were marked by a development of style. What was found in the first composition was found in the last.[40] Moreover, had his illnesses in 1822 or 1826 proved fatal, his legend would have taken its place alongside those of many of his great forerunners; but it would have had little effect on the development or future of violin playing. This influence came later, not as the result of any greater technical mastery or the creation of works more epoch-making than those he had already written and played in Italy, but solely through the change in his environment. As he moved out into the world he scattered round him everywhere a rich and powerful pollen that fertilized in one way or another every object with which it came in contact.

Although close perusal of his early works throws no light on his aesthetic ripening, his growth and training as a composer, there is still every reason to believe that it was during these early Lucca years that he conceived and worked out most of his technical tours de force, viz., revival of the *scordatura*,[41] extending the compass of useful harmonics,[42] developing a new series of bow strokes, per-

40 Most of his works were cast in the form of variations. See Mompellio, (*op. cit.*, 390, n. 1 ff.)

41 The *scordatura* (mis-tuning) was mentioned by Michael Praetorius in 1618 in his *De Organographia* and by Biago Marini in his *Sonata Seconda per il violino*.

42 The advantages of the stopped harmonic of every tone and half tone on the violin was then unknown.

fecting himself in pizzicato for the left hand, and the other "tricks" with which he astounded the world in later years. Disregarding the very early compositions such as the topical Carmagnole Variations, largely extemporized to demonstrate his technical skill, then to be abandoned in a year or two, the Capricci, though undated (according to Lipinsky they were not all written at one time), should no doubt be considered as his first work, and they remained, as with many of the Romantic composers, his finest achievement in the creative field, still wafting to us "the living breath of a genuinely gifted and ingenious composer." While his statement to Lichten-thal that upon his return to Genoa in 1796 he "composed difficult music and worked continuously at difficult problems of his own invention" might suggest that they were worked out at this time, one must also consider that his first four years in Lucca undoubt-edly represented for him a period of insemination, so that the ideas later developed in the Capricci may have been simmering in his brain for some time before they burst forth, all white fire from the anvil, to serve his virtuoso purposes. For there never seems to have been any struggle to discover the proper means of expression. We find no preliminary sketches, no revisions, no touchings and re-touchings, no tentative drafts, as with other composers. Everything was apparently *écrite du premier jet,* in the white-hot speed of execution. Furthermore, unlike other composers he seems to have received no noticeable stimulation from events or people.[43] As Iris Origo wrote of Leopardi, "none of his visions reached him from the outer world";[44] the impact of life generated no personal reac-tions that he was moved to melodize or orchestrate; his passions in-spired no love songs; he knew no ecstacies or disillusionments that were transmuted into music. Hence his compositions sound no subjective note that might help us to penetrate the secret of his emotions.[45] His task, as he saw it, was simply to develop his own gifts—this prodigious technical skill with which the gods had en-dowed him—for his own immediate purposes and not to hand them on for the use of future generations, despite all his protesta-

43 According to tradition (uncorroborated), only Paganini's B minor Concerto owed its inception to an outward impression.

44 Origo, *op. cit.,* 131.

45 See John Addington Symonds, *Sketches in Italy and Greece* (2nd ed., London, 1879, 107 f.), for characterization of Italian genius in this sense.

tions to the contrary. ("A violinist who cannot on occasion produce, and clearly too, a hundred notes a second, should renounce all hope of music—he will never benefit by the revolution my legacy will effect in the world of music.") For it was always his present public that he had in mind.[46] "Composing is not so easy for me as you think [he said.] My great rule in art is complete unity within diversity, and that is very hard to achieve. The public is always clamoring for something new, surprising, and likes to hear long works. This requires reflection before beginning to write."[47]

The Twenty-four Capricci were the only important works to be published during his lifetime, so that those composers on whom he made a deep impression—as in the case of Schumann and Liszt —naturally looked to the Capricci to reveal to them the tremendous fascination of his playing and there discovered themes and ideas that they considered as worthy of development.[48] Indeed, Schumann was so enthusiastic over the "beautiful, tender theme" of the second caprice that he thought this work alone sufficient to insure its creator first rank amongst the younger Italian composers. Brahms, too, who based his wonderful Op. 35 on the twenty-fourth caprice, and also repeatedly showed Paganini's influence in his variations, felt that the Capricci evidenced as great a gift "for composing in general as for the violin in particular." As for the later works, all conceived for virtuoso purposes, they paid heavy tribute to the ephemeral fashion of the day, the composer being pushed more and more into the background by the virtuoso; yet the very elements that make the works now *vieux*—in that they date—contributed then to their success, his playing imbuing them with something not inherent in the notes.[49] In the hands of other violinists they always lost much of their effect, and the change in musical taste

[46] Berri, *op. cit.*, 83, stresses Paganini's lack of interest for any problem touching his art, except that of the box office.

[47] Schottky, *op. cit.*, 274 f. This statement is also not original. He is quoting verbatim Anton Reicha's *Compositions-Lehre* (Vienna, 1818) Part IV, 485.

[48] Kathleen Dale in her work, *Nineteenth Century Piano Music* (Oxford, 1954), 190, states that Schumann and Chopin heard him play the *Capricci* in Frankfort and Paris, respectively. There is no record that he ever played these works in public; in fact, he practically admitted it himself. At his Warsaw and Frankfort concerts, where these composers heard him, he played only his popular numbers.

[49] According to Abraham Veinus (*The Concerto*, 164) "there is little left in the printed score of a Paganini concerto that his contemporaries heard beyond . . . the mechanism of a colossal technique."

has now consigned many of them to oblivion so that modern critics are inclined to keep their main praise for Paganini, the performer.

iii

His obstinate silence regarding his life and pursuits during these early years was unfortunate in that it was eagerly seized upon by envious detractors to surround him with some obscure tragedy, while his biographers, no less eager, have sprung greedily on Fétis' tendentious interpretation of an alleged conversation with him twenty years before, an interpretation influenced by Niccolò's reputation as a profligate, to link this period with an amorous intrigue with a nameless "lady of quality" who "had conceived a violent passion for him, which he reciprocated" and in the course of which they "retired to her estate in Tuscany" for an indeterminate period. It will be interesting to take a look at the origins of this "tradition."

For this biographical article on Paganini, in Volume VII of the first edition of his *Biographie Universelle,* which came out after Paganini's death, Fétis did not draw on personal conversations with the Maestro (as generally assumed) but derived his information exclusively from Schottky and the autobiographical sketch that had appeared in French translation in the *Revue Musicale* in 1830. Taking from the latter Paganini's simple statement, "On returning home [from Parma] I dedicated myself to agriculture and for several years took pleasure in twanging the guitar" (*"Restituitomi in patria mi dedicai all'agricoltura e per qualche anni presi gusto a pizzicare la chitarra"*), he paraphrased it as follows:

Au milieu de ces succès, [the concert tour of 1801] *on remarque dans la vie de Paganini une de ces péripéties assez fréquentes dans la vie des grandes artistes; tout à coup il se dégouta du violon, s'éprit pour la guitare d'une ardeur passionnée, et partagea près de quatre années entre l'étude de cet instrument et celle de l'agriculture.*

The "four years" were of course the period from the autumn of 1796 to the autumn of 1800.

Ten years later (1851), in writing the monograph commissioned by Schlesinger to promote the sale of Paganini's compositions, he played another variation on the theme:

Par une de ces péripéties assez fréquentes dans la carrière des grandes artistes, le violon cessa tout à coup de lui offrir le même attrait. Une grande dame s'était éprise pour lui d'un violent amour qu'il partageait, et s'était retirée avec lui dans une terre qu'elle possédait en Toscane.

Then to reinforce his statement he added a footnote to the effect that "he had paid no attention to the incident when Paganini told him of it since he was only interested in him as an artist. Later it seemed important in order to draw up the calendar of his life." In other words, he was now trying to fill in the gaps in Paganini's early life to which Anders had drawn attention in his monograph, and did not scruple to expand one of Paganini's anecdotes of his youthful amorous exploits to make it cover a period of years on which his source material afforded no information. We know from Schottky that Paganini took great pleasure in spinning tall yarns regarding his rakish escapades, so, inspired either by the notorious liaisons of other Paris artists in the early thirties, or with the deliberate intention of interesting a French public "which must always have a mistress in the case," he may have alluded indirectly to his passing liaison with the Princess Elise at Massa without venturing to link his name with Napoleon's sister. Despite the fact that there is not the faintest allusion to such an episode in either of the autobiographical sketches or in any gossip or slanderous rumor before the appearance of the monograph, Fétis' gloss, which is refuted by its own absurdity, has been unquestioningly accepted by every one of Paganini's biographers, even Codignola, who, in endeavoring to sweep the ground clear of the anecdotal, balks at far more plausible events. In so doing they all overlook the fairly obvious fact that if in that day and age any "great lady" had ever admitted to her company a roving young fiddler of humble origins (yet without fame) and had carried him off to her "estate in Tuscany," it would have so scandalized her world that current memoirs would have rumbled with it. Further, if there had really been a romance of this spectacular kind in his life, we may be sure that he would have related it to Schottky, whom he regaled with stories of alleged adventures that would have done credit to a Boccaccio and the extravagance of which must have strained even Schottky's ready credulity. Another psychological point that it would be well to hold in mind is that there is no record of his ever having inspired a passion in a highborn woman (his brief liaison with Princess Elise, if true, was undoubtedly a purely physical adventure), though, as his letters and recorded conversations very clearly show, he was prone to think every woman with whom he came in contact "was mad about him."

Since the patient torch of research has now illuminated many an obscure corner in his history and finally linked together different epochs in his life, unfounded theories such as this, like many other romantic incrustations, will have to be abandoned.[50] His obstinate refusal, even under challenge, to satisfy the vulgar public curiosity regarding his first four uneventful Lucca years, those years of preparation when his driving ambition gave him the strength, tenacity, and resolution to withdraw from the public stage and devote himself completely and absorbingly to perfecting his technique while maturing as an artist, had probably quite different motives.

Besides considering the obscurity of these first Lucca years as "very little consonant with his glory," a point on which his mind was ever concentrated, he may have believed with Byron that "man's love is of man's life a thing apart" and was silent through a deep loyalty to what was evidently one of the most tender and lovely memories in his life—his first boyhood liaison with the *"ragazza Eleanora"*—and a determination never to throw the spotlight on a period that might cause her any embarrassment. For, to borrow a felicitous phrase from André Maurois, *"le plaisir et l'amour sont, dans l'esprit d'un homme, associés aux premières et inoubliables expériences qui lui ont révélé l'un et l'autre."*

That this assumption is not entirely without foundation is attested by a notice appearing in the *Moniteur Universel* of July 15, 1840, in which the Genoa correspondent of the paper, after listing the principal bequests in Paganini's will, stated, presumably at the request of Germi or Rebizzo, that a life annuity had been left to

[50] Paganini's biographers, in their eagerness to fortify his legend, overlook his own statements. In describing the genesis of his *Duetto Amoroso*, he makes it clear that he wrote the Napoleon Sonata "a few weeks later," a fact corroborated by a close examination of the two manuscripts.

"une dame demeurant à Lucques, mais dont le nom, *selon la volonté express du testateur, ne doit pas être publié.*" (Italics added)

Niccolò was not always so considerate of the various sirens that crossed his path. Hence, the very quality of the silence in which he wrapped this passage of his life shows how permanent and precious the memory of Eleanora must have been.

To both Lichtenthal and Schottky, he skimmed lightly over the surface of these Lucca years but in his interview with Finck, in Leipzig, he was a little more expansive. "While still very young [wrote Finck] he was engaged in Lucca as first violin, where he also did some composing. He stayed there, living only for his art, throughout all the political changes, with which he did not concern himself. This statement, which is frequently questioned and has led many to suppose that there must have been some reason for hiding himself away, is substantiated too forcibly by far from slender evidence for anyone to doubt its authenticity. . . . Paganini remained in Lucca quite undisturbed during all the violent agitations of that bellicose period."

In his conversations with Fétis he was far too diplomatic to publicize his liaison with Princess Elise while Prince Felix was still alive, though the passing affair, which seems to have occurred at Massa (Elise's "estate in Tuscany") was apparently no secret in Paganini's circle, as indicated by the remarks of Jacques Catalani, director of the theatre in Massa.[51] Of course, such testimony at second hand has no corroborative value but it shows the direction of contemporary gossip which, in those days, and particularly in higher circles "easily turned into defamation." Hence, if Niccolò had ever had a protracted affair with any "grande dame" of that period, we may be sure that it would have been aired exultantly in some of the memoirs, letters, journals, and confessions that then flooded the literary market.

It stands to reason that the identity of this fictitious lady has eluded all sleuths, like the murdered wives and mistresses who allegedly preceded her. When Arnaldo Bonaventura published his work on Paganini in 1911, he put forward the theory that she

---

[51] See Paul Marmottan, *Les Arts en Toscane sous Napoléon. La Princesse Elise*, 162, n. 1.

"might have been the Signora Dida" to whom several guitar works are dedicated, though both he and Dr. George Kinsky[52] (in his annotations of Paganini's manuscripts in the Heyer Museum, Cologne) took great care to point out that a number of works dating from the same period were dedicated to other ladies,[53] so that Signora Dida could not have filled his thoughts exclusively nor could he have been "in seclusion with her somewhere in Tuscany."[54] After Bonaventura had advanced this theory, later biographers took it over as fact and from these fragile threads have spun a romance which, if Paganini could hear it from beyond the grave, would make him smile with satisfaction. For unaware that his life was more inspiring than any legend, he bent all his efforts to wind himself in a chrysalis of romance and at the end only succeeded in achieving sensational calumny, to be buried at last, as the indirect result of it, under a veritable monument of denigration.

"Many cities tried to keep me, some as concert artist, others as orchestral conductor [he said]. But my ardent temperament shrank from any fixed position. I liked traveling and it was impossible for me to stay any length of time in one place."[55] These remarks have also been taken to refer to his first Lucca years, when he was enjoying the fragrance of liberation, when liberty to him meant libertinism. Yet, he was evidently speaking of the period between 1810 and 1825, when he was continually on the move, flitting from place to place, for it is doubtful if between 1802 and 1805 his excursions took him much farther afield than the towns within the immediate radius of Lucca.[56] Beyle tells us that in 1801 "the country was armed to the teeth" against the peasants, who as often as not turned into

[52] See Pulver, *op. cit.*, 43, for a characteristic exaggeration of the Dida episode.

[53] These works were written in the period 1822–23, when Paganini was under treatment by Dr. Borda. Bonaventura wrote "Botti" instead of "Borda." (Arnaldo Bonaventura, *Niccolò Paganini*), though he placed a question mark after it to indicate that he was not certain.

[54] Fétis' version is as follows: "As a young man Paganini knew only artistic triumphs, when by one of those sudden twists in the careers of great artists the violin ceased all at once to afford him the same measure of enjoyment. A great lady had conceived a violent passion for him, which he reciprocated, and the two then retired to one of her estates in Tuscany." Fétis wrote that Paganini's Op. 2 and 3 were written at this time. Had he carefully examined the dedications, he might have spared himself an egregious error, and later biographers much extravagant romanticizing. (*Op. cit.*, 40.)

[55] Schottky, *op. cit.*, 255.

[56] Paganini told Schottky of an incident that took place at a concert in Pescia. (Schottky, *op. cit.*, 336.)

bandits, with the result that "violence and death were rampant everywhere," a situation that would not have tempted him to travel. During all this period (up to 1813, in fact) German musicians in Italy supplied the Leipzig and Vienna journals with regular reports of Italian musical activities in which they frequently mentioned instrumentalists, sometimes even describing the brilliant trickery of the perennial crop of prodigies on the violin, the flute, or hunting horn. Yet Paganini's name never figured in their columns till after his Milan début though they could hardly have failed to encounter him had he been traveling at this time. As he was not a person to be easily overlooked, the omission of his name would indicate that he had isolated himself in a little laboratory of his own, perhaps teaching Eleanora the guitar and posting now and then to Leghorn when the sensual demands of his ardent southern temperament demanded an outlet that was not obtainable, or perhaps was inadvisable, in the little shut-in world of Lucca.

iv

Towards the end of September, 1804, a vessel arriving at the port of Leghorn from Mexico brought to these frequently plague-ridden shores the bacillus of a disease hitherto unknown in Italy—the yellow fever. Until then this epidemic had been confined to the hot climates of the New World, so that the Italian physicians were as ignorant of proper curative measures as of the necessary safeguards. It therefore spread like wildfire through the city, and by October 6 —a fortnight after the arrival of the ship—3,033 virulent cases had been reported to the police, while hundreds of persons were dying daily, especially in the slums and crowded poorer quarters where the working classes lived. As usual in such great epidemics, either through superstition, ignorance, fear, or other causes, a large number of cases were never reported, and as the people fled in terror, infection was carried to all the outlying districts. In a desperate effort to stem the spread of a disease with which the existing sanitary conditions and medical knowledge were unable to cope, the theatres were closed and public assemblies of any kind prohibited, since it was soon discovered that the principal victims were robust young men and pregnant women, to whom the plague was mortal, while children, the aged, and the weak were apparently immune.

Antonia Bianchi and Paganini
Portraits by Kriehuber, Vienna, 1828.

Achilles Paganini
Portrait by Deveria, Paris.

Although a medical commission, in keeping with the practice of such bodies, hastened to assure the terrified populace that "they had the situation well in hand," women and young men were urged to take every possible precaution, and preventative measures were at once introduced in all the towns and hamlets within a large radius of Leghorn, even a city as far north as Milan instituting rigorous sanitary measures for the whole province as early as October 17. Lucca, as next-door neighbor, immediately closed the frontiers, prohibited the importation of any food products from Leghorn, and imposed a rigorous quarantine, so that with lightning speed the whole communal life of a very large district was suddenly brought to a standstill. On October 11, Paganini gave a concert at the Teatro Nazionale in Lucca, where he was a member of the orchestra, but as any further professional activities were temporarily suspended, he packed his few belongings and set forth for home over the broken, rutted roads and precipices that formed the only direct overland route from Lucca to Genoa. Here there was certainly no mystery about his sudden reappearance in his native city for anyone who takes a little trouble to read the history of that time. Botta and other Italian historians have described the situation in great detail,[57] so it is easy to understand the terrifying effect it must have had on a young man of Niccolò's emotional temperament. The motive behind the concert of October 11 was undoubtedly to provide him with funds for the journey and the weeks of waiting till the quarantine was raised, while the decision to return to Genoa, it may safely be affirmed, was due either to a hasty summons from his worried parents or a desire to reach a safety zone, and not because some nameless Tuscan Venus, as his biographers so convincingly assure us, "sent him back into the world with strict injunctions to lead a more temperate life." By December 24, Leghorn was declared free of the epidemic and, though the quarantine was not actually raised till January 21, the danger was considered over, at least in neighboring towns. By January 10, Niccolò was already back again in Lucca and on the twentieth celebrated his return by giving a concert in the Palazzo

---

57 Botta: "The plague began its ravages in the lowest, the dampest, and the dirtiest parts of the city, carrying off its victims in seven, five, three, and sometimes in even the brief space of one day.

Guidiccioni (the present State Archives), and two days later renewed his contract as first violin in the Capella Nazionale del Potere Executivo at a salary of twelve scudi a month.[58] There is no record in the papers of his having given a concert in Genoa during his eight or ten weeks' visit, though Gervasoni wrote that while there he gave some lessons to Caterina Calcagno, a talented child of seven. According to Francesco Regli, she always claimed that Bolognese was her teacher and, since Niccolò never mentioned her,[59] it is assumed that Lichtenthal, who at the time of her concert at the Milan Conservatory in May, 1814, wrote the *Allgemeine Musikalische Zeitung* that she "was a pupil of the famous Paganini," took his information from Gervasoni.[60]

Without indicating dates DeLaphalèque wrote that when "General Millot (*sic*) was governor of Genoa, Paganini visited him daily and oftentimes composed the entire music (quadrilles, interludes, etc.) for one of his receptions." This is very probably true, and took place during this Genoa visit at the end of 1804. For DeLaphalèque is here referring to Count Jean Baptiste *Milhaud* (1766–1833), who in 1800 was raised to the rank of brigadier general and sent by Napoleon as chief of mission to the courts of Naples and Tuscany. After being stationed for a time in Mantua, in July, 1803, he was appointed military commandant, or governor, of Genoa, which post he held till he returned to active military service the latter part of 1805. There is therefore no reason to doubt DeLaphalèque's statement regarding Niccolò's contributions since it was in December, 1804, as we now know, that he wrote the two compositions dedicated to Emilia di Negro. This indicates that he was not only in a very creative vein but in close touch with the Di Negro family, which would account for his connections with the Governor of Genoa. After this visit he seems to have avoided his native city till 1808, probably owing to the difficulties of travel and the long, tiresome interrogations at the frontiers of the little

---

[58] This is unquestionably the same position he had been holding from January, 1802. Contracts were drawn up for the calendar year. In this instance the delay was obviously due to the epidemic and to Paganini's temporary absence.

[59] Polko and Franz Farga expand Gervasoni's statement into a romance!

[60] It was a fairly common practice for young musicians to link their names with famous teachers when they may perhaps have had only a lesson or two.

pocket states shackled by papal, French, or Austrian chains. After assuming his duties at the Baciocchi court in January, 1806, he was naturally no longer his own master, but by that time he felt more at home in Lucca and probably had no desire to leave his now familiar haunts.

v

One uncertain point during these early Lucca years is when, and where, he acquired his famous Guarneri del Gesu violin.[61] To Lichtenthal he said: "An owner of a Guarneri violin told me that if I played a certain violin sonata at sight he would give me the instrument, and I won it. . . . Once finding myself in Leghorn without a violin, a M. Livron lent me an instrument to play a Viotti concerto and then made me a present of it." Here the Guarneri is not linked with Livron, nor is there any indication when and where the first incident took place.

To Schottky he was a little more explicit. "One of my excursions that was not a concert tour but a pleasure trip took me to Leghorn, where they wanted me to give a concert. The wealthy business man and music lover, M. Livron, lent me a Guarneri because I had no violin with me. However when I had finished playing he refused to take it back. . . . I had a similar experience in Parma. Signor Pasini, an excellent painter, had heard of my skill in sight reading. He presented me with a very difficult concerto and said he would give me a valuable violin as a present if I acquitted myself of the task in a satisfactory manner. The violin became my property."[62] As already mentioned, the Livron incident must have occurred sometime between 1802 and 1804, when Livron was operating his theatre, while the Parma gift dated, without question, from 1811 or 1812, years when Paganini played in Parma and his "concert announcements always contained a notice that he would perform any piece of music presented to him." Antonio Pasini, donor of the instrument, was a famous miniature painter of the period who in 1805 was appointed professor of miniature painting in the Parma

61 Fétis, *op. cit.*, 38, identified it with the Livron gift.
62 This is always referred to as a Stradivari—probably a surmise of some early biographer.

Academy of Fine Arts.[63] Within the next decade, through his position as court painter and his fame as a miniaturist, he was overwhelmed with orders and was therefore in a position to indulge in such impulsive generosities. He was described by his contemporaries as "quick tempered, disagreeable, and harsh, and rigid in his judgments of his fellow artists," so, since he was an ardent music lover and played the violin himself, he may have been baiting Niccolò in the expectation of deflating this young man's confidence and self-esteem!

At the zenith of his career in Italy, Niccolò frequently played the Stradivari that he purchased in 1818 from Count Cozio di Salabue of Casale Montferrato, but whether he possessed a Stradivari before that time, it is impossible to say.[64] In discussing his career with George Harrys, he told him of a harrowing experience at the gaming table when he was about "to dispose of his excellent violin, the only one he then possessed," which cured him of this expensive pastime.[65] But this incident must have occurred between 1813 and 1818 since before that time, when he was earning a "piffling little salary" at court and playing in relatively small towns, he was in no position to amass "a collection of jewels, rings and brooches," which he claimed to have already "gambled away." It will be recalled that Teresa Quilici testified that in 1811 he was "in straightened circumstances." Given his irresponsible attitude towards life in adolescence and early manhood, it is quite likely that when he got into low water, he often pawned his violin and then redeemed it when in funds, a fact that might also account for many of his professional eclipses. Fundamentally uninterested in politics, divorced from the deep current of the national heritage, he lived from day to day, engrossed in his own interests and pursuits, so that recollection of what later seemed to him irrelevant events became

63 Antonio Pasini (1770–1845), a pupil of Muzzi, first held the post of professor of miniature painting in the Academy of Fine Arts, then in 1822 was made master of "composition and anatomy." See *Gazzetta di Parma*, 1845, p. 515.

64 Cozio di Salabue died in 1840, leaving his collection to his daughter Mathilde; from her it went to Della Valle. It was exhibited at the Milan Exposition of Musical Instruments in 1881, where Giuseppe Fiorini saw it. He acquired the collection in 1920 for 100,000 lire and offered it in vain to Florence, Bologna, and Cremona. He finally presented it to Cremona in 1930.

65 Pulver erroneously attributes this anecdote to Fétis. Fétis took it from Conestabile, who was quoting George Harrys.

blurred in the larger and more important panorama as he crept slowly upwards towards Parnassus. Life in those early years, when he was "drifting with every passion," must have had its frequent ups and downs, its surprises, contradictions, disillusionments, but out beyond was always that mirage of better days to come, which to the very end lay shining in the distance like a sunset.

IV. *THE COURTIER 1805–1809*

*Je suis inexplicable pour tous, nul n'a le secret de ma vie et je ne veux le livrer à personne.—*BALZAC.

MEANWHILE, a new map of Europe was in the making which was to have far-reaching effects on lovely but unquiet Italy and prove, as well, another turning point in Niccolò's career. After the victory of the French in 1800, Lombardy, Piedmont, and Sardinia had been administered as occupied territory under military governors directly responsible to the First Consul as military dictator, while Lucca—formerly a small-scale replica of Venice and Genoa —remained an independent democratic republic under French protection. However, upon crowning himself king, in the spring of 1805, Napoleon at once proceeded to substitute more permanent patterns of government for the previous ad interim arrangements by allotting titles and kingdoms to various members of his family, having at that time—as he told Montholon—*"la bétise de croire à la sainteté des liens de famille."*[1] Eugène Beauharnais, Josephine's son by a previous marriage, was made viceroy of Italy; Joseph Bonaparte was first named King of Naples, and later, King of Spain and the Indies; Louis received the crown of Holland, and Jerome, that of Westphalia; to Caroline Murat and her husband went the throne of Naples; to his favorite sister Pauline, the duchy of Guastalla, and to Elise and her Corsican husband Felix Baciocchi,[2] first the little sea-girt state of Piombino on a promontory spur of the Appenines, and then, upon Lucca's urgent request to be also included in this royal distribution of Bonapartes, the combined principalities of Piombino and Lucca, of which an imperial decree of June 24, 1805, made Elise hereditary ruler.[3]

Although Prince Felix, with soldierly promptitude, set off at

[1] A. Dansette, *Napoléon, vues politiques.* (Paris, 1939), 113.

[2] Felix Baciocchi (1762–1841) came of an old Genoese family. The marriage took place in June, 1798.

[3] The Emperor ceded the principality of Piombino (and Lucca) to Elise as her exclusive property.

once for Italy, Elise, none too pleased with her share of the imperial spoils, which she considered as *"bien petite pour sa tête,"* postponed departure till just in time to be present at her brother's coronation in Milan and accompany him to Genoa, where the Doge had asked, in the name of all Liguria, the *"felicità"* of also being incorporated into the French Empire. *"Les Italiens* [wrote Thiers], *sensible au plus haut point, s'émeuvent quelquefois pour les souverains qu'ils n'aiment pas, séduits comme les sont tous les peuples par les puissances des grands spectacles";*[4] thus, after the nimbus of Milan's investiture, when the Emperor placed on his head the "sacred iron within the golden ring,"[5] with the ancient formula: *"Il cielo me la diede, guai a che la toccherà,"*[6] Genoa—not to be outdone by Bologna, Turin, and Milan—staged from June 30 to July 5 an even more elaborate pageant of hospitality during which, from the harsh, bare background of the Ligurian Alps to the frigates anchored in the bay, the city was a sea of waving banners with parades, regattas, fireworks, chiming bells, and martial music as the municipality swore fealty to the "saviour of the republic" with his parole of "peace, prosperity and permanence," three jeweled words that awakened hope in the hearts of all Italians, particularly the sorely harassed Genoese, who had been deprived of these three blessings for more than a decade.[7]

Although the events in Milan, Bologna, and Turin may have been too far away to reach the ears of Niccolò within the walls of Lucca, we may be sure that *Père* Antonio did not fail to tell him of the "most grandiose and solemn festival the port of Genoa had ever seen" and to remind him sharply of his shortsightedness in failing to participate, as artist, in these imperial festivities, which offered such a rare opportunity of capturing the interest of the Emperor. However, we may be equally sure that Niccolò required no parental promptings to realize the advantages of his position as violinist-leader of Lucca's National Orchestra and the possibilities it offered of winning the favor of the Emperor's sister—an equally

4 Thiers, *Histoire du Consulat et de l'Empire,* (2 vols., Paris, 1846), II, 328.

5 The Iron Crown derives its name from a small ring of iron supposed to be made of a nail of the true Cross. It is placed within a narrow gold band, which is studded with gems.

6 "God has given it to me; woe to him who touches it."

7 Calvini, *op. cit.,* 275; J. E. Driault, *Napoléon en Italie* (Paris, 1906), 337 ff.

great, and for him, far simpler achievement. For such a patron was now the very sponsor that he needed and one that a young and still unknown musician could hardly hope to achieve in any of the larger cities without the tangled web of intrigue and exalted patronage which he knew quite well still lay beyond his reach.

As soon as Lucca's fate was definitely decreed, Princess Elise, who had remained in Genoa during the pending negotiations, set forth with her consort for their new capital, being obliged—owing to the bad roads along the coast—to take the northern route via Tortona, Voghera, Piacenza, Parma, and Pistoia. Although long and fatiguing, the journey was none the less extremely gratifying to her *amour propre* since in every city that she entered, every hamlet through which she passed, she was feted as befitted the sister of the Emperor, as mayors, militia, monks, and villagers turned out in holiday array to offer her appropriate homage. Proceeding by slow stages, owing to the oppressive heat, she finally crossed her frontiers on July 14, entering Lucca by the Porta Santa Maria, accompanied "by all the chief dignitaries of the principality, one hundred horsemen of the imperial guard and four detachments of guards of honor selected from the first families of her little realm. And to complete the picture her own "magnificent coach, drawn by six horses and preceded by Prince Felix on horseback, was followed by twenty-five state coaches and four stupendous coursers," the gift of her mighty brother, who, though he may possibly have had less sympathy with her than with other members of his family, possessed to a high degree *"la sense de la mise en scène"* and wished to guarantee her a royal entry into her new realm.

One can easily imagine Niccolò and his brother Carlo standing among the curious throng somewhere along the line of march, watching under the vertical shafts of a searing July sun the approach of what, in his essentially opportunistic attitude towards personal advantage, prestige, and profit, he must have viewed as the personification of destiny. For in such a small backwater who could possibly overlook him, particularly since Prince Felix's "worst eccentricity," according to his august brother-in-law, was "a foible for the violin"? This alone established a community of interest that might easily, in the magic land of chance, prove the first step on the ladder leading to the actualization of Teresa's dream.

For Luccans of every rank and station it was a week of glamorous pageant, the coronation ceremonies in the cathedral, the horse races and fireworks, the traditional distribution of bread and wine —*panem et circenses*—keeping them engrossed for several days, after which they were content to settle down once more to their customary pursuits while awaiting the promised benefits of the politically stabilized New Order. A fortnight later, after a brief official contact with her ministers, Princess Elise, accompanied by her consort, three ladies in waiting, and two chamberlains, established temporary headquarters at the Baths of Lucca.[8] And here, with the exception of two days in the capital to celebrate the Emperor's birthday, the court remained till September 22, when Elise transferred her residence to Viareggio for the rest of the year. So, for six months at least, the Luccans had little opportunity of getting acquainted with their new sovereigns.

ii

Elise (or Maria, as she was originally christened) was then a young woman of twenty-eight (b. 1777) with an untamable urge for action, which frequently tried her famous brother's patience, one genius of the kind being, in his opinion, quite enough for any family. In addition to her *activité trépidante, son besoin maladif d'action,* she exasperated him still further by bizarre, unaccountable, and sometimes unconventional behavior—an innate tendency to focus the limelight too constantly on her activities. *"Elle faisait* [as he put it] *trop parler d'elle."*

After her first matrimonial plans had failed to materialize, she had married the estimable, extremely likable, but far from brilliant officer, Pasquale Baciocchi,[9] a Corsican of good family and handsome presence, who would probably have remained commandant of the fortress at Ajaccio had his ambitious consort not launched him with energy and feminine astuteness on a more spectacular career. With the independence that came with mar-

---

[8] The Bagni di Lucca comprise several villages in the valley of the Lima, the Bagni alla Villa being at that time the favorite resort of the court and the foreign colonies of Florence and Lucca.

[9] Frederic Masson wrote that before their marriage Baciocchi, Elise, and her mother had resided in the same house for six months, "which explains many things." (*Napoléon et sa famille,* I, 181).

riage, Elise then gave her brother even greater trouble than before, as she went her way without consulting him, indulging not only in deliberate eccentricities that he considered in bad taste and lacking in dignity for the Emperor's sister, but adopting a rude and overbearing manner towards the Empress Josephine, whom she cordially disliked and insulted openly with and without reason. "My sister Elise had the brain of a man and great courage [he said later at St. Helena]. She had noble qualities and a remarkable mind; but there was never any sympathy between us; our characters were at opposite poles. In the College of St. Cyr, where she was educated, she acquired proud and brash manners that accorded ill with Josephine's invariable good breeding."

He frowned and he remonstrated, but she continued on her course, posing as a bluestocking and patroness of the arts, and under the guiding counsel of Louis de Fontanes,[10] cultivating in her Paris salon at 7 rue de la Chaise[11] the company of the most distinguished poets and writers of the day, men like Chateaubriand, the critic Suard,[12] Stanislas de Boufflers,[13] Theodore Bienaimé[14]— in fact all the *porte-aureoles* of intellectual Paris that she could draw into her net. In other respects, however, her caprices took a more spectacular turn, so that it seemed at length advisable to remove her to a less exposed position. Therefore, when Napoleon required someone with initiative and a sense of responsibility, with enterprise and push, to represent his interests at a strategically important post, he packed her off to Piombino, solacing her injured pride with a "gratuity of 500,000 francs and a suite consisting of a chamberlain (Count d'Esterno), a lady of honor (Mme Laplace), two ladies in waiting, (Faustine Gauffier and Mme Rose de Blair, godchild of Richelieu), an aide de camp, a butler, a physician, a personal reader (Ida Saint Elmé), eight domestic servants, and two couriers."

In appearance she possessed none of the striking beauty of her famous sister Pauline. With high cheek bones, prominent eyes, and

10 Count de Fontanes (1757–1821), writer and friend of Chateaubriand.

11 Formerly the residence of the Countess de Maurepas, widow of a former minister of Louis XIV. It is now a clinic.

12 Jean Baptiste Suard (1733–1817), critic and journalist.

13 Chevalier de Boufflers (1738–1813), governor of Senegal, writer of light verse.

14 Theodore Bienaimé (1765–1826), a well-known architect of the period.

a thin pale face, she qualified as the ugly duckling of the family, though the portraits made at the zenith of her career, especially one by her court painter Stefano Tofanelli,[15] by no means support such a harsh judgment. Frederic Masson, writing nearly a century later, described her as having nothing feminine about her, "one of those androgynous beings who, without having acquired the qualities of the other sex, has lost the charms of its own."[16] But her contemporary, Ida Saint Elmé, saw her differently.

She was not beautiful—short, slender, almost lean, she yet possessed the various personal qualities that, combined with cleverness and vivaciousness, make a seductive woman. Her distinguished bearing made her appear well formed. Her feet were small, her hands as perfect as her brother's. The loveliest of black eyes lit up her face, and she knew how to make the most of them when she wanted to be obeyed or admired. None of Napoleon's brothers and sisters resembled him more. She had a quick, alert, penetrating mind, a glowing imagination, a strong soul, and a touch of greatness.[17]

"Between the great brother and the sister [wrote Fleuriot de Langle] there were, no doubt, affinities of spirit, of character, of temperament . . . but one should not stress the parallels too much. Of Napoleon's characteristic traits, Elise imitated only the less sublime. She adopted his lively, trenchant retorts and his often intolerably brusque manner, his habit of posing an abrupt question and then fixing the interlocutor with an intimidating look that seemed to go right through him." With her, as with him, the least contrariety provoked a nervous reaction, the violence of her anger being entirely disproportionate to the cause,[18] making it difficult for her subordinates to get along with her, though all her biographers have stated that "she could be very charming when she thought it worth her while." A person of enormous energy, she was possessed of an inordinate desire to regulate the conduct and activities of everyone around her, exercising her authority in every

15 Stefan Tofanelli (1752–1812), director of the Istituto di Belli Arti in Lucca and instructor at the Liceo Felice. As court painter, he painted many portraits of Elise, which have now disappeared.

16 Masson, *op. cit.*, I, 181.

17 St. Elme, *Mémoirs d'un Contemporaine* (Paris, 1828), 358.

18 De Langle, *op. cit.*, 62.

field of activity—the practical and the commercial, the organizational, the artistic, and the political.

This little city [wrote Noel Williams], which had slumbered for centuries behind its thick ramparts, became on a sudden a brilliant capital, full of life and movement. The aristocracy and the wealthy merchants vied with one another in luxury and extravagance, visitors from all parts of Italy and distinguished foreigners crowded the inns; two theatres were opened, one for Italian ballets, the other for French plays; a casino in which a variety of amusements were provided, and a splendid bathing establishment were built, and the Palazzo Santini was converted into a fashionable gambling hall where faro and roulette were permitted until the small hours of the morning. Elise entertained on a lavish scale and state dinners, balls, receptions, and concerts succeeded one another in rapid succession.[19]

She drew up an elaborate *Etiquette du Palais* of forty pages which in its 203 articles established a protocol more minute and complex than that of the Tuileries. She founded an academy on the pattern of the *Académie française,*[20] with annual competitions rewarded from her privy purse; she demolished churches and other buildings to construct the Piazza Napoleone, stimulated commerce and industry through government orders and financial aid, built highways, roads, and hospitals, drained marshes, introduced the silk industry, coined medals, established a municipal counsel with mayor, etc. on the French model, curtailed feudalism, abolished vexatious taxes, and provided new openings for talent; turned the course of the Fraga, a tributary of the Serchio, to provide water for her fountains; opened a zoological garden; organized schools,[21] revolutionized taste and customs in the principality; reopened the marble quarries of Carrara and commissioned busts of all her family; reviewed her troops; spoke to the soldiers in a dry, military tone; paraded on horseback *"en taille de hussard, coiffée d'une toque ou pointait l'épée d'une aigrette de diamants,"*[22] and tried in every way to emulate her famous brother.

19 Hugh Noel Williams, *The Women Bonaparte.*
20 Based on a former group of humanists and writers calling themselves the Accademia degli Oscuri (Society of Unknown Poets), which was founded in the seventeenth century.
21 A good half of the population could not write. (De Langle, *op. cit.,* 41.)
22 *Ibid.,* 234.

Not content with her summer palaces at Viareggio and Leonardo's "stormy Piombino," she desired another countryseat in the vicinage of Lucca, and on July 5, 1806, purchased from Count Lelio Orsetti the Villa Marlia,[23] two miles to the northeast of the city, which with the assistance of Bienaimé and his Italian colleagues, Lazzarini, Marchelli, and Paolinelli, she transformed into an English countryseat with spreading lawns, an artificial lake with black and white swans, extensive grounds filled with deer, gazelles, and marble statues, and a sylvan theatre in which, assisted by members of the court, she used to recite from the French comedies and drama. "Marlia [Metternich wrote his wife some years later] is really a divine spot. I know of no grounds *à l'anglaise* beyond the Alps that have been laid out with such a luxury of trees and exotic flowers—for example, there are whole groves of magnolia."

Another favorite residence was the former palace of Therese Pamphili Cybo[24] in Massa, where in the process of its renovation and refurbishing she did not hesitate to pull down the adjacent cathedral in "the cavalier manner of a conqueror," because it obstructed the view and darkened her apartments, thereby largely counteracting her positive improvements in furthering the local industries. For the people had a tender sentiment for the incense-laden shadows of their old *duomo* and were disinclined to view the shady square with its trees laid out in quincunxes as in any way an adequate substitute. It was in these two countryseats—and later at Poggia a Cagiano, near Florence, that she spent the major portion of her time. Indeed, to judge by the records of her movements, fragmentary as they are, she could only have resided for short periods in the capital itself, and then only when affairs of state, her annual festivals, and other official acts required her presence there.

iii

On her arrival in Lucca, Elise found, along with a couple of small unimportant military bands, two fully organized and functioning orchestras, viz., the old Cappella della Signoria and the Cappella

---

[23] Marlia is one of the oldest historical estates in the province of Lucca, being mentioned in ninth-century documents. See *Art et Industrie*, May 10, 1928.

[24] De Langle, *op. cit.*, 135.

Nazionale del Potere Executivo, the latter (of which Paganini was first violin) dating from the initiation of the democratic government in December, 1801. It is presumed that the first-named organization, with its long tradition from the days when Lucca was a king's capital, was legitimist in sentiment and unable to share the Jacobin enthusiasms of the new dispensation, whereupon the incoming government organized an orchestra of its own, made up of younger, more democratically minded players. Abbé Nerici, in his work on Lucca's music, does not mention the National Orchestra, probably because in the three and a half years of its existence it had too brief a record of achievement to have attracted a historian, or he looked upon it as an ephemeral political expedient that did not merit a place in Lucca's ancient scrolls. However, that it was an active organization in 1805 is sufficiently attested by Paganini's connection with it and several references to it by contemporaneous writers.

Up to the birth of the principality in the summer of 1805, two opposing parties had alternately exercised dictatorship in Lucca. Throughout the eighteenth century the aristocrats had arrogated to themselves the prerogatives of sovereignty; then the democratic party, propounding the liberal principles of the French Revolution, took over in the late nineties and remained in power till July, 1805, while in between these two extremes were the dissidents, who were merely awaiting a cue to come out before the footlights. In the face of such a situation, for Elise to favor one side or the other, to respect the principles of the revolution and at the same time "adopt the intrepid method of personal government by decree" while seeking to reconcile the two opposing camps and institute the spirit of concord rather than division, was an extremely ticklish task even for a Bonaparte. The National Orchestra, it is presumed, went down with the democratic ship of state; but for Elise to have maintained the *status quo* and to have ignored the older organization might have been interpreted as an affront to the aristocratic Luccans, who were proud of the unbroken record of the Cappella della Signoria for nearly five hundred years and whose sympathy meant, in the beginning, much more to her than "revolutionary," proletarian support. So she solved her problem in a typically Napoleonic manner by dissolving the Cappella and starting, as it were, from scratch. In a decree dated July 31, 1805, she stipulated that all members were to be suspended on half pay till the end of the calendar year. Then from January 1, 1806, all those with thirty years of service were to be permanently retired at one third of their regular stipend; those with from thirty to forty years at one half, and those with from forty to fifty years at full pay. In the reorganization, which took place in the ensuing weeks, Antonio Puccini (b. 1747), till then conductor of the Cappella della Signoria transferred his duties to his son Domenico (b. 1771) while retaining his post as *maestro di cappella* at the Cathedral of San Martino. Giuseppe Romaggi,[25] also of the older orchestra, was taken over as first violin and the second desk allocated to Paganini, the other leading players including Carlo Cancelli, third violin; Germano Bandettini (Paganini's pupil), cello; Jacopo Gerli, viola; Antonio Galli, oboe; Leonardo Martini, contralto; Felici Simi, tenor; and Jacopo Rustici, bass. (Bandettini, Gerli, Galli, and Simi were former members of the Cappella.)[26]

From now on the new orchestra, a much smaller organization than the old Cappella, was at the beck and call of the court and when necessary even had to accompany it on its peregrinations to Elise's several countryseats, so that to a certain extent the Luccans might be said to have lost their orchestra since only those persons having close relations with the court were presumably in a position to enjoy the new, and obviously elite, organization, which might have been a small, ordinary orchestra, though the official records would indicate that it was a real chamber orchestra, that is, with only one instrument to a part. (Nerici wrote that the Luccans felt very bitter over the fate of their old orchestra but had to recognize that the Baciocchis did much to further the fine arts.)

Although Niccolò no doubt was delighted at his good luck, we may risk a guess that it did not please him overmuch to suppress his own personality and hide his light under the bushel of another's mediocrity just because the latter happened to have a longer service record. (In 1805, Romaggi had twenty-seven years' service against Niccolò's three.) That the injustice of this procedure still

25 Giuseppe Romaggi, a Genoese, had been a member of the old Cappella since the end of 1778.

26 Jacobo Chelini. State Archives, Lucca. Ms. 104, p. 83 ff. See also, Nerici, *Storia della musica in Lucca.*

rankled through the years is clearly evident from certain stipulations in his reorganization plan for the Parma orchestra, the purpose of which was "to do away with the obstacle of seniority and prevent an artist's being held down in a supernumerary position because he had a shorter term of service."[27] Even thirty years had not sufficed to wipe out the unpalatable memory.

Since his brother Carlo's name appears on the roster of the court musicians in 1807 and 1808, it is presumed that he too was a member of the National Orchestra since it is hardly likely that the court officials would have sent to Genoa for a second violinist of routine qualifications when, with Lucca's orchestras now reduced to one, there could have been no scarcity of players on the ground. Carlo must therefore have been in Lucca and with also a three-year service record, which gave him the status of a Luccan. For the first two years Paganini's salary with the court was 1146 francs per annum,[28] while his salary under the democratic government had been 12 scudi, or 60 francs, a month.[29] Hence, the court appointment, though a drop in prestige, represented a slight increase in emolument. At the end of 1808 he was receiving 1350 francs a year (granting that he and his brother were receiving the same amount, i.e., 22½ scudi monthly), which, as he said, was "a piffling little salary"[30] in comparison with the sums he was capable of earning at his independent concerts, to say nothing of the greater liberty of action he enjoyed.

We have no reason to believe that his appointment in January, 1806, was owing to any other factor than the recommendations of his former employers and his influential elder colleagues, Antonio Puccini, Romaggi, and the Abbé Quilici. For Princess Elise could have had nothing personally to do with the selection of the players but left the task, like other administrative matters, to her competent ministers since she had had no opportunity as yet of acquainting herself with their capacities except in a general way.

---

27 Codignola, *op. cit.*, 455.

28 State Archives, Lucca. *Intendenza dei Principi e Cassa dello straordinario*, Reg. 17.

29 State Archives, Lucca.

30 In Florence, Elise's personal reader received 2,000 francs per annum, her physician twice this amount, her chef 1,500 francs and his food. A professor of mathematics or of French and Latin received only 1,200 francs.

Indeed, one might say with a fair degree of certainty that at the time of her arrival she was completely unaware of his existence. She had only recently come from Paris, while he for some years had been living in obscurity, and if he enjoyed any fame at all it must have been confined within the walls of Lucca. For he was no longer in the spotlight as a prodigy, and Italy was full of itinerant virtuosi, each town of any size boasting a professor or two of more than local eminence in practically all the instruments. Since up to 1805, as far as intensive research has been able to discover, he had not yet played in Milan, Turin, or Florence,[31] and the memory of the public is notoriously brief, the extent of his attainments as a boy and his early concerts in small towns in Tuscany could never have penetrated to the Tuileries, all the more so since they were not even deemed of sufficient importance to warrant a comment in the local press. Furthermore, as long as the court remained in Lucca, Domenico Puccini was director of the orchestra; for the first two years (1806–1807) Niccolò was merely the "second violin," conducting the opera performances, teaching Prince Felix,[32] and giving the required quota of solo concerts, like the singers and other instrumentalists. Perhaps the panache, the pomp and circumstance that accompanied Princess Elise's entry on the scene intimidated him, or he was vexed over his relatively supernumerary position, so that for over a year he kept in the background. For it was evidently not till the summer of 1807 that he captured Elise's imagination, and she then for a short time (if we can accept his testimony) overlooked the distance separating aristocrat and artist and signalled him out for favors that went further than "solo violinist of the court" and private teacher of Prince Felix.[33]

During the first fetes in celebration of the Emperor's birthday in 1805, Princess Elise announced the organization of an Académie Napoléon on the pattern of the French Academy,[34] which would

[31] Records show that Paganini accompanied the court to Piombino for Lent, 1806, returning to Lucca on Easter Monday, April 7.

[32] Mrs. Henry Sisted, *Letters from the Bye-Ways of Italy,* 28.

[33] Elise's lovers were almost as numerous as her sister's. Many years later Paganini told Achilles of his relations with the Princess. Achilles then passed the information on to his son Attila, who in a letter to Sante Bargellini (February 23, 1930), confirmed the fact. See "Her Majesty Elise Baciocchi and Niccolò Paganini," *Minerva* (July 15, 1931).

[34] De Langle, *op. cit.,* 69, 267.

sponsor regular annual competitions in "music, painting, and literature,"[35] the winning works to be rewarded with a gold medal and public performance on one of the forthcoming official anniversaries (i.e., the Emperor's birthday and those of the Prince and Princess).[36]

The first prize in music was awarded in 1806 to a *Sinfonia sentimentale* and a *Mottetto a Quattro Cori Reali* in the form of a hymn to St. Cecilia,[37] and though the name of the composer was not mentioned, an examination of these two compositions shows that Paganini was not the author since both are not only completely foreign to his style but are a model of notation—"neat presentation" being one of the points to be considered in determining the award—a virtue to which he could never properly lay claim. In fact, he seems never to have captured any of these official distinctions despite his originality and lively creative gift, so it is assumed that the Florentine mosaic and diamond ring that he received from his appreciative sovereign were awarded him either for the sensationally successful Napoleon Sonata in 1807, for his services to Prince Felix, or his performances "off the record" in a less conventional sphere.[38]

Among the regular duties of the orchestra were public and private concerts, theatrical performances, balls, religious services, and any court functions in which music played a part, with once a week a private concert in the hall of the old Palazzo of the republic, the purpose of which was "to keep the pupils in practice,"[39] evidently a recital by the music pupils of the professors, each of whom had to teach two or three students selected by the crown. In addi-

[35] The first literary prize was awarded to Jean Carmignani of Pisa for his dissertation on the poems of Victor Alfieri. The following year the first prize went to Bartolomeo Cenami for a cantata.

[36] Desiring to have Cenami's cantata set to music, Princess Elise commissioned a setting from Giovanni Paisiello (1741–1816), who was then residing in Naples. The cantata was completed on April 24, 1807, but the manuscript has disappeared. See Angelo Bertacchi: *Storia della R. Accademia Lucchese* and Francesco Barberio, "La Principessa Elisa Baciocchi e Paisiello," in *Rivista Musical Italiana*, (No. 3/4, 1936).

[37] An excellent copy of this work is in the New York Public Library. See Bertacchi, *op. cit.*

[38] The Princess was greatly interested in the work of the Florentine *mosaistes*, of whom one of the best known was Andre Marchesini.

[39] These dilettante concerts seem to have been the general custom. Paganini refers to them on several occasions. See Spohr, *op. cit.*, I, 280.

tion, on all Napoleonic festivals, they were required to write a new work and submit it to a special commission which then selected those compositions considered as worthy of performance. Niccolò's first achievement in this field seems to have been his Napoleon Sonata,[40] performed on the Emperor's birthday in 1807, a doubly festive occasion for the court since this official fete day had been chosen by the Princess to break ground for the Via Friedland, the new highway she was constructing across the mountains from Massa-Carrara to Sarzana on the "French frontier."

I had to conduct every time the royal family went to the opera[41] [he told Schottky], play three times a week at court,[42] and every fortnight give a big concert at the formal soirees, but Princess Elise did not always attend or else did not remain all through the concert, because my music placed too great a strain on her nerves. However, another charming lady ["he mentioned her name," added Schottky in parenthesis] who was attracted to me—or at least so it seemed—never missed them, while I had admired her for a long time. Our interest in each other gradually increased, but had to be concealed, which only intensified it. One day I promised her a surprise at the next concert—a little musical prank having reference to our relations. At the same time I announced to the court an amusing novelty entitled *"Scèna Amorosa."*[43] Everyone was very curious till I finally appeared with my violin, from which I had removed the two inner strings, leaving only the E and G strings. The first string represented the girl, the second the man, and I then began a sort of dialogue depicting little quarrels and reconciliations between my two lovers. The strings first scolded, then sighed, lisped, moaned, joked, expressed delight, and finally ecstasy. It concluded with a reconciliation and the two lovers performed a *pas de deux,* closing with a brilliant coda. The musical *Scèna* received great applause. The lady for whom it was intended rewarded me with the most friendly glances;

40 The Napoleon Sonata was originally entitled *Prima Suonata con variazioni per la quarta corda.* The manuscript is now in the Reuther Collection in Mannheim. Paganini was not the first to demonstrate this technique.

41 The state library at Lucca (Biblioteca Governativa) contains a manuscript by Francesco Minutoli (Ms. 3011), which records that Paganini gave a concert in the Teatro Castiglioncello on March 13, 1810, when his assisting artists were Signora Mazzolini, Signor Santini, and Signor Tosi. "Paganini played several violin concertos with great applause and received a fee of 72 *zecchini.*"

42 According to documents in the State Archives in Lucca, Paganini played at a ball at Villa Marlia on September 24, 1807, and at a concert the following Sunday. See Lazzareschi, *op. cit.,* 9.

43 The several movements are entitled: Flirtation; Request; Consent; Timidity; Gratification; Quarrel; Reconciliation; Love Token; Notice of Departure; Leave Taking.

as for the Princess, she was extremely gracious, overwhelming me with compliments and at last saying: "Since you have already performed something so beautiful on two strings, couldn't you let us hear something on one string?" I at once consented, the idea appealing to my fancy, and since the Emperor's birthday *occurred a few weeks later,*[44] [italics added] I wrote the Napoleon Sonata for the G string, which I then played before the assembled court with such applause that a Cimarosa Cantata that immediately followed was thrown completely into the shade and made no impression whatsoever. This was the beginning, and the real genesis, of my predilection for the G string. Later, one always wanted to hear more works of this kind and so I progressed from day to day till finally I had completely mastered this style of playing.[45]

It is regrettable that Schottky, to whom Paganini confided the name of the enamored *grande dame,* was not tempted to fix her for a curious posterity by at least an initial; yet the mere fact that Paganini revealed her name at all tempts one to surmise that he was referring to Elise's beautiful lady of honor, Mme Laplace, the wife of the great astronomer, who accompanied her to Italy and remained with her till the court was transferred to Florence. When Lucca was added to Elise's domain, the Tuileries, not unmindful of Italian pride, requested that the Princess' ladies in waiting be recruited "from the most exclusive aristocracy of the Principality," whereupon the senate selected ten young Luccans "of noble birth and ancient lineage." Of course, it is not impossible that one of these young women was the lady of his dreams,[46] but inductive reasoning would suggest that she was Mme Laplace. The names of the Luccans, even though one was a niece of an archbishop and another the wife of a distinguished diplomat, would have meant nothing to a person of Schottky's background, while Mme Laplace, through her renowned charm and beauty, and particularly her husband's fame, would have immediately intrigued him and have impressed him commensurately.

44 In telling Lichtenthal of the genesis of the Napoleon Sonata, Paganini mentioned no names, since the article was intended for publication.

45 Schottky, *op. cit.*, 368.

46 Eleanora Bernardini, wife of the president of the senate; Louise Mansi; Marchioness Camilla Mansi; Adelaide Sardi; Tommassina Talenti; Louisa Burlamacchi; Rose Trebiliani, later directress of the Institut Elisa; Olympe Fatinelli, sister of the master of the horse; Angiola Matteucci, wife of the lord chief justice; and Marchioness Carlotta Lucchesini, wife of the diplomat.

Be that as it may, the above account, irrespective of all the other circumstantial evidence at hand, should make it crystal clear that the siren who was in Paganini's mind when he was spinning yarns for Fétis was, like himself, part of the princely retinue—in other words, she was either his sovereign, the latter's "charming lady in waiting," or more likely a sylphid of his imagination representing a composite picture of the two.

iv

Although details of his life while "in the service of their Royal Highnesses" are practically nonexistent except for a concert now and then,[47] he must still have enjoyed a fair amount of leisure, in view of Elise's frequent absences on official inspections, her accouchement, and several serious illnesses that for a time interrupted her activities.[48] During these periods, even when his duties consisted principally (and no doubt exclusively) of teaching Prince Felix and the pupils on his official roster, it is not likely that he was permitted to leave the principality though he may often have played in near-by towns to augment his modest income. However, he must have approved (in principle, at least) of such a regulation, since he made a similar provision in his reorganization plan for the Parma orchestra in 1835. Hence, one assumes that when in search of entertainment he never had to wander very far afield, even though the strict line of demarcation drawn between the Bohemian and the aristocrat may have forced him to seek his companions and diversions in circles that were not bound by social etiquette—surely never very difficult for one whose life was in, and of, the theatre.

Be all that as it may, political events taking place around him inevitably had much to do with determining the course of his life in the next five years, perhaps more than he ever realized. For Elise had not been long in Lucca when she began to cast covetous eyes on the neighboring kingdom of Queen Marie Louise of Etruria and commenced, even at that early date, to lay her plans to supplant the Tuscan sovereign and move her court to Florence.

47 In the numerous memoirs dating from the Napoleonic period in Italy, Paganini's name is mentioned only by Boucher de Perthes, Henri Beyle, Colonel Montgomery, Henry Matthews, Massimo d'Azelio, and Mrs. Henry Sisted (among the more important).

48 During the first three years, the court was absent from Lucca for five and six months at a time.

Princess Elise to Count de Champagny.
I strongly insist on an augmentation of territory. Since I cannot reside near His Majesty in Paris, I wish to have a state that will not be unworthy of me. I have very little ambition, but as the Emperor's sister, I've every right to desire and lay claim to more than the 150,000 inhabitants forming the principality of Lucca.[49]

The idea engaged her attention more and more throughout the course of 1807, especially after the "suppression of Etruria" by the Emperor on November 23. But though she had to wait over a year before she obtained the prize on which her heart was set, the eventual issue could hardly have ever been in doubt and must frequently have been discussed within the walls of Lucca. Niccolò was, therefore, presumably very well informed on matters that could not help but have a repercussion on himself. And had he previously been indifferent, a communication from Froussard, Elise's cabinet secretary, to the Intendant General touching the court music would have alerted him at once.[50]

G. B. Froussard to the Intendant General, November 10, 1807.
I have the honor to inform you that, in pursuance of a sovereign decision, the Chamber Orchestra will be dissolved the first of January, 1808. In communicating this decision to His Excellency, the first gentleman usher [Marquis Raffaello Mansi], you will inform him that the budget for the professors of music for the coming year 1808 will comprise only the following appointments:

45 scudi a month for the two Paganini brothers,
25 scudi a month for the tenor,
18 scudi a month for Signor Domenico Puccini, *maestro di cappella,*

in case he can accompany their Royal Highnesses wherever they go; if not, he will be replaced by Signor Rustici, with the same salary.[51] Finally, 15 scudi a month each for two violinists. The total amount involved is 118 scudi a month. You will also have the kindness to inform

---

[49] De Langle, *op. cit.,* 154. Jean Baptiste Champagny (1756–1836) was Napoleon's foreign minister from 1807–11.

[50] Jean Baptiste Froussard came to Italy first with Dombrowski's Polish Legion.

[51] Jacopo Rustici was a member of the ensemble of the National Theatre in Lucca and was the assisting artist at Paganini's concert on January 20, 1805, on his return from Genoa. The same arrangements must have been continued in 1809 since at the end of the year Domenico Puccini appealed to Elise for aid (or a clarification of his position) on the grounds that he had "received no salary since the end of 1808."

the aforesaid that the above professors must accompany their Royal Highnesses to Piombino, to Massa and to the Bagni di Lucca when they are so directed and it is the sovereigns' pleasure. Their traveling expenses will be paid.[52]

Here the court music was reduced to the modest proportions of a string quartet, with Niccolò holding the same position as in the Prince's private quartet. Moreover, the court order manifested a signal disregard of his exceptional capacities and not only made no distinction between "the two Paganini brothers," but instead of entrusting him with Puccini's duties when the latter was unable "to accompany their Royal Highnesses to Piombino, to Massa, and the Baths of Lucca," the post of *maestro di cappella* devolved on "Signor Rustici," a singer! His vexation is easily understandable since such a decision must have made it clear to him that there was little hope of his receiving any greater consideration in the future.

It is therefore reasonable to assume that his mind was set for a decision that would liberate him from such disheartening conditions, for immediately after the carnival, possibly as the result "of some dissension with the court," he applied for two months' leave of absence to return to Genoa, and a passport for this purpose was granted him on March 20.[53]

Something quite out of the ordinary took him on this unusual jaunt at this season of the year and one will surely not go wrong in surmising that the something was self-interest. He had recently been reduced "by a sovereign decision" to a mere quartet player; Florence, with its wider possibilities, was still an "Elise-ian" dream; but how about Turin? For he must have heard that on February 14, Napoleon had appointed Prince Borghèse governor general of Northern Piedmont. If he could therefore "offer his contribution" when the Emperor's favorite sister made her solemn entry during Easter week, might he not achieve the position there that fate was denying him in Lucca?

There is no record of his having played in Genoa during his three or four weeks' visit, and the dates of his two Turin concerts are also not recorded, but since Blangini heard him at this time,[54]

---

52 State Archives, Lucca, *Segretaria di Stato e di Gabinetto*, Reg. 184, n. 4210.

53 *Direzione di Polizia*, Reg. 22, n. 18.

54 Felice Blangini (1781–1841), composer and teacher of singing, enjoyed great vogue at the apex of his career.

we therefore know that they took place between April 23, when the new Governor General arrived in Turin, and May 1, when Princess Pauline and Blangini left for Castle Stupinigi, where she then remained till she returned to France in early June. As this brief Turin *étape* represents another purple patch in the Paganini saga, it will repay us to have a closer look at it.

In his first biographical article (1841) Fétis did not mention the Turin concerts, but in his monograph (1851) he wrote that *"de Livourne Paganini alla à Turin où se trouvaient alors la princesse Pauline Borghèse, soeur de Napoléon, le prince, son époux, et leur suite,"* a concise and manifestly correct statement of the circumstances, producing, moreover, the impression that Turin was the real goal of this particular journey—which was quite evidently the case. Elise Polko, in her quasi-fictionalized biography of 1876, then gave Fétis' simple statement a deliberately romantic twist: "Paganini went first to Leghorn and was later held in Turin for a time by the dangerous Circe, Pauline Borghèse, Canova's Venus."[55] Julius Kapp in 1914, catching Polko's colored ball, tossed it even higher: "Paganini was the guest of Princess Pauline Borghèse in Turin and spent several weeks of undisturbed bliss with this beautiful and wanton woman,"[56]—after which Codignola (1936) brought the theme full circle: "Paganini played in Leghorn and later in Turin, where he captured the interest of Pauline Borghèse, who shortly after this retired with him to a discreet site in the Piedmontese valley."[57] Paganini indeed deserved better treatment from posterity, for here there was not the slightest justification for such distortion of the facts.

When Napoleon parceled out his Italian provinces in 1805, he allocated to his sister Pauline the little state of Guastalla, which was far from pleasing to her. "I warn you that I'll scratch your eyes out if you don't give me a state a wee bit bigger than a handkerchief—it's necessary for me and it's necessary for my husband," she exploded in her first annoyance. So in February, 1808, when fortune's wheel had turned appropriately, he made his brother-in-law governor general of the nine departments north of the Alps (an-

---

[55] *Niccolò Paganini und die Geigenbauer*, 35.
[56] *Paganini*, 12.
[57] *Op. cit.*, 13.

cient Piedmont) and directed his sister to leave Paris immediately and join her husband at his post; which was equally displeasing to her.

Felice Blangini, at that time her music master and reigning lover, who formed part of the royal retinue that left Nice for Turin on Easter Monday, April 18, reported that during the entire four-day journey, and even after arrival in Turin, Pauline, dismayed and angry at having to leave Paris, was *"comme un vrai démon, étincelante de colère,"* a mood that was not soothed by the discovery, a week after her arrival, that her husband had ignored Blangini altogether and, irrespective of her wishes, had appointed another *maestro di cappella* for the court. With that she "fled from the city that was death to her" and on May 1 took refuge with Blangini in the Castello di Stupinigi (formerly the property of the King of Sardinia), which was momentarily preferable to life in the Chablaid Palace with her tiresome husband and the courteous, inimical patricians of Turin. During the five weeks of her Italian sojourn (from April 23 to June 1) we know from numerous letters and memoirs that her nerves and health were in a deplorable condition, her one idea being to escape as soon as possible and return to Paris. In fact, her brother Joseph, king of Naples, who visited her at Stupinigi the latter part of May, wrote the Emperor that he was greatly alarmed *"de l'état de santé vraiment lamentable dans lequel il la trouvait; elle ne mange pas depuis huit jours et ne peut supporter le plus léger bouillon."* After Blangini's rebuff, he too took fright at the possible consequences to his career should he incite the Emperor's ire, and thereupon also deserted his unhappy mistress, returning to Turin, where he shortly after received a summons to the court of Jerome Bonaparte in Westphalia.

It would be absurd to waste words on such a tale if it had not now taken root in the Paganini legend, even those biographers who otherwise show an excessive prostration before Fétis ignoring his simple statement in favor of the cheap romanticism of a Polko whose main object was "to feed the insatiable popular hunger for trashy emotionalism." Needless to say, there is not the slightest evidence, or even probability, that Paganini ever met Princess Borghèse personally unless she happened to attend one of the Turin concerts and he was formally presented at that time. He himself never mentioned her, nor she him. Fétis also wrote that "while in Turin" Paganini had the first attack of the chronic colitis that from then on periodically bothered him; this, if true, he must have learned from Blangini since Paganini could never accurately remember dates and places after a year or two. (Since these attacks were usually precipitated by some emotional excitement, it is more likely that he was ill in Genoa as a result of his "dissension" with the court.) At any rate, if ill in Turin, it could only have been a passing indisposition since by the middle of May he was already back in Genoa, as shown by a letter addressed to Prince Felix on May 20 by the Genoese musician, G. B. Ottagio, who, "having heard from Paganini that the Prince was *un bravo amatore di musica* as well as connoisseur, was "sending him by the hand of Paganini" the first copy of one of his quartets.[58]

We have no record of his activities during the rest of 1808 except a concert at Villa Marlia on August 8 and no doubt another on the fifteenth in honor of the Emperor's birthday. But by this time he must have realized that Elise's enthusiasm for court music, other than a string quartet, had completely evaporated, so that there was little hope of his obtaining a position more commensurate with his prestige and abilities (this, Turin had recently confirmed to his entire satisfaction), even if her dreams were realized and the court was transferred to Florence.

After months of plotting and maneuvering, she too was about ready to abandon hope when on March 2, 1809, Napoleon finally capitulated and bestowed on her the magnificent title of Grand Duchess of Tuscany, with her future seat in Florence. However, though Florence, Pisa, and Leghorn were now added to her kingdom, she soon found that in comparison with Lucca-Piombino her personal authority was greatly curtailed. *"Elise* [wrote Driault] *s'agitait comme si elle avait eu quelque chose à faire, mais ce n'était qu'un vain titre d'honneur abandonné par l'Empereur à une soeur vaniteuse."* No longer might she introduce sweeping reforms without higher authority, independently exercise her administrative powers, display her diplomatic gifts,[59] "discuss, defer, or evade the orders sent from Paris." Even her letters to the Emperor now had

[58] State Archives, Lucca, Reg. 202, n. 75.
[59] De Langle, *op. cit.*, 186.

to be routed through her ministers. From this time on "her powers were limited to transmitting the orders received from the ministers in Paris to the intendant of her treasury, the director of the police, and her chief of staff, all of whom were appointed by the Emperor." And if "she attempted to neglect or amend the instructions of a minister, she was reminded that as a French subject she was liable to arrest." Which sufficiently explains why she spent the major part of her time at her residences in Pisa and Leghorn.

At the beginning of 1809, Niccolò was still on the payroll of the court since official records show that on March 9 he conducted a performance of Cimarosa's *Il Matrimonio Segreto* for the court in the Teatro Castiglioncello and six weeks earlier had first to "ask permission" before he could give a "private ball" at the house of his friends, the Bucchianeris.

The Chamberlain [Ascanio Mansi] to the Chief of Police, January 13, 1809.
I have the honor to advise you that Signor Paganini, professor of the violin in the service of their Royal Highnesses, has received my permission to give a private ball this evening in the house of a certain Bucchianeri, opposite the lateral door of the church of San Frediano.[60]

Paganini told George Harrys that "when in the service of the Baciocchi court he had to suffer many a vexation," probably through the curtailment of his liberties; yet this particular measure may have been imposed by the social unrest arising from Elise's secularization of religious property, which made it advisable at that time to prohibit any large assemblies. Nevertheless, there must have been numerous occasions when he "had to ask permission" for some personal enterprise even though his duties at the court had by then shrunk almost to the vanishing point.

In 1809, Boucher de Perthes,[61] famed as the "father of the pre-history of man," was then in the French customs service and stationed in Leghorn, from where he wrote his father that "Prince Baciocchi is an enthusiastic amateur of the violin. We play quartets together. A Genoese by the name of Paganini plays first violin in

[60] Lazzareschi, *op. cit.,* 13. It will be noted that Paganini is referred to merely as "a professor of the violin."
[61] Jacques Boucher de Perthes (1788–1868) was one of the first French archaeologists.

the quartets and also plays the guitar," and then went on to say that since "Paganini did not live in Leghorn and the Prince was only there occasionally," he did not have this pleasure as often as he wished. Here there is not the slightest intimation that Paganini was in any way connected with the court, so it is assumed that from April, 1809, he was carried on the civil list merely as the Prince's musical instructor. Paganini told Harrys that he "was in the service of the Baciocchi court only three years," which Fétis interpreted as referring to his residence in Lucca, probably because Gervasoni wrote that he "went to Florence with the court and remained some time in that capital." While two further letters of Boucher de Perthes tend to corroborate this fact, one gathers that he was now attached to Prince Felix's personal suite and that his duties, like his residence, were dictated by the latter's movements and not by the wishes of his consort. (In Florence the Prince had a residence of his own which he occupied when military reviews and other official duties required his presence there; otherwise, he spent all his time in Lucca.)

Boucher de Perthes to the Chamberlain [Florence], December 25, 1809. Yes, I declare before heaven and hell that I owe my obesity to the royal dinners that we had with the Prince and to the bad quartets that followed, for the one does not preclude the other, and one can be the pearl of men and even the pearl of princes—as the *maestro di cappella* Paganini says—and have the pearl of chefs without being the pearl of violinists. . . . Paganini is also a royal highness in his way and, if he would only cut up fewer capers and renounce the role of grand clown of the violinists, he would be the grand duke, even the emperor, and could exclaim like another virtuoso: "I'd rather be the emperor of the violin than the violin of the emperor!" Do you know why this chap pleased me so much right from the start? Was it because of his violin, his guitar, his *esprit,* his originality? Not at all! It's because he's so thin! His being so dreadfully skinny consoled me and when I carefully took him all in, I seemed to be almost corpulent. Further, when he plays and draws that enormous volume of tone from his instrument, I have to ask myself whether it's him or his instrument I'm hearing; I'm inclined to think it's him. Certainly he's the drier of the two and when he comes anywhere near the fire I'm always afraid that he'll catch on fire, for please take note, his very members crackle! Therefore, always have a pail of water handy. My compliments to you, to him, and to all the quartet.[62]

This shows that in November and December, 1809, Paganini was in Florence with Prince Felix and was still carried on the civil rolls, though it is obvious that his functions had been reduced to a member of the Prince's personal suite since at this time Elise maintained her residence in Pisa. Before taking up Conestabile's account of Niccolò's final break with his patroness, the underlying motive of which has never been adequately explained, it is interesting to follow the immediate sequel of Boucher de Perthes's letter, which might easily elucidate the mystery.

Boucher de Perthes to the Chamberlain, December 31, 1809.
The affection that I feel for you forces me to tell you that Your Excellency has been guilty of a stupidity—and a big one—in showing my letter to the Grand Duchess! She laughed over it, you say! But I don't like to make Royal Highnesses laugh, and I would be especially annoyed if my chatter should come to the ears of the Prince—who won't listen to reason about his musical talent—and who could easily nourish resentment, not against me perhaps but—which would be ten times worse—against Paganini, whom I bitterly regret having brought into the affair. He needs the Prince and I should reproach myself all my life long for a *plaisanterie* that might make him lose his job and ruin his future.

Perhaps the Grand Duchess, or the Prince, taxed Niccolò with insincerity and disrespect, and hurt and angered by their attitude, or perhaps by some inflicted disciplinary measure, he flaunted his independence and indifference in the manner described by Conestabile.

At a gala function at court at which Paganini had to play [he wrote], he appeared in the uniform of a captain of the Royal Gendarmery.[63] The Princess, upon perceiving this, ordered him to change immediately to black court dress. He replied that his brevet did not specify when the uniform might not be worn and he had no intention of changing. She insisted during the concert, and again he refused, even walking through the ballroom in this costume. However, since he knew that though reason was on his side, might was right at court and strict obedience was demanded, he departed that same night and from then on stood firm against all blandishments.

62 Boucher de Perthes, *op. cit.*, 584.
63 He obviously meant the guards of honor. See De Langle, *op. cit.*, 179.

Here the reason for her annoyance is very easily explained.[64]

Princess Elise to Joseph Fouché, Minister of Police, April 11, 1809.
I left Lucca on April 1. I had learned that there was a revolt at Abbadia San Salvador, and wanted to be in a better position to issue orders and to see that they were carried out.[65] Another reason was that I had heard that there was great apathy in Florence regarding my reception. The Prefect was dying, the mayor had gone to Paris, Count Menou was paralyzing the preparations. With much trouble and many threats they were only able to get the horse guards up to fifteen, the foot guards to twenty-four. Seeing that I would not be received as I should be, I decided to arrive at Florence at night. And I haven't regretted it. Nothing can approach the indifference and frigidity of the nobility. They all refused to enter my guard of honor. Three days after my arrival they offered me a guard of honor. I told them that I would accept it on condition that within a month there were a hundred men in the horse guards. The mayor offered the services of several old chamberlains and old ladies as grooms and ladies of the bedchamber. They also sent me six equerries but their uniform was so indecent that I refused their services. The city offered to give a ball in my honor in the beautiful hall of the Academy. I accepted it. They assured me that the ball would be worthy of me. The hall was beautiful but with the exception of the court of honor, the rest of the company was composed of street girls and the lower middle class whom nobody knew. I stayed a brief half hour and then left. . . . I only remained in Florence three days, and then left for Leghorn.[66]

Given these conditions in Florence, she would have deeply resented it if a mere musician, then ranked socially with comedians and entertainers, appeared in the uniform of her guard of honor (less noticeable in little Lucca) when she insisted on recruiting her new guards of honor from the most exclusive ranks of Florentine society. It is quite improbable, as Conestabile suggests, with the natural reaction of a young man of twenty-eight, that jealousy dictated her action. At that moment her interests lay elsewhere and with the alternation of passion and satiety that was one of the leading facets of Paganini's emotional nature, he too must have long been through with this casual liaison.[67] One suspects that from the

64 Napoleon: "Lively, sensitive, Elise was easily moved—the least contrariety was enough to arouse her anger. However, as she was naturally kindhearted, generous and highminded, she got over it almost immediately."

65 A small commune near Siena.

66 De Langle, *op. cit.*, 197.

67 For a description of the allegedly lax morals at the Lucca Court, see DeLangle, 181.

very first it was for him less an affair of passion than a *pretexte à bons appointments,* for this young man had his way to make and, as the Emperor's sister and a member of the family *qui gouvernait la monde,* Elise presented certain charms that in this particular instance need not be defined to be understood and pardoned.

Men's motives of behavior, we are told, are determined by self-interest and by a careful weighing of the same quality in their opponents. And this was clearly true in Paganini's case since (if Conestabile's description of the incident be substantially correct) he shot his arrow at Elise's weakest spot—her pride and lust for control. In view of the passive resistance of the Tuscan nobility and her own reduced authority, she no doubt now demanded exaggerated obeisance from her personal retainers and was therefore in no mood to regard with indulgence an expression of the more sinister side of her cantankerous fiddler.

Another "tradition" linked with this period and traceable to Fétis' disorderly imagination is that Paganini "was recalled to Florence in October, 1809, to give some concerts in connection with the ceremonies in celebration of the signature of peace between France and Austria." However, from the description of these ceremonies in the Florence papers, Princess Elise took no part, nor direct interest, in the elaborate proceedings and left the task exclusively to the municipal authorities.[68] After an official proclamation on October 21, next day all the theatres in Florence were thrown open gratis to the public and that evening (Sunday) a gala concert took place in the Teatro de la Pergola under the auspices of Gli Accademici Immobili. The Princess and members of her family and suite attended the concert but early the next morning she returned to Pisa, now her favorite residence, where she remained till she left for Paris to attend the Emperor's marriage to Marie Louise of Austria. As she did not return to Italy till September 11th, after the birth of her son, she was absent from Florence for a period of approximately eleven months, six of which were spent in Paris.[69] Thus for her first two years as Grand Duchess of Tuscany she would have had no use for any court musicians.

[68] As records in the State Archives in Florence show, this was her invariable practice after the transfer of the court; whether in a city of some size, or in a small hamlet, she entrusted all arrangements to the local authorities.

[69] In 1811, Elise resided in Pisa from July 1 till the end of December, and again in 1812 for a protracted period.

V. THE WASTREL YEARS 1810–1814

Il y a des moments où notre destinée, soit qu'elle cède à la société,
soit qu'elle obéisse à la nature, soit qu'elle commence à nous faire
ce que nous devons demeurer, se détourne soudain de sa ligne
première, telle qu'un fleuve qui change son cours par une subite
inflexion.—CHATEAUBRIAND.

ALTHOUGH after April, 1809, Niccolò's associations with the
court were obviously only with Prince Felix, the definite revolt—
whether precipitated by overbearance on Elise's part or vanity and
self-interestedness on that of Felix—must have occurred in late
December, when the crown contracts were renewed since from
January, 1810, he was obviously his own master. Whether he temporarily retained his headquarters in Lucca or preferred, at least
when the Prince was in residence, to kennel himself in some rural
solitude we do not know; but at any rate it is not difficult to imagine
how he was now diverting himself since even a quarter of a century later his friends were still "deploring his manner of life,"
still regretting that he was abandoning himself to his daemon and
thoughtlessly taxing strength and physical energy. Yet this insouci-
ant attitude towards his gifts was not a personal frailty. For living
in the passing moment was then characteristic of the age. Moreover—and the point is capital—the unfastidious public to which
he catered from now on, the easily won triumphs in small towns,
often by dubious artistic means, the descent to the vaudevillist
with the tricks of a theatrical mountebank could not help but blunt
his early ambition. Indeed, if in 1813 some inner or outer force had
not hurled him out of this pernicious orbit, he might very easily,
despite his gifts and his far from commonplace technical discoveries, have never transcended his epoch, never towered up in musical history "like some tremendous incredible tree," but might have
remained a local plantlet like so many others.

Boucher de Perthes to his father, Leghorn, February 9, 1810.
I've told you of an Italian with whom I made music at Prince Bacioc-

chi's. He's just been giving some concerts here, which have been a *succès fou*. He's a Genoese by the name of Paganini, and is self-taught; therefore, he plays like nobody else. But he spoils his playing by *panta-lonnades* unworthy of the art and his fine talent. I've heard him add a *point d'orgue* to a concerto of Viotti's in which he imitates a donkey, a dog, a rooster, etc.[1] Sometimes, at the beginning of a number, one of the strings breaks. You think he's going to stop but he goes right on playing on three strings. Then he plays variations on the G string. Where he excels is in his arpeggios, multiple stopping, and a pizzicato that he produces with the left hand. He then performs a mélange of all these things. It is enough to make you lose your mind! The Italians—who love these tours de force—applaud him like mad and, when he leaves the theatre, three hundred people follow him to his hotel. He plays the guitar no less brilliantly than the violin and sings when he is among a few friends. But this isn't his strong point. He has a voice like a cracked pot."[2]

From this we see that early in the new year he was based in Leghorn, where he gave five or six concerts at the Teatro Avvalo-rati during the carnival and aroused the greatest admiration when, after a string broke, "he went right on playing as though nothing had happened, imitating perfectly on the remaining three a dog, a cat, a nightingale, a cock and hen," as the local reviewer put it.[3] In after years ungenerous critics accused him of purposely doctor-ing up his strings beforehand so that they would break and afford him opportunity for an effective number; but, as Pulver justly points out, they overlooked the fact that the very nature of his play-ing placed the strings under a great strain so that if they had not been in good condition, he could never have produced his many exacting effects.[4]

Lillian Day quotes a letter from Paganini *père*, allegedly ad-dressed to Niccolò, in Leghorn round this time, though since she gives neither date, original Italian text, nor source of information, and furthermore offers no explanation as to how this relatively trivial missive escaped destruction through the years when all Paganini's other correspondence prior to 1813 has entirely disap-peared, it is quoted with the greatest reservation.

1 *Point d'orgue (le point d'arrêt)—fermata* or *coronella* in Italian, used here to indicate the cadenza.

2 Boucher de Perthes, *op. cit.*

3 *Corriere del Mediterraneo* (February 13, 1810).

4 Jeffrey Pulver, *op. cit.*, 59.

Signor Figlio:

It seems to me that now that you're so well off, you fail to think of those who are less well to do. Since you are no longer at court, can't you come home for a while? Don't you ever think of those you left at home, your father, your mother, your sisters, and brother? I believe these words will be enough to make you understand what your duty is. I'm expecting you.[5]

Such a message is of course by no means improbable since Antonio must have heard from his old cronies of his son's spectacular success. Nevertheless, if authentic and really dating from this time, the summons must have fallen on deaf ears since after the Leghorn concerts and one in Lucca on March 13 he embarked on his first extended tour to towns along the Via Emiglia, despite the fact that the whole district round Bologna and up as far as Verona was then infested with dangerous bandits driven to desperation by a severe drought in Tuscany.[6] Between March and August, when we next have word of him, he seems first to have made his way to Parma and, from what he said to Schottky, established his headquarters there for the next three years, during which time he in the main kept well away from the dominions of his late patroness.

After two concerts in Cesena (August 29 and 30) and three in Forli (September 18, 19, and 20), on September 23 he played in the little hamlet of Cappi di Piangipane, about six miles from Ravenna. This might indicate that for some reason he was not permitted to enter the city, or perhaps could not secure an engagement at the theatre and there was no proper hall available. Lady Morgan wrote that even when equipped with valid documents it was often difficult to obtain permission to enter a city, or else one was forced to wait for days outside the gates while the papers were being examined by the military authorities. As there is no record of his ever returning to this section of the Romagna, he must have encountered some obstacle that he laid to a lack of interest in his person or his art.

After playing in Rimini on October 28 and November 1, he goes

[5] Lillian Day, *Paganini of Genoa,* 49. The author stresses the "sarcastic salutation" as indicative of Antonio's attitude to his son, but this seems to have been the general custom.

[6] On September 16, 1810, Elise suppressed more than one hundred religious houses in Tuscany, thus adding to the general unrest.

into eclipse again till May, 1811,[7] so he may have returned to Parma, where he fell ill and was incapacitated for a time. Fétis, writing in 1851, stated that in "1815 he returned to the Romagna and after giving several concerts stopped at Ancona, where his nervous troubles detained him for several months." Although the year is incorrect and one cannot depend on Fétis' memory after twenty years, Niccolò might easily have linked a Romagna tour with a protracted illness. The only thing that militates against Fétis' interpretation is that if he ever questioned Niccolò regarding his whereabouts after his departure from Milan, he may have chosen this excuse to conceal events which, as we shall see, would have been extremely mortifying to his pride had they been given wider publicity. A contemporaneous traveler tells us that in those years Ancona was a "town of dirty streets with the stenches and filth of a crowded population living under the most primitive sanitary conditions," and since it drew forth from Niccolò the devastating adjective *miserabillisima* when he stopped there over night in 1825, one assumes that it had not improved and that he could not have been there previously or he would not have chosen to go that way again and even consider for a time the possibility of playing there.[8]

As we find him playing in Modena on May 17 (1811) and in Parma on August 9, he may have been slowly working his way back unless after leaving Rimini he returned to Tuscany for the Florentine carnival of 1811, which was celebrated with unwonted gaiety and extravagance.[9] Be that as it may, after the Parma concert we have no further word of him till he turns up in Ferrara on January 24 (1812) with his friend Giordigiani, who was then engaged at the Pergola in Florence. As the latter's current flame, the ballerina Antonietta Pallerini, was then filling an engagement in Ferrara, Giordigiani readily went along and helped to persuade the dancer

[7] His Rimini concerts were given in the Teatro del Pubblico (now Sala dell'Arengo). At these concerts he was assisted by Giovanni Celli, his own contributions being a "Concerto in one movement by Sig. Creutzer [sic]" and a *"Polacca con variazioni di moderno stile."* Conestabile (Mompellio edition, 116) states that he "played in Rimini on January 22, 1810." Through the recent research of G. C. Mengozzi of Rimini, these statements are shown to be erroneous.

[8] Codignola, *op. cit.,* 230; Lady Morgan, *Italy,* III, 315.

[9] Instead of going to Pisa, Princess Elise spent the winter of 1810–11 in Florence, and did all she could to make the carnival a brilliant success.

to come to Niccolò's aid when the regular primadonna unaccountably deserted him.[10] As she did not pretend to be a singer, her well-intentioned efforts, even with Paganini's guitar accompaniment, were not appreciated by certain persons in the audience, who received her with loud hisses, which evidently disturbed her less than it did her two escorts. When it then came Niccolò's turn to play his popular barnyard fantasy, he informed the ungracious public that the imitation of the donkey was expressly intended "for the person who had hissed," unaware that the people in the surrounding districts had adopted the heehaw as a symbol of the Ferrarese, who were looked upon as very slow and stupid. As a result of this impromptu tour de force he and his two accomplices in calumny had to fly for their lives to escape an angry mob. Codignola (p. 33) dismisses this little anecdote as apocryphal and "typical of the baseless legends" that were "begining to be associated with his name," showing how dangerous it is to theorize; for an old diary in the archives of the Dalla Penna family of Ferrara contains the following incontrovertible evidence:

Ferrara, January 22, 1812 [evening]. Notable concert in the theatre by the very famous Genoese, Niccolò Paganini. Amongst the vocal numbers, we heard the prima ballerina accompanied only by the guitar. She was a very poor singer. She was hissed. As Paganini promised on his program, in his last number he imitated the songs and cries of certain animals. He finished with that of the donkey and called out loudly: "*Per quello che aveva fischiato.*" The police ordered him from the city.

In addition to this confirmation, we know that such an imitation was then a regular item in his repertory and further, Achilles, who often must have heard the story from his father, added a marginal note to Conestabile's account saying that his father "hurriedly left the stage, astounded that his prank had stirred up such a rumpus. He only learned later that this particular joke was very offensive to the people of that city."

Nevertheless, as Codignola rightly says, these were the years of vagabondage when many of the silly tales were started, which then

10 Antoinetta Pallerini was in Venice in 1816–17, during Byron's residence there. According to his friend, Angelo Mengaldo, he allowed himself "*mille plaisanteries*" with her.

clung to him like burrs; for these were the years when he was gradually taking on the external qualities, was developing the mannerisms, poses, affectations, that contributed so greatly to his epic: his
emaciation, something Mephistophelian in his cast of features, his
amazing dexterity, his readiness to exploit but not reveal his personality, the innate showman's instinct, with its *besoin d'étonner,*
and last of all the tremendous magnetism that emanated from his
person and his music and threw his audiences into beatific ecstacies.
All these things, together with his tendency to play the clown, his
willingness to descend from the dignified parallel on which the
mind of the true artist is ever set to the lower level of the prestidigitator, with the resultant popularity that these acrobatic performances brought him in smaller towns and hamlets, helped to mold
to a fixed pattern certain traits that later earned for him, from less
indulgent critics, the epithet of charlatan.

However, many of the mannerisms, the clumsy gestures, the exaggerated acknowledgments with their tincture of humility that were
so frequently criticized and held up to ridicule abroad were by no
means a deliberate affectation. This was evidently the Italian custom, even in the late thirties, as shown by Liszt's letter to the *Revue
et Gazette Musicale* during one of his Italian tours.

*Jusqu'à ce que le malheureux triomphateur se soit montré hors de la
coulisse et que les yeux baissés, la main sur le coeur, il ait exprimé par
une ridicule pantomime une plus ridicule humilité . . . ses révérences
sont gauches, sa démarche mal equilibrée, ses gestes stupides. On dirait
souvent un garçon limonadier qui demande pardon d'avoir cassé une
carafe, plutôt qu'un fier triomphateur qui vient recevoir des couronnes.*

Thus, these seeming "eccentricities, the awkward bows, the
oafish gait, the stupid" gestures, had not been deliberately adopted
to draw attention to himself. He had only carefully modeled his
stage deportment on that of his colleagues, so he had no idea that
according to foreign standards he was conducting himself like *"un
garçon limonadier."* It is only strange that with his pronounced
mimetic gift he did not adopt the more dignified manner of his foreign colleagues, but he seems to have retained many of these national idiosyncracies to the end of his career.

The sparsity of details regarding his movements from 1810 to

1813 is without doubt traceable to some extent to the existing political situation. Hence, it is useless on the whole to speculate even on his whereabouts since his peregrinations must have been subject very largely to forces outside his personal will. Up to the end of 1808, Lucca was a little island where it was simpler to remain than to trouble with passport and other formalities necessary for entering Tuscany or the duchies to the north.[11] But after these provinces were absorbed by the French Empire, once he was fortified with the requisite papers, he was free to roam at will over a fairly large territory, which he soon extended to the Kingdom of Italy (Lombardy), in the north.

After the Ferrara concert and two in Parma during May, he again drops out of sight till the beginning of 1813, when we find him playing in Brescia and Bergamo, two places that he seems already to have visited in the past.

Paganini to Filippo Zaffarini, Bergamo, February 8, 1813.
I'm longing for the moment when I can see you again. My third, and last concert in this city takes place in the theatre [Riccardi] on Friday, the twelfth, in response to a universal demand. I should like to give another in the theatre in Brescia, and that is why I'm asking you to obtain the theatre for me for the following Friday. I appeal to you as the only real patron of music and intelligent amateur. Regards to your wife.

Did he approach these cities from the east, or did his curiosity first take him to Milan?[12] The first hypothesis seems much more likely since once in the Lombard capital he would surely have found it difficult to tear himself away. "After the upheavals of the last few years there was something feverish about the life of the [Milan] cafés, of the balls and theatres, of the clubs where under the green shaded lights, entire patrimonies and new-formed fortunes were gambled away in a night."[13] And Niccolò was not the man to have resisted such temptations once he came within their ambit. The fact that he was tempted and succumbed might of course account for many missing weeks in the two preceding years,

[11] Lady Morgan, *op. cit.*, I, 116n.
[12] Gordigiani, in relating their Ferrara experiences, said that he had met Paganini in Milan, presumably a slip in memory. They evidently met in Florence or Bologna.
[13] Colquhoun, *op. cit.*, 39.

though it is hard to believe that once there he would have failed to give a concert, if for no other reason than to supply himself with funds.

Nevertheless, as far as his music was concerned, one feels that between 1810 and 1813 it was restlessness and boredom rather than an imperative compulsion to parade his gifts that from time to time drove him to leave a familiar patch of ground "where he knew what to expect." Indeed, it was probably this strain in his character, inspired by some inner sense of inadequacy, a disinclination to compete with others in a more exacting forum, that led him to postpone so long the visit to Vienna.

During his three years at court, and even afterwards, he must have met many Milanese who told him of the music, the theatres, the ease and freedom of manners in their pleasure-loving city, where "the luscious Italian women [the words are Henri Beyle's] came every night to their boxes at the Scala, and while the music played, carried on their love affairs *à ciel ouvert*." This makes it doubly strange that the city had not sooner magnetized him to its center. However, once within its gates, and particularly with his pockets full of money, one understands how he overlooked no opportunities, spending himself lavishly and throwing himself with passionate abandon into the amusements and adventures of raffish and irresponsible companions. For the period itself conduced to restlessness. The great changes in the political world, the uncertainty of the future, disturbances at home, the rumblings of war abroad, the social and spiritual chaos following on poverty, intrigue, and oppression, produced an atmosphere that made it difficult to steer a straight and steady course. One simply lived from day to day and, as after all great political *bouleversements* when hopes were constantly paired with disillusionments, one sought a temporary narcotic in a life of pleasure.

However, it was during the next decade that Niccolò sowed his real wild oats, years when "he sought to reward himself for long privation by heaping pleasure upon pleasure," and for which frivolous Milan and, later, "depraved" Venice set the pace.

In my early years [he confessed to George Harrys] I had much dissension with the court at Lucca, and for a piffling little salary had to suffer many a vexation. Then one day I suddenly decamped, living first in one place, then another, and falling into the company of gamblers where I often risked more than I possessed. Several of my accounts of my little love affairs, related in the company of friends, have been repeated and, though the anecdotes are not altogether devoid of truth, they have been so distorted in the telling that I myself no longer recognize them. When I became my own master, I enjoyed life in rich, full draughts—but I was never half so bad as people say.

The theatre and all its doings had always attracted him,[14] a feeling heightened by long association with it, its enthusiasms and unconventional attitude towards life,[15] so that the first thing he always did upon arriving in a city was to spend the evening in the theatre no matter how weary, ill, or footsore he might be. Since there were several in Milan the stranger was always sure to find one open (each theatre played only certain nights each week), though the chief attraction, naturally, was the Scala, the first glance of which was *énivrant* even to such a sophisticated *boulevardier* as Henri Beyle.[16]

It proved equally intoxicating to Niccolò, who immediately decided that it was here his debut must take place; yet, to obtain it was not so simple as it seemed. Since instrumental concerts were extremely rare,[17] an instrumentalist, in order to appeal to a fashionable audience, had to combine his concert with a ballet and several vocal numbers; or play an intermezzo concert between the acts of an opera or the two parts of a double bill. However, unless one had an established reputation or considerable influence with the court or impresario, it was frequently difficult for an outsider to obtain this privilege. Indeed, even later when his flaming music had lighted the Italian sky from Trieste to Palermo, Niccolò often complained of difficulties in securing the Scala for a concert.

The present theatre, designed by the architect Piermarini, had

14 William Beckford, *Travel Diaries of Mr. Beckford of Fonthill* (2 vols., Cambridge, 1928), I, 251–53, wrote that "the hour of the theatre . . . is the happiest part of the day to every Italian."

15 According to Dr. Burney, "a chaste actress and opera singer was a still more uncommon phenomenon in Italy than in Great Britain."

16 See James Galiffe, *Italy and Its Inhabitants*, I, 39 f. Liszt gave a less flattering picture: "*Je ne connais rien de plus sale, de plus noir, de plus fétide, que les escaliers et les corridors de la Scala.*" (*Revue et Gazette Musicale* [May 27, 1838].)

17 Lichtenthal wrote from Milan in 1812 that "instrumental concerts had become very rare."

been inaugurated in August, 1778, to replace the old building destroyed by fire in 1776, and since the future box owners had provided the funds for erecting the new building, their wishes naturally had to be considered when selecting the repertory or other entertainment.[18] Fortunately for Niccolò, he had one powerful advocate within the organization, namely, his old maestro Alessandro Rolla, who was leader of the orchestra.[19] At that time, according to Lichtenthal, this consisted of twenty-five violins, six violas, four cellos, eight double basses, two flutes, two oboes, two clarinets, four French horns, two trumpets, one bass trombone, drums and "Janizary music" (i.e., big drums, cymbals, triangles, and the Turkish crescent), which Spohr found "very large" though still "not large enough for the size of the auditorium." While the "playing was precise and vigorous," he felt that Rolla "subjected his men to too many rehearsals for them to be able to give an effective performance with only one"—a shortcoming that would hardly have disturbed an Italian soloist like Niccolò, accustomed to playing in small theatres with far less efficient bands.

Since the climax of his debut concert (his Streghe Variations) was inspired by a performance of Salvatore Vignano's ballet,[20] *Il Noce de Benevento* (Benevento's Walnut Tree), set to music by Franz Süssmayer,[21] which he witnessed at this theatre, we are able to fix approximately the time of his arrival in Milan, granting, of course, that he had not visited Lombardy the year before.[22]

The work had been brought out in 1812 and proved such an immense success that the following year it was decided to stage another Vignano ballet, this time *The Men of Prometheus,* for

18 See Spohr, *op. cit.,* I, 301, for the Italian custom of "box owners" and their controlling interest.

19 Rolla was also teaching violin at the conservatory, which had been founded in 1808 by the Viceroy.

20 Salvatore Vignano (1769–1821), famous dancer, ballet composer and choreographer.

21 Franz Xavier Süssmayer (1766–1803), Mozart's friend who was at the composer's bedside at the time of his death and to whom the latter gave instructions for completing the Requiem. See W. Pole, *The Story of Mozart's Requiem,* which gives the history of the manuscript and the long controversy regarding the authenticity of the work.

22 Fétis, in his monograph, wrote that "Paganini attended a performance of this work at the Scala"; Kapp added the gloss, "on one of the first nights after his arrival," and Pulver renders it as "on the night of his arrival"!

which Beethoven had composed the music. The première of the new work was set for May 6 but by mid-April it was evident that the production would not be ready for at least a fortnight so, in order to fill in the gap, *Il Noce* was restored to the repertory on April 19 since its undiminished popularity would keep it running on its own momentum till the new work was ready to go on. Hence, Niccolò must have arrived in Milan and have attended a performance some time between April 19 and May 22.

A really admirable witches' dance that occurs right at the beginning of the ballet is being sung here by everybody [wrote Lichtenthal in 1812]. One hears it in all the streets and squares and played on all sorts of instruments. Polli has written some pleasing variations on the tune and has already had them published.

The tune captivated Niccolò as it did the Milanese and, inasmuch as a treatment of this kind was right in line with his ordinary "hits," he followed in Polli's footsteps and wrote a set of variations that he intuitively felt would put all others in the shade.

Possibly he originally intended to play before the end of the season and was unable to secure the theatre; or again he may have deliberately postponed his concert till he had completed the Variations, seeing that this work represented his first major composition in several years and undoubtedly required "great reflection" and very careful working out before presenting it to a fastidious audience. Far too much depended on it to risk spoiling it by hasty craftsmanship or ill-advised impatience, two things that Milan would be the first to discover and condemn. Writing in 1851, Fétis stated that "while engaged in the composition of this work and the preparation of his concerts Paganini fell ill again and several months went by before he was in a condition to play." Was he quoting Paganini here, and if so, was the latter's testimony reliable after eighteen years, or Fétis' memory after twenty? One doubts it very much. It is far more likely that Fétis was again carrying out his self-imposed task of "filling in the gaps" to which Anders had called attention (*"Je me suis attaché à remplir la lacune dont a parlé M. Anders"*), since Lichtenthal in his fairly frequent reports of Niccolò's movements and activities at this time never mentioned a recent illness. In a creative sense the years from 1800 to 1813 had been a period of preparation during which he had produced nothing of importance, nothing that found a place among his leading works: the Napoleon Sonata, which remained outside the perimeter, the trivial *Duetto Amoroso* written a few weeks earlier, several quartets and small works for the guitar, and numerous *pièces d'occasion,* like the horn concerto for Professor Gallo, all improvisations, largely speaking, tossed off quickly and as rapidly discarded. From 1805 to 1809 the pressures of court life, with its many extraneous obligations, represented more a period of ease, almost of lassitude, in which he could not, or would not, call up the genie, while the years that immediately followed were spent in a restless wandering from place to place, when he was unable to settle down, when life meant more to him than art, when serious friends repeatedly urged him to drop the role of the *"grande pagliaccio del violino"* and indulge in *"meno caricature sul suo strumento."* It is a pity that none of his early programs between 1805 and 1813 have survived, for it would be interesting to know to what extent he varied his repertory. He may have essayed some experimental works—the germ cells of his later concertos—but, as he ordinarily limited his program to two numbers, one of which was a concerto by Viotti, Kreutzer, or Rode (a portion of his repertory that he never varied or extended in the three decades of his career), the last number was very likely an extemporization on the order of his *Fandango Espagnol,* or variations on some popular operatic air that ended the evening with a flourish.

Imitative effects of all kinds were then very much in vogue and Paganini, who carried the birthmark of the Romantic Age, had early turned his attention to them, first because they were always immensely successful with the vulgar crowd, and his creative work, being designed to meet the taste of an immediate public, was never conceived—like that of Thucydides—"in terms of eternity." Thus, one single hearing of Süssmayer's amusing little episode was sufficient to spark his dormant inspiration and bring forth a set of brilliant variations in which he imitated the tone of the oboe. "The author of the music in Macbeth [wrote Leigh Hunt] would have hugged him for it. Levity, gravity, the homely, the supernatural, the odd, the graceful, figures in strange combination. And every now and then a voice was heard as of some fearful old beldame venting herself in a strain of feeble mystery, at once humorous and alarming. You imagined a pale old woman, dancing and whining, with a sort of ghastly affectation of the ridiculous."

He had been indulging his fancy for this sort of thing from his early boyhood, but here, dropping the clownish and tastelessly grotesque, the mistakenly conceived, he raised the imitative effect to a higher level and incorporated it in a diabolically difficult and time-resisting work that remained one of the most admired and sensational numbers of his repertory.

ii

As one of Italy's leading musical centers, Milan had a large corps of resident correspondents who sent regular reports of the city's musical activities to the principal Continental journals, the correspondent of the Leipzig *Allgemeine Musikalische Zeitung* being the Hungarian physician and composer, Peter Lichtenthal, who had settled in Milan in 1810 and later played an active local role as composer, lexicographer, and musicologist. By the autumn of 1813, Paganini's name, at least, seems to have been known to him, perhaps through Rolla, Aiblinger, Soliva, or other common friends, though he had obviously never heard him play, otherwise he would have mentioned him when writing of Italy's different instrumentalists. During Paganini's six months' residence in Milan he had quite likely heard the quartet that Niccolò at once had organized, consisting of himself, Moria (second violin), Rolla (viola), and that "angelo del Paradiso," the Viceroy's chamber virtuoso, Giuseppe Sturioni (cello), which had given him some idea of the Maestro's gifts. Be that as it may, after the Scala concert of October 29, when Paganini played Kreutzer's E minor concerto and his own Streghe Variations between the two numbers of a double bill, Lichtenthal's enthusiasm knew no bounds, as comes out clearly in his report to Leipzig, the first extensive criticism of Paganini's playing by a knowledgeable musical critic to reach the German-reading public, and without any of the undiscriminating hyperbole, the extravagant exaltation which then, and for long afterwards, was associated with any Italian comments on his playing.[23]

23 Liszt, article in *Revue et Gazette Musicale* (1838), 102, wrote: *"Les principes essentiels de beau et du vrai ne sont jamais ni posés, ni discutés."*

"Car il ne faut pas se figurer que les expressions simples ou positives soient d'usage dans ce pays-ci [wrote President de Brosses]; *le comparatif même y est negligé, et dans les grands occasions, il faut surcharger le superlatif."* Even today his countrymen approach him with uncritical admiration, it being difficult for them to assess dispassionately any of the achievements of this "Titan." Lichtenthal, however, by putting in the detail, removed the phantom, leaving flesh and blood.

Signor Paganini of Genoa, who in Italy is generally considered as the outstanding violinist of the day, gave a concert at the Scala on October 29, which attracted an extraordinarily large audience. Everyone wanted to see and hear this phenomenal wizard and everyone was really staggered. It fairly took one's breath away. In a sense, he is without question the foremost and greatest violinist in the world. His playing is truly *inexplicable.* He performs certain passage work, leaps, and double stops that have never been heard before from *any* violinist, whoever he might be. He plays—with a special fingering of his own—the most difficult passages in two, three, and four parts; imitates many wind instruments; plays the chromatic scale right close to the bridge in the highest positions and with a purity of intonation that is sheerly incredible. He performs the most difficult compositions on one string and in the most amazing manner while plucking a bass accompaniment on the others, probably as a prank. It is often difficult to believe that one is not hearing several instruments. In short, as Rolla and other celebrities say, he is one of the most artificial [*künstlich*] violinists the world has ever known.[24] I say artificial because, when it comes down to simple, deeply moving, beautiful playing, one can indeed find any number of violinists as good as he and now and then (and not infrequently at that) even some who certainly surpass him—Rolla for instance. One can easily understand that he creates a furore at his concerts. However, musical connoisseurs are quite right in saying that he does not play the Kreutzer Concerto at all in the spirit of the composer, in fact, that he distorts much of it almost beyond recognition. On the other hand, his Variations on the G string aroused universal admiration, for truly no one has ever heard anything to equal it. This in his way unique artist could not satisfy the local public with one concert so he gave eleven within the space of six weeks, some in the Scala and others in the Carcano. He has also frequently played at court. They say that he can play the most difficult Beethoven quartets at sight, but this I should be inclined to doubt without the requisite proof.

24 *Künstlich* means here the extraordinary as opposed to the ordinary—giving an impression of artifice.

In this brief summing up Lichtenthal reveals that even amongst Paganini's own countrymen there were many who were not dazzled by his pyrotechnics and were able to distinguish between purity of style and mere technical display, though at the same time he himself is ready to admit that here the lesser order of beauty, which is technique, was vested in one who, like Napoleon, "had the gift of electrifying men." In short, here the world of music was confronted with a style that must ever remain inimitable since it was inherent in the genius and originality of the man himself.

With Milan's accolade Niccolò had passed from local to international fame, master at last of his own destiny, surrounded by admiring throngs, courted by aristocrats and impresarios, the subject of every *conversazione*. Did he regret, perhaps, the earlier wasted years? or did he look upon his immediate past as a period of development and preparation? Later, in speaking of Vienna, he said that it was "hard for him to bring himself to take the step," a hesitancy that would be easy to interpret as a lack of self-confidence, a feeling of unsureness in some facet of his art; yet, perhaps it was nothing more than his habitual indecision—the typical reaction of the born procrastinator who requires some external leverage to cross the Rubicon. For after these resounding Milanese successes, any subconscious misgivings of his abilities must have melted like mist before the morning sun.

iii

After two more concerts in the Scala on November 11 and 19, there was a pause of three weeks when, if he were not resting, he may have played in towns in the vicinity. Then, resuming his Milan activities on December 12, he gave nine concerts at the Teatro Carcano between that date and Christmas, after which he temporarily retired until the following May. The concerts at the Viceroy's to which Lichtenthal referred, and where he first made the acquaintance of Johann Aiblinger,[25] would indicate that he was not completely at odds with the Bonaparte family, or perhaps Eugène Beauharnais was delighted at this opportunity of dispensing royal favors to a person who had had the temerity to break brusquely with the one of Napoleon's sisters who had been most hateful to his mother.

25 Johann Aiblinger (1770–1867), pupil of Simon Mayr in Bergamo.

Through his connections with the court, he was also brought into contact with Nicholas Henri Jacob,[26] the court painter whose portrait of him was engraved by Luigi Rados and published by Ricordi, afterwards going through numerous reincarnations at the hands of other artists. Although the cherubic youth with tousled curly locks and slightly bravado air who looks out so confidently from this first canvas has little resemblance to the later Paganini, or rather to one's mental picture of the emaciated, high-strung, and surely already dissipated young man who for some years "had been enjoying life in rich, full draughts," the portrait still has its interest and historical importance since it is the earliest that has come down to us. In the former Maia Bang collection in Washington, D. C., there is an oil portrait signed "O. V. 1811," which some previous owner has attributed to Horace Vernet, but this opinion does not rest on adequate proofs. First of all, the picture shows a man much older than the Paganini of the Jacob portrait or even a young man of twenty-nine. Further, Vernet allegedly painted his first portrait in 1818 and did not visit Italy till 1820 and then only for a few weeks. Moreover, there is also no reason for believing that even after going to the Villa Medici in Rome in 1828 he ever italianized his Christian name. Fétis also wrote of seeing a bust of Paganini in Bartolini's studio in Florence in 1841 that was allegedly made in 1808, but if so, this seems to have disappeared.[27]

26 Nicholas Henri Jacob (1782–1871), French painter, pupil of David and DuPasquier, and from 1805–14 court painter at the court of Milan. This portrait, of which a copy of the original lithograph engraved by Luigi Rados (1773–1840) is in the collection of Senator G. Treccani of Milan, was frequently reproduced. After Ricordi announced its publication in November, 1813, Ferdinando Artaria, a relative of the founders of the Vienna publishing house of that name, had a lithograph made by Francesco Caporali, which was published by Artaria between 1822 and 1824. (See *Galleria di rinomati e viventi compositori, cantanti e professori di musica italiani*, 1822.) The original Jacob portrait seems to have disappeared.

27 At the Turin Exposition of 1898 the Paganini heirs exhibited a bust of him as a young man but whether this was by Bartolini or by Leep (Naples) is not known. According to some writers, Paganini gave the Leep bust to Germi. In May, 1932, an alleged Canova bust (formerly in the George Withers collection) was sold in London by Puttick & Simpson. This too shows a man in middle life, somewhat in the manner of the Santo Varni bust of 1831, and bears none of the characteristics of the traditional Paganini. (Perhaps it was the Pistrucci bust to which Paganini referred in 1832.) The anonymous portrait published by Codignola as frontispiece is signed on the back "Genova, 1814, Niccolò Paganini," and was purchased by the Istituto Mazziniano (of which Codignola is director) of a secondhand dealer in 1934. It might easily be the work of Carlo Carloni.

On the whole, these first months in Milan must have proved for Niccolò an active, happy, and inspiring period despite the dull rumble of a changing order as one of the great dramas of the world now hurried to its close. Although he always carefully abstained from politics and concentrated his attention on his music, with little or no interest in the calamities of his native land, he still could not have been wholly indifferent to the fate of that sovereign and his satellites who for fourteen years had swayed the destinies of Europe, particularly of Italy. Did he feel no sympathy for his former patroness when British forces occupied Lucca on December 10? Or did he merely smile and congratulate himself on his good luck? And the following March, when he learned that after abdicating she then rode down to exile, did his thoughts never race back in gratitude to certain memories? Or did he thank the co-operation of his stars that had enabled him to get away before the edifice collapsed? *"L'ingratitude des hommes m'a tellement frappée que je suis étonnée de trouver un être qui s'intéresse à mon sort,"* she wrote Eugène Le Bon after the debacle;[28] but whether her onetime virtuoso was included in this arraignment, one hesitates to surmise, particularly since his actions and his comments on the subject were persistently noncommittal.

Even if the state of the nation failed to touch him personally, political events were now beginning to have their repercussions all around him, making it very difficult to move about. By the spring of 1814 the country had again been rent asunder, the ten Italian states returning for the most part to their former masters; the Bourbons were back again in Naples, Genoa had been allotted to Sardinia (which included Piedmont and Liguria), Venice to Lombardo-Venetia under the dominance of Austria, and the papal states had been restored, with Parma, Modena, and Tuscany as separate states, though also under Austrian dominion. For one thing, Napoleon had made Italian unity have a passionate appeal, so, upon his removal from the scene, the country was infused with an ardent desire for liberation, with the result that when the Viceroy, who hoped to snatch the crown for his own head, attempted in April to give his dream reality, rioting broke out in Milan till the waiting Austrians marched in and claimed the disputed kingdom

28 De Langle, *op. cit.,* 363 ff.

for the House of Hapsburg. Paganini, who had seen enough war and pillage in his youth and believed, like Leonardo, that it was "well to flee from storms," left the city at the first signal of unrest, going first to Pavia and from thence to Turin,[29] after which he returned to Milan for a further series of ten concerts, this time in connection with the *opera stagione* at the Teatro Re.

iv

Reports of this *"miracolo dei suonatori viventi"* having by now reached Genoa, Paganini *père* must have felt that the family had a right to share in this rain of gold and no doubt tweaked the recalcitrant Niccolò by the sleeve to awaken him to a sense of his responsibilities; which turned the latter's thoughts in that direction. Just how close a contact he had maintained with his family since the spring of 1808, we do not know, but it was probably restricted to a laconic letter now and then informing them of his whereabouts and physical condition, in the manner of his later messages. He may also have contributed to their support from time to time when his extracurricular pursuits brought him in additional income; but his small salary in Lucca and the roving, aimless life that followed for some years would have made any regular contribution difficult, if not impossible. He may also have visited Genoa again in 1811 or 1812, two of the most uncharted years of this early period, but the great gulf fixed by destiny between his world and theirs, his protracted absences and silences, his new associates, his aims and activities, even the daily routine of his life had surely loosened all the warmer, closer bonds that have their roots in a community of interests and outlook. Nevertheless, a powerful, ingrained feeling of loyalty towards his own—a defensive rather than an emotional attitude—was a fundamental facet of his nature and it is therefore reasonable to suppose that his decision to turn his steps homeward for a time, though perhaps stimulated by a peremptory summons from his father, was born of sincere anxiety regarding the family's welfare. After Napoleon's abdication, the English occupied the city, which, on British assurances that the Allies intended to restore the Republic's former independence,

---

[29] Among the members of the Turin orchestra in 1814 were Alessandro Molino, Carlo Bruno, Felice Radicati, Giuseppe Ghebart.

also rose against the French. So news of these new disturbances may have hastened his decision to relieve his parents' financial worries till his father could resume his accustomed occupation on the docks, or whatever he happened to be doing at that time.

Genoa had not heard him since his debut as a prodigy, an interim of nearly twenty years. "All this time we have heard nothing but rumors of his prodigious achievements," wrote the *Gazzetta di Genoa* on the eve of his first concert, which took place on September 9 in the scene of his first triumphs, the Teatro Sant'Agostino. However, during the preceding weeks he must have often played in aristocratic drawing rooms and informally among his friends, and thus kept his name in circulation since, when the concert was announced, there was "such a rush for seats" that the municipal authorities closed all the other theatres and even prohibited any private gatherings on that evening.

Once again, as in Milan, he was the most talked-of person in the city. In the *palazzi* of the wealthy and the purlieus of the port with their predatory backwash of humanity, every nook and cranny of the city rippled with civic pride and curiosity; yet there was still no real value judgment of his playing. No one attempted to describe it in terms of technique or of art, to analyze or appraise his compositions, or even to note, with indulgent disapproval, the little lapses of taste and the circus tricks by which he still got many of his effects. But all this mattered little from the economic point of view. If critics and public retreated before his wizardry, the practical-minded Genoese found many ways of spreading the exciting news that "gold was raining down upon him," the publicity value of which, as he was soon to discover to his sorrow, was highly questionable.

Owing to his incommunicativeness regarding his personal affairs, added to the barriers between the city-states of Italy and the brevity of human memory, probably very few Genoese still remembered his early performances or had any knowledge of, or interest in, the later course of his career; which naturally gave rise to all sorts of rumors when he suddenly sailed across the sky in such a burst of glory. Where had he been hiding himself and why had the great world of music had no cognizance of him till the previous winter in Milan? Gifts such as these were a process of development; to spring them suddenly upon the public argued some strange isolation during a long preparatory period, for otherwise some one would have been witness, even if indifferently, of the slow maturing of this astounding *expertise*. It was no uncommon thing, as the political scene shifted in those unquiet days, for a person to be banished to the galleys or incarcerated for some alleged delinquency,[30] and many men far more eminent and influential than Antonio Paganini's son had to waste months and years in prisons that were little better than a dungeon while awaiting a twist of Fortune's wheel.[31]

The legend of his imprisonment that arose about this time was therefore neither fantastic nor improbable, though who or what originally started it, or when, no one probably could say. Maybe it was some trivial human spite stung to irritation by the knowledge that he was on the certain road to wealth, or as he suggested later, some confusion in the public mind with the escapades of Durand, his Polish counterpart. However, that flying rumors were already current in Genoa as early as June, 1814, is testified by a notation in the diary of Colonel Maxwell Montgomery, aide de camp of Sir William Bentinck, who was then commanding H. M. 36th Regiment in Genoa and was intimately acquainted with Di Negro, Mme de Stael, the Durazzos, and their circle.

I have become acquainted with the most outré, most extravagant, and strangest character I ever beheld, or heard, in the musical line [he wrote]. He has just been emancipated from durance vile where he has been incarcerated on suspicion of murder. His long figure, long neck, long face, and long forehead, his hollow and deadly pale cheek, large black eyes, hooked nose, and jet black hair, which is long and more than half hides his expressive Jewish face—all these rendered him the most extraordinary person I ever beheld. There is something scriptural in the *tout ensemble* of the strange physiognomy of this uncouth and unearthly figure. He is very improvident, and very poor.[32]

Since Montgomery presumably picked up his gossip in the small

30 Lady Morgan, *op. cit.,* I, 386.

31 Paganini, to whose freedom-loving spirit, restraint was worse than imprisonment, must have made it plain that the pressures of court life gave him claustrophobia, so that he looked back upon those three years as a period of bondage. Many of his listeners may have interpreted his remarks in the more literal sense.

32 Colonel Maxwell Montgomery, *My Adventures.*

talk of fashionable drawing rooms, a similar report must have reached the ears also of Di Negro, who may have laughed it off as preposterous nonsense. Yet, it still seems strange that he or Paganini's other friends in Genoa did nothing to correct the colonel's false impression, or attempt to silence the malevolent whispers, which they must have realized would prove detrimental in the long run. If at that early date they had taken vigorous steps to stamp out the calumny, they would have spared their friend many hours of worry and depression in the future.

VI. *ANGELINA 1814–1815*

The world's heroes have room for all positive qualities, even those which are disreputable, in the capacious theatre of our dispositions.—ROBERT LOUIS STEVENSON.

IN THE COURSE of Paganini's philanderings under the midsummer moon, in the less respectable quarters of his native city, he made the acquaintance, shortly after his return, of Angelina Cavanna, evidently a polluted little wretch who was doubtlessly aware of his successes and exerted all her wiles to land this Midas in her net. Although to more exclusive circles he seemed "uncouth, improvident and poor," to this pretty little proletarian these qualities would naturally have been less apparent or, at all events, would not have counted in comparison with the potential material advantages. As for Niccolò, the "delicious moments" she promised him must have momentarily turned his head so that he plunged heedlessly into a snare that in the past he must have frequently, and easily, avoided.

Abandoning, in her elation, her customary reticence with respect to her clients, Angelina carried the good news to her impecunious father, a small tailor in the neighborhood, who, scenting an opportunity of enriching himself beyond his wildest dreams, immediately proceeded to indoctrinate her in the proper strategy. At least, subsequent events afford color to the suspicion. "An innocent, ingenuous soul? [asks Professor Berri] or an astute and perverted tool of extortion?" Perhaps a mixture of the two. At any rate, whether ingenuous or shrewd, Angelina posed on a sudden as a paragon of virtue, and refused to be as complacent as Niccolò's extensive experience in this field of human frailty had led him to expect. There was to be no bargaining with her vanities. This time it must be marriage—or nothing.

Given his temperament and sexual drive, he had not lived to the age of thirty-two without being able to recognize at sight the eligibility of the material from the matrimonial point of view or

133

without having developed and perfected a technique of evasion that was then a fairly simple matter when the two protagonists were separated by social or professional barriers. On numerous occasions in the past, like the courtiers all round him, he must have slipped with feline adroitness through the dividing wickets and gone impenitent and whistling on his way, with no ghosts to rise and summon him to an accounting. For the love affairs in which he regularly indulged in his *heures perdues* were always trifling, while life in the licentious ambience of a French court, however unrewarding in a material way, had certainly provided ample evidence that maidenly scruples of this sort presented no grave obstacle to the accomplished amorist.

Assuring Angelina of his strictly honorable intentions, he convincingly explained that since his parents refused to sanction the marriage (a necessary preliminary), the only way to circumvent the difficulty was for her to go with him to Milan where the ceremony could be performed without delay. He was charming and persuasive in his caressing, seductive way, so Angelina, succumbing like her successors, to his magnetism, and forgetting parental admonitions, fell in with the suggestion, whereupon Niccolò bundled her into the diligence and the two set forth on October 11, not for Milan, as she presumably expected, but for the quieter atmosphere of Parma, where it would be easier to preserve his incognito during the several weeks of dalliance that he had in view than in the world of Milan, where such a mistress might prove detrimental to his standing. Be that as it may, it is permissible to wonder if Angelina communicated her decision to her father and, if not, how he was later able to reconcile his seeming indifference to her disappearance and absence for six months with his "agony of spirit" when he discovered her predicament! This point does not seem to have been raised in the ensuing litigation, though it was surely worthy of consideration.

The case is interesting [wrote Codignola], but amongst the many amorous episodes of his life, it was certainly one of the least romantic. We can easily reinvoke it in all its details with the aid of numerous documents, yet even so it does not detract from the figure of the artist. On the contrary; in a biography that makes a point of strictly holding to the truth and is not written *ad usum delphini,* as hitherto has been the case, an incident of this kind makes it easier to penetrate the complex and quasi-mysterious inner personality of Paganini, the man.[1]

In a large seaport like Genoa, such adventures were surely everyday occurrences, and Niccolò may only have been following a familiar pattern from his Leghorn and early Genoa days, one that had heretofore proved quite satisfactory. As an experienced campaigner who knew his way about, he must have been well acquainted with conditions, so it probably never entered his head that such a commonplace little episode with a young prostitute would get him into any hotter water than the many that had preceded it, or that a handsome present would not settle to the entire satisfaction of both parties. This time, however, he overlooked the fact that he was a celebrity round whom were surging the most fantastic tales (particularly regarding his money-making powers), a large part of them being traceable to envy and other ignoble instincts of the human animal; for none could be so conspicuous as he without raising a desire to eliminate him. Completely free of professional jealousy, it never occurred to him that enemies of various kinds might be lying in ambush to discredit and defeat him so that he would no longer represent a serious competitor, or that notoriety of this unfortunate kind, whatever the ultimate outcome, gravely compromised his prestige.

According to the complaint filed by Angelina's father, he "had had anything but platonic relations with her in a room of the convent school to which he had enticed her under the pretext of more readily reaching an agreement regarding the proposed marriage" and then carried her off to Parma without again referring to the subject. There, upon noting from her frequent attacks of nausea that she was pregnant (a condition that in her innocence she ascribed to worms), he did not disillusion her, but promising to cure her, brought her ten packets of a pinkish-white powder and next morning after preparing some sweetened barley water mixed it with one packet of the powder; then telling her to drink it, he went out, leaving her alone.

The concoction (as she stated in her deposition) "soon brought on a violent nausea; indeed it seemed to her as though her stomach

[1] Codignola, *Gazzetta di Genova* (December, 1920).

were turning inside out; and she vomited till evening, also passing blood—a fact that could be corroborated by two servants at the inn whom she told about the powder." Paganini complacently remained away all day, hoping that meanwhile Nature would take its course. But when he finally returned and found that the only effect of his pseudo-anthelmintic was to put the little angel in a belligerent mood, he announced—upon her refusal to continue the drastic treatment—that he had been ordered by the police to send her home at once, a decision she submissively accepted. As she preferred to go to her sister's wet nurse in Fumeri, in the upper Polcevera Valley, rather than to return to Genoa, it is assumed that in the ensuing altercation he at last had disillusioned her.

He must have bundled her off in great haste since she seems to have had no time to gather together her belongings, which he promised "to bring her in a few days." But he "gave her a loaf of spiced bread for the journey" and this, according to her father, was "all she had to live on for several months in Fumeri, where she almost died of hunger and cold in the hut of charitable but miserably poor people . . . a couch of straw here served her as a bed and every day she had to dry her chemise and tattered clothing before the fire because the rain had dropped down on her all night through the leaky roof. Indeed she would have perished had Divine Providence not revealed her whereabouts to her disconsolate father, who hurried to her and found her in a half-dying condition."

Since Cavanna stated in his complaint that she arrived in Fumeri "in the dead of winter," he could only have meant in late December or early January, so the two must have been in Parma for several weeks before she discovered her condition, a conjecture more or less substantiated by the date of the child's birth. After her departure, Niccolò very likely went on at once to Milan, his original destination, hoping perhaps to play there during the carnival or at the Christmas holidays; then upon being unable to secure a theatre he returned to Genoa—to his damnation.

All his biographers here follow Fétis' monograph and send him to Ancona, "where he was ill for several months," merely changing the latter's date of 1815 to 1814 in order to fill in the mysterious gap from the denouement of the Parma episode and Niccolò's arrest in Genoa the following May. But as already pointed out, if he ever gave Fétis the impression that he was "ill in Ancona" round this time, we may be sure that in so doing he was less interested in furnishing his interviewer with authentic details regarding his movements than in concealing from him the mortifying Cavanna incident. He would not even have risked saying that he was in Genoa, for fear lest someone should be tempted to verify his statement and thus reveal the fact that he had been in jail—if only for eight days. It was safer to select a locality as far away as possible and picture himself as a "victim of nervous troubles" than to risk a discovery that, in view of the already current gossip of his incarceration and Fétis' valiant efforts to counter it, would have been calamitous in the extreme. We can therefore dismiss the Ancona *villeggiatura* as a *Fétiserie* since we now know positively that he was already back in Genoa sometime in January, as shown by a notation in Colonel Montgomery's diary, dated February 22 [1815]:

The D's [Durazzo's?] and the impresario got up a concert for Paganini the other night, which was well attended and on which occasion he electrified the audience.

Thus, the interim between Angelina's departure in December and Niccolò's return to Genoa could only have been a matter of three or four weeks at the most, a period during which there is no reason to believe that he suffered from anything more serious than boredom.

ii

During the first three months of his Genoa visit (February to April) he must have avoided the quarter where the Cavannas lived, or Angelina's father would surely have taken action sooner. Either he did not learn of Niccolò's presence in the city till the end of April, when the latter "had the refined cruelty to walk by the plaintiff's house to go to a house next door," or he had been trying vainly to blackmail him. At all events, in the first days of May he lodged a complaint against him "for rape and abduction," and on the sixth the police arrested Niccolò and clapped him in the Tower. In the subsequent trial, the latter, now at bay, readily admitted the intimacy and confessed that he had persuaded Angelina to accompany him to Parma, but denied any coercion, stating that she had offered herself to him quite voluntarily. His lawyer, Gian Maria Figari, after producing her baptismal certificate to show that she was already twenty and not eighteen as her father claimed, struck out bravely in his defense, bringing forward that the girl's father "had turned her out on the streets to earn her living; that she was free to go out alone both day and night; that profiting from such liberty, she had often been seen at advanced hours of the night in public dance halls with foreigners and soldiers, unaccompanied by any member of her family; that the neighbors had frequent cause to complain of her conduct and that she was the object of a great deal of gossip; further that while residing in her father's house she received callers clandestinely at suspicious hours; and on several occasions had passed the night away from home, in places of ill repute, even during her friendship with Paganini."[2]

Cavanna's lawyer then brought countercharges that Paganini "was a person given to promising credulous girls to marry them with the object of accomplishing his libidinous aims, though he never had the slightest intention of honoring his promises; that in order to delude her he made use of these expedients, pretending that he had already obtained his birth certificate and other necessary documents; that in order to support his statement, he told her that because of his parents' opposition, the marriage could not take place in Genoa but would be a simple matter in Milan, whereupon she consented to accompany him on his projected journey; that instead of going to Milan, they went to Parma, from whence, under the pretext of orders from the police, he packed her off to Fumeri, in the upper Polcevera Valley, promising to follow very shortly and they would then be married; that after being thus betrayed, she became pregnant; that her reputation was now ruined and she could no longer follow her profession or hope to find a husband, to say nothing of the heavy expense to which her father had been subjected during her pregnancy and her dangerous and difficult confinement."

The details were sufficiently scurrilous for the case to be tried

2 *Testimoniale di Remissione*, September 28, 1815, and *Testimoniale di Presentazione di Comparsa*, November 31, 1815. Civic Archives, Genoa.

en camera. Yet notwithstanding the scabrous facts and the mutual recriminations, Niccolò's lawyer obtained his release on May 14 upon his signing an agreement to pay Cavanna the sum of 1200 lire,[3] one half immediately, the balance within four months, offering as security the 20,000 lire that he had deposited with Masnata & Son as an annuity for his parents.[4] However, having no serious intention of paying this amount either to Angelina or her father, he arranged to have the first 600 lire deposited with a certain Giovanni Battista Rovere and then a week after his release forbade Rovere to pay it out till a verdict had been rendered in his countersuit against Cavanna.

But the strange temperament of the artist [wrote Codignola] was revealed in his attitude towards the girl who had been his mistress and was soon to be the mother of his child. After suing Cavanna, he seems to have become reconciled with the family and renewed his promise to marry Angelina, Cavanna's subsequent complaint stating that he 'then began to show signs of justice and humanity. He intended to have the child brought up by one of his sisters and he meant to pay all the expenses of the confinement, besides generously recompensing Angelina in addition to the 1200 lire. But right on top of this he instructed an intimate friend to have the agreement nullified and to collect the aforesaid 600 lire, thus retracting all his promises and again showing himself to be an unjust, inhuman creature'.[5]

It is probable, as Codignola suggests, that his tenderness "was

[3] Text of agreement (abridged): ". . . be it therefore agreed that said Paganini disburse and pay to said tailor the sum of 1,200 lire, and in view of the desire of said parties that the agreement reached between them be fully and freely carried into effect, said Paganini has hereby paid in cash to said Cavanna 600 lire, which said Cavanna has duly accepted and acknowledged, thence agreeing to the release of said Paganini, which he begs the Police Magistrate to effect. The remaining 600 lire of the contracted 1,200, Paganini herewith agrees to pay to said Cavanna within the space of four months, offering as security the sum deposited with Gio. Batta Masnata and his son Francesco in accordance with the instrument of September 26, 1814, drawn up by the notary Francesco Maria Pizzorno and duly registered with the Conservator of Mortgages in Genoa, September 28. Genoa: Police Department of the Tower, where Paganini is detained. May 14, 1815.

[4] A few days before his departure, Paganini deposited the sum of 20,000 lire with the bankers, Masnata & Son, to provide an annuity for his parents. His father was to receive 5 per cent interest on this sum for a stipulated number of years "in token of Niccolò's affection, filial piety, and a desire to contribute as far as possible to his parents' tranquillity." The version given to Schottky was a deliberate prevarication.

[5] Codignola, *Gazzetta di Genova* (December, 1920).

for the unborn child," but after the stillbirth (Angelina had to submit to an operation for the removal of her dead child, a girl, on June 24), Cavanna's conduct irritated him and awakened all the panther in his nature, making him "adopt an attitude of open hostility." In view of all the circumstances, Cavanna's action, wherein he claimed 3000 lire damages, really amounted to extortion—an attempt to make Paganini pay, and pay in proportion to his alleged earnings—which resulted in a web of suits and countersuits during which the two haled each other regularly into court. In the end, however, as might have been foreseen, Niccolò as usual was the loser.

Paganini's lawyer seems to have been retained by his father or was recommended by the magistrate, since his friend Germi acted only in an advisory capacity. It is difficult to say, from existing evidence, whether the two were already old friends or whether their acquaintance dated only from this time. Writing in 1836, Germi spoke of a "friendship of twenty-five years," in 1840 of one "of three decades," which would take it back to 1810 or 1811. Did Niccolò perhaps answer his father's summons at that time and return to Genoa, or was Germi referring to the spring of 1808? If so, through Niccolò's long absences and the silence that from time to time enveloped him, the acquaintance must have been allowed to lapse since the tone of his earliest letter to Germi that has survived (1814) is that of a formal business client and not of an old and intimate friend.[6] Four years Niccolò's junior, Luigi Guglielmo Germi was then a rising young lawyer as well as an excellent amateur musician,[7] so when Niccolò returned to Genoa in 1814 he may have revived what was originally a casual acquaintance; for Germi's family obviously stood higher in the social scale than Niccolò's and most certainly did not live in the crowded proletarian quarter. Furthermore, in view of Paganini's lack of formal education, they could never have been schoolmates, so it is difficult to see how Germi could ever have known him as a boy. At any rate, their long

[6] Codignola, *op. cit.*, 117.

[7] Luigi Guglielmo Germi (1786–1870), son of Paolo and Isabella Luigia Germi, graduated from the law school of the University in 1808, became a member of the faculty and for a time took an active part in politics. Although he survived Paganini thirty years, he seems never to have written a line about his great friend nor to have attempted to correct the obvious errors in the writings of others.

correspondence contains no boyhood recollections, nor did Germi's statements in 1836 refer to a friendship of forty years and more.

When the Cavanna storm broke, Germi, no doubt conversant by personal experience with the profligate ways of Genoa's gilded youth, was one of the first to rush to Niccolò's assistance, urging him to patch up the quarrel as expeditiously as possible, however much such a concession might sear his vanity and pride. At the same time, while fundamentally indulgent to his friend's short-comings, he did not hesitate to point out to him the wisdom, in most of life's encounters, of adopting Talleyrand's maxim: *Pas trop de zèle!*

Paganini to Germi, Milan, July 5, 1815.

I can't tell from your letter whether it's a lawyer or a friend who is writing me. With regard to the first point, you know I don't owe anything. A girl who lived in great liberty before she knew me, who offered herself to me, who voluntarily abandoned her own father, doesn't merit any great confidence. You speak of the coincidence of time as regards the date of her resultant confinement. If you're a lawyer, you must know that this isn't enough. The law's expression, "if paternity can be established," means that this one circumstance is not sufficient in itself since someone else might well be the father. Hence other circumstances are required. However, every question is nullified by the death of the new-born child since, supposing that the law attaches any obligation, this applies only to the child. In any case, however, the obligation that you're imposing on me would be totally absolved. This suffices as a reply to the lawyer. Now for the friend.

You are not ignorant of the woman's dubious conduct. You know well enough the trouble and mortification I've unjustly suffered through the police on her account. You know that as the price of my liberty, of which I was unjustifiably deprived, an obligation was extorted from me that was absolutely worthless, particularly since the obligation was unwarranted. With that unpleasant picture before you, I can't understand how you can ask me to be generous, which would be repugnant to my injured soul and my own inner conscience, which in this case recognizes neither obligation, nor debt—much less the slightest crime. I must ask if you've taken steps, as agreed, to withdraw the deposit of 600 lire. I don't doubt that you've kept your promise. Therefore, feeling sure that you have already withdrawn the amount, or have taken action to this end, I would ask you to give it to my father, since he advanced it to me at the time. Moreover, I must point out to you that if the child, as your letter states, was stillborn, or succumbed immediately after birth, this fact is also in my favor since this might indicate that the birth was premature and therefore there is no certainty as to the time between the two events on which to base the pretext of an obligation on my part. Further, please consider that the law gives no rights to the woman, whatever may be arranged for the child. The law has been wise in this case and precisely by this silence (i.e., by making no provisions for her) lays greater weight on her chastity. Otherwise by protecting her it would further her complacency and remove an obstacle to her virtue. You'll laugh at my writing you on legal points, but you must bear in mind that in troubles such as mine, one takes counsel and replies in a manner to promote sincerely and knowledgeably the case in question.

Although Angelina's mode of life certainly offered every ground for his contention, he had been in Genoa since June 20 at least, so his friendship with her was well within the material time in the eyes of the law, thus making him liable for damages in a breach of promise of marriage—unless he could credibly interpose that the child had been conceived after Angelina left Parma and that "the birth was premature." With his proletarian regard for the opinion of others, he was naturally very bitter over the local gossip, even though the case was not mentioned in the papers.[8] In future years also he was silent on the episode, which he ostensibly desired, at any rate subconsciously, to forget. And here his intuition again proved a valuable guide, for with the reports already in circulation any reference to a jail sentence would have convinced the public that all the harrowing tales were true and any effort on his part to disentangle fact from fiction would have been to deliver him over irrevocably to his detractors.

8 In 1816, Angelina married Giovanni Battista Paganini, who, as far as is known, was not related to Niccolò.

Mich hält kein Band, mich fesselt keine Schranke,
Frei schwing' ich mich durch alle Räume fort.
—SCHILLER.

IF THE SHOCK and mortification of his arrest reacted on his spirits and physical make-up like other emotional upsets, he could not have been feeling at the top of his form when he arrived in Milan a fortnight after his release—a surmise supported by the postponement of his Scala concert from June 9 to June 16, which must have been owing to illness or extreme nervous strain. However, the fact that during his six weeks' stay he gave only this one concert was, no doubt, because of the still unsettled and politically tense conditions in the capital, rather than any continued incapacity to appear before the public. "I was in the most miserable of moods and by no means in the best of health," he told Schottky, presumably referring to this period. "My heart was empty and from this arose my melancholy."[1] But we may be sure that the melancholy was accompanied by no remorse, for even without his vigorous denial of a sense of guilt, it is not likely that Angelina engendered any pangs of conscience or that a person of his temperament, after incidents of this kind, was ever sensitive to such interior voices. It was only an outlet that he needed, a balm for aching mind and body, so upon failing to find one in Milan he decided—upon receiving news of the child's death—to return to Genoa, where he was easily persuaded to settle down and await the outcome of the Cavanna suit, which, in view of the altered situation, now presented fewer legal complications. Meanwhile, he resumed his concert work, playing on three different occasions one number between the two parts of a double bill at the Teatro Sant'Agostino, an arrangement that admirably suited him since he received a stipulated fee, or a percentage of the receipts, without financial risk.[2]

[1] Schottky, *op. cit.,* 236.
[2] When Spohr was in Naples in 1817, Barbaja paid him three hundred ducats for two such intermezzo concerts.

In Italy these "intermezzo concerts," as they were known, solved so many problems for the instrumentalist that he introduced them later in Vienna, Paris, and Berlin, though not with an equal measure of success. In Austria and Germany, where they were disdainfully labeled "half concerts," they were dismissed as a questionable Italian importation; but in France they seem to have aroused no unfavorable comment, presumably because they formed a pleasant bridge to the closing ballet. For in Paris, even at his regular concerts, he always strictly adhered to the national custom of rounding off the evening with a ballet, a practice frowned upon in Austria and Germany, where they liked their music neat.

After this brief splurge, for the next four months he merely drifted, probably depending on private engagements to keep him economically afloat—the age-old combination of brilliance and laziness, those recurrent periods when, despite his energy, mists of *far niente* swirled over him, a languor of mind and body after some wild self-expenditure, moments when he was feeling vexed and weary, and completely bored. His health, too, was now beginning to be an increasingly incalculable factor, the result of a "piecemeal process of self-destruction," as sexual excess, illness, and deep depression followed constantly one upon the other with the periodicity of clockwork, one leading irrevocably to the next.

At present [he told Schottky] as a man over whose head a very agitated life has often passed stormily enough, I must admit that my youth was by no means free from the errors of all young people who, after practically the upbringing of a slave, are suddenly left to their own resources and make up for the long privation by heaping pleasure upon pleasure. My talent found great favor everywhere—indeed, for a person of my passionate temperament, far too much so. Traveling about from place to place without restraint, the enthusiasm that almost every Italian exhibits for music, my Genoese blood, which seems to flow just a little more rapidly than the German, all this and many other similar factors often brought me into company that was certainly not of the best. I honestly confess that more than once I fell into the hands of people who played far more skilfully and successfully than I, though their instruments were neither the violin nor the guitar. I often lost in one evening the fruit of several concerts and frequently found myself in embarrassing circumstances through my thoughtlessness. But fortunately these periods were only transitory. I regret them but do not want to appear any better than I am, so I beg you to give your readers the unvarnished truth. There may be some among them who will refrain from casting the first stone till they have weighed the circumstances of climate, a faulty upbringing, Italian customs, and the life of an artist generally.[3]

He went his cavalier way so long as he was solvent; then when funds were running low his energy would reassert itself and he would "turn to his art to rescue him from his predicament." It was only later, when he became enamored of laying up treasures upon earth, that he overcame a youthful propensity that made him appear improvident to those with less fever in their blood.

However, before accusing him too sharply of shiftlessness, of wasting months in one place without serious interest in his art, one must take into consideration that travel, in those days, was fraught with difficulties. The overlords of Italy viewed each other and the subjects under their dominion with suspicion and distrust; royalists and liberals, church and state, were at daggers drawn, the country was overrun with spies, with Austrian and papal agents, so that no man could wholly trust his neighbor. Arrests, flogging, and forced labor, traceable to malicious information, were everyday occurrences, from insignificant underlings to the highest functionaries of the state. Even in little Lucca, well off the beaten track of politics, anyone "suspected of propagating false rumors was immediately arrested and brought before a military tribunal, to be condemned within twenty-four hours according to martial law."

The Sanfedisti [wrote Iris Origo], members of an association founded by the Jesuits to defend the Catholic faith and uphold the temporal dominion of the Pope, had come to include all that was most reactionary in the country—men who had sworn to show no mercy to any man belonging to the infamous rabble of the Liberals, and to bear an undying hatred against any enemy of true religion. . . . Secret societies sprang up all over the provinces and in every class of society; spies and informers hurried to the cardinal's palace.[4]

Weeks must therefore have passed before one was politically screened and obtained the necessary papers, while even then any continued travel back and forth between one state and another was bound to awaken suspicion, particularly in the case of one

---

3 Schottky, *op. cit.*, 257.
4 Origo, *op. cit.*, 69; and *The Last Attachment*, 168.

whose name was linked with some mysterious, criminal past.[5] Besides these political obstacles, it must also have required considerable courage for a person of frail constitution to travel round in crowded diligences, through rough mountain passes, and over detestable roads. For in a country that had recently been one of the battlefields of Europe, with misery, rapine, plague, and pillage on every side, traveling conditions must have been even worse than when Dr. Burney coursed through Italy five decades before;[6] which may explain why Niccolò, after leaving the service of Princess Elise, restricted his peregrinations for a considerable period to the Romagna and Lombardy, where he was now a fairly familiar figure.

Nevertheless, as the year 1815 drew to a close and there was still no prospect of a decision in the Cavanna suit, he began to grow restless and to long for new scenes and new associations. Although at first he may have had no definite goal in view, it is not difficult to guess that Venice was in his mind when, on December 17, he announced a "farewell concert" and his "departure on a long journey," a little publicity trick that he seems to have taken over from the vocal stars and that even at this early date gave rise to some sarcastic comment when he announced another "farewell" concert a week later. "With such a rich offering of music, it would be bold and infelicitous to find fault with Paganini for having announced *one concert only* and then to have given two," wrote the *Gazzetta di Genova* in a tone of mild reproof. But, like Byron, he was always given to "prophesying in too great a hurry." His airy dreams and plans constantly outran his volition, so even after raising anchor, professionally speaking, he still continued to dally till the end of January, when a report reached him that Charles Lafont was to give two concerts in Milan;[7] this instantly crystallized his nebulous plans and he rushed off at once, all eagerness to hear a colleague whose fame till then had traveled faster and farther than his own. Although in his own country he was without a rival, he was still anxious to measure his abilities with those of an artist who had

---

5 By the end of 1818 the papal government was again re-established in the Romagna, bringing with it (in the words of Henri Beyle) a persecution *"exercée par les bigots et les nobles."*

6 Spohr, *op. cit.,* 288; Lady Morgan, *op. cit.,* II, 409.

7 Charles Philippe Lafont (1781–1839).

been solo violinist of two powerful kings: the Emperor of all the Russias and the King of France (after all, something more than the puppet sovereign of a little pocket-state in dismembered Italy).

Quick to sense that his Italian style differed fundamentally from the French and German schools and to recognize that, should he go abroad, he would be judged according to the latter, he looked to Lafont to show him wherein the difference lay. While his public comments on his colleague were always marked by impartiality,[8] two letters written immediately after Lafont's concerts suggest that his feelings were the normal reactions of any popular artist, idolized by his countrymen, who finds his position potentially assailed by an outsider who not only possessed many admirable qualities but was the indisputable master of a genre altogether different from his own.

Paganini to Germi, Milan, February 3, 1816.
Yesterday evening we had a concert at the Scala by M. Lafont. This excellent professor found no indication of anyone wishing to hear him again. He plays well, but does not astonish one. His wife sang quite well but, being French, her pronunciation is not good. Taken all in all, it was not as pleasing as we anticipated.

February 25, 1816.
Lafont played the second time at a concert of a pianist at the Scala, but there weren't three hundred in the audience. However, he pleased more the second time. It is notorious in Milan that his wife came from the Palais Royal and took 100 sequins from one person and twenty from another. Lafont has been trying to hear me but has not yet succeeded. He'll have to stay and wait for my concert.[9]

A great deal has been written on the double concert of March 11, most of Paganini's biographers—taking their cue from DeLaphalèque—presenting it as a title contest rather than an exhibition bout. It was naturally a hazardous venture, "an imprudence," as Fétis put it, for Lafont to attempt to outplay Paganini on Italian soil, for even if he were his superior in "a pure, classic style, in a rich, full, even tone" he was "no match" for his colleague in orig-

---

[8] Schottky, *op. cit.*, 324.

[9] Both these letters are incorrectly dated in Codignola. The Palais Royal was then the royal "red light district," the center of licensed prostitution ranging from famous courtesans to simple prostitutes.

inality and technical skill—the deciding factors, naturally, with an Italian audience. "In a concert at the Conservatoire [wrote Fétis] the palm would perhaps have gone to Lafont; with an Italian public, however, avid for novelty, originality, *entrain*, his defeat was certain."

In Genoa, where I was then residing, I heard that Lafont intended to give some concerts in Milan, and I left at once in order to hear him [Paganini told Schottky]. His playing gave me much pleasure, and a week later I too gave a concert in the Scala so that he might have an opportunity of hearing me. Lafont then suggested that we play together.[10] I tried to evade this by saying that such collaboration was always dangerous because the public regarded it as a duel. And in this case it was particularly dangerous, inasmuch as he was France's outstanding violinist and I was considered (though much too generously) as Italy's best performer on this instrument. But Lafont refused to take no for an answer, and I had no other recourse than to pick up the gauntlet that he tossed to me and allow him to arrange the program. In order to fight with equivalent weapons, I voluntarily waived the right to play on one string. I began with one of my concertos, then Lafont followed with a longish work, and after this we played Kreutzer's double concerto, which Rode and Kreutzer had once played together in Paris. Where the two violins played together, I held strictly note for note to the written text, so that he was ready to wager that we both were products of the same school.[11] But in the solo passages I gave free rein to my imagination and played in the Italian manner—in the style that is really natural to me. True, this did not altogether seem to please my friendly rival, who next played a set of variations (on a Russian theme), and I closed the program with a similar composition of my own (*Le Streghe*). Lafont could perhaps lay claim to a more powerful tone than I,[12] but that I didn't suffer in comparison was evident from the applause. However, Lafont is unquestionably a very distinguished artist.[13]

Basing his account on hearsay from Italian sources, DeLaphalèque, perhaps for personal reasons, interpreted the event as a

[10] Great confusion has existed among biographers regarding the dates of these events, although Schottky gave the year correctly.

[11] When Boucher de Perthes was in Genoa in 1806, he wrote his father that "the amateur here never plays what is written, so that it is truly impossible to accompany a quartet, even one of Pleyel's. As for Haydn and Mozart, there's never any question of them; they are considered unplayable, so that no one even tries to play them!"

[12] According to Fétis, Lafont had "perfect intonation, a pure and mellow, albeit somewhat thin, tone, splendid technique, and great interpretative gifts."

[13] Schottky, *op. cit.,* 300.

sweeping victory for Niccolò, saying that "Lafont did not try to contest his defeat, but cut short his stay in Italy, leaving the field to his redoubtable rival. . . . We are sorry to report [he continued] that Lafont passed through a very trying experience, though it should be said in his praise that today he shows no resentment over it." Lafont, however, seems to have felt far more strongly about it than DeLaphalèque suspected, for when the London *Harmonicon* published extensive excerpts from the monograph, he at once wrote a sharp protest to the editor, in which he set forth *his* version of the case.

As this monograph contains utterly erroneous statements regarding myself, I owe it to truth, to the advice of my friends, and to the favor with which the public has been pleased to honor me during twenty-five years, to give an exact statement of the facts of the case. The following is a narration of what occurred.

In March, 1816, I gave in conjunction with Paganini a concert in the great theatre La Scala in Milan, and far from making a cruel trial of the powers of my adversary or of being beaten by him, as is pretended by the author of this monograph, I obtained a success the more flattering as I was a stranger in the country and had no other support than my talent. I played with Paganini the concerted symphony of Kreutzer in F Major. For several days previously [*sic*] to the concert we rehearsed this symphony together and with the greatest care. On the day of the concert it was performed by us as it had been rehearsed and with no change whatever; and we both obtained an equal success in the passages executed together or separately. On coming to the *phrase de chant* in F minor, in the second solo of the first part, there was a decided advantage for one of us. The passage is of a deep and melancholy expression. Paganini performed it first. Whether the strong and pathetic character of the piece was ill suited to the ornaments and brilliant notes which he gave to it, or whatever else was the cause, his solo produced but little effect. Immediately after him, I repeated the same passage and treated it differently. It seems that the emotion by which I was then agitated caused me to give an expression more effective though more simple, and it was so felt by the audience that I was overwhelmed with plaudits from all parts of the house. During the fourteen years I have been silent on this trifling advantage obtained over Paganini in this instance, only in the symphony and probably rather by the superiority of the school than by that of talent. It is painful to me to speak of myself; nothing short of the misrepresentation of the artist in question could have provoked me to reply. I was not beaten by Paganini; nor he by me. On all occasions I have taken pleasure in rendering homage to his great talent; but I have never said that he was the first violinist in the world. I have not done such injustice to the celebrated men, Kreutzer, Rode, Baillot, and Habeneck. And I declare now as I have always done that the French school is the first in the world for the violin.[14]

For a less biased account we must turn to Lichtenthal's report to the *Allgemeine Musikalische Zeitung:*

A few days ago Paganini and Lafont gave a concert together. There was a great rush for seats. Everyone wanted to witness the duel between the two artists and, as might have been foreseen, the result showed that when it comes to artificiality, to technical mastery, Paganini is without a peer, Lafont being far behind him in this respect. Both, however, are about equal when it comes to beauty of tone and fine sensitive playing, with the odds perhaps on the side of Lafont.[15]

Lichtenthal had either changed his opinion regarding certain aspects of Paganini's performance, or in the three years since 1813, the latter had matured in some of the finer qualities of musicianship, in a depth and refinement of expression, in subtleties that lay beyond the intellectual compass of his former audiences. Association with the more critical musicians of Milan had already had a beneficent effect.

ii

In his next report in early April, Lichtenthal wrote that Niccolò "had left Milan," so in the absence of other information his biographers have assumed that he went direct to Venice. But this was not the case. In fact, inductive reasoning would indicate that at this time he had quite other ends in view.

When he returned to Lombardy he found that many changes had taken place that made it difficult to arrange, or hold to, any fixed itinerary till he had a perfectly clean slate with the Austrian police,

14 Original translation as given in the *Harmonicon* (London, 1830), 177.

15 Leigh Hunt: "It has been said that some portions of the phenomenon are not without *trick*. That is to say, that all which Paganini does is not done by legitimate bowing. It is thought he must use some legerdemain. We have only to say to this that if he does so, a man of his consummate skill has a right to do it, if he increases the effect, because we are to suppose it done not out of his own poverty, but the instrument's." ("The Playgoer," *Tatler* (June, 1831), Vol. II, 1003–1004.)

all northern Italy being now an Austrian vassal state. Up to this point in his career he seems to have had little real ambition for ultramontane fame, being quite content to garner his laurels among his appreciative countrymen; but with the new order in Italy, largely dominated by the Hapsburgs, his thoughts turned more and more in that direction, in response, no doubt, to the urgings of German-Austrian colleagues who felt that he owed it to his genius to present his gifts before a more cosmopolitan forum than that of the provincial capitals of northern Italy. "No one can understand [wrote Lichtenthal] why he doesn't go on tour."

Paganini to Germi, Milan, February 25, 1816.
Day before yesterday I played quintets and quartets with the celebrated Krommer.[16] He is most agreeable and jolly but, as he speaks only German, I have to have an interpreter to understand him. He's fifty years old. He is in His Majesty's retinue in order to play first violin in quartets with the latter, though I don't believe H.M. has played as yet."

The Austrian Emperor had arrived in Italy with his daughter Marie Louise, former Empress of France, who had come to take over the duchies of Parma, Piacenza, and Guastalla, which had been allocated to her in the new subdivision of the country. It is assumed therefore that Krommer and other Austrian musicians with whom Niccolò came in contact in Milan had painted an attractive picture of imperial patronage and Vienna's music, and in particular had described the close ties binding the Emperor and his favorite child, so that Niccolò, with his gaze presently fixed on Venice and Trieste, with Vienna in the distance, presumably set to work to compose a sonata on the G string in honor of Parma's new sovereign, a strategical move that could not fail, in his opinion, to have a favorable reaction in the future, to say nothing of the indirect effect on the local Austrian police who were in a position to make life very unpleasant for a roving virtuoso.

Marie Louise's own plans had been slightly disrupted through the illness and death of her stepmother, Maria Ludovica, which detained her in Verona longer than she had anticipated, with the

16 Franz Krommer (1759–1831), formerly Kapellmeister to Prince Grassalkowitz, later appointed to the sinecure post of doorkeeper to the Emperor, and in 1818 successor to Kozeluh as court Kapellmeister and composer.

result that she did not arrive in Parma till fully two months later than was originally announced. It is not difficult to surmise that Niccolò in Milan kept abreast of all these happenings and that it was his intention to go to Parma "to offer his contribution" to the new sovereign when she "made her solemn entry," just as he had done in 1808 with Prince and Princess Borghèse in Turin, in the expectation that after this loyal gesture, all official Austrian doors would be thrown wide open to him. He may even have thought in his political innocence that his previous connections with the Bonapartes would have a strong appeal for the unhappy ex-Empress of the French and would react to his advantage, for it is not likely that he desired to be tied down by another court appointment or was angling for the post of *maître de chapelle*. It was only the interest and backing of the Emperor's daughter that seemed to him worth playing for. Here, however, he failed to take into account the exigencies of politics. As soon as Marie Louise arrived in Parma, the Austrian government, acting through Count Neipperg, her chamberlain, took drastic action to prevent entry into the duchy of any French subject or former Bonapartist, in particular anyone who had had even the remotest relations with any member of the family.[17] Further, Marie Louise herself was not permitted to receive anyone—her new Italian subjects included—except in Neipperg's presence and not till they had been carefully screened by the police. Indeed, she even requested before leaving for Leghorn for the summer, that Lucien Bonaparte, who was then residing there, be first ordered to leave the city.[18] *"Mon père* [she wrote] *m'a bien recommandé d'éviter tout point de contacte avec la famille et je me suis trop bien trouvée de ce bon conseil pour ne pas désirer de m'y conformer."*[19]

In his very interesting work, *Rome, Asile des Bonaparte,* F. Charles Roux tells with what suspicion anyone was viewed who had, or had had, any connection with the Bonapartes. In Italy not only the different members of the family but their former friends,

[17] Adèle Curti, *Rassegna Storico del Resorgimento* (1922), 445.

[18] When the Austrian Emperor visited Rome in 1819, she wished to join him there and accompany him on his tour, but Metternich would not allow her to come to Rome since Napoleon's mother and his sister Pauline were then residing there.

[19] Imbert de Saint Amand: *Marie Louise and the Decadence of the Empire* (English ed., New York, 1891, 1902), 57.

protégés, and associates were believed to be in collusion with the liberals, French anti-royalists, Italian patriots, and revolutionaries, so that all such persons, like the Bonapartes themselves, were subjected to constant surveillance by French, Austrian, and even papal diplomats and agents.

This therefore adequately explains not only why Paganini, when he left Milan, passed Parma by and went straight on to Tuscany,[20] but why the new sonata bore the title of, though not a dedication to, the new sovereign of the duchy.[21] It also indicates why there is no record of his ever having played it. For even had he received permission to enter her domain, Marie Louise would have surely thought it politic to absent herself from the concert of a former protégé of her sister-in-law and Eugène Beauharnais. *"Rien de plus correct que la conduite de M. la Archduchesse,* [wrote Metternich of her at this time]. *Elle pousse la réserve jusqu'au scruple."* Even when Paganini played in Parma two years later (May, 1818) she excused her absence from his concert on the score of illness!

Thus baffled in his designs, he went straight on to one of Princess Elise's favorite summer residences, the Bagni alla Villa, sixteen miles from Lucca, where during his courtier *étape* he was frequently *en poste.*

Paganini to Antonio Puccini, Bagni alla Villa, July 4, 1816.
In reply to your esteemed communication of July 3, it will be a pleasure to play a concerto for San Croce for eight sequins, just to have the pleasure of seeing you and Signor Romaggi, to whom I beg you to remember me most cordially. Your obedient servant, Niccolò Paganini. Reply promptly for my guidance.

Besides establishing his whereabouts, this little note is also extremely interesting since its very formality, without friendly salutation or other familiar greeting, is indicative of the continuing

---

20 Various biographers have stated that he played in Parma, Bologna, and Ferrara in the summer of 1816, but there is not the slightest evidence that he entered her dominions till the spring of 1818.

21 The manuscript of this work is in the Reuther collection, Mannheim. It consists of a short introduction, *Tempo di minuetto,* in E minor, an *Adagio* in E Major, a *polonaise variato (Andantino)* with theme and three variations, and a short finale. It was an extremely difficult work—in the words of Professor Max Kergl, "the type of music which not only as a composition, but in the truest sense of the word, was written by Paganini for himself alone. Works of this kind are now altogether out of date."

subservience of the supernumerary towards his two superiors, Puccini having been director of the cathedral music and Romaggi violinist leader of the court orchestra at Lucca during the major part of his tour of duty there.

He must then have decided that he did not care to wait so long, or else in the meantime he had received his Austrian passport since three weeks later we find him in Padua, whence he went first to Venice, where he gave five concerts during August, and then crossed over to Trieste, where he gave five more the first week of September.[22] In the article in the Trieste *Piccolo,* to which reference has been made in Chapter III,[23] the author wrote that during this visit Niccolò and his former patroness, Princess Elise, resumed their severed friendship and Niccolò was frequently a guest at Villa Campo Marzio, "where the patricians of Trieste came to relieve her sad exile with fetes, theatrical performances, cards, and conversational banter." It would have been far better if the writer and all those who so trustingly quote him as an authority had informed themselves of the true situation,[24] which has been so admirably documented by Fleuriot de Langle.[25] Driven from Tuscany at the time of Napoleon's downfall, Elise's pilgrimage led her first to Montpellier and Marseilles, whence she returned to Bologna in the hope that she would be permitted to remain there with her family. But this was not to be. Four days after Napoleon's re-entry into the Tuileries, the Austrians arrested her and her little daughter Napoleone and transported them to Austria, then after months of detention in Graz and Brunn she was finally accorded permission in 1816 to establish her residence in Trieste, where she rejoined Prince Felix and her infant son on June 20. Shortly after this she acquired a large villa at Campo Marzio, south of the city, near the promontory of Sant'Andrea, which she at once set out to beautify

22 An "anonymous American" from Baltimore, who was in Venice at this time, wrote of these Venetian concerts (in a work published anonymously): "The astonishing execution of this unrivalled artist extorted such bursts of applause as would in any other country have passed for the ravings of insanity. During some part of the performance, the silence was so profound that the faintest noise would have been easily perceptible. His audience seemed to hold their breath lest a single note should escape them." (James Sloan, *Rambles in Italy* [Baltimore, 1818], 186.)

23 See note 51, Chapter III.

24 His article is based primarily on Tagliapietra's serialized articles in *L'Arte.*

25 De Langle, *op. cit.,* 323 ff.

and make habitable for her family and her still fairly large retinue.[26] Although Paganini was in Trieste from August 30 till
October 15, it is extremely unlikely, for the reasons already given,
that during these six weeks he and the Princess ever came together
since it took some time to renovate the villa and then some months
elapsed before the Austrian authorities would permit her to rent
a box at the theatre. She therefore could not have attended any of
his concerts even if her intense preoccupation with her family and
her own multifarious problems had permitted her to indulge in
such distractions. If, in the halcyon days of Lucca, his music (on
his testimony) afflicted her nerves so greatly that "she could not
remain" all through a concert, she would very carefully have
avoided at this time any extra nervous excitement of this nature.[27]
From her correspondence it can be seen that, as a result of the international ostracism of the Bonaparte family and the close surveillance to which they were subjected, she had practically no contact
with her surroundings, her sole diversions during the remaining
four years of her life being a drive or horseback ride in the vicinage,
the theatre, when the doors were eventually opened to her, and
occasional visits from members of her family. "My health and that
of the Prince and my children is perfect [she wrote her brother
Joseph]. Our house is charming, but we live in the very greatest
seclusion . . . though situated within the city limits, the villa is
completely isolated and difficult to reach during the rainy winter
weather." Desiring a place in the country to replace the lost delights of Villa Marlia, she first tried to purchase a small estate at
Aquilée, not far from Trieste, but when the Austrians pronounced
a veto because the property lay too close to the Italian frontier, she
acquired the Villa Vincentina, about twenty-five miles from Trieste, on the road to Udine (not far from Monfalcone) where from
then on she regularly spent the spring and autumn months.

Princess Elise to Fouché, Trieste, October 18, 1819.
It is easier to find good music masters here than dancing masters. The

[26] After Elise's death in April, 1820, the Villa Campo Marzio was occupied by her
sister Caroline Murat till her death in 1839, whence the later name "Villa Murat."
[27] Her little son Frédéric was born August 10, 1814, while she was being driven
from place to place. She was not permitted to take him with her when she was ex-
pelled from Bologna. She now saw him for the first time after a harrowing period
of two years.

theatre orchestra is led by Farinelli, who enjoys a certain fame in Italy and gives lessons in town.[28] As for society, it is absolutely non existent in Trieste. I see no one but my business executors and I scarcely know by sight the president of the government, who here takes the place of governor. . . . Apart from the isolation in which I wish, and have, to live, I am assured that the natives of the country are not given to visiting. The wives of the merchants that form the well-to-do circles of the city lead a comparatively retired life and only go out on Sundays. On other days, the few promenades we have are entirely deserted. Nevertheless, the theatre, which is beautiful, is open all year round and often gives elaborate performances in the Italian manner.[29] The merchants have a very well-arranged casino where they dance in the winter. . . . During the carnival there are some masked balls at the theatre, but they are sad, doleful affairs. . . . The interior of my home re-echoes this monotonous life to some extent. I pass two months in the spring and two in the autumn in the country, and the rest of the year at my Campo Marzio house in Trieste. I've told you that I see no one. One spends the day in his apartments or in the general living room, where each person amuses himself just as he likes, according to the weather and the season. We go for a drive every day and in the evening we go regularly to the theatre, or if I stay at home, we have some music, play billiards, or else we all sit round a large table where one plays cards, or draws, or works at something that interests him. Last winter we played some comedies, our only audience being the persons of whom I have spoken. On those days we danced and had a little supper, which prolonged the evening till midnight, a very late hour at Campo Marzio, because we ordinarily retire very early. . . . Although serious, I like to have the people round me amuse themselves; but I take no part in it any more than is absolutely necessary for the pleasure of the others.

One of the music masters of Princess Elise's daughter was Paganini's friend Velluti,[30] who arranged the quiet musical evenings at Campo Marzio and the Villa Vincentina, to which Princess Elise referred. But all these events fell in the years 1817 and 1818, long after Niccolò's departure, though it is highly doubtful if such an engagement would have attracted him. In fact, one suspects that he may even have deliberately avoided any contact with the Baciocchis during the six weeks of his visit (granting that he was aware

[28] Giuseppe Farinelli (1769–1836), opera composer in the style of Cimarosa.

[29] Teatro Nuovo (now Verdi), inaugurated in 1801.

[30] Giovanni Battista Velluti (1781–1861), the last famous male soprano. He sang at the première of Rossini's *Aureliano in Palmyra* in Milan in December 1813, from which time Paganini must have known him.

of their presence in Trieste) so as to keep in the good graces of the Austrians till his Vienna dream was realized. With the memory of his Parma experience still fairly keen and with his characteristic avoidance of any political complications, he would have taken particular care not to become involved in any way with a person who was politically *persona non grata* both to the Austrians and the French, one who, as Metternich phrased it, was now *"tellement insignifiante et son insignifiance de telle notoriété publique dans toute Italie que la choix de son séjour n'a plus guère d'importance."* (She was now known as the Countess de Campignano.) In the pursuit of advantage, or when his ambition was involved, Paganini remained always the arch-opportunist.

iii

While in Trieste he learned that Louis Spohr had arrived in Venice and was to play there on October 18. This was another concert he could ill afford to miss.[31] So, returning to Venice on the sixteenth, he went next day to call on the German maestro of whom his German-Austrian colleagues had so often spoken. However, what he really thought of Spohr is not recorded. Although he always spoke of him with great respect, anyone so sensitive as he must immediately have noted the German's patronizing attitude, as though he were one of lesser breed.

Yesterday Paganini returned here again from Trieste [Spohr wrote in his journal], having, it seems, thrown overboard his project of going to Vienna. He came to see me early today, and so at last I've made the personal acquaintance of this wizard whom I have heard spoken of nearly every day since I arrived in Italy. No instrumentalist has ever charmed the Italians as he has done and, though they aren't fond of instrumental concerts, he nevertheless gave more than a dozen in Milan and has also given five here. If you ask how he really hypnotizes his public, you hear the most extravagant praise from unmusical people to the effect that he is a real magician and brings forth from his violin tones that were never before heard on this instrument. On the other

---

31 Spohr was not in the employ of the Elector of Hesse-Cassel at this time, as stated by De Saussine. He left his post at the Theater an der Wien (Vienna) in 1815, and after spending some time at the countryseat of Prince Carolath in Bohemia, left on his continental tour, which opened in Milan on September 27, 1816. He was not engaged at Cassel till January, 1822.

hand, connoisseurs say that he undeniably has great technical facility in the left hand, in double stops and all kinds of passage work, but the very qualities that captivate the crowd debase him to the level of a charlatan and cannot compensate for what he lacks: a full tone, a long bow stroke, and a tasteful cantabile style. However, what thrills the Italian audiences and has won for him the name of the "Insuperable" (which is even placed under his pictures) is, when one goes into it, a series of marvellous tricks which, in the dark ages of good taste, the once-famous Scheller was wont to perform in the small towns and capitals of Germany, and which at that time equally excited the admiration of our people,[32] such for instance as harmonics, variations on one string (whereby in order to make a greater impression he removed the other three), a peculiar kind of pizzicato produced by the left hand without the help of the right hand or the bow, as well as sounds quite alien to the violin, such as imitations of the bassoon, the voice of an old woman, and other things of the same kind.

As I never heard the magician Scheller . . . I wanted to have an opportunity of hearing Paganini in his own style, and all the more so since I presume that so admired an artist must also possess some more sterling qualities than those of which I have just spoken. His present virtuosity is said to be traceable to a four-year imprisonment to which he was condemned for strangling his wife in a fit of violent rage. At least, that's what they say quite openly in Milan, and also here. Since with his entirely neglected education, he couldn't entertain himself with writing or with reading, boredom led him to think out and practice all the little tricks by which he now astonishes the Italians. Through his ungracious and rude behavior he has alienated many of the local music patrons, and whenever I've played something for them at my house, they have extolled me to the skies at the expense of Paganini in order to injure him, which is not only very unjust (since a parallel can never be drawn between two artists of such divergent styles) but is also detrimental to me because it turns all Paganini's friends and admirers into my enemies. His adversaries have published an open letter in the paper in which they say that my playing has recalled the style of their veteran violinists, Pugnani and Tartini, whose great and dignified manner of playing is now a lost art in Italy and has had to make way for the trifling and childish style of their contemporary virtuosos, while the Germans and the French have understood how to adapt to contemporary taste this noble, chaste style of playing. This letter, which was published without my knowledge, will do me harm rather than good with the public, for the Venetians are now firmly convinced that Paganini has absolutely no peers, much less any superiors.

[32] Jakob Scheller (1759–1803) was described as a strange mixture of genius and charlatanism.

Paganini came to see me early this morning [he continued three days later] to say many nice things to me about my concert. I begged him very urgently to play something for me, and several musical friends who were present joined their entreaties to mine, but he flatly refused, saying that he had had a fall which he still felt in his arms. Afterwards when we were alone and I pressed him again, he said that his style was calculated for the general masses and never failed in its effect; but if he were to play something for me, he would have to adopt a different style and he was now far too little in practice for this. However, we would very likely meet in Rome or Naples and then he would no longer refuse. I shall therefore probably have to leave without having heard this wizard.[33]

As Spohr surmised, Paganini gave him no opportunity of hearing and judging him. Although born only two years apart, the two were divided by an unbridgeable chasm in their attitudes towards art: Spohr fundamentally the classicist, Niccolò *"eine ganze Milchstrasse von Einfällen"* in the virtuoso sense.[34] Then too, Spohr already had a redoubtable reputation as executant, teacher, conductor, and composer, a renown that far transcended Niccolò's in northern Italy. Conscious of his limitations and that his art till now had only this single facet, the latter realized that here he was facing a more formidable opponent than Lafont since he knew by hearsay that the flamboyant soloistic style that "was natural to him" was anathema to the German artist; in other words, an interior voice warned him that the chemistry of their musical souls was too divergent for them ever to meet on common ground, a fact substantiated fourteen years later when he played in Kassel, where Spohr was leader of the orchestra.

iv

Paganini to his mother, Venice, October 16, 1816.
I shall always comply with your wishes, not only with regard to the money that's left over, but I want to give you a monthly allowance so that you can provide yourself with the things you need for the maintenance of yourself and the rest of the family. Tell me how many Genoese lire you need per day so that I can send them to you. I'm only anxious to see you and my sisters happy and contented. Perhaps I shall spend the winter in Naples and then in the spring go to Germany. I

[33] Spohr, *op. cit.*, I, 299 ff.
[34] G. C. Lichtenberg: "A whole Milky Way of ideas."

shall have as traveling companion an excellent tenor, a real friend, whom I've already tried out.[35] My uncle, your beloved brother, and his family are well. Mother, dear, don't put any trust in relatives. They cunningly try to make use of us, but it's better that we talk of our affairs. Please remember that I shall do everything to make you perfectly happy. Write to me and send your letters to Verona, where I'm going next Saturday.

The only record of this first Verona visit that has come down to us is a questionable anecdote in connection with Valdabrini,[36] violinist leader of the theatre orchestra there, which despite its obvious absurdity is still a prime favorite with biographers.[37] Perhaps Valdabrini was connected in some way with the anti-Paganini clique to which Spohr referred and this Verona visit was inspired by Niccolò's desire "to put this presumptuous person in his place" since, according to the story, he went to quite elaborate pains to deflate his colleague's egotism.[38] Schottky borrowed the anecdote from DeLaphalèque, obviously for padding since he was of the opinion that it was too absurd to be taken seriously, apart from the fact that Paganini had never mentioned it. While the episode is of no consequence, it is typical of the wonderful string of anecdotes that had already grown round him and were to be found in all the literary journals outside Italy, a country still throttled by various kinds of censorship which prevented their publication, but not of course their exportation. Although Codignola (p. 28) justly dismisses the Valdabrini story as a ridiculous canard, he accepts (in a footnote on page 362) an even more incredible tale "taken from the memoirs of an anonymous contemporary"[39] which shows that in that romantic age Italian raconteurs were in this respect no more reliable than their French and German counterparts.

Early in December, Niccolò was back again in Venice, where he gave six concerts,[40] some in the Teatro San Luca and one at least in

35 Luigi Granci.

36 It has been impossible to verify any of the Verona dates since the *Gazzetta di Verona* ceased publication on July 1, 1816, by order of the Austrian police and no local paper was allowed to appear for ten years.

37 Schottky, *op. cit.,* 311.

38 G. Grassini in *Rivista Universale,* Vol. 8 (Florence, 1868), 82 ff.

39 In DeLaphalèque's anecdote Niccolò employed a reed cane as bow; in Codignola's, his impromptu G string was the "cord of his monocle stretched over the punch bowl."

the Fenice,[41] on which occasion Byron must have heard him since he "had taken a box at that theatre" for the season. There is a well-established tradition that Paganini was a great admirer of the English poet, yet no one has ever said with certainty if, or where, they ever met. However, they were both in Venice from December, 1816, till the end of March, 1817, and since their lives, allowing for the difference in rank and riches, were following the same pattern, they could hardly have avoided bumping shoulders in the half-world of Venice.

Byron and his friend Hobhouse, "accompanied by the menagerie, the dogs, the cats, the monkeys, the guinea hens and the Egyptian crane," left Milan on November 4 and, after stopping briefly at Verona, rolled into Venice on November 10. So Niccolò must have witnessed their arrival in Verona, "which created an enormous flurry" because of Byron's "great, gaudy traveling coach." This would surely have captured Niccolò's attention. At any rate, when he returned to Venice he must frequently have caught a glimpse of the "mad, revolutionary, and atheistical Mylord"; and even if such occasions had hitherto been lacking they must both have been present at the masked ball at the Teatro Fenice that closed the carnival, an event where the demarcations of wealth and title played no role.

Escudier, quoting "a lady who had traveled in Paganini's company," wrote that he had met the poet, but if here he had Antonia Bianchi in mind, her friendship with the Maestro only dated from 1824, after Byron had left Italy, which would tend somewhat to weaken the value of her testimony. However, some comments in Niccolò's letters shortly after leaving Venice would indicate that he was either quoting the poet or had heard his cynicism discussed, and finding it applicable to his present state of mind had at once adopted it. For, as we have seen, he had what Chateaubriand called *"l'opulent aptitude à recueiller les idées des autres."*

Some day, Byron supposedly told him, he too "would become

40 The diary of Emanuele Cigogna in the Museo Correr, in Venice, contains the following entry: "Sunday evening (March 20, 1817) I was at the Teatro San Luca to hear the violinist Paganini. He is incomparable. It's a pity he's such a very dissolute character."

41 The Teatro San Luca was owned by Count Vendramin. Wagner died in the Vendramin Palazzo in Venice.

silent and reserved." At present, the poet said, "the acclamations of the crowd, love, wealth, popularity, seem to you delectable, yet when through genius and hard work you will have savored all these alleged delights, you'll soon find them cloying. This will leave a fearful, atrocious void within you and you'll then say with me 'why all this effort for nothing but disgust and satiety?' " "I'm not at all contented with this world,"[42] sighed Niccolò in one letter. "I feel a void within me that frets me terribly," he lamented in another.[43] Hence, if Escudier's quotation is substantially correct, it is not difficult to trace the parentage of Niccolò's reflections, though the cause of his depression at this time was something less impersonal than Byron's pretended *Weltschmerz!*[44]

According to Paganini's later biographers, it was in Venice at this time that he made the acquaintance of Antonia Bianchi, the mother of his son, a statement quite without foundation and traceable, apparently, to the romantic fancies of Elise Polko, who wrote:

They say that it was here [Venice] that he first met the woman whose jealousy later made her the evil genius of his life—the singer Antonia Bianchi. She was then a very charming young girl, a little supernumerary at the San Samuele Theatre, who was entrusted now and then with an unimportant role. Love for the wonderful artist sprang up in her heart like a bright flame. But at this time Niccolò was bound by other chains—held fast by the white hand of a distinguished aristocrat.

Here no sense of loyalty to her source material prevented her from blithely altering the date and locality of Fétis' "violent love affair," with the result that many biographers, loath to abandon her pretty fiction of Bianchi's Venetian past, link their liaison with the second Venice visit in 1824. Since his 1816 letters refer to a Venetian flame, his Italian biographers take it for granted (on Polko's evidence) that he is speaking of Bianchi. However a long

---

42 *"Non sono contento di questo mondo."*

43 *"Trovomi con un vuoto che mi crussia assai."*

44 Byron to Hobhouse: "I am not tired of Italy but a man must be a Cicisbeo and a Singer in duets and a connoiseur of Operas—or nothing—here. I have made some progress in all these accomplishments, but I can't say that I don't feel the degradation . . . better be a hunter, or anything, than a flatterer of fiddlers, and fan carrier of a woman." (Byron: *Letters and Journals* [6 vols., London, 1898–1904], IV, 357.)

letter written from Rome in 1819 and a comment in a previous letter,[45] in 1818, make it crystal clear that the sole object of his interest during the Venetian visit of 1816 was a Signora Lauretta, who rejected his attentions because "she did not love him," a most unusual episode in his amorous career and one that unquestionably enhanced her interest in his eyes. For even after nineteen years she still seems to have occupied a secret corner in his thoughts. At least he was very curious to know what had become of her!

Paganini to Antonio De Pagliari, Genoa, May 2, 1835.
The memories that will pass through my mind on reseeing you and Venice will no doubt be tinged with the serious and the delightful [*"avranno senza dubbio del serio e del dillettevole"*], the Naiads . . . and our sirens who will now manifest the ravages of time. No doubt you'll be generous and provide me with a gallant dictionary, with the annals of our many heroines and the private life to which they are, and have been, condemned. I should love to know what seat Petrarch's Laura holds in this hierarchy! [*"Amero di sapere ancora quale sede tenga in questa hirarchia la Laura del Petrarca!"*].

As regards Polko's assertion that "Bianchi was then a little supernumerary at the San Samuele Theatre," she was extremely unfortunate in her choice of theatre because we know from James Galiffe, who spent the autumn and winter in Venice at that time, that during the season of 1816–17 "the San Samuele Theatre was closed." Niccolò unquestionably made her acquaintance during his Milan-Como *étape* in 1822–24, for had he known her previously and she had declined his friendship (as Codignola and others assume from a comment in a letter dated November 7, 1818),[46] she would never, six years later, have resumed a relationship that she had previously severed because "she did not love him and his friendship meant nothing to her." For anyone with any knowledge of the feminine heart knows that an antagonism of this kind is seldom, if ever, exorcised. A woman's feelings are rarely capable of such reversals. Further, as several of Paganini's letters quite distinctly show, he was paying for the vocal lessons of Lauretta and continued to do so for some time in the future. Bianchi, he taught himself. "Suffice it

45 Codignola, *op. cit.,* 45.
46 *Ibid.,* 46.

to say that when I met her, she was an insignificant little singer and I taught her so that she could sing at concerts," he wrote Carli. At his Milan concerts before he left for Austria she was also distinctly designated on the program *"scolora di Paganini."* As the excess of physical energy that boiled in his blood and broke out in satyriasis was a matter of propinquity, the object of his ardor always faded quickly from his mind when absence interrupted the two currents, which shows how deep an impression Lauretta must have made upon him, when the mere name of Venice reinvoked her image after the passage of nearly twenty years. At all events, these two hitherto unpublished letters permit us to correct the false statements made by his biographers regarding the person of his Venetian mistress. And further it is highly improbable that Bianchi was ever in Venice before 1824.

v

While in Verona he finally received word that on November 14 the Genoa senate had pronounced a judgment in the Cavanna case and had sentenced him to pay Cavanna damages in the amount of 3000 francs plus costs. As usual, the verdict went against him.

Paganini to Teresa Paganini, Verona, November 28, 1816.
I'm delighted that you received the sight draft and power of attorney; even if they didn't arrive in time, they'll come in handy in some way. I don't feel bad about the 3000 francs because I know what scoundrels the lawyers Figari and Ciocca were. Please give my regards to my most excellent defender, lawyer Mangini, and my friend Ottagio, and beg them to continue to extend their kindness to me. I think it might be well to obtain the King's permission to appeal for a revision of the verdict brought against me through the subterfuges of the lawyers. I'm ready to pay you any sum you'll need, so go ahead and do exactly as seems best to you since I give you all the authority set forth in the power of attorney. I'm happy but should be even more so if you would treat yourself well at table. I want you to buy yourself the good Monferrato wine and provide yourself with good food and make all the family contented. Otherwise, I shall be unhappy. I don't lack means to send you whatever money you may need.

But meanwhile he did not let the matter worry him. The courts in those days evidently had no way of forcing payment of such debts, so, even without submitting an appeal, when the time came round, he did not hesitate to return to Genoa since his only property (his bank account) was safe in Lombardy and could not be attached by the Ligurian courts if he refused to pay.

During all these pleasant and engrossing weeks he seems to have been unaware of, or indifferent to, his father's failing health, though the fact that his mother had been managing the Cavanna affair since the early autumn would indicate that Antonio had been incapacitated for a considerable time. In his will, Antonio's illness was described as "pleurisy and inflammation," which may have been tuberculous pleuritis, and thus might easily account for Niccolò's tubercle baccili. Be that as it may, after receiving the viaticum on April 1, Antonio, "sound in spirit, senses, mind, memory, eyesight, speech, hearing, judgment, and understanding," sent for a notary public and drew up his will,[47] a document that later played a role in a suit brought by Cavanna's widow to obtain the payment of Niccolò's still outstanding damages. After leaving instructions for his burial, he stipulated that, having "received the sum of 2200 free Genoese lire as dowry from his wife without covering deed of gift," his heirs were now to repay this sum to Teresa when, or if, she ceased to live with her children. Then, after bequeathing to his two daughters 500 lire each, which was to be paid them "within two months by his proprietary heirs, Carlo and Niccolò," he instituted Teresa general usufructuary of "all his property consisting of furniture, real estate, gold, silver, money credits, and whatsoever he possessed, so long as she remained unmarried," after which it devolved on the two sons to pay the designated legacies. The total sum amounted approximately to the damages and costs in the Cavanna case, which suggests something other than pure coincidence! Indeed, Cavanna's lawyers did not hesitate to insinuate that the will was an elaborate subterfuge to enable Paganini to delay or avoid payment of this debt. Thus, if these allegations were true (and one suspects they were) it would indicate that Antonio and Teresa had very capable legal advice, or they would hardly at such a time have worked out this elaborate strategy unless, of course, Antonio had already had some training in such matters.

47 *Ibid.*, 190, n. 1.

Leaving Venice early in Holy Week, Niccolò went first to Ferrara, where he played on Easter Sunday, April 6; then, after dallying a month along the way, he arrived in Milan early in May and remained there till after the première of Rossini's new opera *La Gazza Ladra* on the thirty-first—still in no haste to go to Genoa though by then he must have learned of his father's death on April 1. It was while arranging some financial matters with his banker Carlo Carli at this time that he purchased through the latter a 1724 Stradivari from Count Cozio di Salabue, which was apparently his first important acquisition of this nature.[48] In the unsettled period when Italy was subjected to pillaging by the invading soldiery and heavy contributions were being levied by the French, Count Cozio had placed his valuable collection of instruments in Carli's safekeeping, which explains how this transaction came about. These business matters settled, he set forth at last for home and remained in Genoa till mid-December, where life was seasoned with a brief flirtation with a friend of Germi's.

Paganini to Germi, Turin, December 20, 1817.
If I was sad during the journey, it was because of you and Mme Tadea, whom I left with the desire of seeing soon again. Here they want to hear my violin again and I shall be proud to give a concert on Christmas night if they will grant me permission for this holy day. This evening I'm going to the rehearsal at the Teatro Regio to file my application. . . . I'll write to you by ordinary post regarding my law suit, having already found a lawyer—an amateur violinist, who has taken full charge of it.[49]

[Four days later] I hope you've seen the Signora and will let me know how she is, since her health is a matter of great moment to me. I shan't give a concert on Friday because the boxes at the Teatro Carignano are not at disposition. I'm going to see if the Queen will let me have her theatre for January second. Yesterday evening I went to

48 At the time of his death he had two 1724 Stradivari violins (the date of one was later given as 1727).

Cozio di Salabue (1755–1840) began his collection in 1775 but started to dispose of it before his death. After his death the remainder passed to Marquis Dalle Valle of Casale Monferrato, and from him to Giuseppe Fiorini, who presented it to the city of Cremona. Carlo Carli, descendant of a distinguished Milanese family, was an accomplished amateur violinist and a great patron of the arts.

49 Paganini seems to be referring here to another legal matter in which he was involved and with which Germi had nothing to do. Or it may be that Germi was merely an attorney and did not plead cases in open court.

the concert of two dilettantes but I was horribly bored and left after the third number. . . . Here the tradesmen and people of means are making an awful row because the boxes of the big theatre have been allocated to the nobility.[50] Today I started to practice a bit and my fingers sting. Don't forget to remember me to the adorable Signora Tadea and tell me how she is.

Turin never seems to have been a very fortunate city for him. Indeed, he soon decided that "the stars in that sky were all against him," for nothing ever worked out quite as he expected, the music and the theatres were a disappointment, the noise and commotion during the performances spoiled all pleasure, even the authorities adopted a hostile attitude.

Paganini to Germi, Turin, January 7, 1818.
Thank you for the cordial interest manifested in your news of my mother. You can well imagine how it saddened me to hear that she hasn't yet recovered. I wrote her a letter, not by my own hand, but dictated from my heart. . . . The uproar that goes on in the Teatro Regio prevents anyone hearing either the singers or the orchestra. Therefore I'm silent.

The noise in the Italian theatres at that time was a matter of general comment and conditions had changed little since the days of Dr. Burney and President de Brosses, whose descriptions of the boisterous behavior of the audiences were in no way exaggerated even for the first half of the nineteenth century.

In Milan [wrote Dr. Burney] every box was furnished with a complete room with a fireplace in it and all conveniences for refreshments and cards.[51] In the fourth row is a faro table, on each side of the house, which is used during the performances of the opera. The noise here during the performance was abominable, except while two or three airs and a duet were sung, with which everyone was in raptures.[52]

In the evening we went to the opera [wrote President de Brosses].[53]

---

[50] Lady Morgan, *op. cit.*, I, 81.

[51] This condition was also to be found at the small German courts where the court chamber orchestra was expected to perform while the guests were playing cards.

[52] Burney, *The Present State of Music in France and Italy*, 81.

[53] Charles de Brosses, *Lettres familières écrites d'Italie* (Paris, 1858), II, 317.

They were giving a piece for which Leo had written the music.[54] I suspect that I might have found it very charming if I had been able to
hear it, but the pit was either mad or drunk, or rather both at once. I
don't believe there is anything so distressing and at the same time so
impertinent as the noise that goes on. The public market is no match
for it. Everyone not only carries on a conversation at the top of his
voice, but they applaud with loud shrieks, not alone after the arias but
as soon as the singers appear, and all the time they are singing—and
this without ever once listening to them. Even the gentlemen in the pit
have long wooden canes with which they pound on the seats as hard as
ever they can to express their admiration. They have associates in the
fifth-tier boxes who at this signal throw down millions of leaflets containing printed sonnets in praise of the primadonna or virtuoso who
has just appeared. Everybody leans half way over the boxes to catch
one of them. The pit leaps to its feet and the scene finishes with a general Ah!—resulting in a terrific headache for everybody present.[55]

Probably a great many of the musical offerings did not demand
very close attention either as music or as entertainment. In Italy
the impresarios were usually wealthy amateurs (like Duke Vis-
conti in Milan, Count Vendramin in Venice, Count Guiccioli in
Ravenna) who, when the repertory lagged, would commission a
work from some composer of repute who was not always inspired
by real creative genius. In the smaller towns the works were performed by "scratch companies," and after the composer had been
selected and all the business details completed, he would pay a visit
to the town, hear the singers who were to interpret his opus, be
handed a libretto, usually written by the local playwright, and
then in two or three weeks would concoct an opera made up of the
barrel scrapings of earlier works. If the opera were successful, it
might be produced in other places but, since these compositions
were rarely or ever printed, it was a simple matter for a routine
composer to turn out eighty or ninety lyrical works, which seems
to have been the average output in those days.[56] All he need do was
to reshuffle his own or other men's ideas and serve them up in a
different order with a dash of new material, hoping for the best.

[54] Leonardo Leo (1694–1744), one of the leading composers of light opera and
church music of his day. Jommelli and Piccini were among his pupils.

[55] This behavior was not limited to the opera but occurred even at concerts.

[56] Carafa wrote thirty-five operas, Pugni ten, in addition to three hundred ballets,
Blangini thirty, Nicolini forty-eight, Generali forty-five, and Mercadante sixty.

In the words of Glinka, "they had the right to catch the most talented opera by the wings, chop off its legs or tail, cut its throat, and cook a fricassée of their own invention." As a result the system of copyists who could produce exactly the number of copies required was both a highly developed trade and a very profitable business, even though their fees were very small. For they not only supplied the theatres and churches and local amateurs but were also employed to prepare whole musical libraries. Hence, as copyrights were then unknown, the possibilities of pirating other men's ideas were unlimited, so it can easily be seen what a lot of crudities, imperfections, and refurbishings of old material passed as opera and how natural it was to look upon such music as an accompaniment for conversation. This will also explain in part Paganini's reluctance to have his manuscripts fall into the hands of strangers.[57]

During the ensuing fortnight he received negative answers from Turin and Milan, showing how dependent he was, despite his popularity, on the favor of the impresarios. If he could only have made his plans with a fair degree of certainty, he might not have wasted so many weeks frittering away his time in places and pursuits that were far removed from music. Such a passionate temperament as his required, besides diversion, constant emotional excitement; thus, when the latter was not provided by his art and he grew bored with his surroundings, he did not seek relief in a round of hard work but instead turned his mind to the pagan delights of life and set forth like Pan to stroll through woods and fields in search of the only effective balsam for his spirit.

Paganini to Germi, Turin, January 21, 1818.
I intended to go home for the present carnival, since I can't get a theatre for a concert, even in Milan. But now I've decided to stay here and prepare at least three concerts that I'm going to give during Lent. . . . I'm terribly bored here. The music at the Teatro Regio is murderous. [Jan. 31, 1818] I don't go to the theatre here any more so as not to be bored—and thus I live a lonely life. I've been practicing now for several days but all my dexterity is of no use. However, I mustn't get discouraged. . . . Almost all women are endowed with a certain dash of artifice,

[57] Percy Scholes, *The Great Dr. Burney:* "When Dr. Burney visited Italy . . . he wrote that he was 'shocked to find that the art of engraving music had now entirely disappeared.'" See also Henry Matthews, *Diary of an Invalid.*

which experience has taught them is necessary in order to gain empire over a man. But I rarely find united in one person grace and modesty, simplicity and astuteness, sentiment and insensibility, an angelic face and an infernal heart. This is the physical and moral picture of a girl in the flower of her youth, whose acquaintance I've made through a friend, already a victim of her wiles. Fortunately for me, forewarned of the dangers to which I exposed my heart in associating with this new Helen, I've known how to resist the darts that shot from those eyes, bringing inquietude and death to the soul. But I confess, dear friend, that after having once set eyes on this seductive creature, I pass my days in sadness, fighting a thousand painful thoughts that keep me in a continual state of dejection. My crisis is terrible and it's imperative that I absent myself forever from a house where I should never again have set my foot.

Although his concert at the Teatro Carignano won the undivided enthusiasm of the public, one of the critics was inclined to cavil at his want of feeling and his uncanonical technical feats, but Turin was, of course, the old Pugnani stronghold where for twenty-three years musicians had been trained in the pure grand style of Tartini, Corelli, and Vivaldi. As Pugnani had been dead only two decades, the critic may have been a onetime disciple and incapable of appreciating Paganini's bravura style. That the political factor may also have influenced his judgment is suggested by the drastic action of the Governor in refusing Niccolò a license for a third concert on the alleged ground of his refusal to repeat a number in response to his listeners' clamorous demands.

Paganini to Germi, Turin, February 25, 1818.
My stars in this sky are all against me. Just because I wouldn't repeat the variations at the second concert, as the audience wished, the Governor has seen fit to suspend the third one, which was scheduled for Sunday next. . . . Here are twenty louis d'or, which you will receive at the office of the diligence. I should like to have this small sum forwarded to that person—if you think she is still without means. But I beg you to use all possible secrecy in this matter so that no one ever hears about it. Confiding in your honesty and friendship, I beg you to accept my thanks in advance while awaiting your dear letter as well as news regarding the object in whom I'm interested. I must thank you for your counsel regarding human temptations. Please take note that I no longer have anything to do with the aforesaid lady, to my peace of mind. And I hope to keep away from her.[58]

A fortnight later the wheels had turned again and he was once more completely absorbed in music, having for the moment put the various ladies out of mind.

Paganini to Germi, Turin, March 11, 1818.
To the devil with all the sirens in the universe—I only wish your continued friendship. I hope never again to play my violin in this kingdom. I want to get away and shall leave on Saturday for Piacenza, where I know what to expect.

The Piacenza visit, when it eventually materialized, recompensed him in a measure for the vexations in Turin since it was here that he made the acquaintance of Karl Lipinsky, who had come to Italy especially to hear him and after vainly wandering from one place to another finally caught up with him in Piacenza.[59] Dr. Franz Gehring, of the Vienna University, who contributed the article on Lipinsky for the first edition of Grove's Dictionary,[60] wrote that Lipinsky played with him on April 17 and 30. This was probably an error for April 17 and May 24 since there is no record of a concert on the thirtieth. Moreover, Lipinsky's name is associated only with the concert of April 17, though, since he also spoke of playing a second time "several weeks after the first concert," it is possible that his name was omitted from the program of the May concert.[61] One of the numbers was "Kreutzer's violin sonata," though the double concerto may have been meant.

Many years have elapsed since I was challenged to play with Paganini [Lipinsky told Count von Krockow in Dresden in 1849] and numerous were the letters of introduction pressed upon me by kind friends. Among others was a letter from Spohr to an old gentleman living in Milan, who in his youth had been one of the most promising pupils of

[58] Paganini is here obviously referring to three different persons.
[59] He may have gone to Milan to hear Mayseder, Boehm, and Pixis.
[60] Gehring wrote that Lipinski was in Italy twice, first when he went to hear Paganini and then some time later when he "returned to study with an old pupil of Tartini." G. W. Finck, who contributed the article on Lipinski to Schilling's *Lexikon* (1835), does not mention a second Italian visit, and states that Lipinski's attention was first drawn to Paganini by Lichtenthal's articles in the Leipzig *Allgemeine Musikalische Zeitung,* and his interest further whetted by Spohr, with whom he studied for a time.
[61] Schottky (*op. cit.,* 408) wrote that Lipinski remained nearly a year with Paganini—an obvious exaggeration. Did Paganini give him this impression?

Tartini. . . . Taking my letter of introduction and my violin I repaired
to the house of Signor Salvini. . . . After listening to me for about a
quarter of an hour, he got up, looked intently first at me and then at
my violin, and exclaimed: "Basta!" However I was somewhat reassured
when he asked me to come and see him the next morning. . . . In this sad
mood I almost regretted having consented to play with Paganini for
I knew that to a certain extent it was to be a trial of skill between us.
Next day I went to Signor Salvini's house at the appointed time. He
received me with great cordiality and before I had unpacked my music,
he said: "Please give me your violin." I handed it to him and was
amazed to see him grasp it firmly by the neck and strike it with all his
might on the edge of the table on which it fell, smashed to atoms. But
with the greatest coolness and tranquillity the old gentleman then
opened a violin case that was lying on the same table and carefully
taking from it a violin, said to me: "Try this instrument." I took it and
after I had played one of Beethoven's sonatas, Salvini held out his hand
to me and said with some emotion: "You are doubtless aware that I
was formerly a pupil of Tartini.[62] On one occasion he gave me this
large and genuine Stradivari which I have cherished as a souvenir of
his memory. You know how to use such an instrument and to give expression to its hidden power." "But," I exclaimed, "there is the world-
famous Paganini!" "Don't speak to me of him!" cried the old man ex-
citedly. "I've heard him, that one-stringed magician, who has no great
musical depth, but who can merely astonish his listeners by his great
technical dexterity, without being capable of any noble, full, round
tone. Paganini is admired, but your playing thrills and transports one.
You alone are a worthy follower of Tartini. Therefore accept this violin as a present from me and at the same time as a souvenir of Tartini."[63]

Although eight years younger than Paganini, Lipinsky was already an artist of high reputation and attainment, a fact that Paganini instantly recognized, so, "after playing together nearly every

[62] Lipinski used the violin all the rest of his life. After his death it went to the
dealer Richard Weichold of Dresden and was then purchased by Professor Engelbert
Roentgen of Leipzig. On the suggestion of Joachim, the instrument was sent to Hill
& Sons in London in 1899 for needed adjustment and after a short sojourn in the
ownership of an amateur player in Holland, it passed into their possession. Later it
was for a time in the Hamma Collection. Coming then to America about 1922, it
passed from the Wurlitzer Collection to Roger Chittoline and then to Dr. Martinez
Canas of Havana, Cuba. It is a 1715 Strad, well covered with rich reddish color. Since
it was too narrow to produce the width desired by Stradivarius, he pieced out the
block of maple, noticeable at the lower flanks. (Information furnished by the late
Ernest Doring.)

[63] Krockow's article in this translation appeared in the *Violin Times,* December
15, 1895, and January 15, 1896.

day" he invited the Pole to play Kreutzer's double concerto with him at his second concert. All biographers, with the exception of Pulver, have interpreted this as another virtuoso duel, which, judging by Lipinsky's remarks, would seem to be the way he also looked upon it, at least in later years. Yet, in view of Paganini's personal attitude towards "competitions" of this kind, which he frowned upon as futile and serving no good ends, it is only natural to suppose that his invitation was inspired by admiration, for he was still young enough himself to take genuine pleasure in the enthusiasm of his colleague and was probably delighted to share his music with a receptive and appreciative disciple. Where he read censure and skepticism in the eyes of Spohr and Lafont, he read only large-orbed wonder in Lipinsky's.

Paganini to Germi, Piacenza, April 25, 1818.
From Turin I wrote to the tenor Granci of Bologna with the idea of engaging him for the Naples tour. I've had no reply of any kind. Maybe he wasn't there, but for that tour he would have been a nuisance. In Italy I seem to be everywhere at home and wherever I wish to give a concert, I find singers who will give their services for a few scudi.[64] That's why I shall go without him. . . . In Turin I was lazy because a young girl of thirteen or fourteen, a Protestant of cultivated family, made such an impression on me that I asked her parents for her hand and they told me that when she has finished her education they will offer no objection if the girl reciprocates my feelings. So there's time to think it over. I'm living here with friends and there are some very charming nuns who are educating some very beautiful young ladies, one of whom I had the good luck to meet on the stairway—but such an accident is *difficult and rare. O Dio, qual piacere!*

As the record of his career discloses, he never demanded fine musicianship or worldly reputation from his assisting artists, a little idiosyncracy for which he was much criticized abroad. Perhaps his motives may have been of a financial nature, or he may have disliked (subconsciously, maybe) to share his stellar rank with an eminent singer who might prove a formidable rival for the favor of the public. Then, too, the habit may have developed from a practical consideration. As the audiences demanded variety, he was able, by keeping his expenses to a minimum, to engage several

[64] According to Spohr, in 1816 and 1817 assisting artists received one carolin.

artists, and for much less than he would have had to pay a Pasta, a Catalani, or a Cortesi, and besides was spared the cost of traveling expenses.

Tibaldi-Chiesa (p. 149) asserts that about this time he visited Antonio Rolla (son of his old master) in Milan and entrusted to him the publication of a number of his works, which were brought out by Ricordi in 1820 as "Op. 1—5." As far as can be verified, Paganini during this period was in Milan only twice, namely, in the spring of 1816 and again in May and June, 1817, when on his way to Genoa. In 1818, when the arrangement with Ricordi was presumably effected,[65] Antonio Rolla (1798–1837) was a neophyte of twenty, Paganini a mature artist of thirty-five, so, if he entrusted the matter to anyone at all, it was surely to Antonio's father. Be that as it may, it seems logical to believe that the real inspiration for this move lay with Lipinsky, who after listening to the Capricci undoubtedly wished to have them made available to other violinists like himself and therefore persuaded Niccolò to have them published, a surmise more or less confirmed by Lipinsky's later statement that "Paganini wrote the Capricci at different times and in different places and had distributed copies of them among his friends so that when Ricordi came to publish them, he had to write them out hastily from memory." Since he was in daily contact with Paganini at this time, his information was undoubtedly correct.

Paganini to Germi, Bologna, July 1, 1818.
At Turin just because I couldn't repeat the Variations at my second concert because of not feeling well, the Governor wouldn't let me continue the recitals, so I decided never to play in Piedmont again, and that's why I didn't give the promised concerts in Vercelli or Alexandria. At Piacenza, as you know, I gave three. At Parma I gave one, but the weather was bad and Her Royal Highness was ill, so I left at once for Cremona, where the Philharmonic Society, after making me an honorary member,[66] guaranteed the expenses of two evening concerts at the theatre. . . . If my violin once pleased like ten, now it pleases like a hundred. Tell my family . . . I forgot something: a certain Lipinsky, a Pole and professor of the violin, came to Italy from Poland expressly to hear me. He caught up with me at Piacenza and was with me almost

65 Ricordi published the *Capricci* in 1820, not in 1818 as Tibaldi-Chiesa states.
66 The Accademia Filarmonica of Bologna was founded in 1666 by Count Vincenzo Carrati.

constantly. He played the Carrega, Raggi, and Germi quartets most marvellously.[67] Now he's going back to Poland to study my genre for some years and says he never wants to hear any other professor of this instrument. Cavaliere Crescentini,[68] the musician, honored me by attending my concert last Thursday. He called on me in the impresario's room, asking me to give him the pleasure of dining at his country place. I went and amused myself enormously in the company of Mme Colbran and another signora—an amateur—who, beautiful as Eve, bewitched me with her rendering of a duet *Per mari, per fonti, cercando di luce.* Signor Barbaja,[69] impresario of the Naples theatres, asked Mme Colbran to invite me there, promising me all the theatres *gratis;* so I'm going the end of September. . . . Radicati,[70] first violin at Bologna, accompanies beautifully and is a first rate professor. The other evening he played a Haydn quartet and I played another, just as it was written. But to tell you the truth, there emanates from my playing a certain magic that I can't describe to you.

There has been much uncertainty among Paganini's biographers regarding the date of his first meeting with Rossini (owing to Fétis' erroneous statements),[71] though there would seem to be no reasonable doubt that their acquaintance dated from Paganini's first winter in Milan. He was then the lion of the hour, and Rossini must have been in the city several weeks previous to the première of his *Aureliano in Palmyra,* which took place at the Scala on December 26. It is therefore safe to say that Niccolò was often in the theatre and was surely present at the first performance, or at least the general rehearsal; so, even though Rossini may not have been interested in instrumental music, Niccolò, as an ardent opera fan, would have been eager to meet this famous colleague who for

---

[67] His quartets Nos. 7, 8, and 9 were evidently written between 1816 and 1818.

[68] Girolamo Crescentini (1766–1846), a celebrated sopranist, possessed a beautiful mezzo-soprano voice and a perfect method of vocalization. He was the last great singer of his school.

[69] Domenico Barbaja (1778–1841). After the political disturbances of 1820, Barbaja went to Vienna, where he had the direction of the Kaertnerthor Theater and the Theater an der Wien. During the eight years he was in Vienna, his company embraced all the finest talent of his day. His agreement with Rossini called for one new opera annually for the San Carlo and del Fondo Theatres, for which Rossini was to receive two hundred ducats a month, with a small share in the gaming tables.

[70] Felice Radicati (1778–1823), served first at the court of King Victor Emmanuel V. After going to Bologna, he became director of the orchestra of the Basilica di S. Pietro and violin instructor at the Liceo Filarmonico. He was killed in a carriage accident in Vienna.

[71] Fétis, *op. cit.,* 46.

some years now had coursed through the Italian sky "like an un-
hooded eagle of the empyrean," the whir of his wings being heard
in the smallest provincial town that maintained a theatre. So we
may be certain that if they did not meet in the theatre, their many
common friends would not have failed to bring the two together.

During this Bologna visit, Rossini happened to be home on holiday and as here too they moved in the same circles, they must have
seen each other frequently, so that it was natural for Rossini to
bring his colleague into contact with his impresario Domenico Barbaja, who proved so helpful to him later on. Starting his career as
a waiter in a Milan café, Barbaja laid the foundation for his future
success by obtaining the concession for the gaming tables in the
Scala; then on going to Naples he made a similar arrangement at
the San Carlo Theatre, where, after surrounding himself with a
galaxy of brilliant stars and harnessing Rossini also to his chariot,
he became, as Henri Beyle put it, *le premier homme du Royaume.*

Besides Rossini and his circle, Paganini discovered many other
musical interests in Bologna, so, had he settled there, as for a time
he thought of doing, he would have found himself in a most congenial atmosphere. Among others, there was Radicati and his wife
Teresa Bertinotti, who allegedly sang at Niccolò's debut. However, since neither Radicati nor the latter's biographer, Carlo Pancaldi, ever referred to any previous collaboration between the two
and since Paganini also never mentioned her in any of his letters,
one is more than ever convinced that he deliberately fabricated
this detail to impress Schottky with his early connections. If true,
such a bond would surely have had a sentimental value for the two
participants (in view of Paganini's present fame), yet on neither
side was there ever the slightest reference to shared recollections
of this or of any other nature.

Conestabile, who drew largely on Pancaldi's unpublished memoirs, written long after the events described, quoted him as saying
that Paganini had come to Bologna for "treatment by the two celebrated physicians Tommassini and Valorani,[72] and remained there

---

[72] Tommassini was one of the leading pioneers in clinical instruction in Italy.

Vincenzo Valorani was a graduate of the Bologna School of Medicine. He became
a member of the faculty in 1827, and in 1830 was appointed to succeed Tommassini
when the latter was called to Parma.

eight months," both of which statements are manifestly incorrect. For six weeks seems to have been the limit of his stay and there is no evidence that at this time his health was causing him particular worry. When he visited Bologna in 1827, after his recent illness in Naples, he may have seized the opportunity of consulting these two famous diagnosticians but, if so, he never mentioned either of them in this connection, so far as can be learned from available and entirely trustworthy documents of the period.

Among his many Bologna friends was Annibale Milzetti, a person of distinction and considerable influence, who was very fond of him. Presumably concerned over his irregular mode of life, his lack of inner discipline and high seriousness, with the resultant drain on his delicate constitution and its possibly detrimental effect on the exercise of his great gifts, Milzetti seems to have taken him in hand and persuaded him that it was time to stop his philandering and to marry and settle down. One assumes that he suggested a young friend, Marietta Banti—evidently with an excellent family background, for, since her only charm, in Niccolò's eyes, seems to have been her love of music, his brief, synthetic infatuation must have been inspired by suggestion or some material factors effectively presented by an interested advocate. As for some time now, in response to the urgings of his family, he had been thinking more seriously of marriage, Milzetti probably had no trouble in selling him the idea, and all the more so since the prospective bride was evidently very young. "In Italy [wrote Henri Beyle] *les femmes jouent un tout autre rôle qu'en France; des l'âge de quinze ans une jeune fille est jolie et peut compter dans le monde.*" At any rate, after more than a decade of promiscuity when there could have been very little in the voluptuary's manual that was unknown to him, Niccolò's overwrought emotional organism now demanded the surprise-invoking quality that comes only with sophistication; so, after the first fine careless rapture that youth afforded him, his curiosity was quickly satiated and it therefore took more than a love of music to keep his interest at high pitch. Furthermore, he rebelled so strongly against the marriage tie that at the moment of decision he invariably declined to walk so tight a rope, which was the situation in this case. During his few weeks in Bologna, under the influence of "Papa" Milzetti's persuasive personality and his own faculty of self-delusion, he played the lover's role convincingly, yet the mere fact that he failed to share his hopes and plans with Germi till some time had passed makes one suspect that from the very first he was parading a false plumage for motives of his own.

Paganini to Germi, Bologna, August 4, 1818.
It was the greatest pleasure to hear that you are disposed to join me at Florence; I'm leaving tomorrow and shall give three concerts there. Friend, I recommend that you also leave at once since, besides the pleasure of your dear company, I have things to tell you regarding my future happiness. . . . I'm in ecstasies and dying to see you. . . . My decisions, *figlie della fortuna,* are going to surprise you. . . . Please give my regards to all my family and tell them that I'm not going to Venice any more because I've broken off my friendship with Signora Lauretta.

Florence, August 11.
Here I am, feeling first rate. . . . In case your affairs won't let you get away now, you'll find me at Leghorn within a fortnight or three weeks and Signor Puccini, professor of violin, will give you my address.[73] I've got lots to tell you—much that will give you pleasure. I'm off now to play some quartets with Signor Tinti, professor of violin.

Judging by his next letter, Germi must have voiced his conviction that while in Genoa he had committed himself in some way to the "adorable Signora Tadea," an obligation that could not be lightly shunted aside should he now be contemplating matrimony. For taking in his reply a self-justificatory tone, Niccolò definitely dismissed the lady.

Paganini to Germi, Florence, August 16, 1818.
I always told Signora Tadea Pratolongo that I appreciated the cordiality she extended to me in her country house, and in fact I think I've entirely repaid it by lending my professional services—and also as far as my finances permit; *this you know.* Many other women would like to lay claim to my heart and my money, but I've quashed their hopes by a much more pertinent gesture, that is, I could not but detest them from the very first moment. But I only beg Signora Tadea, so different from many others, to put me altogether out of mind since duty and religion demand that I live in perfect silence.

After this he evidently did not have the courage to pursue the

[73] Angelo Puccini (b. 1781), Leghorn violinist, pupil of Salvatori Tinti.

subject of Marietta, preferring to postpone discussion till he could plead his cause in person. For the present it was best to let Germi believe that he was temporarily through with womankind.[74]

Paganini to Germi, Florence, August 20, 1818.
I believe you won't disapprove of a resolution I made some time ago to consign all the ladies of my acquaintance to the devil, seeing that they are only bent on my destruction. You will have received a hint of this in the last mail. Dear friend, don't deprive me of the much-longed-for pleasure of seeing you. To make this possible I've decided to give only one concert here . . . and then leave at once for Leghorn, where I shall give three concerts on the evenings of the twenty-seventh, twenty-ninth, and thirtieth,[75] returning then to Florence—in your company, I hope. . . . A certain M. Grasse[t] of Paris,[76] first violin at the Théâtre des Italiens, on hearing me at Bologna, uttered such blasphemies that it is impossible to write them. . . . In Bologna, Maestro Rossini was unable to accompany me on the cembalo in the Waltz in E, which in Genoa is thought to be his composition; so that I knew that he had not composed it, but Maestro Romani, who is now here in Florence.[77]

Germi joined him in Florence, as he hoped, and then went on to Lucca with him for the Festival of San Croce,[78] where Paganini may have played since he gave two concerts at the Teatro Pantero on September 4 and 18. Then after Germi left, he went on to Pistoia, where he also played before returning to Florence on October 1. But the days that he and his friend spent together seem to have been slightly marred by one of the heated little squabbles that regularly enlivened, and perhaps fortified, their friendship. Since we have no record, during the long years of their association, of any unpleasantness over financial matters, the present annoyance

74 In many ways Germi and Paganini were cast in the same mould. For many years the mistress of Germi's house and heart was Camilla Beretti, a *lavorante domestica*. Germi finally married her on November 17, 1837, after living with her for at least twenty-five years.

75 These concerts were not announced in the papers, probably because they were intermezzo concerts. The Vivoli correspondence in the Biblioteca Labronica in Leghorn shows that he played at the Teatro San Marco on September 6 (then known as the Teatro dei Floridi), so it is reasonable to suppose that he gave the others also.

76 Jean Jacques Grasset (1769–1839), a distinguished violinist of his day, and pupil of Berthaume.

77 Pietro Romani (1791–1877), pupil of Fenaroli, was appointed conductor in Florence in 1817. He composed a large number of successful ballets. Rossini used to sign a lot of his photographs, *Pianiste du troisième classe.*

78 In a letter of October 2, 1823, Paganini refers to their presence at this festival.

was undoubtedly traceable to what Germi considered as inexcusable fickleness towards a personal friend.

Paganini to Germi, Florence, October 1, 1818.
I thought you were angry with me for having caused you so much suffering during those, for me, blessed days when you honored me with your company. But instead, you've given me the pleasure of such a dear, such a beautiful letter that I am never done reading it, and read it yesterday evening at a brilliant *conversazione* and made the listeners laugh. . . . I've received three letters from Milzetti in which he tells me that Signor Zaccaria has received iniquitous and false letters from Genoa and that it's certain that the young lady's sister and brother-in-law are my greatest enemies, but all will be in vain because my dear Marietta replied to the writer of the letter that all these calumnies only made her love her dear Paganini the more.

October 10, 1818.[79]
A most interesting letter from my adored Marina! Here's a copy of it! First of all I must tell you that her father keeps a sharp lookout and won't let her have any paper or ink; but in spite of all that, with the help of one of the maids she wrote me the following on half a sheet of paper: "My one and only love! My pen can't describe my joy on receiving your kind letter. It's true that your departure caused me the greatest grief that a more-than-enamored person like myself can know. But patience! Please do all you can to return to Bologna as soon as possible, which will be the greatest pleasure my dear lover can give me. I understood everything in your two letters but I have so little time at my disposal that I can't express myself in any other way. As for myself, I am up against a thousand obstacles, which is why I beg you to come back just as soon as you can. I hope you'll get what I'm trying to say, that is, that my brother-in-law and sister are raising Cain because nothing happens, but nothing will come of it. Addio, my life and my all." In reply I stressed the hitherto unknown pleasure of receiving her precious letter, which I kissed a hundred times because it was written by the hand of *mio bene* (how do you like that expression?). I told her that I shall see her at Bologna (which contains the object of my thoughts) after my trip to Naples, that no other city means so much to me as Bologna, a city that will be blessed for me if Heaven lets me unite my destiny forever with that of my darling Marietta. I stressed in the same way my pleasure in hearing that she is so assiduous with her singing—when she

[79] Mompellio, guided by Paganini's statements that he was going to Rome by way of Arezzo and Macerata, states that he played in Arezzo. This may be, though there is no documentary evidence of it.

was in the country, she went through all the Crescentini studies, and her papa scolded her because she studied so much.

This letter was no sooner in the post than he dashed off another, urging Germi to procure an additional document needed in connection with his marriage. "Do me the favor of sending it as soon as possible, because I want to make a good showing before my Bologna friends, as well as marrying into a good family. I hope my expectations will materialize because I know how much my glory means to you."

His concerts over, he returned to Bologna, not, as might be assumed, to see the lovelorn Marietta and sign the marriage contract, but to withdraw his money from Pegnalver's bank and transfer it to Milan, Milzetti having dropped a hint that certain persons connected with the bank were "crooks and gangsters." This transaction completed, he calmly resumed the role of the itinerant musician and set out for Rome, where the morning after his arrival he dropped a note to Germi in which he unblushingly confessed to a complete change of heart.

Paganini to Germi, Rome, November 4, 1818.
I arrived safe and sound yesterday evening in this *Dominante,* as the Romans call it. The city surpasses the liveliest imagination. The air is heavy but I've got a good appetite. . . . Dear friend, I must tell you that my feelings have entirely changed. I stayed in Bologna about six days and grew so indifferent to the lady that I'm no longer thinking of marriage. She adores me but I can't make up my mind to marry, which is why I want you to tell me how to write and prepare her for such indifference. . . . Dear friend, I'm not at all content with this world. Console me, you who have so much power over the soul of your true friend.

What happened during the week in Bologna to have engendered this sudden dissatisfaction with the world? Had he only been trying to make Lauretta jealous, and her continued indifference had disgusted him with mankind? Four days later another letter reiterated his aversion to matrimony and revealed, between the lines, that his thoughts were still with his Venetian friend Lauretta, and probably had been all along.

Paganini to Germi, Rome, November 7, 1818.
In this city you have to change your shoes ten times a day because of

the downpour. . . . I was a little enamoured of the lady in Venice, but letters reaching me from Venice have told me so many things about her that I can't think of speaking to her any more. She's given up her music. She says she doesn't love me, that my friendship means nothing to her, and that she's therefore perfectly happy. I believe she's gone to her sister in Brescia. . . . My aversion to marriage still continues. Therefore, no more love letters—only formal ones. Freedom is a treasure.

Perhaps if Lauretta, who had obviously made a profound impression on him, had exacted marriage as her price—for every feminine instinct must have sensed that he was dangerous and undependable—she might still have galvanized him into action, and his emotional life, by the mere process of habituation, would then have proved a more fructifying one, even though the underlying motive for his capitulation—as with so many Don Juans—might have been in the nature of an oblique revenge.

VIII. *ROME AND NAPLES 1818–1820*

When the blood burns, how prodigal the soul
Lends the tongue vows.—SHAKESPEARE *(Hamlet).*

AS HE INTENDED to spend the winter in the south, there was plenty of time to acquaint himself with conditions—to get his bearings, in other words. For with only four weeks till the theatres closed for Advent, he realized that it would be unwise, in a city where he was still unknown, to give a concert if he could not immediately appear again while the air was electric with his magnetism. Otherwise, the public might lose interest, and the machinations of envious competitors ripen to his disadvantage. Besides, the Roman climate favored lassitude; the air was "heavy" and the rain, soft and enervating day after day, tempered his ambition, leaving him content to drift awhile in this *"Dominante* that surpassed the richest imagination."

Although for six years he had been earning enough to supply all his material needs, he could not have given that impression since a Count Moscati later claimed that he "arrived in Rome with no shoes to his feet and no coat to his back, and even had to borrow money from a fellow artist to buy himself a suit of evening clothes before he could give a concert."[1] Although obviously a malicious exaggeration, the jibe attested nonetheless to that indifference to externals that was so often commented on by those who felt that such royal gifts as his demanded a certain panache to enable him to impose himself upon an insolent society that looked with inherited disdain upon the professional musician.[2] For by now there was no need for him to feel the pinch of poverty, unless, of course, the fickle gods tripped him at the gaming table, and even then his

---

[1] It is quite possible that Paganini's story of the prince who wanted to buy his violin occurred at this time. He said that after this episode he gave up gambling, but he was evidently still addicted to it when he first arrived in Rome. Pulver and others attribute the story to Fétis, but Fétis took it from George Harrys.

[2] See Giuseppe Baretti's *An Account of the Manners and Customs of Italy* for a description of the attitude of aristocratic Italians to musicians, particularly singers.

embarrassment need not have been for long. Therefore, if he ever "found himself without a paolo," it could only have been because the lusts of the flesh were more imperious than vanity and worldly ambition. "He is a man of eccentric character and irregular habits [wrote Henry Matthews].[3] He has no fixed engagement, but as occasion may require makes a trading voyage through the principal cities of Italy and can always procure a theatre upon the condition of equal participation in the receipts."

In Rome, however, it was just this question of the theatre that confronted him with a dilemma. He always insisted on playing in the leading theatre and on a Friday when there would be no competition—an idea that Antonio must have planted in his head. But during the carnival (December 26 till Ash Wednesday) it was difficult to secure the Teatro Argentina, while Friday was a frank impossibility since here the clergy were in full control, and on this weekly day of abstinence all theatrical entertainment was banned in memory of the Sacrifice on Calvary. Even had he been willing to dispense with the Argentina or the Valle, there were no regular concert halls, the only alternative being a private drawing room or a deserted *palazzo,* and the latter could hardly have been a satisfactory solution, in addition to the trouble of organizing an orchestra and engaging soloists. When Spohr was in Rome in 1817, he was able through the influence of the Austrian Ambassador to secure a room in the vacant Ruspoli Palace, but it was impossible to use it as it was since the whole building was in a ruinous condition.

First of all the windows had to be reglazed [he wrote], the holes in the marble pavements filled up with bricks, and then I had to hire the necessary furniture, chandeliers, chairs, music stands, etc. But first and foremost it was necessary to remove the filth and rubbish that extended from the entrance to the concert hall and cluttered up the vestibule and the wonderful marble staircase. Whole wagonloads had to be carted away. I then had to hunt out and engage the singers and musicians, one by one, in the big city. Although composed of the best instrumentalists in Rome, the orchestra was nonetheless the worst that I had had. The ignorance, want of taste, and stupid arrogance of these people beggared all description. Of dynamic nuance they knew absolutely nothing. One might have overlooked this, but each player made

3 Henry Matthews, *Diary of an Invalid* (London, 1820), 245.

whatever ornamentation came into his head, with turns on almost every note, so that it sounded more like the noise of an orchestra tuning up than harmonious music.[4]

Things were evidently not much better at the Argentina, to judge by the comments of James Galiffe, who attended a performance of Rossini's *Tancredi* at that theatre. "I saw only the first act, which was bad enough, but Rossini, who saw the second, assured me that it contained only one piece of his composition and that the rest, though it bore his name, was perfectly unknown to him. One thing is truly shocking in all the theatres of Rome—their disgusting filthiness and the horrible stench which pervades them, of which no one who has not experienced them can have any idea."[5]

In addition to the local regulations, it is again possible that politics may have played a part in the obstinacy of the ecclesiastical authorities, inasmuch as the situation in southern Italy was then rapidly narrowing to the final contest between the Liberals and the papal government, and every stranger was looked on with mistrust, especially anyone formerly associated with the Bonapartes. "The oldest and the latest news is—Holy Land and a cuckolded people," commented Paganini in a betraying phrase which suggests that, while ordinarily giving a wide berth to politics and affecting an air of studied indifference as though his mind were closed to the political currents of his time, he had become strongly anticlerical—a risky attitude at any time since in the midst of so much intrigue, where every second person was a spy or an informer for one side or the other, it must have been extremely difficult for a person in such a conspicuous position to have escaped suspicion even when practicing the greatest caution. And the two years' delay in granting him the papal decoration he so devoutly coveted, as well as his admission to the St. Cecilia Society, for which he had to wait three years,[6] may well have been traceable to derogatory reports filed against him during these first weeks in Rome when some impulsive remark, sparked by his impatience and personal annoyance, might very easily have attracted unpleasant interest in his person.

4 Spohr, *op. cit.,* II, 50; C. A. Eaton, *Rome in the Nineteenth Century,* III, 3.
5 Galiffe, *op. cit.,* 418–25.
6 Paganini's name was proposed by his friend Pietro Costagini on March 10, 1836, but he did not receive the diploma till February 12, 1839.

Paganini to Germi, Rome, December 23, 1818.

Although I've been silent for so long, you've been constantly in my thoughts and to prove it to you, I must tell you that I've not only scored the quartet for you but I've written you another in A minor [No. 14] which I hope you'll like. One of the movements—a *largo con sentimento,* the whole well worked out—will please you, I hope. If your Naples friend is a trustworthy person, I can give him the originals. Let me know. Here I haven't played one single hour. But tomorrow I'm going to begin to practice so as to get ready for the concert that I'm to give here the eighth of next month. My friend, you can't imagine how solitude weighs upon me now that I've changed my mind about marrying, because I should like to marry some very beautiful girl who is not interested in material advantages or singing. I feel a void within me that frets me terribly and I only wish that I might have the good fortune to find somebody to my taste so that I could marry. Yesterday evening I saw the most beautiful Englishwoman, to whom I lost my heart on the spot, but when I learned that she was a Jewess, I sighed and could almost have wept, knowing that a union was virtually impossible. I'll bet that if you'd seen her, you would have perhaps renounced religion in order to get her. The young lady in Bologna, who is sighing for me, sees from my last letter that I've cooled off a bit, so she wants to know the reason. Tell me what to say to her. I don't want to tell her that she no longer occupies my thoughts, but I've got to tell her something. Her papa is as strict with her as ever. Milzetti finds himself a little exposed, but I absolutely don't want to hear anything about it because she doesn't interest me.

"I still haven't played anywhere," he wrote Milzetti on December 30,[7] an unusual situation that must have worried him because it gave him no opportunity of parading his gifts in just those influential quarters that would have been most helpful to him with the Vatican. C. W. Eaton, an Englishwoman who spent the preceding winter in Rome, wrote that the only music to be heard there was "at the opera—certainly the worst in Italy—or at a reception or concert given at one of the embassies." But Niccolò still had no entry into this exclusive social world. However, as the theatres reopened on December 26, life from then on was a little more exciting, though he soon came to the conclusion that the "Roman public didn't care for scientific and philosophical music"; it liked only

7 This letter, No. 25 in Codignola, is incorrectly dated October. Paganini wrote the characteristic abbreviation "10" meaning the tenth month of the Roman year. (Decem – 10. The meaning of -ber is obscure.)

works "in waltz style played with a solo flute and *una mezza chitarra."* In comparison with Milan and other places, the musical atmosphere of the Eternal City left, in Niccolò's opinion, much to be desired.

Whilst his letters convey no information regarding his extra-professional activities, now and then a name slips through that shows that he was gradually getting acquainted, particularly in artistic circles. There were numerous distinguished foreign artists in Rome that winter and it is very likely that he met many of them at one time or another in the studios of Canova[8] or Ingres, amongst them Johann Friedrich Overbeck, Peter von Cornelius, and Wilhelm von Schadow,[9] who worked in Rome from 1810 till 1819 and whom Paganini was to meet again in Germany, where Schadow was then one of the leaders of the so-called Berlin school. It was also at this time that Ingres made his well-known crayon portrait of him. According to an article in Bénézit's *Dictionnaire Critique et Documentaire des Peintres* (Vol. 5, p. 65), Ingres made about three hundred such little crayon portraits *"qu'il faisait payer 40 francs et dont un grand nombre lui furent procurés par l'entremise de son barbier."* Paganini, however, seems to have merely served as model since there is no evidence that he ever acquired the portrait. Although greatly idealized and departing drastically from the traditional conception of the Maestro through the serene gaze, the poise and spiritual calmness, the apparent ease and opulence, the portrait has some points of resemblance (suggested rather than actual) with the Patton portrait of 1832. There is the same high brow, the same dignity, the same un-Italian look, yet still the end effect is formal, cold and artificial, a model *"gonflé d'une matière molle et non vivante, étrangère à l'organisme humain"* which Baudelaire considered as the hallmark of all this artist's portraits.

ii

After six years of resounding successes in northern Italy, where he had become "an archetype in the public mind" of what a virtuoso ought to be, he no doubt felt that he need only voice a wish to see it gratified, with the result that the delays and obstacles he encoun-

---

8 C. A. Eaton, *op. cit.,* III, 314.
9 *Ibid,* III, 330.

tered irritated him till he was prone to exaggerate every passing vexation (as when the Spanish violinist Teodore Segura called on him with a letter of introduction from Milzetti and on the strength of this inveigled him into playing for him "for five minutes") till it even spilled over into his correspondence.

Paganini to Milzetti, Rome, December 30, 1818.
It grieves me greatly, not only that Segura concealed his status from me, but to see how little probity there is in the world. I also hear that he gave concerts in Spoleto, Terni, and Narni with a certain Morandi, a professor of violin who took him to America. If he should return to Bologna, don't let him know that I'm so well informed. And if he ever wants the Stradivari that I have in Genoa, tell him that I've refused 500 louis d'or for it. They say in Rome that at his concert in one of the aforesaid towns he used my name instead of Segura, and I can well believe it because one day here a wretched guitarist announced himself as Paganini and received all the congratulations.

It was infuriating to think that despite all his precautions he had been so easily taken in, and the circumstance rankled for some time. Thus, it was probably one or two experiences of this kind, in a period of tension, that led him later to take such extreme measures to checkmate prospective eavesdroppers.

Waiting vainly day after day for the desired permission, he finally came to the conclusion towards the end of January that there was little chance of his ever obtaining it. The clergy were still silent and unyielding and as the question narrowed down to a contest between two inflexible and resolute opponents and he realized that he had only four more weeks "before the darkness of the Cross fell across the carnival city," he "made up his mind to leave for Naples" and mark Rome, like Piedmont, off his books. In fact, he was all ready to set off when "various distinguished persons who had undertaken to secure the requisite permission" begged him to postpone his departure till they made one final effort to persuade the obstinate authorities. Then a few days later, to his great delight, the papal secretary of state, Cardinal Albani,[10] granted permission for a single concert on Friday, February 5, at the Teatro Argentina, which proved such an overwhelming success that, contrary to all

[10] Cardinal Albani (1750–1835), created cardinal by Pius VII in 1801, and appointed cardinal secretary of state and librarian by Pius VIII.

precedent, the Vatican capitulated and extended the permission to the two remaining Fridays. According to Chateaubriand, Albani was the *"executor des hautes oeuvres de l'Autriche"* within the Vatican—"rich and extremely avaricious, he is involved in all sorts of enterprises and speculations. . . . *Un homme d'esprit, faux par caractère et franc par humeur; sa violence désoue sa ruse; on peut en tirer parti en flattant son orgueil et satisfaisant son avarice."*[11] Thus we have every right to assume that Paganini's powerful Austrian friends resorted to diplomacy, or even to more practical measures. At any rate, though wisely silent on his tactics, as with his "title" later, he was immensely proud of the achievement and never failed to emphasize it when speaking of these early years.

Whether through opportunism or natural bent, yet in keeping with his always servile attitude towards the regime in power, Paganini's conduct at this time suggests that he was more sympathetic to Metternich and his policy than to a united Italy; for besides nursing a frank disdain for the Carbonari,[12] which would have made it impossible for him to have taken their oath of "eternal hatred against all monarchies," the independence of Italy, to which they were pledged to give their lives, seems to have meant very little to him. Since his mid-adolescence, when he and his father had taken active part in the brief Jacobin uprising of 1797, he had passed through much political unrest; so the smouldering fires in southern Italy evidently did not impress him. His patriotic fervor, as distinct from a strong feeling of national solidarity, had burnt out long ago, or had been summarily stifled by some unpleasant personal experience of which we have no record. After he had grown to manhood, his tendency was always to move on to quieter scenes as soon as thunderheads appeared on the horizon. On more than one occasion during the next two years he found himself in the midst of a cauldron—in Rome, in Naples, and in Sicily—yet he always slipped through without mishap by preserving a cryptic silence respecting his personal opinions.

Besides establishing his position in the Roman musical world, the three pre-Lenten concerts netted him the handsome sum of

11 Chateaubriand, dispatch to Count Portales, April 2, 1829.

12 The Carbonari, or charcoal burners, were an offshoot of the freemasons, probably originally related to the secret society of the Charbonniers, an early form of trade-union.

1350 *colonnati* (between 6750 and 8100 lire), which, in addition to the prospect of some lucrative private engagements after Easter, made him feel unusually generous and called to mind once more his Venetian protégée, Lauretta, whom he now hoped—by holding out material bait—to entice to Naples on the pretence, of course, of furthering her singing.[13]

Paganini to Antonio De Pagliari, Rome, February 24, 1819.
I'm too convinced of your sincerity and of your splendid friendship to doubt what you say in favor of Lauretta. However, I agree with the last paragraph of your letter in which you say that women are too cunning, so that it is almost impossible to know exactly what is going on in their hearts. It often happens that a woman refuses the honors of a king to amuse herself with a mule driver, and whoever is ignorant of the latter considers her as a heroine. I don't want to put Lauretta in that class but very often certain refusals are publicized so as to enjoy more tranquilly secret love affairs. Let us take her, however, from her good side and let us with good conscience give praise where praise is due. As you will already have seen from my previous letter, I'm breaking with Lauretta completely, owing to her proud and far from good character. But I intend to go on helping her, and before long you'll note the effects of my assistance. Today I'm writing to Naples to try to get her into the conservatory of music there, where, if she really has the will and disposition to study, she can achieve something within a short time. Without being unjust to your friend Mayr, I've in general a poor opinion of him. Some of those with little musical talent and less science only try to swindle their pupils—others interest themselves solely in the individual without caring if they succeed or not. However, bearing this in mind I've made my decision and within a short time I'll let you know the answer I receive. Therefore, tell Lauretta of my idea and see what she thinks of it. Friday evening I gave the third big concert in the Teatro Argentina, and here, too, important people say that I've been a most fortunate artist in having so greatly pleased such a difficult public. Tuesday I'm leaving for Naples.

Did Lauretta respond to these renewed overtures? Apparently not. She evidently had a more attractive *mulattiere* nearer home!

13 Paganini wrote Milzetti that the first concert had brought in 412 scudi, the second 616 and the third 600. Pulver (*op. cit.,* 67) wrote that the first "concert was not a very brilliant affair, the locale was very unsuitable and the audience far from numerous." He derived his information from Finck's article on Paganini in the 1835 edition of Schilling's *Lexikon* which was based on a description by G. E. Sievers of a concert given by Paganini in Rome in 1826! The 1819 concerts all took place in the Teatro Argentina.

iii

That he had "found favor" with a Roman public was doubly gratifying since he often must have heard that Naples, the real goal of
this southern tour, was the hardest place in Italy to achieve an
unchallengeable triumph, particularly for an instrumentalist, the
opera-loving Neapolitans being fundamentally less interested in
music of this type. In addition to this local attitude towards art,
which made every debut problematical, the great underground of
politics in this part of the peninsula was now shaken by violent
tremors that presaged imminent revolution, with the result that
every stranger was regarded as a spy till he had proved the contrary.[14] It was therefore more than ever imperative to walk warily
and not only be careful not to alienate any of the music patrons
"through rude and discourteous behavior"—one of his most frequent transgressions in these years—but to keep his opinions to
himself, something that, with his acquired caution, was less difficult to do. The days between his arrival and his opening concert
he therefore spent reveling in the beauty of the city, wandering
amidst the milling crowds of "barefoot monks and richly robed
prelates, soldiers and fine ladies, misshapen beggars and prostitutes, fishermen and sailors, artists, and foreign milords" that
thronged the Via Toledo, admiring the "carriages and coaches with
their horses adorned with great scarlet feathers and bells," enjoying the suaver climate after the moist, warm Roman sky, and in
between expending all his charm in a coterie of musicians whose
opinion he respected and whose approval he was most anxious to
obtain.[15]

Conestabile recounts a little episode told him by Onorio di Vito
and confirmed later by Mercadante, which shows the hidden ani-
mosity he had to overcome during his first weeks in Naples—the
meed of every artist who had garnered his bays elsewhere.[16] According to the story, a musical club numbering among its members all
the leading instrumentalists, planned to subject this boasting
Ligurian to an acid test by making him prove himself at an official
trial by his peers, if possible before his debut. To this end he was

14 Continental Italy was French in sympathy, while Sicily was in the British orbit.
15 Origo, *Leopardi*, p. 237.
16 Onorio di Vito, born in Arpino, 1792.

invited to a musical gathering where he was asked to play at sight the first violin part of an extremely difficult quartet specially fabricated for this purpose by the young composer-violinist, Giuseppe Danna. Long accustomed to taking hurdles of this kind and probably suspecting the motives behind this overeagerness to hear him play this particular work, Niccolò was in no wise disconcerted and, after glancing at the score, attacked it with his usual air of sovereignty, even playing a portion of it on three strings after his E string broke; which left his auditors speechless with amazement. They thereupon decided that the reports from northern Italy were not exaggerated after all, so from that moment he might be said to have conquered the Neapolitans even before his appearance in the theatre.

Nevertheless, he still hesitated to take the big San Carlo theatre for his opening concert on March 31, preferring instead the smaller Teatro del Fondo;[17] which Fétis interpreted as an indication of temerity, a lack of self-assurance. But he was gauging the Paganini of 1819 by the artist of 1831, whose fame had reached international proportions and who felt that only the "largest and most distinguished theatre" in the city was in keeping with his prestige. Barbaja may also have persuaded him to play first in the smaller auditorium, a measure that was evidently fully justified since, according to the leading critic, "the first audience was more select than numerous." At all events, he was in the impresario's hands, for it was just as difficult in Naples as in Rome to find a proper auditorium— a point emphasized by Franz Kandler some years later, who wrote that for the average artist, the only alternative to a theatre "was a private drawing room."[18] As a friend of Barbaja's, Paganini naturally had no trouble in obtaining one of the court theatres but, even so, his application had to be routed to the King via official channels since Barbaja was unable to accord him the privileges of the orchestra and singers without the King's permission.

After arranging tentative dates at the San Carlo for June and July, he then returned to Rome in time for Easter, and nine days

---

[17] The Teatro Fondo was no less elegant than the San Carlo but usually gave operetta and ballet. Rossini originally wrote *Otello* for the Fondo, where it was produced for the first time.

[18] Franz Sales Kandler (1792–1831), German musicologist and critic, and at one time sopranist of the Vienna Court Opera.

later played at two official functions at the Teatro Tordinone in honor of the Austrian Emperor, the first on April 20, the second on May 4.[19] The day before the first recital he finally, after several months of silence, got round to writing Germi, though he told him very little about himself except to drop a hint that he had lost his heart—no news surely to this wise, discerning friend.

Paganini to Germi, Rome, April 19, 1819.
I wish two things for myself, first, that I might live with you—granting that I shall have money enough; the other—I want to leave you a little curious—but no! I'm in love with a young girl here in Naples with the education of a princess—and a *virtuosa*. I should be happy if she could reciprocate my feelings. In Naples I hope to have the Teatro San Carlo full for my second concert, which I shall give on my return, in view of the great uproar they made at the first one in the Teatro del Fondo. Tomorrow evening the government is giving a big function for His Majesty in the Teatro Tordinone, or Apollo—illuminated *a giorno*—with a concert by Paganini. . . . The fee (for two concerts) has already been fixed at 2500 *scudi-colonnati*. . . . As regards my sister Domenica, do something for her; anything you do will be well done. But one should never do good deeds, so as not to be repaid with ingratitude. However, I leave the matter entirely to your wise judgment.

The Austrian Emperor, accompanied by Metternich and the latter's daughter, Countess Esterhazy, had arrived in Rome at the end of March, and ten days after Easter, Prince Kaunitz,[20] Austrian ambassador to the Holy See, gave a large reception in their honor and engaged Niccolò to entertain the six hundred guests. This represented the Maestro's first appearance before the influential circles of Roman diplomatic and patrician society. A passing indisposition having prevented Metternich from being present and his curiosity having been aroused by his daughter's enthusiastic account of Niccolò's performance, he sent for him, probably with the intention of inviting him to Vienna since Niccolò appeared without his instrument, indicating that the flattering summons was not interpreted as a "command performance." However, soon succumbing

19 Mary Shelley must have heard him on one of these occasions. In September, 1822, she resided for some time at Albaro, near Genoa, and also might have heard him there since he was in Genoa at this time for about six months.

20 *Diario di Roma* (April 24, 1819). Friedrich and Dorothea Schlegel were in the Emperor's retinue. Grillparzer was also in Rome at this time.

to the Chancellor's charm and to the Countess Esterhazy's complimentary assurance that he had been *"toute la fête,"* he voluntarily
seized the Chancellor's violin and played for him. Then later in
the day he returned with his own Guarneri to play the works performed at the reception, no doubt for an informal gathering of
members of the Emperor's suite. (In Paganini's autobiographical
sketch he referred to Metternich's companion as "his wife," but
Princess Metternich was already fatally ill and did not accompany
him to Italy.)[21]

Nearly all Paganini's Italian biographers frown with grave disapproval on such subservience to the conquistadors and spoilers of
his country. But it would be obtuse not to recognize that first of all
he was a plebian and had none of the aristocrat's fierce pride before
the conqueror. Then, too, it must be borne in mind that he was a
member of a socially despised profession—that of the theatrical
world of entertainers who lived to please and were accustomed to
bow humbly to their betters, since their career and even their
existence hung largely on the favor of the great.[22] His attitude on
this and other similar occasions was of a piece with his philosophy
for, though a democrat at heart, he was a royalist by ambition and
always subordinated his patriotic emotions to a calculating self-
interest. That he should have been courted by the aristocracy notwithstanding his "deficient education" and modest family background witnesses not only to his genius but to the presence in his
personality of that rare glamor known as charm. For in those days
the musician was only beginning to be treated as something a little
better than a lackey; hence, to be singled out by the world's great
and accorded some personal attention was an achievement of which
he had every reason to be proud. In this particular instance, it must
also not be overlooked that Metternich himself was an extremely
able violinist and at his musical soirees, formal and informal, often
performed with Vienna's most famous artists. Thus, there was here

21 Princess Metternich died later in the year. Countess Marie and her sister Clemen-
tine died in 1820.

22 Liszt wrote that "in the aristocratic houses of London, artists of the first rank,
such as Moscheles, Rubini, Lafont, Pasta, Malibran, and others, were forced to enter
by the service stairs and when they reached the drawing room were separated from
the guests by a cord stretched across the room." In 1835, Liszt published six articles
in which he made a plea to "raise and ennoble the position of artists through abolition
of the abuses and injustices with which they were faced."

a distinct community of interest, Niccolò's enthusiasm taking fire from the Prince's admiration and true appreciation of his gifts, whilst Metternich's compliments were grounded on something more satisfying to the born musician than the usual obliging condescension of the aristocrat.

iv

The middle of May saw Paganini back in Naples, where for well over a year he then divided his time between the mainland and Palermo. The climate, the people, "the vigor and violence and clamor" of Neapolitan life suited him in every way, and he was very happy and contented, wasting—with the exception of two concerts and a little sporadic composition—many months in quasi-idleness.

Paganini to Germi, Naples, July 20, 1819.
My health is good, except that I suffer from the excessive heat, which has now let up a bit. Nothing is more flattering for me than the praise and the applause I received at the three concerts I gave here in the royal theatres before a fastidious public which prides itself on being able, and with good reason, to pass judgment on musical matters. I need only mention that the first evening I played at the Teatro San Carlo this public, in thus applauding me, contravened a regulation of the court which provides that when the court is present there shall be no sign of approval or disapproval till the latter has begun to applaud. They didn't wait and with incessant clapping and cries of "Evviva!" enthusiastically applauded me and called me out three times in succession. I'm living very economically; therefore, you needn't fear that I'm squandering health, peace of mind, and money. This city is beautiful, enchanting. A splendid climate, magnificent scenery, the finest food and wines, luxuriant carriages, public parks as riant as the gardens of the Hesperides, charming women. But Paganini lives half Stoic and half prudent Genoese. I shall give a couple more concerts and then when the weather gets cooler, I shall go to Palermo. From there I shall make a musical tour of Italy on my way to Vienna (invited by Prince Metternich) and then on to Paris and London. And from this advantageous peregrination will spring that honest leisure that I wish to achieve for the impotent years to come. There, dear friend, you have my plans if Heaven lets me live. . . . Meanwhile I'm doing myself honor and adding to my little treasure . . . and don't bother about the malicious. Keep well, and let me in return give you some good advice: cut out Bacchus. This god is as much to be feared as that charming prostitute Venus.

After three more concerts at the smaller Teatro dei Fiorentini,[23] he left for Palermo, where he remained uninterruptedly till the end of March, 1820.

Paganini to Germi, Palermo, January 31, 1820.
I see that you've received the quartets . . . Signor Bollasco will deliver the others to you, i.e., Nos. 11, 12, and 13. Play them patiently and you won't find them bad. The finale of the last one you will have heard in the first quartet without guitar. However, since it's not yet printed, I thought I ought not to forget it. In Turin you will have suffered from the cold though not from boredom. There are lots of prostitutes there. Milzetti tells me that Banti sends me her regards. What a pity she isn't as beautiful as she is good! In Naples I made the acquaintance of a very charming girl of eighteen, beautiful as an angel, with the education of a princess and a heavenly voice and an interpretative gift that bewitches everyone. She sings divinely and her name is—guess! Catalani, daughter of one of the leading and most successful lawyers in Naples. The young lady would gladly marry me but I don't know if her parents would consent, because the Neapolitans don't like to see their daughters leave home. Well, we'll see! I too will think it over before tying myself up. Liberty is the best of all things. [He is here quoting the medieval Latin proverb: *Libertas optima rerum!*] I gave my first concert here in the Teatro Carolino. I can't describe to you the enthusiasm of the audience. The Princess, who doesn't like to applaud,[24] overwhelmed me (with applause), as did also the public, and said that if I gave forty concerts she'd go many miles to hear them. When I'm out walking, the people crowd round me, encircle me; in short, I very rarely leave the house. . . . Rolla's son is an excellent player—an astute rascal who has profited greatly from my style when I played duets with him at his father's request. Up to now I've kept that girl in Venice supplied with money so that she could take singing lessons and because I thought she was true to me.[25] But here in Palermo there's a lady who was in Milan when I was there. As she thought I was definitely through with the Venetian for all time, she let out everything to me about the latter's conduct. She's in love with a painter and went to his house and was seen and reproved by this lady and the painter's landlady. And their clandestine meetings lasted for a long time, that is, for over a year. The painter himself, a certain Signor Carloni, *my friend,*[26] still has her pic-

23 At the concert of August 18 he played his variations on *Non più mesta* for the first time.

24 The Duchess of Calabria, Maria Isabella, Infanta of Spain, second wife of Francesco, Duke of Calabria, who later became Francesco I.

25 He is here referring to Signora Lauretta, not to Bianchi as has hitherto been assumed. Since Lauretta's family lived in Brescia, he may have made her acquaintance when he played there in 1813 and then took her to Milan with him.

ture. At last I'm free and happy, and all the more so when I think of my dear Germi. *Io t'amo di tutto cuore.*[27]

Carlo Carloni, a well-known portrait painter of that day, was a friend of Henri Beyle, who wrote that "he had the real instinct for portraiture," all his pictures being remarkable for their pronounced fidelity to the model. "He makes large miniatures in black and red crayons and has had the wit to keep copies of all the portraits of the remarkable women he has painted during his lifetime." This explains the picture episode that Paganini and his no doubt envious informant interpreted as proof of Lauretta's infidelity.

Up to now he rarely mentioned his health, so that it was not till his return to Naples in the spring of 1820 that we learn that in Sicily he had been ill enough to require the services of a physician. Although his letters give no hint of the nature of the illness, one senses that the suspicion had begun to force itself upon him that his ailment was of a very serious nature. For from now on he complains more and more of his miserable state of health, that winter marking the real beginning of his preoccupation with his infirmities, which increased as his ills mounted and his vitality decreased. His intemperate use of powerful laxatives also dates from this period, when his Palermo doctor prescribed the Roob cure;[28] at least this unnamed medico effectively planted in his mind the idea that this was the only way to eliminate from his system the "hidden poison" that was attacking his organism and threatening prematurely to incapacitate him both physically and professionally.[29]

26 One of Carloni's most notable works was a copper engraving of the French war minister, Count Achille Fontanelli. He signed his works: *CC dip. ed incia.* He settled in London later.

27 Dr. Julius Siber in his work *Paganini, a Psychological Study,* which appeared in the *Jahrbuch für Sexuelle Zwischenstufen* in 1914, advanced the theory that Paganini's "hysteria, tendency to tears, irritability, carelessness in dress, vanity, femininity, the mania of posing as sick in order to arouse the sympathy of others, and his negative reaction to women" represented the indisputable hallmarks of the homosexual.

28 Roob (from the Arab *robb,* or the Persian *rob, rub,* meaning fruit syrup) is the juice of a fruit reduced by boiling to the consistency of syrup and preserved with sugar, the product being similar to the electuaries with a base of fruit or vegetable juices.

29 When he left for Vienna, he took with him, according to his notebook, an envelope containing prescriptions "for shortening one's life." Perhaps he had heard of the sometimes dire effects of venereal infection and was taking the necessary precautions. It would therefore appear that at this time the possibility of suicide was ever present with him.

One of the favorite "Paganini anecdotes" is associated with his failing health and an unpleasant experience that allegedly befell him at this time, though, if there is any foundation for the tale, which seems extremely doubtful, it could only have occurred much later and under entirely different circumstances. According to Pancaldi, the original narrator, Paganini could get no relief for his nervous, hacking cough, so upon the advice of his physician he took two rooms in the suburb of Petrajo, "under the fortress of St. Elmo,"[30] where he would have the benefit of fresh country air and greater tranquillity. His condition, however, continued to grow worse and, as the rumor spread that he was suffering from consumption, the fear of contagion so alarmed his landlord that he had the "inhumanity" to turn his poor bedridden guest out into the street.[31] Just then, Niccolò's pupil, Gaetano Ciandelli,[32] fortunately happened to pass by and, after administering a good drubbing to the landlord, carried his helpless friend off to comfortable quarters and cared for him till he was well.

Codignola was the first to question the authenticity of the incident (which apparently rested on no better authority than hearsay),[33] pointing out that apart from the fact that Paganini's correspondence gives no hint of any protracted illness at this time, he was far too prominent a figure for the Neapolitans to have countenanced such treatment or for any landlord to have attempted it— a statement fully substantiated by a later letter showing that Niccolò resided in Petrajo, not in 1820 but in the spring of 1826, when, of course, he was accompanied by Antonia Bianchi and his little son.

Paganini to Vincenzo degli Antonj, Naples, March 10, 1826.
Having moved to a house in the country very close to Naples on the

30 A corruption of St. Erasmus. The fortress was constructed in 1329 by Robert d'Angio.

31 Belief was so strong that consumption was contagious that many leading Italian physicians of the eighteenth century refused to perform autopsies on patients who died of phthisis, and in 1699 the Republic of Lucca was the first in Italy to promulgate antituberculosis legislation. See *The White Plague*, by Réné and Jean Dubois (Boston, 1952).

32 Gaetano Ciandelli taught cello in the Conservatory of San Pietro a Majella from 1844 to 1865.

33 Codignola (*op. cit.*, 33) attributes the story to Schottky. Schottky does not mention it. It appeared first in Conestabile (*op. cit.*, 152, n. 1), who took it from Pancaldi's unpublished memoirs.

slopes of Petrajo in order to cure my cough, which torments me fiercely, I'm here under the care of the excellent Dr. Calisi and after two or three months of treatment I shall be entirely cured.

However terrified the landlord might have been, he would hardly have attempted forcibly to eject his famous tenant while the temperamental Bianchi was standing by, though he might, of course, have requested him to seek other quarters in view of the general superstition that consumption was dangerously contagious. It is also possible that Niccolò may have had such an experience in some small town or posting station while touring northern Italy, since inn and tavern keepers along the way, who thought nothing of robbing and killing a man, would not have hesitated to turn a *jettatore* out of doors if they thought him capable of casting an evil eye on their activities or visiting them with some incurable disease.

v

After the verdict had been brought against him in the Cavanna case in November, 1816, he managed for a time to avoid both the clutches of the law and the payment of the damages, but in June, 1818, Cavanna's widow, who had remarried after her husband's death, instituted suit to collect the outstanding sum and again won the case, the court sustaining the first verdict and condemning Niccolò to pay not only the costs of the litigation but interest on the outstanding damages from November, 1816, to September 26, 1820, the date when his 20,000 lire at Masnata's reverted to him and could be attached by the court in the event of his continued failure to settle the obligation. With all avenues of escape now barred he wisely agreed to settle for 4400 lire, though actual payment, for some reason, was not made till August, 1820.

Paganini to Germi, Naples, May 3, 1820.
You could not have made a more advantageous adjustment. Bravo, Germi! I never thought such a tiresome business could have been interred with such an insignificant sum as 4400 lire. . . . I'm glad to hear that my mother can use the remaining 2600 lire. Give her my most affectionate greetings. . . . Here they wallop certain so-called Neapolitan Carbonari on their behinds, and none too gently; but in my opinion they merit even worse.[34] Why don't you come to Naples? If you came

34 When the Carbonari revolution failed in 1821, the leaders went to France, where

by sea, you could go back with me by land after having a look at all these sights and wonders. If you could see Rome with all its elegance, it would divert you enormously.

May 29, 1820.
My quartets will perhaps be consigned to the flames.[35] Keep away from bad guitarists. In Palermo there are only mediocre guitarists, who play waltzes, variations, and other pieces by ear; but they can't produce a chord; which is why I haven't heard the quartets. I tried to have a go at them at Naples. There was Zefferini, cello, a discreet viola, and one of the best guitarists in Naples, but to my surprise he couldn't bring forth a proper tone and hadn't any idea of a chord. So we stopped offending the ears. . . . I must take great care of myself for about two months (on the advice of the leading doctors in Sicily). I want to regain my health for the tour I wish to make . . . and then perhaps we'll take a wife and even produce a *bambino* or *bambina*. The Naples lawyer—who is really a bonehead—informed my spokesmen that he refused his consent because he was convinced that I'd make a woman of the theatre of his daughter. So perhaps they'll marry her off to a Calabrian.

While in Sicily he had had ample opportunity of observing the activities of the Carboneria, which was there a popular movement;[36] so his lack of sympathy with its aims may have been one of the principal motives for his return to Naples, where he arrived just in time for drama. The Naples revolution, which was intended to sound the tocsin for a general uprising, was initiated on July 2 by Don Menechini's "little insurrection," followed on the sixth by the proclamation of a constitution and the entry into the city of General Pepe's army, which kept the populace in a state of agitation for some time. By July 16 the unrest had spread to Palermo and, by August, civil war in earnest was raging in the Isola di Sole, though the Naples revolt, which had been looked upon "as the dawn of liberty and independence," turned out to be little other than a fizzle. Nevertheless, for those living in the midst of it, the

---

they became associated with other radical circles. This may explain in part Paganini's later refusal to play at any of the benefits for Italian refugees in Paris. According to Giuseppe La Farini, eight hundred citizens were condemned to death for the cause of liberty, and more than twice that number were sent to prison or the galleys.

35 Paganini's quartets are not real quartets in the strict sense of the word since the first violin predominates while the other instruments play more the role of an accompaniment.

36 Iris Origo, *The Last Attachment,* 201, states that in southern Italy the party "consisted almost entirely of the prosperous but discontented middle classes."

weeks before and after the upheaval must have been fraught with nervous tension; yet in none of Paganini's letters—even one written at the height of the excitement—is there evidence of a direct impact of events.[37] Indeed, he might well have been a hundred miles away; though an accident that befell him in May, if not occasioned by an attempt to escape an irate father or husband, might have been traceable to his disinclination to align himself with the revolutionary party. "My bodily fall was all too true! [he wrote Germi on July 7]. I can still feel those damned twenty-nine steps![38] A human fall would perhaps have cost me less."

It was while convalescing from the fall that he wrote his quartet No. 15, dedicated to Marquis Niccolò Crosa di Vergagni, of Genoa.

Paganini to Germi.
Only you may have a look at it. I'm quite satisfied with this work, written during my convalescence. If you'd like to copy it, or send it along as it is, it is all up to you. I'll trust to your discretion. . . . I believe this music will prove pleasing because it is well written and well sustained. Add a word to the Recitative; it should be: *Andante sostenuto con sentimento.* The word *sostenuto* is missing. The best professors here make the mistake of hurrying the tempo and this drives me wild.

Whether or not the fall had anything to do with it, he now decided that he was through with women, though as usual the mood rapidly vanished as soon as he was able to move about again.

Paganini to Germi, July 7, 1820.
My heart is rendered impervious to love. I'm beginning to appreciate men, since I'm now beginning to think better. As for the women, though I at times despise them, they occupy a place in my heart because they afford me delicious moments.

[August 8]
The other day I saw a nice young girl in a church and I fell a little in love with her. I followed her to see where she lived. She's the daughter of a notary. What do you advise? Shall I marry her or remain a bachelor?

37 It is quite possible that he referred to political events but Germi cautiously destroyed the letters to prevent their falling into the hands of informers who might have made trouble for his friend.

38 Boucher de Perthes wrote that in Leghorn the "apartment on the ground floor was the cheapest."

During the day it was too hot to expend either mental or animal energy, but in the cool of the evening, after the recuperative siesta, he spiced his existence with music making, the opera, convivial evenings with his musical colleagues, or with some black-eyed, racy Neapolitan nymph who "afforded him delicious moments." "I can't leave at once for Genoa [he hastened to assure his friend]. I've suffered two months and a half of almost intolerable heat. Let me get a little fresh air, which we are anticipating shortly."

But it was not only the hot weather that delayed him. After the long convalescence following his fall, he developed a painful boil on his thigh, which laid him up again for nearly a month and banished all thoughts of concerts for the rest of the year. Yet with all his aches and pains, his worries and exasperations, his infatuations and disillusionments, he was never physically too miserable or emotionally too engrossed to lose his sense of practical obligation towards the members of his family, to forget their needs, their comfort, and well-being. Although he was often behindhand in his correspondence with his private almoner in Genoa, the thought of any of his kin was always sufficient to twitch him into galvanic action. Indeed, his constant solicitude for his mother and his sisters in the midst of worries that would have lamed a lesser will had a touch of sweetness in it—an almost feminine tenderness.

Paganini to Germi, September 5, 1820.
I feel exactly as you do and will gladly comply with all my mother's wishes. Let her have a place in Genoa that's suitable for any time of her life and I'll increase the capital to 30,000 lire.[39] I hope you'll close that unfortunate account and tell me how much is left. As to the Vigne house, if my mother likes it, I'm also ready to contribute to it, and thus I shall have a place ready in case I come to visit her sometimes and eat the good *ministrone* that she makes so divinely. I'm annoyed to hear that she shares her allowance, which should go to her alone. . . . Since my little house in Ramairone is in such an inaccessible spot, I think it would be well to sell it, that is, if it doesn't suit my mother. If my brother-in-law could repay the 6000 lire, I could increase my mother's capital. Dear friend, tell me, advise me, arrange things so that I can do everything properly and without reflecting so as to be more worthy of my mother's love and that of my family,[40] as well as of my dear Germi.

39 He is referring to the original annuity of 20,000 lire, which he had taken out for his parents before leaving Genoa with Angelina Cavanna in 1815. Referring to this letter, Pulver (106) wrote that "Paganini sent Germi the respectable sum of 30,000 francs to be invested for his mother's benefit," an error due to ignorance of the annuity.

vii

If political events in Naples had no immediate repercussions on Paganini, this was not so with his friends Barbaja and Rossini, for whom the change in government, by depriving Barbaja of the King's powerful patronage and his own monopoly of the gaming houses, represented a sudden and drastic turning in their lives. During the carnival of 1820, Barbaja had produced Rossini's latest work, *Mametto II,* while Paganini was in Palermo; then, during the uncertain weeks when it looked as though Rossini must seek another backer, he received a commission from the Roman banker Torlonia to write a work *(Mathilde de Shabran)* for the inauguration, during the coming carnival, of the Teatro Apollo (the former Teatro Tordinone), which Torlonia had purchased and completely renovated. This for the time being took care of Rossini; then Barbaja, presumably through Count Wenzel von Gallenberg,[41] who was later associated with him at the Royal Opera in Vienna, was appointed impresario of the Vienna court theatres, which gave his career also a new turning. It was Paganini's original idea to leave Naples with Rossini the middle of November, maybe on purpose to be present at the première of a work whose composition he no doubt had followed closely scene by scene during its inception and development. But at the last moment his departure was postponed so that he did not reach Rome till the end of January, literally just in time to come to the aid of his now distracted friend. Immediately upon Rossini's arrival, Luigi Vestri, impresario of the Apollo, had put the new work into rehearsal but a nemesis now seemed to stalk behind Rossini—a continued round of annoyances and petty frustrations that culminated on the eve of the dress rehearsal in the sudden death of the conductor (Bolle) and the disastrous discovery that there was no capable substitute in Rome.

With his emotional temperament, Rossini was naturally at his wits' end when Paganini then gallantly stepped into the breach and offered to direct till a suitable conductor could be found.

40 In 1821, Germi rented an apartment for Teresa on the third floor of Piazza Sarzana, No. 1514.

41 Wenzel von Gallenberg (1783–1839), pupil of Albrechtsberger, lived in Italy from 1802–1803, where he married Countess Giulietta Guicciardi, to whom Beethoven dedicated the Moonlight Sonata, and who for a long time was thought to be Beethoven's "immortal beloved."

"Through bonds of tender and disinterested friendship [according to the *Diario di Roma*] he not only conducted the rehearsal but the first two performances, and with a mastery and *élan* that swept all the performers off their feet, bringing out the very finest that was in them."[42] He even played on a viola a difficult horn solo, in the absence of a horn player who suddenly had been taken ill, and not only led the orchestra but "acquainted both singers and instrumentalists with the composer's intentions in the fullest sense of the word,"[43] thereby rendering Rossini a service that he never forgot.

The second of Paganini's own concerts at the theatre, which had been announced for March 2, was postponed a day "by reason of extraordinary circumstances," the "circumstances" being nothing other than a little carnival prank that he and Rossini had planned with two other friends, the singer Pisaroni and young Massimo d'Azeglio,[44] showing that like most great geniuses they could now and then gracefully descend from their pedestals to enjoy an unconventional lark.[45]

On the last Thursday of the carnival, the four dressed themselves as *ciechi,* the blind musicians who plied their trade in groups of two or three, one strumming a guitar or scraping a fiddle to accompany the others as they passed, singing, up and down the Corso between the brocade and flower-bedecked frontages of the palaces that formed the scenic background for the gay masquerade without. "Rossini [wrote D'Azeglio] increased his already rotund form by sheathing himself in voluminous folds of material so that he looked positively inhuman, while Paganini, already thin as a rail,

---

42 Leigh Hunt: "It is curious to observe with what masterly precision he gives the cue to the orchestra, how exact to the time his memory is, and with what instantaneous and easy nicety he takes up, as it were, the whole of the weight of the accompaniments on the tip of his bow and hangs it on the right peg. The official conductor at the pianoforte seems to sit staring in pure wonder, and the people that crowd behind the musicians on either side the stage turn around to one another with lifted hands and smiles of astonishment. All the orchestra appear mechanical and he the soul standing in front." (*Loc. cit.,* Vol. II, 1011.)

43 After the second performance Paganini relinquished the baton to Giovanni Campi.

44 Massimo d'Azeglio was Manzoni's son-in-law. His father was head of the Taparelli family.

45 This episode is badly garbled in Pulver's biography. He makes two incidents out of it, the first time associating it with Rossini and Meyerbeer in December, 1817, and the second time giving the D'Azeglio version and dating it February, 1822.

with a face like the neck of a violin, looked even thinner and more cadaverous than ever in his clinging feminine attire." As they made the rounds of the Corso, clowning and singing as they went, they were even invited into several patrician homes to sing their little ditty:

> *Siamo ciechi; siamo nati per campar di cortesia.*
> *In giornata d'allegria non si nega carita.*[46]

viii

After the Battle of Antrodoco (March 7) had brought to a tragic conclusion the first attempt to free Italy from the fetters of the Treaty of Vienna, Paganini returned to Naples, arriving at his destination shortly before General Frimont's Austrian troops (in response to the King's appeal to Metternich) took over the city on March 23. On the eve of his departure from Rome, "where everything was tranquil," he had sent his mother 3000 lire, part of the proceeds of his Roman concerts; which was a fortunate inspiration. For, as a result of the latest unrest in the southern part of the peninsula, in a world of brewing conflicts and the various restrictions attendant on the Austrian occupation, he could not resume his concert activities till the end of July. Meanwhile, the Neapolitan spring, combined with many weeks of idleness, precipitated him once more into an impassioned love affair in which the object of his infatuation incorporated for a season all the feminine graces he desired in a wife. At last he was prepared to marry as soon as the requisite formalities could be arranged.

In linking together his widely separated letters and trying to piece together a pattern of his day-to-day existence, one is tempted to surmise that when he was last in Genoa his family (like his Bologna friend Milzetti) had seriously urged him to abandon his restless, rudderless course and, like all Italians of his station, to marry, settle down, and raise a family, now all the more imperative in view of his rapidly increasing wealth. After breaking off his friendship with Lauretta and abruptly terminating his synthetic interest in her substitute Marina, he resumed his aimless philander-

---

[46] Translation: Blind from birth and dependent on your charity to live,
On this happiest of days, don't refuse a donative.

ing till his family again attempted to bring about a shift of focus in his attitude towards life and its responsibilities, which may explain his revived decision "to take a wife," a reaction quite in keeping with his quick responsiveness to any suggestion thrown out to him.

Paganini to Sebastiano Ghisolfi, Naples, January 18, 1821.
I was so delighted to get your letter and I appreciate more than ever my mother's very cordial sentiments, as well as your thanks for the little remembrance to my mother. Tell her that she will soon have more ample testimony, since a great fortune awaits me. I'm no longer going to break my neck in rushing off to London but shall proceed slowly, as follows: within a week I shall be in Rome to remain there for the carnival. I shall then play in Milan, Graz, Vienna, after this in Prussia and then on to London. There are indications that I am impatiently awaited everywhere and that my violin will bring me in the sums that will guarantee a good existence. Since I must travel for about two years more, a wife would embarrass me and for that reason there's time to think it over. . . . A kiss for my mother.

But by mid-June he had finally come round to the family's point of view.

Paganini to Germi, Naples, June 22, 1821.
I have finally decided to follow the dictates of my heart and also of my station and take a wife—a charming girl, the daughter of a most excellent family, who combines beauty with the most thorough education, has really touched my heart and, though she has no dowry, it has pleased me to choose her and be happy with her. Yes, if Heaven so wills I couldn't desire a greater happiness. My years will glide by happy and contented and I shall see myself mirrored in my children. Meanwhile, I require a certificate that I am unmarried, and I don't know a better friend than you to whom to address myself in order to get it as soon as possible. Therefore, do me the favor and obtain first of all my baptismal certificate from the parish priest of S. Salvatore, which should be round the year 1780. Then find someone else who knows me . . . and go to the Archepiscopal Chancery and file an affidavit that I'm unmarried. . . . Rush the matter through and banish my worries, because delay is directly fatal for me. . . . The civil statute of the French Code is still in force here so that I must have my father's death certificate. . . . My mother will best know where you can find it at once. You know that it is also necessary to have my mother's consent. Mine, as you know, can't write and I should be sorry if this should come to the ears of the

courteous family of my beautiful fiancée. Therefore, do me the favor and tell my mother that when she goes to the notary to file the certificate of consent, she should bind up her right thumb and when asked to sign she should say that she can't because she has a felon on that finger. Thus in this way we'll both save our bacon. In accordance with the French regulations, I must also furnish proof that my paternal grandparents are not living; please get this for me, since you know how it's done. Now comes the hard part. As to the baptismal certificate, I'm sorry to say that I've entered my fortieth year. If you could make an arrangement with the parish priest of S. Salvatore and it were possible to put me on the sunny side of forty, it would please me immensely. . . . You know my nature and can well understand the physical orgasm that has taken possession of me, excited by the most hypersensitive nerves and an exalted imagination. Now, if you don't want me to be devoured by desire carry out my wishes with the utmost dispatch, and crown the sweet destiny that is now in store for me. . . . I'm looking forward to presenting my Venus to you and making you confess that Paganini shuns mediocrity in everything. . . . Remember, I'm all in a stew till I have everything.

Nervous, impulsive, burning with desire, this impatient lover whose previous facile love affairs had not accustomed him to wait, was like an enamoured schoolboy. With the "adored Marina" still in mind, Germi may have felt that it would save him time and trouble if his giddy friend in Naples were obliged to reduce his speed a little till he had resolved the old conflict in his soul between the sensual and the ideal. "Heaven seems to wish this marriage— therefore, we're looking forward to happiness," wrote the optimist in Naples. Germi, the cynic, was not quite so sure. First of all, he must have more data. What, by the way, was the name of this divine creature with all the queenly graces?

Paganini to Germi, Naples, July 10, 1821.
Here you have the name of my beloved: Carolina Banchieri, daughter of the couple Teresa Ruiz and Romualdo Banchieri. I admire more and more the friendly and philosophical remarks in your letter. And while the friends to whom I read it laughed, my heart was filled with happiness because here a solicitous friend is speaking to me of my bride. What sweet names! I see indications everywhere that God wants to make me happy in this way. Beauty, education—these are the dowries that my taste demands. Heaven seconds my desires. . . . You, my mother, and whoever sees the object of my affections cannot help but admire

her and join with me in praising Heaven for having created a girl embodying all the physical and moral graces.

And there, as though fate wished to tease us and pique our curiosity, the correspondence ceases! It would be interesting to know if, and when, Germi supplied the necessary documents and why the marriage did not then take place. Although it might have required both time and patience to locate the baptismal certificate, all the other papers were at hand, so a fortnight at the most would have sufficed to gather them together. What was opposing the "sweet destiny" that Heaven had in store for him? Was this ardent Don Juan not so serious as he pretended and had he merely adopted this elaborate ruse to break down Carolina's maidenly defenses?

Further details of this hectic love affair remain unrecorded, but whatever happened between mid-July and the early autumn, he seems to have persuaded Carolina to join him on an excursion early in October, during which he abandoned her—to all intents and purposes a prosaic repetition of the Cavanna episode. Had her solicitious parents finally refused consent through his inability to furnish the most important document—a clean and satisfactory bill of health? The letter in which he informed Germi of the outcome of the "marriage that Heaven seemed to wish" is dated Parma, November 17, and was no doubt written a fortnight or more after the rupture, for it is quite obvious that Carolina never even got as far as Rome.[47] There were then four overnight stops on the post road from Naples to Rome—Capua, Gaeta, Terracina, and Velletri, at which latter place he presumably dropped her since he states that "four days" was the extent of the liaison. He then continued on his way alone, possibly stopping a day or two at Rome, Florence, and Bologna and arriving in Parma (a distance from Naples of about fifteen days' continuous traveling) sometime early in November.

---

[47] It took something over four days to cover the 148 miles between Naples and Rome. "There are no houses or villages to be seen in the whole extent [wrote Mary Shelley of the sector between Terracina and Velletri], if you except three miserable post houses. The people appear to gain their livelihood by sporting or robbing, where they dare."

Paganini to Germi, Parma, November 17, 1821.
I'm truly sorry not to have written you before now. For you alone I'll say that I found that object a real *sans-souci,* who disappointed me on every score; which is why I freed myself after four days, which seemed like four years to me. She's now with a peasant who will swear to everyone that she's been with her from the very moment she left home, so maybe in this way they'll think that nothing has occurred. I promised to return home, which I'll do at my convenience. Tomorrow I'm leaving for Vienna. . . . The moment I sent one packing I recalled the other one you know.[48]

Once more the "object" failed to tally with the invoice, but this time, fortunately, there was no unpleasant sequel to disturb his peace of mind, which suggests that Carolina may have been as relieved at the denouement as her tempestuous lover. But to whom was he referring in the last sentence (the postscript of his letter)? Presumably to the recalcitrant Lauretta or another rejected flame with whom he "had broken off relations" (*richiamai* is a revealing word!). If so, however, she must have declined his invitation since something obviously happened at this time to accelerate, if it did not cause, a serious nervous crisis. Given his reaction to Carolina— *her* loss could have occasioned no very deep regrets—his innate cynicism would have taken care of that, and had Bianchi been the recipient of his summons, as assumed by Codignola, the immediate results would not have been so serious. Nor, given his incalculable and wayward nature, would he have remained faithful to her for over two years before establishing a quasi-permanent relationship. For no one, even in self-interest, and surely no one so untamed as La Bianchi proved to be can transcend indefinitely the bounds of his own character or alter his innate temperament. Hence, long before the spring of 1824, Niccolò would have discovered those "great defects" that ultimately made life with her impossible.

48 There are certain things in this letter that might indicate that Carolina's parents were aware of the break. It was often customary at that time for the engaged couple, after the formal betrothal, to live together as man and wife. This may have been so in the present case and the parents may have made the arrangements with the peasant so as to prevent any possible gossip. For it is hardly likely that Carolina was in a position to force Paganini to "promise to return home to Genoa." This may have been the condition on which Carolina's parents agreed to the breaking of the engagement.

IX. *"TWO YEARS PASSED IN SADNESS"* 1822–1823

Was mich nicht tötet, macht mich stärker.—NIETZSCHE.

THE QUESTION of Paganini's movements from mid-November, 1821, till February, 1822, is infinite in conjecture. All we know from the scanty material that has come down to us is that in the early spring he was gravely ill, a condition no doubt induced by unbridled dissipation; for after the debacle of his matrimonial plans—with the previous feverish exaltation—it would have been characteristic of him that he plunged headlong into a licentious course, which then resulted in the usual reactions—emotional, nervous, physical.

It is presumed that Parma detained him till he received a reply from Carolina's prospective successor, with whom he could have had no personal relations for three full years at least. And it seems rather more than likely that his invitation was rejected, whereupon he went on to Milan, where either intemperance, a feeling of frustration, or the rapid progress of his maladies—the linked chain of cause and effect—ended in a serious and alarming breakdown that brought his mother and Germi hastening to his side so that Teresa could nurse him back to health.

Codignola advances the theory that he fell ill in Parma and returned to Genoa before going to Milan.[1] But an article in the Leipzig *Allgemeine Musikalische Zeitung* (No. 16) of March 23, which must have been written four to six weeks previously—the customary time lag with the Italian correspondence—reported that "Paganini is back again in Milan and is going to give a concert." We may therefore not unreasonably infer that up till then he was in his usual state of health. Moreover, in a letter of April 20, he distinctly refers to a "two months' bill" at the inn for himself, his mother, and his brother-in-law (who by April 17 had returned to Genoa), so that his illness must have occurred after Lichtenthal had

[1] Codignola, *op. cit.*, 197.

dispatched his article. Since, in his unsuccessful love affairs, he was not given to instinctive resignation, one cannot imagine his going home to Genoa to lick his wounds; and furthermore, his correspondence very clearly shows that, after returning to northern Italy, he was in Genoa only once, namely from the late autumn of 1822, when he took his mother home, till the end of May, 1823. In his letters from April to August, 1822, there are no references to his native city, as would surely have been the case had he recently been visiting there after an absence of five years. Then, too, the name of Camillo Sivori is not found till June, 1823, it being evident from this that their acquaintance dated from the preceding winter, which confirms the statement of Sir George Grove, who knew Sivori well, that Paganini taught him first in the winter of 1822–23.

By mid-April, when we again emerge from surmise into certainty, he was already convalescing, though still under his mother's watchful care—a wise provision on Germi's part since the flame ignited by Carolina's "physical and moral graces" must have threatened to consume everything before it till the rapid development of his tubercular heritage and acquired infection enforced a measure of self-restraint and brought him back, perforce, to a saner adjustment of his life.[2]

"My health is continually improving [he announced on April 30], but convalescence takes time." Although always immensely optimistic, he now had no illusions regarding the true nature of his malady, for his worst fears had recently been confirmed by Dr. Sira Borda (1761–1824)[3] of the University of Pavia, one of the most renowned Italian physicians of his day, who after making a thorough examination had frankly told him his "opinion." "Suspecting a syphilitic infection of fairly long standing," he first or-

[2] His chronic colitis was probably psychosomatic in nature. Berri: "Of a highly emotional temperament, Paganini now manifested a slightly neurotic tendency, which was probably accentuated by his tuberculosis. The *elettricismo*, as he called the tension and exaltation necessary for playing . . . has certain points of contact with mediumship on one hand and epilepsy on the other. It was not in vain that the ancients called epilepsy *Morbus sacer*, and looked upon epileptics as seers and prophets." J. F. Nisbet, in his *The Insanity of Genius*, also maintained that Paganini was epileptic.

[3] Borda was at first a disciple of Giuseppe Rasori and his theories of counter-stimulants. By 1822, Borda had changed his opinion very materially and even went so far as to burn many of his writings on the subject.

dered a course of treatments that could be followed in Milan, and till the opium and mercury "prescribed in murderous doses" (Paganini's phrase) began to react disastrously on his organism,[4] Niccolò seems to have profited slightly from the cure and to have had sufficient energy to interest himself in various professional matters, which kept at bay those doldrums of the spirit that ordinarily followed his serious bouts of illness and made any enforced idleness so fraught with danger for him.

Paganini to Germi, April 30, 1822.
You will have heard of Rossini's marriage to Colbran—they made a fool of Barbaja. Further, Colbran extracted twenty-four ducats from Barbaja a short time before the marriage took place on a sudden in Rome. . . . [5] As soon as I can I'm going to Field Marshal Pino's on the Lake of Como,[6] where I hope to get perfectly well. I also need to get away from the inn, which is a little too much of a drain on me financially and physically. Just imagine, after reaching an agreement about the rent, they charged me 50 lire for extra linen just because I was ill, with everything else in proportion. My bill for two months, without having eaten hardly anything; and with no wine whatever, amounted to about 400 lire, not including medicine and coffee. And the same with the bill for my mother and brother-in-law. I'm awaiting the speedy dispatch of the cello, which you should register by diligence and consign to the Locando del Pozzo, where I shall go to fetch it as soon as I receive word. . . . I have company continually but I'm not happy when I don't see you or have the hope of seeing you.

His elderly friend, General Domenico Pino (whom he was unable to visit till the following summer) had made a brilliant record in Napoleon's service but in 1814 his distinguished military career had unfortunately terminated under a cloud, he having alienated the sympathy and esteem of many of the Milanese through equivocal conduct during the April tumults following Napoleon's abdica-

4 Berri, *op. cit.*, 54. "Medicine at that time was empirical, fantastic, often deleterious."

5 In 1822, Metternich summoned Rossini to Verona to write a cantata for the festivities in connection with the Congress of Verona. In spite of his great admiration, he does not seem to have invited Paganini to participate. Although Paganini's health would have prevented his accepting such an invitation, he would surely have mentioned it with pride had he too received such a summons.

6 Domenico Pino (1769–1826). He left his property to his sister's son, Galeazzo Fontana (d. 1860), who took the name of Pino after his uncle's death. See Emilio Legnani, *L'ingresso trionfale in Milano del generale Domenico Pino.*

tion. Enlisting in the French army after the revolution, he had risen rapidly and was in command of the French forces entering Milan on Whitsunday, May 14, 1796. From then on he mounted continuously in the good graces of the Emperor, who, after his coronation in 1805, ennobled him and conferred on him the portfolio of Minister of War when a broken leg temporarily interrupted his military service. Two years later he returned to active duty and after taking part in the campaigns in Pomerania, Spain, and Russia was entrusted, at the time of Napoleon's downfall, with the military command of Milan, where he was then stationed. However, during the April revolts, he was accused of connivance with the Austrians in the hope of being appointed Viceroy, the suspicion being entertained, and even voiced quite openly, that he had offered them his services as an informer. Be that as it may, during a visit to Vienna in July of that year, he was raised by the Austrians to the rank of Field Marshal and then retired, after which he took up his residence on his wife's property in Cernobbio, on the Lake of Como, and from then on interested himself solely in the arts.

In June 1808, he had married Vittoria Peluso, known as La Pelusina, former prima ballerina of the Scala, who, though ten years his senior and by no means a beauty, had the immense advantage of being the wealthy widow of Marquis Bartolomeo Calderari, from whom she had inherited a palace in Milan and the Palazzo del Garrovo in Cernobbio (the present Hotel Villa d'Este), which had been originally built by Cardinal Tolomeo Gallio. After her marriage to Pino she greatly beautified the property and then sold it in July, 1815, to Caroline of Brunswick-Wolfenbüttel,[7] Princess of Wales, who resided there till her departure for England in April, 1820, at which time it was acquired by the Duke of Bracciano. After the sale of the estate, General Pino and the Countess retired to a smaller property in the vicinage, the so-called Villa Nuova, where he resided till his death in March, 1826.

I wrote a lot of music for General Pino [Paganini told Schottky], and I left with him a good part of my works for violin, guitar, and piano,

[7] Princess Caroline of Brunswick-Wolfenbüttel (1768–1821) married the Prince of Wales in 1795, and in 1813 left England and settled on the Continent. She returned to England in 1820 upon her husband's accession to the throne, and died a month after the latter's coronation.

which were sequestrated at the time of his death; but I still hope to find them when I return to Italy. I left some more of my musical manuscripts in Parma, which were unfortunately stolen while I was on tour. Pino, a friend who was like a father to me, also played the violin, his manner of performance being modeled on my own. When I was ill in Naples in 1826, I composed thirty-six works within a very short time, the first of which was a *Marche Funèbre* for Pino, who was longing for death, which came to him just as I had finished the march. I then sent it to another friend, the Genoese Antonio Botto, but before the manuscript reached him, he too was struck down, so I cursed the ill-fated composition and threw it away.[8]

As so often with his plans, he now found a number of obstacles that interfered with his departure. First of all, it was probably difficult to leave his mother, and then he had a succession of annoying minor ailments, which upset his personal arrangements till he ultimately had to postpone the visit altogether. Although Como was only two stages from Milan, the fortified barriers, customhouse officials, and police faced the traveler with many slow and tiresome formalities, while the Austrian garrison also shut the city gates and locked up the inhabitants at an early hour of the night, which could not have been a tempting thought for Niccolò

Paganini to Sebastiano Ghisolfi, Milan, May 14, 1822.
Mother isn't going to Pavia any more because her brother arrived here the very morning that you left for home. I shan't write you of his perfidy, but shall let Mother tell you about his dishonest behavior during the two days he was in Milan. I'm about fed up! I was just getting over a sty on the lid of my right eye, and now I'm laid up because a stupid ass of a surgeon injured the big toe of my right foot—he couldn't cut the nail without drawing blood. So now I've got to call in another with more experience to remedy, if possible, the botchings of the other. I should like to leave for the country a week from Sunday because General Pino is impatiently awaiting me.

His condition must then have taken a sudden turn for the worse and have become sufficiently grave for Borda to summon him to Pavia for a systematic course of rubbings with mercurial ointment —an unexpected development, which, after more than two months of silence following an announcement that his health "was con-

8 Schottky, *op. cit.*, 276.

tinually improving," naturally filled Germi with alarm. Why had he not written? What had happened? Was Borda's prognosis favorable?

Paganini to Germi, Pavia, August 7, 1822.[9]
I've just this moment received your letter and this very minute am replying as best I can. As regards my health, it's not too bad but it's going to be marvellous. The divine Borda is exactly of your opinion, but adds that my malady is out of the ordinary and is something quite new. They call it hidden syphilis. One thing, however, we should be glad that through a miracle I'm not dead and that I'm going to recover *perfettissimamente,* but it's going to take time. Therefore patience! . . . My mother is taking the mineral waters and must continue the cure through the autumn, so she isn't going home till later. Since I've been in Pavia, I haven't written a line to anybody. I'll bet everybody in southern Italy thinks I'm dead.

Three weeks later there was little change in his condition. Discouragement was now beginning to creep in.

Pavia, August 24, 1822.
I laughed so much over the Rossini story that my jaws swelled and I had to skip the frictions a second time. What a tiresome business this cure is! I've had fifty-five frictions; the first thirty of one dram; ten of four denaro; and fifteen of five denaro—without any sign of improvement! Professor Borda is astounded to see so much hidden poison in me, and dating from so long in the past. God knows how many months more I shall have to pass in this position. But there's hope of a complete cure; therefore courage! However, I regret to say that I suffer almost constantly from an erratic and febrile pulse. Yet when I read your delightful letters, I seem to be quite well and my cough doesn't bother me. Dear friend, I beg you above everything in the world not to come to see me, but go to your good mother in the country, if you don't want

---

9 The autograph of this letter is dated August 7, 1823, but as on several other occasions Paganini has obviously written the year incorrectly. In August, 1823, he was in Cernobbio, his mother, home in Genoa. After receiving the above letter with the news that Teresa was "taking the mineral waters," Germi sent her an amphora of mineral water mixed with wine, which Paganini acknowledged in a letter of August 24, 1822, and in his next letter (October 2, 1822) again refers to the recent gift. The last-mentioned letter is also incorrectly dated in Codignola, though this time Paganini has distinctly written "22." Additional evidence is provided by the inductive method. For instance, the letter of August 24, like that of October 2, opens with the unusual salutation: *"Amico più che carissimo,"* which is found nowhere else in his correspondence.

to see me suffer. Pavia is a dead hole—no students—few people that I care to know. Everybody is away in the country—the theatres closed. Let me look forward to the joy of embracing you when I'm well and can travel about with you—when we can make music together, and raise the devil. The amphora of wine and mineral water that you sent led to a most curious dialogue with my mother; but I calmed her down and, laughing like a lunatic, she thanks you for the joke.

We have relatively few letters dating from this first Pavia period of 1822, owing no doubt to the doctor's directions not "to exert himself too much," so we can only conjecture how he filled in the dreary weeks from June until October. He had an attack of jaundice sometime during this period and seems to have composed a number of small works for a "Signora Dida," another siren his romantic biographers have tried so zealously to weave into his legend. However, of the few letters that have come down to us, two only contain any reference to a lady, the first, written from Pavia early in July, mentioning a "Signora Faggini," and the second from Cernobbia a year and a half later, in which he asks Germi to find a guitar for a friend.[10]

Was it for Signora Faggini or a friend of General Pino's that he wrote the two minuets, one a *Menuet e Perigourdine* with the subtitle *Minuetto che va chiamando Dida,* and another with the message:

It's no use sighing. Jaundice leaves me a heritage of weakness, so that Dr. Borda forbids me to play for several days. Am I happy? Patience— the days pass; I'm gaining strength and will show you [six words crossed out] that I'm truly your obedient servant and most implacable friend.

Whoever Signora Dida was, she certainly played no important

---

10 *Paganini to Giacomo Manzino, Pavia, July, 1822.*
"The queen of cordial ladies, Signora Faggini, will bring you this letter. How can I thank you for having recommended me so well?"

Paganini to Germi, Como, January 7, 1824.
"A lady here desires a beautiful guitar, but an especially fine one. If you can find one there, send it to me; otherwise ask my brother—have him ask my copyist where or in what city in Piedmont such a thing can be found. I can't think of any excellent guitarist from whom to order one that is well made and sonorous. Therefore, please interest yourself in the matter."

role in the affairs of his heart, for neither of these dedications reveals the hand of an impatient lover. Indeed, a number of his notes in autograph albums in later years were far more inflammatory than these two innocuous messages, which might have been addressed by any teacher to any pupil.[11] The second might even have been a noncommittal gallantry by which he sought to cover his tracks in evading an obligation to some hostess who expected him to dedicate his "profession" to her guests.

By the end of October he had sufficiently improved to interrupt his treatment for a time and take his mother home to Genoa, where he remained till the end of May, 1823, a conjecture that, along with his statement that his "mother lived with him seven months,"[12] is adequately rooted in demonstrable fact since on May 15 he played at a musical soiree at the Sivoris,[13] in Genoa, and on the twenty-fourth executed a document there in which he appointed Germi his legal administrator. And it was also during these six months that he taught Camillo Sivori.[14] "This young man was only about seven years old when I taught him the rudiments of music. In three days he executed several pieces perfectly and everybody exclaimed, 'Paganini has performed a miracle!' At the end of a fortnight, he played in public."[15] Although he wished Schottky to understand

[11] Among the many dedications of this kind is one dated London, July 29, 1832: "If some day it will be granted me to know the adorable object who will preserve the present [portrait], I shall esteem myself happy." In 1833, when he was in Birmingham, England, the authoress Louisa Anne Twambley, then twenty-one, sent him a "rapturous poem" after hearing him play, which brought him "immediately to her feet." He then expressed his homage by giving her his picture with a suitable dedication and by writing in her album the first eight measures of the *Campanella Rondo*. Her poem, entitled "Extemporaneous Sonnetta, with variations, composed for, and inscribed to Baron Paganini," was published in a volume of her poetry in 1835. He also wrote in the autograph album of Mrs. Benjamin Curtis, wife of a wealthy American silk merchant in Paris: "O Love—why ignite this sweet flame in my breast if you are then to rob me of this dear object!" And to Mme d'Obrée: "How happy the original of this second portrait would be if he could express orally what the pen can never utter."

[12] Schottky, *op. cit.*, 259.

[13] On this occasion they played a *Cantabile e Valzer* for violin and guitar, which had been written for, and dedicated to, Camillo. This composition is now in the Reuther Collection. He may have had the work copied for Sivori, retaining the original himself.

[14] An old Genoese biography of Sivori stated that "he was born on October 25, 1815, in a box of the Teatro Sant'Agostino, at the last bar of Paganini's *Agitato*." There is no record of a concert on that date, though Paganini was then in Genoa.

[15] Schottky, *op. cit.*, 282.

that here he had an unusually apt pupil whose "innate musical sense" taught him how to apply at once the precepts of his master, he wished to make it equally clear that the real secret behind this startling progress was a "discovery" of his own which, when known, would enable artists "to study more profoundly the nature of the violin—an instrument a hundred times richer in possibilities than is commonly supposed."

Sivori's father, a well-to-do merchant "dealing in Neapolitan wares" (according to an old Genoese almanac), was at first strongly opposed to a professional career for his young son, though he allowed him at the age of five to begin the study of the violin with Restano, a local musician who was then teaching Camillo's two sisters the guitar. By the time Paganini arrived in Genoa in the autumn of 1822 the youngster had begun to show more than the customary native talent, so his father, still unable to decide whether his gifts were remarkable enough to warrant his abandoning a promising commercial career for the uncertain, and in many respects opprobrious, one of a musician, brought him to Paganini, whose interest and enthusiasm then seem to have decided Camillo's fate.

On leaving Genoa he recommended that the boy be sent to Costa, with whom he then remained till Paganini returned to Genoa in 1824, when he advised him to work with Agostino Dellepiane, who gave him the finishing touches and three years later accompanied him on his first foreign tour to France and England. As Sivori's name was later bracketed with that of Paganini for "his prodigious command of difficulties," it was undoubtedly Dellepiane who taught him the practical application of Paganini's principles and style since, according to reliable authorities and the evidence of Paganini's Op. 2,[16] Dellepiane had also come under the

---

[16] In Paganini's correspondence Dellepiane's name is mentioned for the last time in 1831. In order to determine Paganini's relationship with the Sivoris, Codignola endeavored to consult any manuscripts and correspondence still in the possession of Sivori's heir, Signora Clelia Ferrando Sivori of Genoa, but all his efforts were in vain. Belgrano, who knew Sivori personally, spoke only of a *Concertino* in his possession, though Paganini refers to six *Cantabiles* and Minuets as well as a Waltz written for Camillo. The fact that these works were once in Sivori's possession is attested by a letter written by Belloni (Liszt's former secretary) to Leon Kreutzer, on December 14, 1858, to the effect: "I found among Sivori's music six little pieces and a *Concertino*— in manuscript, with accompaniment of guitar, composed and written entirely in Paga-

latter's influence in Lucca in the very early days of his career. As for Paganini's own contribution to Camillo's education, Sivori gave David Laurie the following account:

He was probably the worst teacher of the violin who ever lived. He was short and bitter in his remarks when I showed any deficiency in playing the studies he gave me to practice, which generally consisted of his own compositions written hurriedly in a very cramped hand, as if he disliked to write anything so simple, especially for his own pupil. His general mode of teaching was to walk up and down the room while I was trying to play the last new exercise that he had given me, with a mocking smile on his face and uttering a depreciatory remark now and then. When I had finished, he would come close up to me, still with the same mocking look on his face, and remain silent for a few moments looking at me from head to foot, and then ask if I thought I had played the study at all in the way I had been shown. A trembling "No" was my reply—"and why not?!" came the query. After a few moments' silence I would venture to say that I couldn't play it like him because I hadn't the ability. "Ability was not required—all that was necessary was perseverance and application." However, he was willing to give me another trial, and seizing the violin like a lion seizing a lamb, he would play the study again without ever looking at the manuscript, walking about and playing it in a way that filled my heart with despair. However, one great lesson I carried away with me was not to neglect even for a day to practice scales.[17]

A large number of pupils must have passed through his hands during his eight years in Lucca, yet none of these "aspirants" ever seem to have claimed him as their master, while the only disciples he himself acknowledged were Sivori and Ciandelli, sometimes one, sometimes the other being given the distinction of "his one and only pupil." As we have said, he never spoke of Calcagno, so she may only have played for him to get his verdict on her talent,

nini's hand and bearing the following dedication: *sei pezzi facili, composta espressamente per il bravo Ragazzino Camillo Sivori. Niccolò Paganini.* Here in Genoa they still remember the concerts that Paganini and Sivori gave. If you think you could make some use of them, to your advantage, let me know; Sivori is disposed to let you have them. Furthermore, he is now restudying them with the intention of playing them. They are very easy, with charming melodies." It is therefore possible that Sivori gave the works to him and they have since been lost. In 1872, Achilles Paganini issued a circular to various Italian and German music publishers offering them a number of his father's unpublished works, but none of the Sivori works were listed on it, not even the *Cantabile* now in the Reuther Collection.

17 David Laurie, *Reminiscences of a Fiddle Dealer* (London, 1924), 60 ff.

in the process of which he may have made certain criticisms (as with Clara Wieck later), his aim here being suggestive rather than didactive. The absence of any reaction on his part to the use of his name in this respect would indicate that he thought the circumstance of no importance since, when two other young violinists, Giacomo Filippo and Agostino Robbio, advertised themselves as his pupils, it brought forth, at least in Filippo's case, a most vigorous denial.

Paganini to Vincenzo degli Antonj, Milan, March 2, 1828.
As to the boy Filippo, I can state that he never was a pupil of mine. On the contrary, I believe that the help of a good maestro would have enabled him to make greater progress in the musical art, since he has the natural talent for it. He is now here in Milan to give some concerts and is then going to Paris and London. The boy Sivori, *the only one who can call himself my pupil,* has given a concert in Paris, where he received enthusiastic acclaim.

He probably taught Sivori for a longer period than any of the others and therefore looked upon him as the only pupil he had really moulded to his pattern. In discussing Ciandelli with Schottky, he said that for many years he had been a monotonously mediocre player and "quite rightly no one took any notice of him. . . . He interested me greatly and I wished to help him, so I showed him my discovery, which produced such a great effect that in three days he was a different person and the sudden change in his playing was pronounced a miracle. In fact, in the beginning his playing was torture for the ears and he used the bow like a novice, but after my lessons his tone was full, pure, and graceful; his bowing showed authority and he made the greatest impression on his hearers."[18] Here again, his assistance was probably more in the way of criticism, with an occasional suggestion regarding execution, which enabled Ciandelli to master some of the technical problems with greater ease than by traditional methods.[19] In his

18 Schottky, *op. cit.,* 281.

19 Michelangelo Abbado: "Paganini employed the *scordatura* to astound the technicians, playing in this way works that would have been unplayable with normal tuning. He carefully guarded these works in manuscript since if he had published them the 'trick' would have been revealed. . . . Furthermore, the *scordatura* had the merit of making the timbre of Paganini's violin more dazzling in comparison with the accompanying violins of the orchestra; whereas, today this effect would be lost since his

several letters "recommending Ciandelli" as his "pupil," one gathers that his object was rather to help his friend to better his position, obtain outside engagements, etc. than to claim any particular credit for his accomplishments. At all events, neither Ciandelli nor Sivori ever spoke of his having revealed to them any particular short cut or "secret," so they must have felt that his suggestions had a "rational basis," as he himself took pains to emphasize.

On his way back to Lombardy he spent the night at Novi, where a Genoese acquaintance gave an elaborate banquet in his honor, though he "was very careful not to overdo." Novi was not only the first posting station with a comfortable inn, but during the Genoese Republic had enjoyed the status of a sort of free port for foreign products of all kinds so that many of the Genoese merchants also maintained a residence there. During the Napoleonic period, this thriving import trade was interrupted, the warehouses closed, and the beautiful country homes on the neighboring slopes boarded up and allowed to run to ruin; but by 1821 and 1822 commerce was once more in full swing, which will explain the extravagant libations that were offered there in Paganini's honor.

Paganini to Germi, Pavia, June 7, 1823.
To celebrate my arrival in Novi, the very courteous Signor Castiglioni must have opened more than 300 bottles of imported wine. However, I wished to eat and sleep at the Locanda. The celebrated Borda has prescribed asses' milk for me and has prohibited wine. The cough, which bothers me more or less, arises from an acidity that will disappear as a result of the great negative cure. General Pino is expecting me at his summer home in Como and I shall go there the end of next week. I'm just back from Milan, where I went for diversion. Yesterday evening Catalini gave a concert there at the Carcano. . . . Greetings to my mother. I'll write you from Milan.[20]

The promised letter, one of the longest that has come down to

works are now generally played with piano accompaniment. Finally, he also used gut strings of soft and mellow quality, while today the E string is steel wire and the majority of violinists use second and third strings overspun with plated copper or silver wire. Paganini's tuning would therefore result in a more metallic tone but it would not be more brilliant." (Condensed from an article in *La Rassegna Musicale*, [May, 1940]).
[20] Angelica Catalani (1780–1849), one of the great sopranos of her day.

us, touched on various matters, and contained many messages for his Genoese friends who had extended hospitality to him during his recent visit—"Botto, Riva, Mainetto, Mercante, Dellepiane, Degola, Rebizzo, and his brother Carlo," whom he had not seen since 1817.

Paganini to Germi, Milan, June 18, 1823.
I could tell you many things about my laziness, but I hold my peace so as not to blush. I spent twelve days in Pavia, which was a waste of time. The announcement of Catalani's second and last concert finally roused me and I returned to Milan to hear her. The Scala was almost packed, at an admission of 4½ Milanese lire, a reduction of 2 lire from the first concert at the Carcano, owing to the small audience (on that occasion). I was terribly bored. Her powerful, flexible voice is a most beautiful organ, but she lacks the grand line and musical philosophy. . . .[21] She can sing a *mezzo voce* up and down and everything that she sings *forte* she can also sing *pianissimo,* and with great sweetness; and from this springs all the magical effect. . . . She would have more soul if she had been trained by such celebrated masters as Crescentini, Pacchierotti,[22] Babini,[23] and our celebrated Serra. . . .[24] Borda tells me that he by no means expects my cough to affect my lungs, that with time and wolf's—or rather asses' milk and no wine I shall be able to make my tour and I shouldn't fail to play and enjoy myself. . . . Who in the devil told you of '*giri e regiri*' and a fiasco?![25] I don't understand you and wish you'd explain the matter to me better. . . . Your Guarneri had a superb reception in Milan, and Mantegazza is taking extraordinary pains with it.[26] There's a piece in the belly that's badly made and of the poorest wood; now this has been changed and I hope it will be an astonishing success.

[21] Paganini frequently made this point. A correspondent wrote in the London *Harmonicon:* "I quite agree with Paganini that there is a philosophy of the violin, though many people will smile at the expression. . . . A writer in the *Court Journal,* who has published recollections of Paganini, states that he had read to the violinist some remarks on his playing that had appeared in the *Harmonicon.* He explained to him how eloquently they had spoken of the truth of his intonation, etc. 'And (interposed Paganini with a triumphant smile) of the philosophy of the violin.' "

[22] Gasparo Pacchierotti (1744–1824), a famous *evirato,* settled in Padua after his retirement.

[23] Matteo Babbini (1754–1816), a pupil of his uncle Cortoni, was one of Italy's most famous tenors.

[24] Giovanni Serra (1787–1876), an eminent composer and conductor.

[25] An uncomplimentary phrase meaning intrigues with women, evidently referring here to Paganini's dissolute behavior where women were concerned. The comment also no doubt refers to temporary sexual incapacity, which Henri Beyle called *le fiasco.*

[26] Mantegazza, a well-known family of luthiers.

Your Amati is not an Amati but a Cappa of Saluzzo.[27] Pugnani changed all Cappa's labels to Amati and you won't find any Cappa violins with his name. But yours is a Cappa and one of the most beautiful I've seen. Mantegazza has never taken such a violin apart. Your violins and viola, as well as my cello, have been examined by the celebrated, and only intelligent, connoisseur, Signor Zonabuoni (*sic*) and his judgment is sacred. Your viola is a Gasparo di Salo. My cello is very beautiful and is a Stradivari made by his assistant Bergonzi—in short, a Strad out of his workshop.[28] Sivori has written me a long letter in which he wants to persuade me to write a concerto for Camillino to play in the Oratory next January.[29] I'll answer his letter on Saturday and hold out hope for it. Sunday, I'm planning to go to the country, to General Pino's. I'm going to be prudent and devote myself to the violin so as to be able to satisfy the desire of all Milan.

Although he was trying to live prudently and follow the regimen laid down by his physician, it would appear that his return to Pavia must have been necessitated by a recurrence of certain symptoms that Germi, and possibly his Genoese physicians, considered as sufficiently grave to require a resumption of his "cure"—a condition that did not respond to Borda's treatment and that must have continued to grow worse, since four days later he had his first relapse.

Paganini to Germi, Milan, June 28, 1823.
I'm almost frantic. Here it's raining and hailing *maledettamente* and last Sunday [June 22] I came down with gastric fever and rheumatism, which has prevented my leaving for Como. Borda came to see me and now I'm over it and almost entirely recovered. I'm only eagerly looking forward to the moment when I can leave for Como, where a most beautiful ass and a graceful cow (which the General has procured especially for me) are awaiting me.[30] Next Thursday is the day set for my departure for that delightful country place, where I want to get fat; but in a week or two I'll go to Milan for your violins and will order for you some G strings overspun with silver. Signor Tagliavacche has promised

27 Goffredo Cappa of Saluzzo (b. about 1647, died 1717), a famous luthier and pupil of Nicolo Amati.

28 Carlo Bergonzi (1690–1747), pupil of Stradivari. See Franz Farga, *Violins and Violinists*.

29 He is probably referring to a religious ceremony held in the Oratorio di S. Giacomo il Maggiore, Genoa, on February 19, 1824, in memory of the late King Vittorio Emmanuele I.

30 Asses' milk was then a favorite curative for tuberculosis, one of the first records of its use dating from the eleventh century. (Dubois, *op. cit.*)

to take you one of my books, which you are to read so as to get an idea of Greek and modern music.[31] He's also taking you a bottle of vermouth that was given me at Novi by Signor Bendinelli Castiglioni, which I beg you to accept. You know I'm not allowed to drink either wine or beer. . . . Tell my brother to see that his pupils pay him well.

Some time in July he was at last able to go to General Pino's but after a few weeks Borda recalled him to Milan so that he could see why he was deriving no benefit from the repose, fresh air, and nutritious food, which he had hoped would speed his convalescence.

Paganini to Germi, Milan, September 2–3, 1823.
Borda having sent for me, here I am back from the country. The day before yesterday they bled me because the food, instead of nourishing me, went into the blood. I've stopped the milk diet on account of the excessive heat but I shall resume the cure (any kind of milk) the first cool days and in about three months Borda will then see if there are any tubercules. My cough is still fierce, but the sputum isn't bad. Therefore, we have hopes. I write, but I can't see very well, so excuse my brevity. . . . My eyesight is getting so bad that I can't see what I've written and that's why I ask you to excuse my bad writing. I'm stopping in the house of Signor Fontana, the General's nephew and not in the *palazzo* of Countess Pino because she's an old hag—but she'll pay for it.

What had happened between him and his hostess? Had perhaps the rumors of the *giri e regiri* also reached her ears, or did she fear contagion? She was now an old lady of seventy-three, ailing and probably intolerant and overbearing, who may have attempted to interfere in matters that this incurable amorist looked upon as strictly his own affair. While the above letter was written from Milan, he was undoubtedly referring to Cernobbio, unless of course the General's nephew was temporarily in Milan. The latter did not reside in Cernobbio but at Borgo Vico (a part of Como), his villa being situated at the very edge of the town, in a large vineyard running down to the lake. Alongside the villa (described by Lady Morgan as a "simple white building") was a pavilion of the same size where Fontana entertained his guests, and it was here no doubt that Paganini took refuge from the Countess. When he

[31] Emanuele Tagliavacche, a wealthy Genoese with whom Paganini frequently stopped.

returned later in the year, she had presumably gone to Milan for the winter, so that he could resume his residence with the General in the Villa Nuova, which looked down on the silent and deserted Villa d'Este, now in charge of a caretaker who added to his income by showing foreign travelers through the recent residence of the "notorious" Princess of Wales.

ii

While superintending the repair of Germi's instruments in Mantegazza's workshop (he had evidently brought them with him on leaving Genoa) he ordered a quantity of bows, probably made to his own specifications, which Germi was to sell for him in Genoa. For two years now he had been living on the interest of his capital and felt the need of bolstering his finances, so, since concerts were still forbidden by his physician, he turned, like *Père* Antonio, to the commercial side of music. *Genuensis: ergo mercator!* Although his friends in Milan were "continually pestering him to give a concert," he still felt his technique creaking under him, so they would have to wait till the "divine Borda" had wrought the miracle—a thought that buoyed him up through all his tribulations. For after nearly two years of exhausting illness a profound depression was beginning to spread over his spirit, and as he took note of his condition and compared it with that of even a year ago he was disconcertingly aware that, despite all his own and his physician's efforts, there was very little improvement to be noted. In fact, he often had a feeling that his cough and accompanying symptoms were getting worse instead of better.

During this visit to Milan, while tormented by interminable broodings over his unhappy fate, he chanced to make the acquaintance of Dr. Maximilian Joseph Spitzer,[32] a young Viennese physician who had been called to Italy to treat one of the Austrian officials. For some reason, Paganini mistook him for an American, probably because of Spitzer's inadequate command of Italian and French, added to an accent (Hungarian) that was difficult to identify. Upon learning his profession, Niccolò at once poured forth a

32 Maximilian Spitzer (1792–1868) studied in Prague and Jena, and graduated from Vienna University in 1820. In 1829 he settled in Marseilles and acquired a great reputation as an oculist.

full history of his case, his chronic and organic ailments, Dr. Borda's treatments, his own hopes and fears; whereupon, Spitzer, noting his extreme emaciation, his nervousness and corpselike pallor, gave him the shrewd advice to build up his physical strength with wholesome food and proper exercise or "he would be dead within a month," which was enough to destroy the waning remnants of his confidence in Borda and confirm him in his opinion that all doctors were ignoramuses.

Paganini to Germi, Milan, November 26, 1823.
Fortunate is he who can depart for the other world without depending upon doctors. I'm alive by a veritable miracle. An American doctor has saved me. According to Borda, he prescribed the mercury cure and the five bleedings in order to find out what was causing my cough. Now I ask you if tests of this kind should be made for experimental purposes! Just as if I'd sold my body to him! In my opinion this is iniquitous, ignorant, and rascally. Toward the last, Borda gave me large doses of opium and, though this relieved my cough a little, it deprived me of all my powers; in other words, I couldn't stand on my feet and couldn't digest a chocolate even in twenty-four hours. I developed a light asthma, my stomach became bloated and my color cadaverous. Having had the good luck to meet the aforesaid American doctor in a café, he gave me a shock by convincing me that I'd be buried within a month if I didn't follow his advice since he knows what's the matter with me and that my cough is due to nervous debility, such maladies being unknown to our doctors. Here I am, I said, I'm in your hands. He gave me some pills, a tisane of his own concoction, and for food I'm to eat only good grilled veal chops and good wine. In a few days I was a new man—and now I feel marvelous. Milan is talking of nothing but the American who performed such a miracle. The cough will disappear little by little. The end of next week I'm going back to General Pino's Villa Nuova, where I shall have better care and I'll be able to ride horseback as the American advises.[33] I detest Borda—as does everyone else—for not only having ruined me physically and financially, but for having made me lose almost two years in sadness. . . . Tell my brother to write to me without embarrassment and when the winter is over it won't be difficult for me to have him come here to play the guitar in my quartets, which they would like to hear. Meanwhile I'm looking about for a good violin for him and, if you think it advisable, you might lend him one of your castoff bows, fetching, however, his bows with brass inlays. The Sivoris never show any judgment. I had grand proof of their simplicity when

33 At that time horseback riding was also prescribed as a curative for dyspepsia and constipation.

I was in Genoa and wrote six cantabiles and minuets and a waltz for them—all very difficult and instructive, not only as regards the mastery of the instrument, but for forming the soul of Camillino, who gives no evidence of possessing one. . . . They never said a word to me about other pieces such as sonatas and duets for violin and guitar! . . . Pardon my bad writing, dearest friend, but since the American only allows me to occupy myself five minutes at a time, I shall therefore limit myself to a single kiss on your sweet lips.

"The invalid who will not, or cannot, realize the seriousness of his own condition [wrote Professor Berri] usually has blind faith in the doctor who feeds him with illusions, and he even does not hesitate to resort to quacks. In this respect Paganini was no different from others. Like all artists and actors, he was a bundle of prejudices, superstitions, and ridiculous fears."[34] But the object of his present enthusiasm was by no means a charlatan or a quack. Spitzer already had an established reputation in Vienna and was very highly esteemed in medical as well as army and official circles. Born in Vamos near Miskolcz in Hungary, in 1792, he had studied medicine in Prague and Jena and upon receiving his degree from Vienna University in 1820 was appointed head physician of a division of the military hospital there, which post he held till 1828. During the autumn of that year he was compelled (or thought it well) to leave the country, and he then went to France, where in 1829 he received from King Charles X permission to reside and practice medicine, and where during a long and active career he achieved considerable renown. Déschamps describes him as a *médicin distingué,* so that Paganini's confidence in him, which he retained up to the last, was evidently fully warranted.

The mercury and opium to which Borda had resorted had induced the usual secondary reactions (toxic, digestive, and renal) which brought on the stomatites and jaundice that added to his miseries and subsequently led to foul ulceration of the mouth and loosening of the teeth. However, by reverting after the debilitating bleedings to a copious diet of wholesome food, his nerves improved and he regained some of his lost strength, which gave the superficial observer the impression of a "miracle," particularly since the renewed confidence in his physician also tended to dispel

34 Berri, *op. cit.,* 57.

his profound depression. "Was his anger justified?" asks Professor Berri. "Diagnosing his case as syphilis, Borda prescribed mercury, the oldest antisyphilitic known. Rasori and his disciples . . . prescribed it in murderous doses in the form of an ointment. But it would be unfair to condemn Borda, who acted in good faith, with the knowledge then available, and in accordance with the principles that he conscientiously preached and taught in Pavia University. . . . At that time purging and bleeding were considered as the twin pillars of the temple and, since the practitioners were barbers and phlebotomists, the practice was greatly abused. In the light of present medical knowledge, repeated bleedings in a case like Paganini's were really wicked. Opium acted as a sedative for the cough when administered in large doses, but here had the usual detrimental effects, making him anaemic, destroying his appetite, and paralyzing his intestines."[35]

Feeling stronger as the result of Spitzer's nutritious regimen, he returned to his *villeggiatura* at Cernobbio the beginning of December and remained till early March, making music with his friends, writing occasional pieces for the General, enjoying the food and country air, benefiting from the regular existence, and ticking off the hours in a leisurely and beneficial manner while still not losing sight of his commercial venture with the bows.

Paganini to Germi, Cernobbio, January 7, 1824.
The bows should be worth two louis a piece, owing to the precision of workmanship. They are—I repeat—excellent for everybody. As for myself, however, I prefer more hairs with maximum elasticity, which is impossible to attain without altering the design of the stick. This would be hard to do without experimenting beforehand and my being present at the tests.[36] But for the moment what difference does it make if they don't happen to suit me? They do beautifully for anyone who wants to use them—and they suit you, don't they? If you order the others, you'll have to pay at least half as much again. . . . Why doesn't my

---

[35] *Ibid.*, 38 f.

[36] Ole Bull described Paganini's bow as being "made after the old Italian style of a somewhat later shape than that of Tartini's. When the hair was tightened to the proper tension, the stick was nearly straight. Vuillaume, when he saw this bow, laughed and inquired who could play with such a thing. When Paganini brought it to him to be repaired (he had broken the upper end), Vuillaume offered to make him another, but he was much displeased with the idea and declined the gift in a very decided manner, saying that he could never think of using any other."

brother write to me? Tell him to write to me without fear—that I shall know how to take his letter. . . . In March, I plan to try out the Pollini Water. . . .[37] The *Ghiribizzi* for guitar were written for a girl in Naples and I only wanted to scribble something and not really compose;[38] but there are some clever themes among them that will not prove displeasing, and to pass the time you will do well (if you have a copy of them) to show them to Signor Botto's charming daughter.

February 29:
The American's cure has nourished me, but my cough is fiercer than ever. Although not cured, I now feel strong enough to undertake the Pollini Water cure . . . so I hope to get perfectly well. Thanks for the good news about my mother and brother, to whom give many loving messages from me; and please buy some ink and the necessary writing materials and give them to Carlo so that he can write to me and send me his news. . . . I practically never play, but I accompany the General very, very often on the guitar in some sonatina that I've written for him. I'd have this music copied and send it to Signor Botto if I were sure he wouldn't lend it to anyone.

By the middle of April he was at last strong enough to resume his concert work and gave his first recital in the Scala on April 23, with sensational success. Although beforehand many of his old admirers were prepared for disappointment in view of his long illness, he seems to have demonstrated with supreme ease that, even though "he hardly ever played," his musical resiliency was in every way commensurate with his physical recuperative powers.

We do not know when or where he met Antonia Bianchi but there is plenty of evidence that at this time she was residing in her birthplace, Como, and was a friend of Carlo Carli. So it is a tenable supposition that he met her through Carli or the General's nephew. At all events, their liaison dated from this period and in the beginning was evidently nothing other than the customary casual affair between two artists. For the question of matrimony seems never to have arisen, either at this time or even after the child's birth. With his emotional flux and reflux, he had presumably concluded, after

37 Pollini Water was a much advertised antisyphiletic preparation manufactured in Milan by Francesco Pollini and his wife Marianna.

38 Evidently the young "girl of eighteen, beautiful as an angel" who first captured his attention in Naples. The *Ghiribizzi* are forty-three small pieces written in Naples in 1820. They are now in the Reuther Collection.

the affair with Carolina, that it would be wise in future to keep a loophole of escape. He would help Bianchi with her singing and, as his assisting artist, she would share in his acclaim; he might even take her with him on his European tour—all of which, by his masculine code of reasoning, should be sufficient compensation for any sacrifices entailed by her unconditional surrender.

After the Scala concert and two at the Teatro del Condominio in Pavia, he left for Genoa, taking her with him as his assisting soloist,[39] an entirely new departure, so that Germi and his family must have known that here the relationship was based on something other than professional considerations. At any rate, during their three weeks or more in Genoa, Bianchi had ample opportunity of getting acquainted with the different members of his family, who at this time were making especially heavy demands upon him. While he was in Genoa in 1823, his sister Domenica's husband had been arrested and upon his release several months later had gone abroad, leaving his family to its fate, so that Niccolò was now expected to shoulder this extra burden since Domenica's children were still too young to come to her assistance. One can therefore easily imagine Bianchi taking in the situation and enlightening Niccolò on certain points that had hitherto escaped his observation to the end that his generosity would not be played upon to the detriment of her own interests.

Paganini to Germi, Milan, July 5, 1824.
My brother tells me that they smashed your windows. Now for God's sake, don't, out of the goodness of your heart, fail to take action against Ghisolfi, who certainly is the accomplice! Regards to my brother, to whom I'm not writing, for lack of time, but let him get his money and not mind the scoundrels; but do try to obtain for him the necessary satisfaction through the courts, and let the whole be a lesson to him for the future. If my . . . family doesn't love you, I adore you. *Ciao.*

Germi apparently took his advice seriously and instituted legal action on his own and Carlo's behalf, which proved unpalatable fare for the rest of the Paganini family, who lost no time in relay-

39 At the first concert he was assisted by Clelia Pastori, Bernardo Winter, Luigi Zuccoli, and Giovanni Coppini, all of whom gave their services gratis. On May 24, he was assisted by Mlle Barette, a young cellist of fifteen, and by Bianchi, who was advertised as a *virtuosa forestiera*. It poured rain on both evenings.

ing their complaints to Niccolò. This drew from him an exceedingly truculent note in which—forgetting his distinct instructions—he irrationally sacrificed his friend to his tribal loyalties.[40]

Paganini to Germi, August 14, 1824.
From my angle I must ask you to refrain from any intermeddling with my mother and my family; and I myself will write mother directly. In view of this, I wish you to desist from any intermeddling if you wish to remain a friend of mine, confining yourself solely to the task of looking after my financial interests. Otherwise, you'll force me to renounce your friendship. I flatter myself that you will comply with my wishes, which have no other aim than to insure our reciprocal tranquillity.

It is regrettable that Germi's reply to this testy riposte (if he deigned to make one!) has not survived; but whatever its tenor, it took some weeks before the officious but well-intentioned steward and his inflammable ward resumed their old relationship, which Paganini seems to have done in his characteristic way, by merely picking up the threads where he had dropped them, without other conciliatory gesture. It was in his nature to resent interference on whatsoever score and, since fierce loyalty towards all of his own blood was one of his dominant qualities, an angry reaction was, of course, inevitable, though he was never hesitant about dropping uncomplimentary hints himself if some member of the family annoyed him. His two sisters, Nicoletta and Domenica, with their respective families, their envies and cupidities, emerge clearly from his correspondence. One can easily picture them in their sordid surroundings, quarreling among themselves, scheming brazenly to extract money from Niccolò, and spending hours in gossip with their neighbors in the street. His brother, Carlo, however, for whom he had a sincere affection, remains—despite his frequent messages and references to him—elusive and mysterious, a shadowy figure in the background, hampered and harried by insurmountable obstacles that life had sown along his path. Although he married twice and held the post of second violin in the San Carlo orchestra, one gathers that for the most part he lived a plodding,

[40] At the time of Paganini's birth, the moon was posited in Cancer. See Frederic van Nostrand, *The Influence of the Moon* (New York, 1942), 28. "Among the mistakes one should avoid in dealing with these people is to indulge in any open criticism of their kindred, their country, or their friends."

unlovely existence with neither the ambition nor the opportunity
—perhaps not even the ability—to raise himself above the environment in which he had been born. One thing, however, can be said
for him, he evidently hesitated to impose on his famous brother's
liberality, appealing for financial aid only when overwhelmed by
some misfortune. On the other hand, one notes with some surprise
that, while Paganini was indefatigable in recommending and furthering the professional interests of his musical friends (Ciandelli,
Sivori, Bignami, and others), there is no record of his ever having
taken any steps to teach his brother, to help him perfect his technique by imparting to him the famous "secret," or to do anything
to assist him in bettering his position, a neglect due possibly to
certain intellectual deficiencies that he was perceptive enough to
recognize, but too loyal in his tribal instincts to admit, or to embarrass Carlo or himself, by placing the latter in an exposed position for which the mediocrity of his abilities did not qualify him.

X. *FULFILLMENT 1824–1827*

Some one to cast your glory on, to share
Your rapture with.—BROWNING.

AFTER A CHARITY concert in Como, Bianchi's birthplace and present home, the two left on July 6 for Venice, where, with the exception of several days in Udine and a concert in Padua, they remained till the end of October, when they transferred their activities to Trieste for several weeks before going south the end of December. What took them to the Adriatic at this time? Merely Paganini's restless desire for a change of scenery, or as the first *étape* of the Vienna journey? Some biographers infer that like many others down the ages they considered it as an ideal setting for a honeymoon. Perhaps. But may it not have given Niccolò deep spiritual satisfaction to show a certain insusceptible Venetian siren the worldly advantages of being the *maîtresse en titre* of a Paganini?

Although this Venetian-Trieste period is fairly well documented, his concerts and their programs all recorded, and several anecdotes regarding friends and minor incidents incorporated in the local folklore, three letters of Matthäus Nikolas de Ghetaldi, the last chief magistrate of Raguse (Dalmatia), who was then visiting in Venice and made the Maestro's acquaintance there, add a fresh, informal, and in some respects unusual, note to the familiar picture, showing how wayward and eccentric he was in many ways.

September 21, 1824.
Yesterday I made the acquaintance of Signor Niccolò Paganini of Genoa at Messer Naldi's. He looks unwell. Of moderate height, he carries himself badly. He is also very thin, pale, and dark complexioned. He laughs a lot, and enjoys it. His head is too large for his body, and he has a hooked nose. His hair is black and long, and never dressed. His left shoulder is higher than the right, probably owing to his playing. When he walks he swings his arms. We spent a very jolly afternoon. In the beginning I was under the impression that he was an uncanny, taciturn, and morose man—he was so described to me. But he is very lively and

talks almost incessantly. When he laughs he slaps his shoulders with his thin hands. He is really very homely.

October 2, 1824.

After the concert we chatted for a long time with Paganini, who was very exhausted. Probably because when he plays, he uses his whole body; and he is physically very weak. While playing he gave the beat continually with his left foot, which was very disturbing. Then he would bend the upper part of his body, and straighten up again. Twice he waved his bow in the air and made fearful grimaces. I think he's a charlatan, even though he's very accomplished. His style of playing pleases the people enormously. In the evening he showed his left hand to Dr. Martecchini (who had just arrived from Trieste). It's astounding what he can do with it; he can move the joints laterally and can bend the thumb back till it touches the little finger. He moves his hand as flexibly as though it were without muscles or bones. When Dr. Martecchini remarked that this must be the result of his mad passion for practice, he flatly contradicted him. Yet every child knows that he still practices seven hours a day, only his vanity won't let him admit it. However, Dr. Martecchini stuck to his guns, whereupon Paganini began to rage and shout, calling the doctor a thief and a robber. It was very unpleasant but we had to laugh. . . . How he can have such a demonic effect in the concert hall is beyond me. When he tore round the room swearing, he looked very ridiculous. Later, he quieted down when Mme Bianchi arrived round ten o'clock. He then showed us some astounding tricks on his violin. For instance, he plays a melody with two fingers while he plucks an accompaniment with the three first fingers. It often sounded as though three people were playing. His passages in double stops are dazzling, and I've never heard anyone run over the strings so fast. . . . Then he imitated a donkey, a parrot, and a thrush—all wonderfully natural. This annoyed Messer Naldi, who whispered to me that that was something for the village fair but not for the concert hall. Later, Dr. Martecchini tried to play on his violin and found, to his astonishment, that it was completely out of tune. Whereupon Paganini simply doubled up with laughter, and said that he always played on a mistuned violin.

October 18, 1824.

Yesterday evening Messer Sorgo told us that Paganini was now playing every evening in the cemetery on the Lido. So we went over and found a big crowd sitting and standing round listening to Paganini play. Some people were amused but most of them—with tears in their eyes—said that it was touching that this great artist played every evening gratis for the dead. On the way home there was a Dominican monk in the gondola who said that Paganini had sold his soul to the devil, and the Bishop had given orders not to allow him in the cemetery any more because he profaned the holy place. With that we threw him overboard. . . . Towards midnight Paganini and Bianchi arrived. Paganini was in a very gay mood. He couldn't sit still a minute. Finally, he took his violin and began to play and I've never heard him play so beautifully. He played harmonics with incredible ease, and then he struck the strings with his bow till you thought they would break. Dr. Martecchini called my attention to his posture. He holds himself differently from other violinists. When he begins he stands perfectly erect, the right foot forward. The right arm is pressed tight against his body and even in the wildest passages he never moves the right elbow. He plays only from the wrist. When he plays for us, he goes through no antics. His antics seem to be for the benefit of the public. . . . As a man he is incredibly disagreeable, impolite and impertinent. He showed Dr. Martecchini some little tricks on the violin and then charged him a high fee for this lesson, though he was Dr. Martecchini's guest for weeks, and the latter also treated Bianchi for nothing when she was ill. . . . He spends practically nothing, though he earns a lot. He lives with acquaintances and takes his meals with friends and is always bringing strangers along with him.[1]

The "impoliteness and impertinence" that struck the writer so unfavorably was here evidently not an isolated case, as substantiated by Pancaldi's now well-known anecdote regarding his "disagreeable behavior" to Count Perucchini, father of one of his particular friends. He had accepted an invitation to a *conversazione* at the Count's and had crossed from Trieste especially, yet, though "Bianchi (after arrival) had donned an evening gown," Paganini appeared in the Count's drawing room (filled with a distinguished company in evening dress) wearing the same outlandish costume in which he had arrived from Trieste—a yellow nankeen coat over his black suit. When the host then asked Bianchi to sing, she very graciously responded, but Paganini on the contrary brusquely refused, saying "that the Count had deceived him—that he had been given to understand that it was to be a quiet musical evening with a few congenial friends and he now found himself confronted with a formal concert audience." From the artist's point of view, he

[1] Communicated by the writer's granddaughter, Eugenia Maria de Ghetaldi, and published in the Berlin *Acht Uhr Abendblatt* of March 19, 1934. I am grateful to Mr. Rizo-Rangabé of London for calling this interesting material to my attention.

undoubtedly had a legitimate grievance, yet the situation must have been familiar to him, for in keeping with the manners of that age and the feudal customs still largely in existence artists were expected to regard it as a privilege to place their art at the disposition of their betters, to act as entertainers, with or without the bejeweled *tabatière*. In many instances, as we have seen, he manifested the natural subservience of the vassal, that is, to a qualified extent. He was always visibly flattered by marks of aristocratic favor, smelled no condescension in their praise and was ever ready to bend the knee in homage to receive the accolade. But when the circumstances were reversed and it was *his* royal pleasure to dispense his music, he demanded an equivalent obsequiousness. Therefore, the sense of social inferiority and servitude implied by Perucchini's attitude whipped him into fury. For in the composition of his character, despite its pliancy, there was a streak of iron. One had only to touch his pride and he was ready in an instant to stand upon his dignity, and the more pressure brought to bear upon him, the more intractable he became.

ii

In November, as the Adriatic visit was drawing to a close, his thoughts turned southward and he began to long, after several months' silence, for a letter from his friend.

Paganini to Germi, Trieste, November 27, 1824.
It seems a thousand years since I heard from you. You promised to write to me before leaving for the country. But I've seen no sign of any letter. I'm therefore all impatience to hear how you enjoyed yourself—and how you are. After the concerts in Venice, which were none too lucrative because of the excessive heat and the fact that all the wealthy people were in the country or away on holiday, I'm now here in Trieste, where the impresario of the opera house is jealous of me. For this reason, I'm giving him a fifth of the filthy receipts, as rent, since he didn't want to let me have the theatre for fear lest the throngs coming to my concerts should draw away the public from his opera. I must tell you as a friend that even before hearing me play, the Philharmonic Society in Laybach sent a deputation to call on me and give me a diploma, making me a member of the organization. The leading members of the society, including the classical professor of violin, Signor Benesch,[2]

[2] Joseph Benesch (b. 1793), teacher of Sigmund von Praun. In 1822 Benesch was appointed orchestral conductor of the Philharmonic Society in Laybach.

came here on purpose to hear my violin. They and Philharmonic members from different places in the vicinity all sat together in a special part of the theatre. To give you a good laugh, I must tell you a clever retort that another skillful professor of violin, a certain Signor Jaell,[3] a German residing here, made to Benesch that evening in the theatre. After hearing me the latter said: "We can all make our wills." "Oh no!" said Jaell, "because I'm already dead." . . . The celebrated professor (dilettante) Signor Samengo,[4] as soon as he learned that the *virtuosa* Bianchi and I had arrived, very kindly carried us off to his house where we have had superb quarters and food for two months. . . . Valenzano is here and has made a lot of money.[5] He charged Signor Samengo forty-five florins just to change the nut on his Strad. Tell Mainetto to write to me, not only about himself but also about my brother and the rest of my unfortunate family. My mother has never written to me again, and I don't know what has become of my nieces. I should love to hear how Camillino Sivori is getting on.

Leaving the Adriatic in mid-December they set forth for Naples, stopping first in Bologna, where he gave two concerts in the Teatro del Corso on December 24 and 25; then, following the Via Emiglia to its termination, "rolled into Ancona," the first glance of which convinced him that "he did not care to play there." To have chosen such a route to Rome at that season of the year is a strong argument for the contention that he had never been in Ancona, since, after leaving Loreta and Macerate, the road to Foligno through the mountain passes of the Apennines was exceedingly rough going in the depth of winter, with snow and mud and frequently stormy weather, which sometimes made it necessary to cover some parts of it on foot. That the week's journey must have been an arduous enterprize is attested by the fact that upon arrival in Rome he found his violin with "the fingerboard off and the sound post down," which "took much patience to put back in shape again." "But here I am in the processions [he reported gaily on January 22] singing the litanies, because it's Holy Year. The strangers, though few in number, are begging me to give a concert, which I shall do if I can get a hall."

[3] Edward Jaell, a Viennese violinist then residing in Trieste.

[4] Agostino Samengo was a native Genoese composer whose works were given in Milan and Venice.

[5] Giovanni Maria Valenzano (1771–1825), a famous luthier of his period.

Sievers,[6] the German musicologist and journalist, who was then in Rome, attended these pre-Lenten concerts and sent a long report to Gottfried Weber's *Caecilia* in which he described with convincing accuracy the far from flattering background:

If anything tended to demonstrate the lukewarm attitude of the Romans towards instrumental music, especially towards so-called "concerts," it is the lack of interest shown for three concerts given by Paganini during the pre-Lenten season. . . . The first glance at the hall showed what he might expect of the Romans. The place was a stable—not in the actual sense, but it was a place far more suited to grass-eating animals than to decent human beings. It was a room in a great *palazzo*, for here you will find unoccupied palaces at every step. The orchestra consisted of half a dozen persons whose toilet showed whence they came and in what haste they had been assembled. The vocal part of the program was provided by several artisans, members of the chorus of the Teatro Argentina, who sang choruses from Rossini operas, the solos being sung always by two persons so that one could help the other out. The public was on a par with the orchestra. There were barely fifty people in the house and of these no more than twenty had paid the half scudo admission. . . .

Paganini's playing is well known outside Italy, by report. He is a silhouette, but nothing more, of Alexander Boucher.[7] The two, so far as I know, have never seen each other, but they are such kindred souls that Paganini has become Boucher's son. . . . There is style to Boucher's madness, but with Paganini this is wanting. His performance on the G string reveals indefatigable industry, but it lacks the ultimate finish. The same is true of his octaves, which he plays much better than other violinists. But here too the finishing touch is wanting. He even trills in octaves, though the trick does not always come off. In short he is not a consummate artist, either in the serious or the baroque manner, for from no angle is he entirely satisfactory, because from no angle is his playing perfect. He has remained his own pupil. . . . He is undoubtedly gifted—a genius even, in his way, and the only outstanding violinist here in recent years. But the point at which the artist in him has come to a standstill denotes an innate weakness and shortcoming—an inability to advance any further.

Paganini's letters do not mention these Roman concerts, except

6 George Ludwig Sievers (b. 1775) served as Italian and French correspondent of several German publications.

7 Alexander Boucher (1778–1861), a well-known violinist of the period. He bore a remarkable resemblance to Napoleon, on which he capitalized to an exaggerated degree.

one at the Teatro Argentina on February 11, so he too was evidently none too pleased. In addition, one suspects that his first passion for Bianchi had already flickered out and that he was now toying with the idea of terminating their association, when Antonia, determined more than ever to retain her prize, foiled any incipient plans in this direction by announcing that she was pregnant.

Paganini to Germi, January 22, 1825.
How is the pregnant Madamigella? I know someone else I believe is in the family way. Please pay whatever sum you can to my friend Mainetto so that he can get my mother everything she needs. I've told my mother that I don't want to hear any more about the Passadores and Ghisolfis, so she should never mention them to me again, and as a reward for her silence I've told Mainetto to give her ninety-six Genoese lire a month, and you are to give my brother thirty-two instead of thirty.

Chafing under his companion's "lack of heart and head" and yearning for a change in his domestic atmosphere, the moment he learned that Lucrezia Cortesi was singing in Florence, he undertook the long six-day journey just to hear her, no doubt with the idea of finding another soloist.[8]

Paganini to Germi, Rome, February 3, 1825.
I was in Florence for two days—and why? To see a divine creature— well educated, very beautiful, and a very gifted singer—La Cortesi. I should like, if it were possible, to associate myself with a person of this caliber; but I don't know if it would be successful. True affinity is a rare thing. . . . My health is magnificent. I've always been thin, but I feel a void in my heart. If you were near me, I should be happier.

But Bianchi well knew how to safeguard her own interests and had no trouble in breaking down this incipient opposition. He was so easily led that in those early days—till her jealousy had taunted him into rebellion—a person of her determined will had no trouble in keeping him in harness, particularly so long as his heart was not otherwise engaged.

On his return to Rome, he played at several soirees in the houses

---

[8] Letizia Cortesi, a popular soprano of that day. When she gave a benefit concert in Venice in 1818, Byron sent her his purse containing fifty gold napoleons.

of the Roman aristocracy but none of his appearances were noted in the press, probably in deference to the Holy See. For the rumors of his alleged incarceration, which had previously lapped the shores of musical Rome, had now crystallized into a campaign of calumny, with the result that when some friends suggested that he be given a papal decoration he found to his dismay that the ragged old tale of the *ex-galérien* was now standing in his way.

Although Rome's attitude towards this old slander had brought home to him the world's arrogant uncharitableness towards one considered a moral delinquent, it is not unlikely that his quick, hot flush of anger on learning that Henri Beyle was now propagating it in print in his recent biography of Rossini was directed more at the individual than at the fact itself.[9] The two must have been frequently thrown together when Beyle was circling in the orbit of Rossini and Carloni, yet, while the friends that populated Beyle's life in Italy were frequently in, or of, the theatre, he quite evidently was not drawn to Paganini. Pique arising from artistic pride may therefore have had much to do with Niccolò's reaction since Beyle's long residence in Italy and their many common friends had, in Paganini's eyes, afforded him sufficient opportunity of discovering the falsity of such baseless rumors. "With your sagacity you'll be better able to write an appropriate letter to point out in good time the inconsistencies of such an absurd assertion and thus prevent the public from indulging in any indiscreet reflections," he wrote Germi on July 26. Germi then seems to have tickled him with the suggestion of suing Beyle but, since publishers and authors in those days had little to fear from libel suits, Beyle—if the subject was ever broached, which is unlikely—presumably offered a gentleman's apologies and considered the matter "closed." Even Paganini never mentioned it again.

9 The following footnote appeared in Beyle's *Vie de Rossini:* "This ardent spirit did not achieve his sublime talent by eight years of patience and the conservatory, but through an *erreur de l'amour,* which is said to have caused him to be cast into prison for many years. Solitary and abandoned in an imprisonment that might terminate in the gallows, nothing remained to him but his violin. He learned to translate his soul into music and the long evenings of captivity afforded him the time to perfect himself in this language." Rossini, who claimed that the biography was unauthorized, also threatened to bring suit. Beyle based the work on that of G. Carpani, taking over verbatim large sections of it.

Paganini

Charcoal portrait by Jean Ingres, Rome, 1819.

Cabinet des Desseins, Musée du Louvre, Paris.

Helene von Dobeneck

From a private collection, Heidelberg.

Paganini to Germi, Rome, March 27, 1825.
His Eminence, the Cardinal Secretary of State [Giulio Maria della Somiglia],[10] a man of eighty-four, after hearing my violin at a concert that I gave in the house of Marquis Giuseppe Origo, confessed that never in all his life had he passed such a delicious evening. He is disposed to get me a decoration from His Holiness, but is undecided on account of the rumor saying that I learned to play in the hulks. Therefore, you must do me the favor of having our governor[11] make me out a certificate denying such a report and stating that I'm of honorable birth and that my birth was duly registered, so that I can receive the decoration. Of course such a decoration doesn't mean much, but outside Italy it is highly esteemed. The sooner you get the certificate from the Governor (requesting it in my name), the better pleased I'll be. As soon as you get it, send it here to Rome to my particular friend, Marquis Giuseppe Origo, who will deliver it to the Papal Secretary of State, and we'll obtain everything.

Today it seems astonishing, indeed incredible, that a native born Italian of Paganini's eminence, a man who was admittedly an ornament and glory to his land, should have had to produce certified documents to prove that he was not an ex-criminal besmirched with a police record. With the power of the Church of Rome and the infinite ramifications of its authority and influence, it should have been a simple matter (even when exercising understandable caution) to have checked the records quickly through competent clerical channels and not only have saved him the mortification of having to prove his innocence, but also have shown the world and the faithful that the highest Christian institution still "conducted its business with regard to its Master's Sermon on the Mount." The fact that Paganini did not receive the order till April 25, 1827, fully two years later, would suggest that the Cardinal Secretary of State viewed the eloquence of the Governor of Genoa with equal skepticism.

iii

On Monday in Holy Week he and Bianchi left for Naples, where he announced a concert at the Teatro Fondo on April 16, assisted by the singers Adelaide Tosi, Morselli, and Fioravanti, with

---

[10] Giulio Maria della Somaglia (1744–1830). He was made a cardinal in 1795, and accompanied Pius VII to France.

[11] Ettore Veuillot, Marquis di Yenne.

Bianchi also contributing a solo "for the sake of the publicity"; which no doubt ministered to her mounting self-esteem. As it happened, Lily Paltrey of Berlin, a relative of Friedrich Nicolai (one of the leaders of enlightened thought in Germany) was then visiting in Naples and has left us, in her Italian diary, her impressions of this concert.

April 11.
Dined with Count Fleming, the Prussian ambassador. We stayed for some time after dinner and then drove to the Teatro Fondo, a most charming little theatre, really quite adorable, where we had a very good box with the secretary of the legation, Ignaz von Olfers. The famous Paganini played. He is very gifted, but there is still a good deal of charlatanism about it all. He played among other things a *Concerto Militaire* on the G string. There was lots of singing, for the most part by quite ridiculous singers. We were simply convulsed with laughter.

As far as Paganini was concerned, the charming Lily was evidently echoing a current German rumor based on the reports of German or French violinists who were unable, or unwilling, to explain his wizardry in any other manner. Her criticism of the singing was obviously more sincere, and traceable in part to a difference in national taste; for Italian music and Italian artists were never as popular in Berlin as in Dresden and Vienna.

The warm, moist air of Rome in the early spring seems to have had an enervating effect on him, aggravating his hacking cough and giving him renewed ground for worry. "I'm feeling so-so [he reported to his friend]; I'll let you know what the doctors have to say about my annoyingly persistent cough." He had no heart to undertake a European tour under such a heavy handicap, so from now on went wandering from one doctor to another in the hope of finding some remedy that might at least alleviate it. When the tour was over, he then wished to settle down, perhaps in Genoa, where he hoped to have the direction of an orchestra. As his thoughts dwelt more and more on his condition, he longed for something less fatiguing than the life of a roving virtuoso, an ambition perhaps originally planted in his mind by his companion, who preferred a life of ease and luxury to the cheap hotels and mean lodgings that satisfied her unfastidious mate.

Paganini to Germi, Naples, April 12, 1825.
When I return from abroad—a matter of three years, I should very
much like to have the direction of the orchestra of the new theatre in
Genoa, with charge not only of the theatrical performances as a whole,
but also of the selection of the singers and the repertory.

What an opportunity lost to his native city, and perhaps even to
the development of music, at least in his own country! But the
question seems never to have arisen then or later and, if Genoa ever
really gave it serious consideration, his six years' absence meanwhile brought other figures to the fore and gave them time and
opportunity of seating themselves so firmly in the saddle that
nothing short of a revolution could have cleared the way for him.
Perhaps, if the post had been offered to him at this time, the tour
might have been abandoned to the advantage of both sides. For
him in giving his life a quiet routine in a climate to which he was
accustomed, with a continuing incentive that would have spurred
him to constant effort without too great physical fatigue. And for
the theatre by entrusting the lyrical wing to an artist and a personality far above the ordinary theatrical practicians of that day.
But, as an inscrutable Fate so often wills, the suggestion fell on bar-
ren ground, and now, as later in 1835, Genoa and its distinguished
theatre were the losers.

iv

After a three-day voyage in the little steam packet "San Ferdi-
nando" he and his companion arrived on April 20 in Palermo,
where they had decided to await her approaching confinement.
Since expenses in the immediate future promised to be unusually
heavy, Niccolò therefore lost no time in applying to the Duke of
Serradifalco for permission to give some concerts at the Teatro
Carolina, the first taking place on May 16, the second on June 17.
When he then submitted a third request, the cautious Intendant,
Marquis Ugo delle Favari, who had no doubt learned that he formerly had been associated with the Bonapartes, now deemed it
wise to have him shadowed and his activities checked before according him any further privileges.
"Wrote the Director General of Police to watch Paganini's activ-
ities carefully," he noted on the margin of Niccolò's application.

Naturally, the latter had no idea that the police were spying on him but ten days later Don Mariano Camizzero, director of police, was in a position to assure the Intendant as follows:

Filharmonico Niccolò Paganini has been under surveillance ever since I received your verbal instructions. Nothing has been discovered to date except that he receives frequent visits from Don Domenico Testa and the notary Pingitore, who both wear their hair like Paganini.[12] As far as can be learned, these visits seem to have no criminal intent. They are often in the company of the painter Sanzo, who visits Paganini solely for the purpose of painting his portrait, perhaps for business reasons in view of the sitter's fame. I shall continue the surveillance and if anything new crops up, I shall not fail to inform you immediately regarding any necessary measures.[13]

So he was able to give his concert as planned, before the intense heat put an end to further activities till the autumn. Then a fortnight later another of his great ambitions was realized when Antonia, on July 23, gave birth to a son, whom his friend Don Testa carried that same evening to the font where Paganini, believing probably as did Busoni's father, that a child's career is mysteriously fashioned by the names bestowed upon it, proudly challenged fate by christening his first-born: Achilles Cyrus Alexander.[14]

After the child's birth, did the old dream arise again from the already flickering flames that his "years would now glide by happy and contented and that he would see himself mirrored in his children"? One is inclined to doubt it. It is idle to speculate as to what extent he continued to fondle the illusion that this liaison would "bring the much-needed calm into the troubled waters of his inner life" (Codignola's phrase); for at no time does he seem to have thought of legalizing the union—an eloquent omission that very probably proved one of the principal bones of contention between him and Antonia later on, particularly as the only obligation on his part (as he stressed so strongly at the time of the Cavanna suit)

12 R. M. Johnston, *The Napoleonic Empire in Southern Italy*, II, 66 ff., states that at that time "tonsorial fashions" were of great importance.

13 Archives of the Minister of the Interior, File 63, Doc. 928. (Communicated by Ottavio Tiby.)

14 The choice of names might also have been an aftermath of the French revolutionary theories Paganini absorbed in his youth, when parents were enjoined to give the future heroes of the republic the names of the heroes of antiquity.

was "to provide for the child." Antonia's position was unquestionably far from envious, and that she may have brooded over it and
taunted him with his refusal to regularize the relationship is fairly
obvious from the celerity with which she married a more amenable
suitor as soon as opportunity arose. Nevertheless, the situation in
itself could not have been unusual. Even Germi arranged his life
on a similar pattern, postponing the bonds of matrimony with the
woman who had been his housekeeper and was the mother of his
son till there was no longer any desire on either side to break them.

"The need of a sincere affection [wrote Codignola] had led
Paganini to pass rapidly from one brief but violent passion to
another, in each of which he sought the tranquil peace of married
life; but in the end they all proved illusory and he came out of
them more disturbed spiritually and physically than before."[15] The
analysis is flattering, but the "need of a sincere affection" could by
no stretch of the imagination be offered as the ground for Niccolò's
"brief but violent passions," and none of the adventures that engaged him give one the impression that they were inspired by
visions of domestic bliss. On the contrary. The determination to
preserve his independence was so powerful that the moment the
mirage came clear through the clouds of "exaltation" he shied
away like any bronco that hears the swish of the lasso. True, he
played at times with the idea when in a Byronic mood, but his
needs were paramountly physical, not spiritual; and when the first
was satisfied—as with all libertines—any casual thoughts of domestic happiness immediately lost their appeal, so that it is difficult to
feel quite sure that "starved affections" were in any sense responsible for his "morbid inquietude."

Bianchi no doubt—for a short time at least—exercised a strong
hold on some passional facet of his nature, but that he ever sought
with her "the tranquil peace of married life" is also highly con-
jectural. Was he in reality a nympholept "ravished by visions of
immortal beauty," forever seeking an ideal? Or was not pride the
beginning and the end of every matrimonial quest? Was the search
not just another aspect of his ambition? The acquirement of wealth
gave rise to a passion for glory and position and as he moved into
the ever widening circles of the social world and saw the leisured

15 Codignola, *op. cit.*, 21.

and cultivated ladies with their sophistication, their patrician graces, one suspects that he viewed them, not as the embodiment of an ideal in the sense of his spiritual needs, but as a witness to his good taste, as the suitable complement of his own superlative endowments, those gifts that required a glittering framework, the setting of birth, education, social distinction, inherited wealth. For did not "Paganini, in all things, shun mediocrity"? He was definitely not cast in the monogamist mold and no one knew it better, as can be seen from his readiness to admit his own two unreconcilable and essential needs, the pull of two opposing tendencies—the desire for woman, and an imperious demand for absolute freedom. It is therefore hard to picture him in a stereotyped domestic role, "going home from the glittering theatres to a happy, peaceful fireside," as Pulver puts it. That this would have been infinitely healthier for him there can be no argument. It is equally true that he often played with dreams of feminine perfection, some beckoning sylph like Chateaubriand's, sparkling as his *staccati,* profound as his adagios, bearing—like his playing—the hallmark of uniqueness, a dazzling enigma like his tours de force. But when the moment of decision arrived, no materialization of the image was ever permitted to encroach upon his liberty, till he finally came to accept the situation as one of the insoluble contradictions of his life.

v

In the early autumn they returned to the mainland and established a temporary residence in Naples, but not even the presence of the child could prevent the already badly shattered romance from going on the rocks.

Paganini to Germi, December 17, 1825.
Please give my regards to my brother, to whom I'm not writing because of anxieties that I cannot go into here; but I loved his letter, and especially to hear that he had recovered from his fall. . . . By the way, Bianchi, who's still with me, has one great fault. She flies into a rage over nothing. The other evening she took my violin case and banged it up and down on the floor four times till she smashed it to pieces, just because I didn't take her along with me to a merchant's where I only had to go for a quarter of an hour on business. Fortunately my man-

servant grabbed it, or rather tore the violin from her hands, and saved it; and by a miracle I found it safe and sound, though a little shattered. Another thing, the day before yesterday, Bianchi was with me in the evening at the house of some Spanish friends; The son and his mother . . . called me aside to ask my opinion on the originality of a fanatical dilettante of the violin who was there. Bianchi interrupted us (I think from jealousy perhaps) and asked me to take her home. On my asking why, she gave me a violent slap, accompanying it by infernal shrieks that shocked all the company. She screamed till she nearly burst, and none of us thought she would come to her senses.

After their removal to the country away from Naples, "where sirens lay in the waters and satyrs played in the sun," she seems to have quieted down and, with her eyes fixed on Vienna and Paris, now turned her attention seriously to her singing.

Paganini to Germi, Naples, April 6, 1826.
Dr. Calisi, who is famous here in Naples, is absolutely going to cure me. I'm taking the roob and sulphur cure in the country near town and am counting on recovery within two or three months. . . . Bianchi, who is improving greatly in her singing,[16] will accompany me on my grand tour of Europe, which I shall make as soon as I have got rid of my insupportable cough. Catalani wanted to sign me up for London, but I didn't care to.

At the turn of the year he had come down with influenza and catarrhal fever that settled in his chest, causing severe attacks of suffocation which, added to his "fierce cough" and the debilitating effects of Leroy's Elixir,[17] which had been brought to his attention round this time, reduced him almost to a phantom. When he first fell ill, he was probably residing in one of the crowded quarters of the city within convenient distance of the theatres but, as soon as he had safely weathered the first crisis, his doctor recommended that he leave the inner city and take lodgings on the slopes below

16 Kandler wrote that "Bianchi's voice was beautiful and impressive. The tone is mellow, full, round, subtle, and when necessary, of considerable power." (*Allgemeine Musikalische Zeitung* [1828].)

17 Some of the Leroy-Pelgas edicts were: "Bleeding is an abominable practice. The use of leeches is the most pernicious of all human inventions. Mercury is one of the worst enemies of the human race. Quinine is the cause of an endless number of incidents, almost all irremediable. Diet is unnatural. There is only one effective medicine: the purge—loosen, remove, refine, rarify, expel, clean, purify, eject the material that irritates and aggravates."

the old fortress of St. Elmo, where the air was purer, the sun more ardent, and the peace and quiet that he needed less disturbed by ambient Neapolitan noises.[18]

Did his prolonged ill-health through these long, taxing weeks have a blighting effect on Bianchi's affection? As the healthy partner did she rebel against tending a sick, nervous, irritable man with, so far as could be seen, no immediate prospect of a cure? Maybe. At any rate, as sensual passion subsided, sharp differences in character manifested themselves. On her side, avarice, inordinate ambition, and overweening jealousy. On his, reckless self-indulgence, harshness, with probably a touch of cruelty, brusqueness, and tremendous pride. With a personality "that moved like a magnet creating its area of attraction," added to a fickle strain, he could not avoid arousing her jealousy, particularly if she suspected any intent to elude his conjugal responsibilities before her future was secured. So, since neither education nor upbringing had taught her restraint, her tantrums became more frequent and violent, making her a constant source of strain, for she could not let this turbulent lover go till he blessed her—either with matrimony or an annuity for life.

Paganini to Germi, December 12, 1826.
After Christmas I'm going to give a concert at the Teatro San Carlo and will play my First Concerto, which I haven't yet played in Naples. I will play my second (with a bell obligato) if I give another and have finished orchestrating a third with Polacca. I want to play these concerts for my countrymen before performing them in Vienna, London, and Paris.[19]

The projected recital did not take place till January 30, after which they left for Rome, where he gave at least four concerts before another severe attack of influenza laid him low for several weeks. "I've had a fierce cold that made me think that I was done for [he wrote on May 7] but in spite of the doctors, who thought I was doomed, I recovered very quickly as soon as the fever left me;

18 Origo, *Leopardi*, 230. Leopardi's Neapolitan landlady also made trouble for him owing to his "sickly appearance."

19 In a letter to the Intendant of the Royal Theatres dated October 7, 1826, he applied for a renewal of the permission granted to him early in the year, since *una lunghissima malattia* had prevented his availing himself of it, showing that for ten or eleven months at least he had done no public playing.

and I've now regained my lost appetite."[20] Such relapses were indeed discouraging but on the whole he was now in a stage of his career when he must have felt that his existence had suddenly taken a new turning. As far as his music was concerned, achievement had always come easily, but ambitions of various kinds now fell like ripe plums into his lap, as though the gods, relenting past asperities, at last wished to make amends. The current of his life had taken a new and exciting twist, showering benefits and fruition on the virtuoso and the lover, the composer and the financier. The only drawback was the beastly, aggravating cough for which, seemingly, there was no remedy.

vi

Germi had finally produced the desired certificate from the governor of Genoa, testifying to his unblemished record and exemplary life—in the police-court sense—which evidently satisfied all the demands of Leo XII, who on April 3 conferred on him the coveted splendor of the Order of the Golden Spur,[21] which included the title of Knight (*Cavaliere*) and was the oldest, and for a time one of the most highly prized, of papal orders, awarded only to those who "by feat of arms, writings, or outstanding deeds had spread the faith and championed the Church." Although the chief solicitude of the pontiff was to enforce by inquisitorial supervision strict observance of Catholic morality, the fact that Niccolò was overtly living in sin and that his son and heir, as the Irish say, was "born on the wrong side of the blanket" was quietly overlooked, since in those licentious days to have brought up the issue would have been to wreak havoc in a far more rarefied atmosphere than that of professional musicians. For the living, worldly honors were not contingent on the virtuous conduct of one's life. All that was needed was a clean slate with the police. However, for the dead —when the frailties of life are over—such distinctions (as the future was to show) had a different scale of values. Yet, once upon a time there was place for both the Magdalen and the repentant thief in the Divine Compassion.

20 In the discussion of Paganini's health at this period of his life, some confusion has arisen, due probably to his own contradictory accounts.

21 Gluck received the Golden Spur in 1756, Mozart in 1770 from Clement XIV, Morlacchi in 1816 from Pius VII, Liszt from Pius IX.

At last a *cavaliere,* he turned his steps northward, intending to play in Perugia en route but, finding on arrival that the theatre was occupied by a theatrical group till the end of June, he arranged a date for July 1 and went on to Florence, where he played on June 27, returning then to Perugia, regardless of the long, hot, fatiguing journey. The sheer excitement of the concert and of being "ridden home in triumph, accompanied by a band, flaming torches, and a vast concourse of people" seemed to have afforded him a compensating satisfaction that drove all other considerations from his mind.

It was his original intention to play again in Florence and then proceed to Leghorn, "where his physicians had ordered him to take a course of baths,"[22] but shortly after his return Achilles fell and broke a leg; which in those days amounted to a major mishap. He therefore canceled his pending concerts so that he could look after the injured youngster and keep him quiet till the tiny bones had knit.[23] Since Achilles' birth and, in fact, as long as the liaison with Bianchi lasted, nothing in Paganini's letters would indicate that the child meant anything to him or indeed played any part in his plans or the ultimate arrangement of his life. For only once is his name mentioned, and then obviously in response to Germi's inquiry regarding his recovery from this accident. So perhaps it took the latter to awaken his paternal love and to show him how much this little son might some day mean to him. The ways of destiny are strange, and the later years might have been sadder and lonelier for this *grand solitaire* if for several days and nights he had not felt the tug of tiny arms around his neck and his heart touched by the helplessness and pain of this, his own, bambino. Perhaps, too, this close communion showed him that he could be both father and mother in one, and from this clairvoyance sprang the courage that seven months later enabled him to sever bonds that by then had become more than "an embarrassment" to him.

After three concerts in Leghorn, he continued his journey northward to Bologna,[24] where he had some business matters to attend to before leaving Italy for an indefinite time. True, he gave Germi

22 In 1808, a Sieur Turi had opened an establishment at Leghorn for sea bathing.

23 Paganini's assisting artist in Florence and Leghorn was Giudetta, not Giulia, Grisi as erroneously stated by Tibaldi-Chiesa and Emilio Gragnani. Giulia was then only sixteen years old and did not make her debut till 1828.

unlimited authority to act for him, but the final decision always rested with him and even when gravely ill he never failed to maintain an astounding grasp of his financial interests. ("I beg you to invest my money as you think best and tell me the necessary details when it comes time to negotiate a contract.") For he was a shrewd and patient accumulator and not even tormenting private problems could confound his calculations or confuse him—with the sole exception of his dates, which always seem to have been mere senseless symbols for him. He evidently did not intend to go to Genoa again but, as there were several details he wished to discuss with his "administrator," he had no other recourse when Germi was unable to meet him in either Turin or Milan. But it proved a rewarding solution after all since it enabled him to bid his family good-bye, give some concerts to defray the unavoidable expenses, and consult his old physician Dr. Giuseppe Garibaldi.[25]

He remained in Genoa till the latter part of November and besides playing at several private soirees gave two concerts in the little Teatro del Falcone (in the Durazzo Palazzo) that were honored by the presence of the royal family. Just then final preparations were being made for the inauguration of the new Carlo Felice Theatre and he was surely more than justified in wishing, and expecting, that on this great occasion he would be invited to participate. "If it were given me to take part in the inauguration of our new theatre, I should rejoice no little," he wrote Germi— a comprehensible reaction for, as Gibbon said, "there is no more exquisite gratification than to revisit in a conspicuous dignity the humble and laborious scenes of one's youth." But his name was never even suggested, which must have seemed to him a peculiar way for his birthplace to voice its loyalty. However, he was an expert in hiding his real feelings, so, as far as Genoa might ever know, its attitude failed to touch him. Fate was reserving him for more resounding exploits and a broader, vaster stage.[26]

24 Paganini's friend in Bologna who looked after his affairs was the lawyer Vincente Degli Antonj, who held a distinguished position in Bolognese society.

25 Garibaldi was a pupil of Niccolo Olivari, founder of the Genoa Medical Clinic. He was on the faculty of the School of Medicine of Genoa University and when the university was closed in 1821 at the time of the revolutionary uprisings, he was one of those authorized to give private instruction.

26 The committee in charge of the orchestra appointed Giovanni Serra conductor and Carlo Sampiero first violin. Although five years Paganini's junior and by no

On his return to Milan, his schedule was disrupted by what seemed a multitude of difficulties that disturbed the repose and tranquillity so badly needed at this time. First the Scala "revoked the promised permission for the theatre" till after it closed for Advent, and then at his first concert the nonappearance of two of his assisting singers threatened "a serious disturbance," which luckily was obviated by the "magnetism of his presence." An injury to his thumb next forced the cancellation of the second concert but at the third he permitted Bianchi to enjoy the recently unappreciated honor of being his assisting soloist—a confidence she seems fully to have justified. "At last Sunday's concert [he wrote Germi] Bianchi sang a rondo with such mastery that she received clamorous applause," which though immensely flattering to his pedagogic methods undoubtedly made her more exigent than ever.[27]

After a charity concert in Milan and a concert in Pavia "to comply with the wishes of the students" he was all prepared to set off for Vienna, when another severe cold again delayed his plans. Perhaps even then, and despite the fine new carriage he had ordered for the journey, he might again have changed his mind had it not been for his companion.[28] For long before Achilles' birth he had promised to take her with him to Vienna. Yet as the day drew near she came more and more to the conclusion that she would never be able by seduction, threats, or tantrums to hold her magic fiddler, much less lead him to the altar. At the thought of crossing the Alps into a foreign country and into a different moral climate where she could not foretell what was in store for her, and realizing that with-

---

means such a formidable artist, Serra was highly esteemed as a composer. This may have influenced his selection since the tendency was then to prefer opera composers as conductors rather than trained orchestral leaders. Previously, the control was divided between the maestro at the piano (or cembalo) and the first violin, but in the late twenties the leader had nominally replaced the keyboard director and had begun to use his bow as baton, though he still conducted from a part written on two staves rather than from a full score, and enforced his beat (in the words of Otto Nicolai) "by stamping his foot, which often made more noise than the playing of the orchestra." The Carlo Felice Theatre was inaugurated on April 7, 1828, with Bellini's *Bianca e Fernando.*

27 Paganini told Schottky (*op. cit.,* 296) that he played thirty-seven concerts in Milan in three different *étapes.* These were of course 1813–16; 1822–24; and 1827–28. We have a record of only thirty-one. The other six must have been at court or with such an organization as Gli Orfee.

28 When Paganini left for Vienna, he left his instruments with Carlo Carli, including the Cozio di Salabue Strad (1724).

out a legal bond he was saddled with no obligations, she was probably very seriously concerned about her future and did not relish the prospect of being stranded on strange shores with a tiny child, should Niccolò suddenly elect to treat her in the summary manner of her predecessors. For to employ Santayana's phrase, he could never "distinguish between affinity and proximity." Since she evidently thought she could only get what she wanted by behaving violently, she now gave him no peace till he guaranteed her future. "Bianchi is at last tranquil [he wrote on January 2]. I've given her a document that guarantees her a life annuity of 100 Milanese scudi."

Given his highly nervous temperament, these frequent scenes must have worn him out. For she was an untamed, passionate creature consumed by a jealousy that knew no peace in the presence of a man whose long slender fingers on the strings "could charm away a soul." Yet it must be said that both past and present history gave her every ground for apprehension, and Niccolò, overstrung himself, was certainly no model of restraint, as testified by De Ghetaldi. When sensing his precious liberty attacked, we may be sure that he retorted in a way to bring out all the feline in her nature. For that shadowy smile that played at times about his lips was not all affectation, and when vexed and wearied he could surely drive the dagger of his sarcasm with a killer's venom. Moreover, with such a creature of mere appetite as she, he held a powerful weapon with which to taunt at will. "For over two years now [he wrote later in the year] I haven't touched a woman." So her frustration may have been sexual and physiological, and for this reason all the more disruptive if she suspected that he was deceiving her.

For the time being, however, the annuity had a palliative effect and the skies remained serene, no untoward events or sudden illness arising to delay the great adventure. On the morning of March 6, the three then finally took their places in the new traveling carriage and were off at last on the ten days journey to Vienna, a goal that, had it not been for Bianchi's egoism and determination, might, for Niccolò, have remained forever sparkling in the distance like the phantom Irish isle of Tir-na-n-Og.[29]

29 Paganini followed the ordinary post route, as shown by his notebook.

PART II

Sext

Awake, my sleeper, to the sun,

. . . .

The fences of the light are down,
All but the briskest riders thrown,
And worlds hang on the trees.

—DYLAN THOMAS.

XI. *VIENNA 1828*

They threw their caps
As they would hang them on the horn o' the moon,
Shouting their emulation.—SHAKESPEARE (*Coriolanus*).

WHEN PAGANINI arrived in the Austrian capital on March 16,
he was no stranger to the Viennese. For more than a decade reports
of his dazzling performances had crossed the Alps, part of the
esthetic baggage of every returning Austrian, whether official,
musician, or soldier in the ranks. Indeed, one might say without
exaggeration that his name was almost a household word, even
though to the general public it suggested less the virtuoso of supreme attainments than a sort of Latin Kreisler whose instrument
possessed the gift of sorcery should one venture, unprotected by a
talisman, within the radius of its mysterious spell.

Such a reaction was clearly conditioned by the atmosphere of the
age, for in Vienna, as in all northern Europe at that time, the young
romanticists, desirous to be free to work in their own way, had declared uncompromising war on the restraining formal discipline
of classical tradition and in lowering their sights and seeking
simpler, less elevated paths had returned to the ancient national
sagas, the folk tales and folklore with their burden of black magic,
incantation, diablerie. With "the out-and-out fabulous [in Hoffmann's words] making its pert entry into everyday life," it was not
strange that these travelers' tales from Italy should find susceptible
ears among the Viennese, particularly since nothing authentic was
known of Paganini's early life and antecedents.

In Austria and Germany, the twenty-five years following the collapse of Napoleon's empire were further characterized by a way of
life and an artistic taste derived from the Philistinism of the middle classes, of which a frugality of living, a culture of limited proportions, and great economic depression were the outstanding hallmarks. In addition, it was a period when poets, dramatists, and
other writers, under the impact of the revolutionary changes taking

257

place in the political and material worlds, began increasingly to occupy themselves with politics and place their gifts more and more at the service of advanced ideas. In consequence, from the early twenties Vienna's coffeehouses had become more like political clubs where personalities, events, and trends were eagerly discussed, especially since newspapers were not yet general and even when existent conveyed, as instruments of autocratic government, very little information of the sort the people wished to hear. Moreover, it was a period in which there was an exaggerated cult of the personality, when noted artists, actors, writers, and musicians played an inordinate role in public life, not only in the literary salons that were then in fashion, but in the modest haunts of the *petite bourgeoisie:* in the *Tabagien,* or taverns frequented by the submerged tenth, in the *Konditorien* outside the city gates, in the *Weinstuben* within, where writers, actors, and musicians congregated and where, along with political discussions, the lions of the day were a conversational topic of never ending charm, their lives —like those of popular Hollywood stars—everybody's plunder. Pedestaled in triumph, their gifts were frequently exalted, their persons invariably idolized, thus making Vienna, in the words of Reichardt, "the richest, happiest, and most agreeable residence for the musical artist."[1]

For the "musical artist" in whom mystery and magnetism were inextricably intermingled, "the time, the season, the protagonist, and the scene" were therefore all in delicate accordance so that Paganini immediately found himself the fashion—the most talked-of person in the city—and all without the slightest effort on his part.

When accounts of his incredible feats first struck Vienna, the city's august critics reached automatically for the salt, since the familiar Latin lapses into hagiography, with their tendency towards partiality, hyperbole, and extravagance were here looked upon as the reaction of infatuates, of a public less musically cultivated than themselves—an attitude traceable, perhaps, as much to national as to musical prejudices. Yet, even so, the Viennese were not self-sufficient like the Neapolitans. They had "more sympathies than antipathies," were open to persuasion, and did not decline on prin-

1 Johann Friedrich Reichardt, *Vertraute briefe geschrieben auf einer Reise nach Wien* (1810).

ciple to accept another's verdict. They only felt that if all these wonderful reports were true, the man could be no normal human being. However, if there was any charlatanry in this artistic mixture, if (as some said) he rode his genius like old Scheller, principally for comic ends—in other words, if he subordinated art to entertainment—they were convinced that no place would unmask him sooner than Vienna. To compete with Hoffmann's Kreisler might require collaboration with the devil but when it came down to music as an art, in the grand tradition of their beloved masters, it would take far more than an ordinary dash of talent to delude their connoisseurs.

As for Niccolò's personal habits and the etiquette of his private life, that was quite another cup of tea. Here there were no reservations whatsoever. Of such an enigmatic individual anything might be expected. This man had throttled wives and mistresses in crises of thwarted passion, had dissected them, like Leonardo, in the interest of his art and from their delicate intestines had fashioned strings for his magic instrument. He was mean and unpredictable. He had languished in the hulks for his political opinions. He had been for years in the nameless oblivion of a dungeon where ball and chain had left a permanent mark upon his gait. Like Faust, he too had made a pact with Mephistopheles—in fact, he was the devil's spawn, the Wandering Jew incarnate. The most appalling allegations were laid to him; nothing was too far fetched or too preposterous for the popular imagination; so, while the papers kept his name constantly before the public, all the antique fables, the hoary scandals (which he thought had once for all gone underground when he gained the Golden Spur of papal favor) now emerged on every hand to be bandied about in hundreds of versions—in cafés, salons, theatres, and concert halls, indeed even in the market place.

In the beginning, owing to the barrier of language, the leading actor was probably unaware of all this swirling gossip, most of it not even within hailing distance of the truth. Anyhow, at this particular moment his mind was wholly taken up with his forthcoming debut, though he could have had no real misgivings regarding his reception. Albeit in alien territory, both in concepts and evaluations, he now felt well prepared to storm this formidable citadel, for his art had ripened into grandeur and he was supremely confident of his skill—a comfortable feeling that boded well for victory. Besides, he could never have had the lonely, helpless feeling of a stranger anymore so than in Milan or Rome or other musical centers that he entered for the first time. On the contrary, for while these earlier ventures were the result of sudden impulse, for twelve years now his thoughts had been directed towards this Austrian goal. During a particularly impressionable period of his life Vienna had opened wide the door of his imagination and he had meditated on it so constantly and for so long a time that his reaction on arrival was surely one of recognition. Moreover, he had come well provided with influential introductions, among others, to Count Joseph Esterhazy; Count Moritz von Dietrichstein,[2] the "music count"; Count Charles de Zuchy; Baroness Rosalie von Geymueller, the singer; Baron Emanuel von Doblhof, director of the Society of the Friends of Music; and the Austro-Italian publishing house of Artaria,[3] which acted as his private counselor in all his personal affairs.[4] Then, too, there were the many Austrian musicians whom he had met at various times in Italy: Joseph Wiegl, whose operas were frequently given in Milan and other musical centers; Böhm and Mayseder, who had concertized in Italy; Joseph Panny, whom he knew from Venice and Trieste; his countryman Dr. Francesco Bennati and his old miracle-worker Dr. Spitzer; Prince Metternich and the Archduchess Marie Louise, who had accompanied her husband Count von Neipperg to Vienna for the spring military maneuvers. In addition, everywhere he went, on foot or in fiacre, crowds swarmed round him, which was gratifying to his vanity and a brilliant augury for his success. And to add to his well-being, there was no need for him to feel lonely on account of the strange language, for on every hand he heard the melodious sound of the Italian tongue.[5]

2 Count Moritz Dietrichstein (1775–1864), intendant of the royal theatres.

3 The head of the firm at that time was Domenico Artaria, son-in-law of Carlo Artaria, one of the original founders.

4 Other letters of introduction were to Signor Targeani, Mme Lucie de Laitan, Signor Fenini, Marquis Vincenzo Zappi, Antoine d'Épine, and Mme Teresa Levi.

5 Edward Holmes (1797–1859) wrote of his visit to Vienna in 1826: "The people are Rossini-mad, with good ears they tolerate the worst of music. They out-Herod Herod in their noisy and vociferous applause of their favorites . . . everything Italian

Here, too, as in Germany later, he found halls and theatres easily available, with disciplined orchestras and a musically intelligent and receptive public,[6] without the necessity of routing requests through endless official channels, of reconditioning dilapidated buildings, of organizing his own orchestra, engaging soloists, etc. Although Barbaja's lease of the royal theatres was about to terminate and was soon to be taken over by Count von Gallenberg (whom Paganini also knew from Naples), he was still in control and it was through him that Niccolò obtained permission for the large Eidotto Room (Redoutensaal) in the Hofburg Palace, where some of the most famous concerts in history had taken place, especially in Beethoven's day, though now it was rarely used except for world celebrities like himself and Catalani.

After several days in a hotel, he moved (with Artaria's help) to suitable lodgings in the Trattnerhof (a large building complex on the Graben just opposite St. Stephen's Cathedral),[7] which was less expensive than a hotel and not only offered greater privacy, but also greater comfort and convenience in caring for a toddling youngster who was probably by that time fairly spoiled. A week after his arrival he then announced his first recital for Friday morning, March 28, but upon learning that Fridays in Lent were observed by the court as vigils, he postponed it till the twenty-ninth since otherwise the court could not attend—a most important desideratum for a debut.[8] Thus, for the first time he had to bow to circumstances and waive his Friday preference, it probably being explained to him that outside Italy it was immaterial since the theatres were usually open throughout the week. At all events, from now on he abandoned this requirement. Yet, even with this concession to the court, the hall for the opening concert was by no

is in fashion at Vienna—the language, music, and singers." (*A Ramble Among the Musicians of Germany* [London, 1828].)

6 In 1821 the court orchestra numbered approximately fifty and was probably not much larger in 1828. For ordinary concerts not favored with the support of the court orchestra, the orchestra was composed of musicians drawn from the different theatres, supplemented by amateur string players. His Vienna concerts were conducted by Hildebrand, Schuppanzigh, and one by Karl Fradel.

7 The Trattnerhof was a large building housing at that time 321 families. See Richard Groner, *Wien wie es war* (1934).

8 The placards and newspaper notices said simply that the concert was postponed "owing to an obstacle," without further explanation.

means filled,[9] though he still had every reason to be gratified since his audience included all Vienna's important arbiters of art and letters, the most influential members of the Italian colony, and all the leading connoisseurs—from the professional critic, through the knowledgeable amateur, down to the oracular *bas bleu*, while all the city's best known violinists were congregated together on the stage, this *corps d'élite* including Joseph Benesch,[10] Joseph Khayll,[11] Mathias Strebinger,[12] Joseph Mayseder,[13] Joseph Boehm,[14] Leopold Jansa,[15] Joseph Slavik,[16] and Leon de Saint Lubin,[17] as well as many lesser lights, most of whom he knew from Milan or Venetia.

Notwithstanding this sophisticated public, the atmosphere in the hall (the journalists tell us) was suffused with excitement so that the strains of the opening Leonore Overture had scarcely died away when the attention of the auditorium was focused on the door at the back of the stage through which the wizard was to make his entrance, a portion of the audience springing to its feet and even standing on the chairs in order to obtain a more unobstructed view. With the born showman's eye for effect, Paganini (at least abroad) made it an invariable rule to heighten suspense by delaying his appearance, so after the conclusion of the overture there was a protracted pause that seemed to the eager Viennese like an eternity. At last, as they were beginning to manifest impatience, the door on the balcony level opened and revealed "a cadaverous figure in sombre, old-fashioned black dress clothes," who, before descending

9 The admission was two florins *"Conventionsmünze,"* or five florins *"Wiener Währung,"* which led the Vienna cabmen to call a five gulden note a *Paganinerl.*

10 Joseph Benesch, Paganini's friend from Laybach, now a member of the court orchestra.

11 Joseph Khayall (1781–1829), solo oboist in the court orchestra.

12 Matthias Strebinger (b. 1807), violinist in the court orchestra.

13 Joseph Mayseder (1789–1863), pupil of Suche and Wranitzky. He became a member of Schuppanzigh's quartet while still a boy. Ludwig Strauss (1835–99) wrote: "I once plucked up courage to ask Mayseder what he thought of Paganini. 'We never heard anything like it before (he said) nor shall we ever hear anything like it again. All of us wanted to smash our fiddles.' "

14 Joseph Boehm (1795–1876), a pupil of Rode and teacher of Ernst, Joachim, Grün, Remenyi, and many other notable artists.

15 Leopold Jansa (1795–1875), member of the court orchestra.

16 Joseph Slavik (1806–33), pupil of F. W. Pixis at the Prague conservatory. He was a member of the court orchestra.

17 Leon de St. Lubin (1805–50), born in Turin, studied with Polledro in Dresden and with Spohr in Frankfort. At the time of Paganini's Vienna visit, he was first violin at the Josephstädtischer Theater.

the several steps leading to the stage, paused once more to survey the auditorium with a look half weariness, half imperious disdain. Yet this unusual and carefully calculated ritual by no means dampened his reception, for the door had no more than closed behind him than waves of welcoming applause swept towards him, increasing in fervor as he moved at glacier pace to his place before the orchestra. Framed in straggling black locks and curly side whiskers, the face—seamed and scarred by bodily and mental suffering—gazed out into the hall with an immobility that was in striking contrast with the vivacity of the sparkling eyes. "His face has much less expression than might be looked for [wrote Leigh Hunt later], it first seemed little better than a mask, with a fastidious, dreary expression." However, his bow had no sooner brushed the strings than "a higher spirit seemed to take possession of him. His features became animated, his eyes lit up, and his movements, so far as they had to do with his performance, became assured and definite. His expression seemed to mirror an inner conflict; the most unspeakable pain, the most ardent longing, the cruelest jest, even the most cutting scorn became discernible, all inevitably reminiscent of Hoffmann's Kreisler." (*Theaterzeitung*).

Next day even such critics as Ludwig Halirsch[18] and Ignaz Castelli[19] were at a loss to describe intelligibly his playing and the delirious enthusiasm of the audience. They tapped the deepest sources of their eloquence, only to admit that "what they heard was simply indescribable in words."[20] To form any idea of the disturbing emotional atmosphere he had generated in the hall, one must (they said) have experienced it personally.

We can appreciate their difficulty for, even though accustomed to walk with wonders daily till they have become for us familiar

[18] Ludwig Halirsch (1802–32), an employee of the Austrian government who was *en poste* in Italy at different times.

[19] Ignaz Franz Castelli, (1781–1862), popular dramatist and journalist who founded the *Allgemeiner musikalischer Anzeiger*.

[20] The program of the first concert was as follows:
1) Overture to Fidelio (Beethoven).
2) Concerto in B minor. Paganini.
3) Aria by Paer. Antonia Bianchi.
4) Sonata Militaire on the G string. Paganini.
5) Rondo *Non lusingare a barbaro* (Romani). Antonia Bianchi.
6) Larghetto and Variations on *Non più mesta accanto al fuoco* (Rossini). Paganini.

deities, it is well-nigh impossible to grasp the effect and manner of his playing as it struck the ears of his contemporaries. The Italian reviewers exhausted their superlatives without applying attention to the performance from the critical angle, yet even abroad, where patriotism represented no obstacle to detached appraisal, hyperbole was just as frequent and even more impressive through the critics' desperate endeavors to present sane and well-grounded reasons for it. All the same, to be able to form any conception of his art, and the impact of his personality on the public of his day, we must still look to the more factual of the reviewers, in countries other than his own—to men like Halirsch and Castelli in Vienna, Rellstab and Marx in Berlin, Guhr in Frankfort, Fétis in Paris, Chorley in London. For even to turn to the printed music, to hear it performed by our own great virtuosos, heirs, in fact, of his electrifying innovations, cannot solve for us the secret since the notes are no longer charged with the potencies of his enigmatic personality, with the genius of a man who was almost a species in himself.[21]

Allgemeine Theaterzeitung, April 5, 1828.
Paganini handles his instrument according to a method of his own, and for this reason his achievements remain inexplicable to violinists of even the first rank. . . . Gifted by nature with the keenest sensitiveness, endowed with artistic sense and perseverance, and placed by fate in situations where only the uninterrupted study of his instrument made him conscious that he was still alive, he was able to turn to his advantage things that would completely disconcert more ordinary mortals. . . . He immersed himself in exercises that constantly led him to new technical ideas and their combination. Only in this way could he tread paths that were unknown to his predecessors, because they were nonexistent. He literally detached himself from himself by continuously pacing back and forth. In this way he developed a technique that raised him to heights from which he could survey the entire realm of his art. . . . To analyze his performance is sheerly impossible and numerous rehearings avail but little. When we say that he performs

21 R. Lewin: "The way to hear this music [*La Campanella*] is to put up the score and play it in imagination. Only then can you realize the wild speed of the passage work and the weird, mesmeric nonchalance of that remarkable second theme in G Major. . . . Take the painfully difficult double-stopping harmonics in *I Palpiti* and the two concertos. Today with the most perfect of modern strings, if these are perfectly in tune, if the artist has a colossal power of stretching and a certain amount of luck, these passages are only just possible."

incredible difficulties with as clear and pure an intonation as another, when we say that in his hands the violin sounds more beautiful and more moving than any human voice, that his ardent soul pours a quickening glow into every heart; when we say that every singer can learn from him, this is still inadequate to give an impression of a single feature of his playing. He must be heard, and heard again, to be believed.

Ludwig Halirsch.
Paganini's whole being, as composer and virtuoso, is permeated with the most elevated spirit of poetry, in the noblest sense of the word. This is no momentary magic; the impression is deeper and more lasting the oftener one hears him and comes to appreciate his greatness. I have known him for seventeen years, have often heard him play in Italy and have missed none of his concerts here. With each new achievement the conviction deepens that he is the greatest instrumentalist the world of music has ever known.

Ignaz Castelli.
Never has an artist caused such a terrific sensation within our walls as this god of the violin. Never has the public so gladly carried its shekels to a concert, and never in my memory has the fame of a virtuoso so spread to the lowest classes of the population. After his first two concerts, there was only one name on everybody's lips and it seemed as though the people had lost all interest in politics, art, society, and even local gossip. There was only one thought, one topic of conversation—even amongst the tradesmen—indeed, I believe the children also momentarily forgot their toys.

ii

For the second concert, which took place after Easter, the Viennese literally arrived in shoals, the Empress and her children being present in the balcony and Franz Schubert among the commoners in the hall. Schubert had just given his first and only recital with a net gain to his exchequer of 800 gulden, which enabled him to indulge in this expensive treat and even go a second time and share the pleasure with his friend Edward von Bauernfeld.

I wasn't able to manage the five florins demanded by this concert-pirate [Bauernfeld confided to his diary]. Of course, it goes without saying that Schubert had to hear him, but he insisted that he wouldn't go again without me. "Stuff and nonsense!" he said. "I've heard him once al-

ready! and I was very cross because you weren't there. Believe me, such
a chap won't come a second time, and money is now as plentiful as
blackberries—so come along!" Such being the case, he took me with
him. We heard the infernal-divine fiddler and were no less charmed by
his wonderful *Adagio* than astounded by his other diabolical tricks.
The awkward bows of his Mephistophelean figure, which resembles a
lanky black puppet, had a slightly comical effect.

After he had paraded his sensational tours de force in two or
three more recitals, the violinists were especially keen to hear him
in some familiar work so that they might take his measure musically, leaving aside for once this dazzling and incomprehensible
technique. Although he disliked to abandon his fixed policy of
playing only his own music, this time he yielded to the universal
demand, performing first the Rode and then the Kreutzer concerto
that had long been in his repertory, but adding to the first an
Adagio religioso (composed "especially" for the Viennese) and to
the second an *Adagio*.

I've often sworn off playing compositions by others [he told Schottky],
and I've already destroyed all such music. But in Vienna they made me
break my vow. For it is foreign to my nature to play the works of others,
to perform borrowed material. Not that I can't play these works. Everybody knows quite well that I can play the most difficult music at sight,
but I want to maintain my own individuality and no one can blame
me for this since it seems to satisfy the public.[22]

As Goethe said, "There is no violinist who would not prefer to
play his own melodies," so Niccolò's attitude was not unusual. Why
play other men's music if he could write his own?[23] Certainly his
Vienna colleagues were of the same persuasion, yet they still felt
that on being suddenly confronted with such a trajectory of re-
valuations they could not gauge his achievements as an artist—or
their own, for that matter—till they met on common ground. The
reactions of his colleagues have never been recorded but the critics
on whom devolved the task of appraising his performance on the

[22] Schottky, *op. cit.*, 278.
[23] In this he had the example of Beethoven before him. According to Paul Bekker,
"Beethoven, as far as we know, never—except in his earliest days—played the compositions of another; and he never wrote a work for the pianoforte of which he did
not conceive himself to be the best possible interpreter."

basis of direct comparison were not displeased with the result, even with his interpolations and with what they looked upon as a complete disregard of the composer's intentions.[24] "He added a *Scherzo* to the Kreutzer *Rondo* [wrote the *Zeitung für die Elegante Welt*] which the work stands very well, even if the original composer never thought of it."

To date we have only heard him play a work of Kreutzer's and one of Rode's [wrote the *Theaterzeitung*], but on both occasions the composer's individual style disappeared in the ingenious treatment of the executant, and the composition might easily have been taken for his own. The author's ideas were all there, but in a more spiritualized, deeper, more powerful, and nobler speech, which etherealized the formal beauty of the original.

Fétis, however, felt quite differently about it.

In order to judge Paganini [he wrote in 1851] one had to hear him in his own works, in the compositions that characterized his talent. In his Paris concerts he thought he had to pay the French a compliment by playing a concerto by Kreutzer and one by Rode. He did not rise above the mediocre. As he said to Harrys: "I have my own personal method and I write my compositions in keeping with it. To play the works of others, I must mould them to my style, and I should much prefer to write an original work in which I can give the reins to my musical sentiment." The unfavorable impression he made in Paris with the two aforesaid works was a lesson to him. Since then he stopped playing any music but his own.

As for his own compositions, in Germany and Austria they were never disdainfully dismissed as "Italian music" even by those who

24 If he wove his own creations into the woof of other artists' works, he also frequently reversed the process. Hugo Hermann in his memoirs tells an interesting story regarding a competition that took place in the Cirque Napoléon in Paris, between Alard and Sivori. "When Sivori sounded the first notes of Paganini's second concerto, which I knew very well from the printed editions, Sivori's rendering departed very drastically from this. In fact, it was scarcely recognizable. In the last movement [the Bell Rondo] he even introduced a theme from a Spohr string quartet, which was very cleverly interwoven with the typical Paganini wizardry. I was naturally very interested and as soon as I had an opportunity I questioned Sivori about it and asked his permission to copy out his version, which increased the work's effectiveness to a sensational degree. However, he told me that he had learned this version directly from Paganini without one single note having ever been written down. Evidently, Sivori wished to guard the secret for himself!"

had strong feelings on the subject. And with one exception he was never accused, as was Liszt, of "making music cheap and trivial." Not till he arrived in Prague was his own taste seriously impugned.

In Trieste he had made the acquaintance of the Austrian violinist Joseph Panny and seems to have taken a great fancy to him, helping him in numerous ways in his friendly and not overly critical enthusiasm, but most of all, no doubt, through personal championship, which redounded to Panny's professional credit.[25] Despite many excellent connections, Panny was a poor devil who had passed through many difficult times during which he had essayed various occupations till one or two unexpected strokes of luck had brought him back to music, which he originally had to drop in order to earn his living. In the first stages of his musical career, he had written a number of works, principally for his own performance,[26] which were of little value. But when he resumed his music later, he gave more care and thought to composition and after settling in Mainz wrote a number of instrumental works for Schott, which were popular in their day, even though Fétis dismissed them as containing *"plus de fautes contre les règles de l'art, et plus de réminiscences que de beautés originales."*

Paganini told Schottky that before going to Vienna it was his fixed intention to ask Beethoven to write a "storm" for him to which he himself would add a set of final variations—a project that would undoubtedly have met with a rebuff![27] But, be that as it may, the idea had taken such hold upon his mind and he felt so keenly Beethoven's loss that he evidently confided his disappointment to Panny, who, scenting an opportunity of earning some badly needed cash, easily persuaded him that he was quite capable of filling the role originally designed for Beethoven.

25 Joseph Panny (1794–1838), after many years as a roving violinist, finally settled in Mainz, where he opened a school of music and resided till his death. Peter Cornelius studied with him at one time.

26 Adam Carse: "At that time the soloist was expected to show off his executive skill rather than his interpretative power or musicianship. The soloist who did not make a great display of mere execution was not ranked very high, the concert music being designed only with a view to exhibiting the performer's virtuosity. Large quantities of trivial variations, fantasias, and similar media for display were performed by soloists who very often composed their own pieces and in such a way as to exhibit the devices in which they particularly excelled."

27 Schottky, *op. cit.,* 337.

Shortly after Paganini's arrival in Vienna, Panny borrowed 200 florins from him[28] and in return allegedly gave him a Mozart manuscript; which may have been a simple commercial transaction and might explain why Paganini, according to Schottky, "never mentioned the amount again." Yet, knowing the Maestro and his almost invariable custom in such matters, added to the similarity of the two sums, which would seem to be more than mere coincidence, one suspects that when he selected Panny to fill Beethoven's intended role and on the completion of the "dramatic sonata" required him to write on the manuscript that he "had received 200 florins in payment of it" he was here referring to the loan, having in this way afforded Panny the opportunity of working out his debt "in kind."

A "storm" was one of the themes especially dear to the hearts of the Romantics, since it afforded the performer with a gift for embellishment and improvisation almost unlimited opportunities of demonstrating his descriptive powers. As Paganini was then in a very creative vein (several of his most successful works date from this period), he could have wished only to recover his outlay or to compliment the Viennese by selecting as collaborator an Austrian composer. For otherwise there would seem to have been no plausible reason for his not having written it himself.

The suggestion has been advanced that after leaving Italy the scoring of works in large form may have presented for him certain problems; that, having devoted his career and his creative gifts to the technique of his solo instrument (when he had his audience always in the forefront of his mind), he lacked the craftsmanship to meet the high requirements of a large and well-trained orchestra. For the orchestra he heard in Vienna was no longer the modest instrument he had studied under Paer thirty years before, nor had he since been in a position to learn the amplitude of orchestration, since in this respect Italy had contributed very little to the orchestra's development. Therefore, to hear works like Beethoven's Seventh Symphony after the crude means of the average Italian "symphony" and the thin accompaniments of contemporary Italian opera was probably bewildering and may explain why some of

[28] Panny's receipt with notarial certification was listed in Nebehay's catalogue (Vienna) some years ago. The present whereabouts of the document is unknown.

Beethoven's music sounded *"extravagante"* to him. (One wonders if he ever heard Weber's little gibe at Italian orchestration! *"Oboi col Flauti, Clarinetti col Oboi, Flauti col Violini, Fagotti col Basso, Viol.*²ᵈᵉ *col Primo, Viola col Basso, Voce ad Libitum, Violini colla parte."!*) The changes he undertook in the wood winds and the brass during his short association with the Parma orchestra in 1835 were no doubt traceable to the experiences he had garnered in Austria and Germany, where instruments were then constantly undergoing improvement in volume, range, and nuance. Whereas orchestration had formerly been a simple matter when writing works for local Italian orchestras, his letters from abroad suggest that it was now difficult for him to settle down to it, owing perhaps to some psychological inhibition, some inner feeling that here a certain technique was required that he had not yet adequately mastered, his only error in Panny's case being that he thought any German musician was capable of it.

The Panny work formed the climax of his farewell concert on July 24, but the effect did not measure up to expectations. It "fell flat, with not a hand of applause," and was not even "a successful virtuoso vehicle for Paganini," the critics unanimously rejecting it as trivial and out of place on a serious concert program. While they gave courteous consideration to Paganini's small share in the work, they summarily dismissed poor Panny as "lacking intelligence and soul," which probably decided Panny to hitch his chariot, if possible, to Paganini's star and to accompany him on his German tour as "traveling conductor." At any rate, he left Vienna in Paganini's company but upon arrival in Carlsbad²⁹ they had a serious falling out, Panny then departing on a concert tour of his own through Germany and Scandinavia. Paganini's intuitive flair for recognizing a master when he met him unfortunately did not always function in reverse, which frequently led him to expend his enthusiasm on quite unworthy objects. Yet, in all such cases his heart no doubt overrode his better judgment, a little human frailty that Schottky attributed to a lack of discernment.

29 Paganini told Schottky (*op. cit.,* 275) that the reason he parted company with Panny was that he "did not want to give people the impression that, like Catalani, he required a composer to travel with him and could not write his own music."

iii

We must now retrace our steps and take up the main threads of his life in the Austrian capital—the Viennese reaction outside musical circles, his several problems, emotional and clinical, the complete change wrought in his existence, the transformation of the Italian virtuoso, formerly content like Wordsworth's skylark "to soar but not to roam," into the restless cosmopolitan with henceforth no desire to sink his roots into any soil, not even to become a Genoese again amongst the Genoese.

"The great novelty and prodigy of the day is Paganini [reported the Vienna correspondent of the *Harmonicon*]. He is not only the finest player on the violin but no other performer upon any instrument whatsoever can come within a mile of him; in short, he bids fair to outdo the giraffe."[30] This was not mere facetiousness; for from the moment of his debut the city was in a ferment. And despite stories of boisterous actions unconnected with his art, of mysterious crimes and their still more mysterious punishment, his popularity waxed from day to day. Wherever he appeared he was at once encircled by a flying squadron of infatuated women; and even the proletarian ranks, as Castelli noted, were intoxicated to delirium. If he hesitated, for fear of being crushed or ogled, to pursue his inconsequential way like other ordinary mortals, and retired into seclusion, his admirers turned to lithographs, china cups, or other bric-à-brac decorated with his portrait, which were then given a place of honor in the *Servante,* along with other Biedermeier *objets d'art*. Immediately after his arrival, Kriehuber painted his and Bianchi's portraits, which were at once published by Artaria. So within a fortnight there was no shop in all Vienna without his portrait framed in laurel or bearing floating streamers of lyrics written by well-known sonneteers down to mere poetasters whose enthusiasm was more obvious than their poetic gifts. His gaunt visage with the straggling locks and prominent nose appeared on practically every salable object, themes from his works

---

30 A giraffe had recently been presented to the Emperor by the Khedive of Egypt, and had been the talk of the town for some weeks, since the animal till then was unknown in northern Europe.

could be heard in all the cafés and dance halls, and if he were obliged to take a fiacre, next day it was labeled like a sacrarium. Anecdotes sprang up like mushrooms and no newspaper appeared without the "latest Paganini quip," many of which—offspring of some lustrous imagination—have now been consecrated by tradition and can be accepted, even by the purist, as at least symbolical.[31] He took it all good-naturedly and was often "convulsed with laughter" over some audacious jest or *"caricatura buffonesca,"* though for some reason he missed a more ambitious bit of raillery of a type that usually afforded him great amusement, namely, a musical comedy *Die falsche Virtuoso,* which had been hastily concocted by Karl Meisl and Frank Gläser,[32] one of the most successful musical comedy teams of that day, and presented for the first time on May 22 at the Theater an der Wien. (He had a concert of his own on the opening night.) Taking advantage of the reigning enthusiasm, they turned out a witty, tuneful little operetta which, barring the haste in which it was written, was immensely successful, owing to the clever way in which the authors had adapted many of the current anecdotes and had woven several of the most popular Paganini themes into the overture. The work had only two or three performances during the remaining weeks of his Vienna stay and either no one called his attention to it, or his many worries drove it completely from his mind since, when someone mentioned it in Berlin, he at once wrote off to learn if it was in "any way uncomplimentary to him," a point on which he happened at that time to be particularly sensitive. Otherwise, when health and personal affairs permitted, he enjoyed the theatres both from the public and the working side of the footlights, executed commissions for his friends,[33] and played quartets with his Austrian colleagues,[34] which afforded them further opportunities of studying his playing at close

[31] One of the most charming stories (probably apocryphal) current at this time told of his hearing a little lad scraping a fiddle in one of the courtyards and upon learning that the boy was trying to earn some pennies for his mother, Paganini took the instrument and played it himself. The music drew all the tenants of the building to their windows and resulted in a rain of pennies for the delighted little minstrel.

[32] Gläser was a very prolific composer of this type of musical entertainment. The Paganini skit had a total of only twelve performances.

[33] Among other things he purchased a Graff piano for his Trieste friend, Agostino Samengo, paying 400 thalers for it, exclusive of shipment charges.

[34] The leading quartet at that time consisted of Ignaz Schuppanzigh, Mayseder, Weiss, and Linke.

Charlotte Watson

Grand Duchess Marie Louise of Parma

range. Further, he was greatly interested in Vienna's many concerts and, when not ill, was present at all the more important ones, especially those of the singers and the violinists. (Strange to say, his letters do not mention his attending the concerts of any violinists, with the exception of Lafont and Signora Raggi-Pallavicini, but we know from others that he was rarely absent on such occasions and always applauded vociferously, in the Italian manner.)

On Thursday, May 1, he was present at the opening concert of Schuppanzigh's Augarten concert series, on which occasion he heard Beethoven's Seventh Symphony for the first time. These matinee concerts, which took place in the public park on the Au, or meadow, lying between the Danube and the Danube Canal, went back to 1782, when they had been founded by Martin (a well-known Vienna entrepreneur) in association with Mozart. By 1828 they had fallen greatly from their high estate but they were still one of the typical aspects of Vienna's music, which naturally would have appealed to Paganini, quite apart from Schuppanzigh's connection with them. According to an eyewitness, he sat perfectly immobile while the symphony was being played, but when it was over and his companion turned to make some comment, the latter was surprised to see the tears streaming down his haggard cheeks. "*E morto!*" was all that he could say—in Pulver's words, "surely one of the highest and most sincerely felt signs of homage the memory of Beethoven ever received."[35]

A fortnight later Prince Metternich's young wife, Marie Antoinette Leykam, a beautiful Viennese with a touch of Italian blood whom he had married in 1827, engaged the Maestro to play at a reception on May 15 in honor of the Prince's fifty-fifth birthday.

She had prepared several surprises for the Prince [wrote Baron von Andlaw], though they were not all equally successful. First came a short concert, Paganini playing for the first, and only time, at a private party. Everyone was extremely eager to see this strange figure and hear his demonic playing at close quarters. . . . Before he appeared, Prince Dietrichstein led a blond young man to the pianoforte, but just as he began to play, refreshments were passed round which distracted the attention of the company. Suddenly Prince Dietrichstein called out angrily: "Stop playing! Nobody is listening to you!" And it took a great

35 *Wiener Theaterzeitung* (May 20, 1828).

deal of coaxing before the young man could be persuaded to resume the interrupted sonata. This embryo virtuoso was . . . Thalberg! Paganini then followed with *Le Streghe*.[36] [Thalberg was the illegitimate son of Dietrichstein and Baroness von Wetzlar.]

As an ardent music lover and one with a notable weakness for the Italian muse, Metternich could not have received a more pleasurable birthday gift, for as he wrote to Princess Lieven, "Nothing moves me like music. After love, or more exactly, combined with love, it is probably the best of all possible influences. Music both stirs and calms me, it revives the memory, it lifts me out of the narrow circle of daily experience. The heart expands, its urges become timeless, all comes to life, the joys and sorrows of the past—those that I desire and those for which I wait."

Paganini left no record of any special gift on this occasion, so he may have contributed his services in homage to the Prince's anniversary because "he was mad about the violin."[37]

Paganini to Agostino Samengo, Vienna, May 15, 1828.
I had no sooner appeared here than I saw a musically cultivated public most kindly disposed towards any musician with an enthusiastic interest in his art. I've given five concerts in the large Redoutensaal and day before yesterday gave the sixth, this time in the Royal Theatre for His Majesty, the Emperor. . . . If it were legitimate for me to tell you how greatly the public honors me, I should have to add that the press is even more flattering, a translation of which I read also in the Trieste paper.[38] But I shall restrict myself to saying that I'm truly encouraged by a really unanimous acclaim, the most flattering to which I ever could aspire. This evening I'm playing at Prince Metternich's; tomorrow, again in the Redoutensaal—for charity.[39]

Yet his path was not all strewn with roses, gratifying as might be the universal adulation paid him by people in every walk of life. He had come through the formidable ordeal with flying colors but soon to his dismay he discovered that his legend and his career were now impossible to disentangle; and the realization was anything

[36] Franz Freiherr von Andlaw, *Mein Tagebuch* (Frankfort, 1862).

[37] Metternich wrote that at the time of the Congress of Vienna "he conducted the orchestra, symphonies and concertos, and played in a quartet so successfully that people still remembered the occasion."

[38] *Osservatore Trieste* (May 8, 1828).

[39] There is no record that Paganini ever played at court.

but pleasing to him. The *Theaterzeitung* had alluded in thinly veiled terms to the old scandal of his imprisonment and, if allowed to pass unchallenged, the report might prove disastrous.[40] For in pietistic Germany and puritanical England, should such calumnies be spread abroad and be given credence (as they here seemed to be) they might stand between him and certain dreams that meant far more to him than a papal decoration on his breast. The days when he was happy to exploit such gossip for the sake of the receipts were long past, so as soon as the *Theaterzeitung* article appeared he at once rushed off to his countryman, Marshal Camillo Vacani,[41] of the Imperial Austrian Army, who wrote in his name a letter to the editor in which he emphatically denied the slanderous report, hoping by this categorical denial to silence the gossip once for all.

While warmly thanking the writer of the article in the *Theaterzeitung* of April 5 reviewing his first concert before the highly cultivated and estimable Viennese public, Paganini feels that he must clarify an expression employed therein and seemingly alluding to vague rumors falsely disseminated by those ignorant of his origin. In the interest of his own honor and the truth, he must therefore state that at no time, in no place, and under no government whatsoever was he, for any reason, compelled to lead a life other than that proper to a free man, a respected citizen, and a faithful observer of the laws. This fact can be substantiated wherever necessary by all the authorities under whose protection he has lived in freedom and with honor for himself, his fam-

40 When Schottky was gathering material for his book he received a letter from a friend in Modena, giving him the following version of the alleged imprisonment: "Paganini was a very inexperienced youth and loved to gamble. He was very easily led astray by boisterous companions who were not exactly models of virtue. One day he and Marquis P—— (a good friend of his) called on a lady who was not only very good-looking herself but who had a beautiful daughter, with whom Paganini immediately fell in love, while his friend was equally infatuated with the mother. Upon leaving, they compared notes and, both being convinced that their feelings were reciprocated, they proceeded to confess their love to the ladies in a not altogether delicate manner. The latter were horrified and had the two importunate lovers arrested. The Marquis succeeded in regaining his liberty within a week, but Paganini who had been more daring in his advances than his friend, was imprisoned for three months." Might not the memory of some little contretemps of this nature have been behind his refusal to play in Modena in the early summer of 1818 when the "presence of five crowned heads made the occasion otherwise propitious"? (Codignola, *op. cit.*, 147.)

41 Camillo de Vacani (1785–1862), son of an aristocratic old Milanese family. He entered military service when very young and in 1808 served with the Napoleonic troops in Spain for five years.

ily, and the art which he is now fortunate enough to present to a public of connoisseurs as indulgent as the Viennese—the first before whom he has had the honor to play since leaving Italy.

Vienna, April 10, 1828.

The letter was published, without comment, in the issue of April 19 but, like future *pièces justificatives,* its only effect was to give the scandal wider publicity than ever. Although official circles were too well informed to give serious consideration to such accusations, the journalists regularly had recourse to the story since it added an aura of mystery to his personality. And for the most part, he seems himself to have realized this fact, that is, when his nerves were not unstrung; yet an inner voice still warned him not to let it pass unchallenged, that in the end it was far more likely to be maleficent. And such proved to be the case when after his death the effect of this and kindred libels robbed him of the spontaneous and universal homage of his countrymen.

iv

Meanwhile, he proceeded with his concerts, giving five in May, five in June, and one in July, making a grand total of fourteen.[42] After the recital on May 11, he consented, in recognition of the favors shown him by the court, to play two intermezzo concerts at the Burg Theatre,[43] where the receipts were to be evenly divided. But since the amount fell short of the anticipated figure, the Intendant on both occasions rounded off his fee to one thousand florins, so that again he had no reason to complain. In between these appearances he also gave a charity concert for the benefit of St. Mark's Almshouses (for which Haydn and Beethoven had done so much) and received in recompense from the city the large Salvator Medal, which was conferred on him July 10 by the chamberlain Count Rudolf von Czernin.[44]

---

[42] Paganini's receipts for his first eight Vienna concerts were 2,464, 5,138, 3,418, 3,802, 2,098, 2,817, 1,000 and 1,000 florins.

[43] The first concert in the Burg Theatre was *auf allerhöchsten Befehl,* one of the brilliant occasions when the sovereigns and court were in attendance in full regalia. For this he received a *"wahrhaft kaiserliches Gnadengeschenk"* in the form of a gold snuffbox with the Emperor's monograph in diamonds.

[44] He was also presented with a silver and bronze medal engraved by Joseph Lang

After the second concert at the Burg Theatre, the Emperor also bestowed on him the honorary title of Chamber Virtuoso, which, as long as he was in Austria and Germany, he displayed on all his programs, though he dropped it when he went to France, maybe because he hoped to receive an equivalent recognition from Louis Philippe. At his next five concerts at the Royal Opera (Kärtnertor-theater) the attendance was much smaller than heretofore, and in addition he was required to pay two hundred florins each time to the Burg Theatre, probably on the theory that his concerts affected the attendance at the other house.

The concert on June 12 was a benefit for Bianchi (some say, at Artaria's suggestion) and it was on this occasion that he played for the first time his variations on the Austrian national hymn.[45] His next concert had to be postponed from the nineteenth to the twenty-fourth because of illness, and after another on the thirtieth he finally had to cancel all engagements for three weeks. For he was now suffering from a variety of ailments, aggravated and climaxed by his stormy break with Bianchi and by an unpleasant lawsuit with his dentist Vergani. In fact, a veritable "world of ills came down like snow," so that he must have often wished with all his heart and soul that he were once more safe at home in the *Land wo die Zitronen blühn.*

with the motto: *Periturus sonis non peritura gloria* (Sounds die away, fame is imperishable). He also gave violin students of the Vienna Conservatory free admission to all his concerts. At the charity concert he was assisted by Bianchi and the young pianist Leopoldine Blahetta. When the concert was announced, one of the Vienna papers commented: "Such a *donum gratuitum pro bonum publico* should appease even the inveterate patriots who never want for anything and yet have begun to shout for help over the inhuman sums that a foreigner is taking out of the country."

[45] Paganini's fourteen programs in Vienna afford an interesting picture of the tastes of that day. The first concert opened with the Fidelio Overture, in homage to Beethoven. In the course of the series the overture to *Zauberflöte* was played three times, that to Mozart's *Titus* once, the overtures to Beethoven's *Egmont* and Weber's *Oberon* each once. The other concerts presented French and Italian works. At the concert of May 13, the orchestra played Mozart's Jupiter Symphony, opening with the first movement. Then between Paganini's numbers the other movements followed in this order: Minuet, Andante, Finale. The concert of May 16 opened with the first movement of Beethoven's Seventh Symphony, followed by the first movement of the pianoforte concerto in A Major, played by Henri Herz. The last number was the Andante of the symphony. On May 22, the orchestral offerings included the Allegro from Beethoven's Symphony in D Major, the Andante from Haydn's Paukenschlag Symphony and the Scherzo from the Beethoven work. The farewell concert on July 24 presented the Minuet and Andante from Mozart's E flat Symphony.

v

Not long after their arrival in Vienna the relationship between him and his "charming companion" had sharpened to a crisis; indeed, within a fortnight he seems to have been ready to sever the partnership on condition she give up the child in return for a financial settlement, as shown by the Vienna dossier on Achilles' adoption, which contained copies of two communications addressed by Paganini to the Tribunal of Justice in Milan, the first as early as March 31.[46] As the weeks went by, things reached such a state of tension that any question of further life together had become a sheer impossibility, and while natural incompatibility of temperament and the rapid downward trend in Paganini's health obviously played a role therein, the real forces that caused the lady's tantrums derived unquestionably from her colossal vanity, her demands on his person and his finances, her pettiness and lack of balance, and very probably from her fierce resentment of his popularity in aristocratic circles where attention would have especially gratified her vanity and from which (unless she appeared as assisting soloist) she would naturally have been barred. With passion spent and no reciprocal regard or deep affection to make one patient with the other's frailties, with Bianchi a termagant by nature, lazy, and possessing none of the domestic virtues, and with Paganini harrassed by physical pain so that trifling vexations induced volcanic emotional reactions with a brisk exchange of insults, continued life together was clearly inconceivable. For without harmony and peace of mind he could never summon the concentration, the nerve control, and self-possession necessary for the practice of his art. "Bianchi has been separated from me for some time [he wrote Germi on July 5] because she is an iniquitous beast and I never want to hear her name again. But I'll tell you the rest when things are more tranquil."

As already mentioned, she was a friend of Paganini's Milan banker, Carlo Carli, who corresponded with her regularly till his death and seems in some way to have been instrumental in bring-

46 The documents themselves are no longer in existence, but a tabulated list of the "official enclosures" now in Vienna indicates the nature and the date of the communications. See n. 2, Chapter XXXII.

ing about her marriage to Carlo Felice Brunati in 1830, since a decade later Paganini "blessed the letter Germi had drafted for him to Carli, which led to her marriage,"[47] thus relieving him of any further responsibility. Carli now also interposed a word for her and ventured a reproof for Paganini's summary dismissal and violation of a mother's claims, which so angered him that he was unable for some weeks to control his feelings sufficiently to make reply.[48]

Paganini to Carlo Carli, Berlin, March 1, 1829.

That part of your kind letter in which you speak of Bianchi put me in such a state that I've postponed answering you from day to day, from week to week. So you think the lady would have been helpful to me if I had fallen ill! My friend, it's just when I'm ill that I realize what an advantage it is to me not to have her about! Whether through lack of heart or intelligence, at such times she never did anything she should have done. I don't wish to reopen at this time the many painful wounds. The wretched creature never wanted to practice or do anything at all. When she had to undertake even the slightest task, she complained that I treated her like a slave. She told God and all creation of her ignominy. I tried in vain to restrain her; but again and again everything she did provoked me. This sad story would be too long and painful to relate here. When I met her she was an insignificant little singer and I taught her so that she could appear in concert. She had scarcely a rag to her back. Now she has a magnificent wardrobe, jewels, and money in the bank! She embittered my life as long as she was with me and now that I'm rid of her, she has, as I know, only one aim in life—to blacken my character. Honorable men will judge between us. To a friend like yourself I wanted to explain my position once for all—not to justify myself, but to relieve my feelings.

Outlines of the sordid story are a little obscure but the two must have parted company by mid-April at the latest. In moving to other quarters she evidently took the child, together with her other

47 *"Devo dover bendire la lettera chi mi dettasti per il fu Carli, avendu fruttato il matrimonia della Bianchi."*

48 Paganini's notebook contains a preliminary draft of this letter in Rebizzo's handwriting, dated Berlin, February 28, 1828. In the margin Paganini added a note to the effect that he had written the latter in his own hand. Kapp took his quotation from this source. The actual letter was dated March 1 and was received by Carli on March 20. The original is now in a private collection.

worldly possessions, Paganini in turn withholding all her music,[49] presumably to keep her from returning to Italy with Achilles before he had been able to arrange for his adoption. After the initial application, the magistrate's court designated the child a ward in chancery under the guardianship of Carl Joseph Hammer, a city alderman in charge of civil sequestrations; then on August 4 it handed down a decision in which Achilles was turned over to his father. In a preliminary arrangement on July 22, Paganini had paid Bianchi the sum of 3531.02 florins (10,953 lire), whereupon she waived all further claims upon him and relinquished the child on the court's orders, on condition she be kept informed from time to time of his well-being and be allowed to visit him, should they ever find themselves in the same town. At the same time, the agreement signed in Milan on December 4, 1827, guaranteeing her an annual allowance of one hundred Milanese scudi was automatically revoked, the court directing Paganini to return to her "within twenty-four hours all the music belonging to her," which she now looked upon as her indispensable working tools if she were obliged to support herself by singing.

Paganini to Germi, June 11, 1828.
You will have learned from the Vienna papers of my triumphs; but I won't be happy without your friendship and your love. I've deposited 60,000 Austrian lire in Eskeles Bank so as not to have the money lying idle. I've given my ninth concert at the Italian opera and the posters were no sooner up than all the boxes and seats were sold, so now I have to stay in Vienna all this month and next to give five or six more concerts. I've written two adagios for double stops, which are effective; the one makes you weep and the other—entitled *Religioso*—makes the auditors contrite. Here they relish true music and all the best players and composers have gone to the country to study in private. I've composed a grand sonata on the G string in which at the end I play variations on the Haydn theme, *Gott erhalte den Kaiser,* which I'm now

---

[49] Pulver (*op. cit.,* 147) wrote that "Paganini allowed her to take with her all the things he had given her . . . but made her return all the music he had written for her." Codignola (*op. cit.,* 272) gives an Italian translation of the alleged verdict of the Magistrate's Court wherein it is stated that Paganini "agreed to restore to her within twenty-four hours all the pieces of music belonging to her." Codignola does not indicate the source, or present whereabouts, of this document (i.e., whether he was quoting a translated copy, or reproducing the original). Since the official Austrian copy has been destroyed, it is impossible to verify which version is correct, though Codignola's agrees with Schottky's (*op. cit.,* 346 ff.).

going to orchestrate. I've heard two new quartets of Beethoven played in my house by four of the best professors; I shall soon return the compliment by playing these works for them myself,[50] but this music is very extravagant. . . . I have to send Bianchi away because I'm disgusted with her; but I'll tell you about it later. Meanwhile, we've separated and tomorrow I'm giving my tenth concert in the Italian Opera, which will be for her benefit, as stated on the posters.[51]

Like the born opportunist that he was, he now introduced a custom that he followed throughout his continental tour (France and England excepted)—that of paying homage to the sovereign and people whose guest he was by composing variations on the national anthem. But once more the "idea" was derivative! Here he was plagiarizing Catalani, who had introduced the custom in Germany and Austria, where the public were still talking of it. His Anglo-Saxon listeners, however, were much less impressed.

Leigh Hunt (June 27, 1831): Paganini's playing of *Gott erhalte den Kaiser* appeared to us altogether a mistake. This composition of Haydn's is surely a point of severe and simple playing and not a subject for whining and chromatics. The style in which Paganini gave it was rather what we should have expected from some unthinking shower-off than a great master. It should have been affectionate, but only in such a way as to be compatible with a Hymn, and with the modesty of a religious petition—fervent, cathedral, deferential, yet at the same time self-collected; conscious of a presence, before which there is to be no unseemly weakness or overweeningness. Yet to those who were aware of the nature of the subject, Paganini's chromatical, fond, and effeminate manner of playing it resembled a caricature of some morbid loyalist who had got maudlin with the Emperor's wine, and must needs go sighing and dying through the National Hymn. Here was a deficiency in that judgment which implies the very deepest taste, or the perfection of the sense of truth.

That he was able in the midst of the huge convulsion that rent

50 At that time the quartet was looked upon as a solo work, with three accompanying instruments. See Ernest Newman, *The Life of Richard Wagner,* I, 130–33.

51 In her biography, (*Paganini of Genoa,* 141) Lillian Day writes that "Bianchi complained to Domenico Artaria, Paganini's manager, who kindly headed a group of indignant citizens who compelled the artist to give a concert for the benefit of his abused mistress." The Artaria Archives are in the Vienna Stadtbibliothek but are not yet available for research, so it has been impossible to verify the Day statement. As usual, the author quotes no sources. In this connection she quotes a portion of the Carli letter but incorrectly identifies it as a letter to Germi.

his life asunder to give his mind to creative work is all the more astonishing in view of his state of health and the alarming symptoms that now overwhelmed him like evil genii rising from a bottle. Shortly after his arrival in Vienna his teeth began to give him serious trouble, the obvious aftermath of Borda's mercury-opium treatments. Starting first with a prolonged and very painful toothache, he discovered that an abscess had formed, which soon caused him such excruciating pain that upon the recommendation of Domenico Artaria, he sought the services of an Italian dentist, one Dr. A. M. de Vergani, who advertised himself as the "dentist of Archduchess Marie Louise and their Royal Highnesses Karl and Joseph Palatin," so Paganini felt confident that he was in the right hands. Upon examining his mouth, Vergani (as he stated later in his deposition) was "horrified" to find that all Paganini's teeth were "literally hanging by a thread"; in other words, they were all loose and to make it possible to masticate he had threaded them together! With the lack of proper hygienic care, added to the foul infection of his teeth, his mouth was in a frightful condition and Vergani, in attempting to open the abscess and remove the offending molar, either injured the bone or the tissues became infected, whereupon Paganini refused to pay him, after which Vergani sued, and eventually won his case on the grounds that infection was already pre-existent.

With present medical knowledge of the serious and far-reaching consequences of dental infection on all the functions of the body, one is appalled on reading Vergani's testimony that the results were not more serious than they were. But things were still quite bad enough and it seems strange that practitioners as able as Bennati and Spitzer (who were treating him at this time) did not discover it or that Bennati failed to mention the condition in his subsequent analysis.

After studying at Padua and Pavia, Francesco Bennati had gone to the University of Vienna under a special scholarship granted by the Austrian authorities in Italy, and remained there till May 15, 1828.[52] "*Je vous recommande M. Bennati qui accompagne le*

---

[52] Francesco Bennati (1788–1834) studied at Padua, Pavia, and Vienna. Among his many works was *Du mechanisme de la voix humaine pendant le chant; Études physiologiques et pathologiques sur les organes de la voix humaine.* He also collaborated with Savart and Cagniard-Latour in studies of the vocal chords and the human voice.

courier de ce jour [Metternich wrote his son Victor on May 15]. *C'est un jeune médecin né à Mantoue—très joli homme et fort bon garçon. Il voyage pour son instruction. . . . Il chante à merveille, qualité qui n'est pas trop de la faculté."* His musicianly bents evidently had much to do with his specializing in the functions and maladies of the vocal chords and brought him rapidly to the forefront of his profession as a laryngologist, which secured him his appointment as consulting physician of the Théâtre des Italiens in Paris. In 1831 he spoke of having been "on an intimate footing with Paganini for over ten years" (counting evidently from 1822 when Paganini was ill in Pavia) but, since he did not receive his degree till 1826, it is unlikely that Paganini ever consulted him professionally in Italy unless he passed through his hands in one of the therapeutic classes in which the students made the examinations under the supervision of a medical instructor. Music and common friends may also have brought them together so that Bennati was familiar in a general way with his fundamental disorders. After Bennati's departure, Paganini evidently consulted Spitzer, who examined his eyes (which were now giving him really serious trouble) and directed him to wear blue glasses when playing in artificial light, which he must have found beneficial since he frequently used them at his concerts from this time on. After Spitzer left, he called in Dr. Matthias Marenzellar,[53] a homeopathic physician in the army medical corps, who after treating him for several weeks advised him to take the waters at Carlsbad which might indicate that his sluggish intestines were again involved, leading to the evils that always caused him so much pain and discomfort. It is not unlikely, in the light of present-day knowledge, that a condition probably brought about in early childhood through carelessness and ignorance and the unhygienic living conditions of that time was aggravated later by an inherently tense and high-strung temperament, since, after each emotional crisis in his life, he suffered for weeks afterwards from intestinal disorders and of course only made things worse by resorting to violent purgatives. His repeated scenes with Bianchi were alone sufficient to keep all

---

[53] Matthias Marenzeller (1765–1854) was on the staff of the Vienna General Hospital for twenty years. He was a great opponent of "bleeding and the use of purgatives."

his organs in a chronic state of spasm; therefore, it is no wonder that the condition finally reached a point where he had to resort to medical advice.

Just at that time Dr. Hahnemann,[54] the founder of homeopathy, was very much in the public eye, owing to the growing popularity of his principles and the obstacles placed in their dissemination by the authorities and his medical colleagues who remained unconvinced by his theories. So, true to his practice of trying every new curative measure that came to his attention, Paganini for a time was an enthusiastic disciple, though whether he ever consulted Hahnemann himself in Germany seems doubtful unless he chanced to run across him at Carlsbad or Baden Baden. Hahnemann had settled in Leipzig in 1799 but owing to the hostility of the apothecaries he was obliged to leave in 1821 and took up his residence in Coethen upon the invitation of the Prince of Anhalt-Coethen, whom he later accompanied regularly to Carlsbad for the cure. After Paganini's first introduction to the treatment in Vienna, his six weeks in Carlsbad later must have thoroughly indoctrinated him in Hahnemann's principles, owing to the latter's numerous patients and proselytes there and the winds of controversy that whistled through the pines of the famous Bohemian resort.

With his teeth and gums in such a deplorable condition, dosing with mild medicaments only increased his general malaise and must have made him an exceedingly difficult house companion. Conestabile wrote that he "lost many teeth as the result of a poor dentist," though if his mouth were in as bad a condition as Vergani's deposition stated (of which there is no reason to doubt) the mere extraction of a molar could have represented no great difficulty, even for a tyro.[55] What is far more likely is that the infected condition, obviously of long standing, had affected the bone of the jaw, and the dentists of that day, not understanding the treatment of such cases, failed to scrape the bone, so that the infection spread through the blood stream, making his condition even more serious than it was.

[54] Samuel Christian Hahnemann (1750–1843), founder of homeopathy.
[55] The *Intelligenzblatt zur Prager Zeitung* of November 15, 1828, announced Vergani's arrival in Prague, where he would be available for consultation for six weeks.

Paganini to Germi, July 5, 1828.

I should have given a fourteenth recital if I had not been extremely ill, but I shall give it next week or the week after in order to comply with the gracious wish of Her Majesty, the Archduchess Marie Louise,[56] who wishes to be informed of my recovery. There is still a desire to hear me. How many Paganinis are there in the world?[57] I don't believe it is to my advantage or to my glory to give recitals in small places; so in August I shall go to Munich, Prague, Dresden, Berlin, Frankfort, and Stuttgart; and to Strasbourg, Chalons, Paris, and London next April. Meanwhile, I am preparing two pieces of dramatic music on the G string to be played with full orchestra, and the *Sonata drammatico* entitled "The Tempest" is practically finished.[58] I shall play this work along with my Third Concerto (which I have not yet played) at my farewell concert for the Viennese.

Since, despite his great success, he never thought of returning to Vienna,[59] it is to be supposed that the quarrels with Bianchi, the upheaval in his personal life, had left a corrosive residue that spoiled the episode for him and obliterated other, pleasanter memories. With his exalted ideas of a mother's love, of the meaning in the life of a little child of a mother's adoration and indulgence, he would probably have gone to the limits of the possible to have preserved this treasure for his son. But Bianchi was not modeled of such heroic clay. As for himself, fated to tread great heights alone, the depths of his unconscious dictated his reactions, urging him onward to a solution that was irrevocable because it had been cast for him by destiny. For the most imperative demand of his nature was to maintain the haughty freedom of his spirit; he dared not sacrifice it, even for his son, to one who in a fit of anger "smashed his violin" and "boxed his ears in public." For three years now he had been torn continually between two powerful and conflicting

---

56 Liszt wrote of her: *"Marie Louise, qui joue fort bien du piano, accueille des artistes avec la plus gracieuse bonté."*

57 This remark also seems to have been taken over from Beethoven! See Frimmel, *Ludwig van Beethoven* (1st ed., Berlin, 1901), 40.

58 The following note appears on the manuscript: "Composed for Niccolò Paganini and commissioned by him on May 25, 1828. Vienna, June 14, 1828." The manuscript is now in the Reuther Collection.

59 In December, 1834, the historian Angelo Pizzana wrote Count Dietrichstein that Paganini had arrived in Parma, to which Dietrichstein replied: *"Ah, s'il y retournait,"* in recalling the Vienna days.

emotions—his desire to preserve a relationship for the child's sake and his need to safeguard his own liberty. *"Sono stato niente fortunato,"* he sighed to Germi in a moment of depression. But his love of music was more fundamental and profound than his love of woman. Thus when Fate once cast the die, he was emotionally ready to spread his wings and like a bird soar once more into the open.[60]

60 Before leaving Vienna, Paganini had the Polish luthier, C. Nikolaus Savicki (1792–1852), put a new fingerboard on his violin. ("I hereby certify that Signor Savicki is an extraordinary genius not only in making violins but he also repairs all musical instruments marvelously. I have seen and scrupulously inspected all his instruments as well as others that he has repaired and take pleasure in stating that he is the outstanding artist [in this field]. Moreover, *I entrusted my violin* to him to change the keyboard, which I should never have done with any other artist.") Hill wrote of Paganini's Guarneri now in Genoa: "The fingerboard, which is of Italian work and dates from 1800–30, is throughout noticeably rounder in form than those used by the player of today and this strongly arched board naturally carried a similarly curved bridge. The construction from start to finish is beyond reproach, if judged from the Guarneri standpoint. . . ." Savicki may have imported his fingerboards from Italy, or Paganini might have had another put on when he returned to Italy.

Io intrepido soffersi, ma no volli dar segno di sentire.—PAGANINI.

LEAVING VIENNA round August 13, Paganini arrived in Carlsbad on the morning of the eighteenth,[1] and the very next day gave
a concert in the Sächsische Saal, where his receipts amounted to
860 florins.[2] Taking this handsome sum as an indication that he
had struck a vein of ore, or wishing perhaps to earn sufficient to
defray the costs of the "cure" before the physicians restricted his
professional activities, he announced another on the twenty-second,
this time in the theatre—overlooking the fact that Carlsbad was a
small watering place and the summer too far spent to fill the larger
auditorium since by the end of August most of the transient guests
had gone. Hence, while approximately the same number of tickets
were sold, the proceeds, because of heavier expenses, netted only
495 florins—a loss he laid to the ineptitude of his new secretary,
Antonio Caccio, and he thereupon abruptly terminated their association. Caccio, however, held a valid contract executed in Vienna as recently as July 1, so when his temperamental employer
declined to recognize its obligations, he took the document and his
troubles to the police, who pointed out to the Maestro that it was
far more to his interest to compromise than to force his secretary
to take legal action. So, bowing to superior force, he gave 150 florins
to the chief of police, Adalbert Antonio Graf, who on September 11
turned it over to Caccio "in full satisfaction of his claims." And the
issue was amicably closed.

For a person who so pertinaciously insisted on his own con-
tractual rights, such total disregard of others argues in his nature
a strain of a less excusable quality than absent-mindedness. But

1 The journey from Vienna to Carlsbad took forty hours continuous traveling, so
Paganini must have traveled by short stages and stopped along the way.

2 For the first concert the hall rent was 9.36 florins; he paid the orchestra 40 florins,
and 198 tickets were sold. For the second concert, the theatre cost 60 florins, and 225
tickets were sold.

such actions were all of a piece with the brusque severance of his Lucca contract, the only excuse for him that can be made being that up to now he had had little experience in such matters. For the flattery of which he had long been the object in his native land, the adulation of the public in Italy and in Vienna, implied the submission of the multitude in which formalities of justice were neither imposed on, nor expected of, him. In his entire career in Italy there had never appeared on his horizon any competitor or adversary powerful enough to divert him from his course, and his popularity was such that no menial or manager whose claims he might elect to disregard would have dared to raise his voice against him. Abroad it was a different matter. The possession of wealth, or the likelihood of acquiring it, stimulated envy and made him, through inexperience, an easy mark for those with sagacity enough to protect their own interests and to provide themselves with an instrument of revenge should he fail in the conscientious performance of his agreements or attempt to make them victims of his cupidity or some unaccountable whim. A year outside the confines of his native land sufficed, however, to change his attitude in this respect, though not, be it said, without some painful bruises to his pride and pocketbook.

As the European tour gradually emerged from the land of dreams into reality, his friend Lazzaro Rebizzo expressed a wish to accompany him, offering—for a commensurate recompense—to stand between him and the *tracasseries* of life as friend and secretary. Yet, when the time to leave eventually came round, he had more pressing interests nearer home so that the Maestro had to go without him after all, a defection that seemed to cause no disappointment, at least Paganini's letters made no reference to it. In any case, after Bianchi's departure he more than ever needed a companion, so, when Rebizzo still failed to answer his repeated summons, he engaged Caccio on the recommendation (it appears) of Artaria. Caccio, however, through poor judgment and inexperience, coupled no doubt with soaring financial ambitions of his own, was led to fling his roses a little too riotously, which resulted in the aforesaid "loss" for his employer and summary dismissal for himself.

Paganini to Karl Fradel, Prague, October 20, 1828.
Having tried out Signor Caccio at Carlsbad and having found him both
brainless and heartless, I got rid of him with a gift of 150 good florins.
He's now in Prague giving language lessons.

Besides miscalculating the musical response of a smallish town
whose activities ran in totally different channels, Paganini was now
in a very shattered state of health, which made it impossible for
him to summon up the old-time "electricity." His dental trouble,
too, was so deep seated and Vergani's ministrations so disastrous
that the abscess at the root of the molar was affecting his entire
system, his suffering increasing and his condition worsening day
by day. After the abscess had been lanced several times to no avail
and "forty-eight poultices day and night for a month and a half"
had also failed to bring relief, the physicians advised him to go to
Prague, where there were several noted specialists who would surely be able to help him. He therefore "raced there with all speed,"
leaving Carlsbad on October 3 and arriving next day at Prague,
where he alighted at the Hotel Schwarzes Ross till he learned what
fate next had in store for him.

As soon as he had rested a little from his journey, he called on
Dr. Julius Vincenz Edler von Kromholz[3] of the Prague General
Hospital and Dr. Franz Willibald Nusshard,[4] assistant in the surgical clinic, who after giving him a thorough examination ordered
an immediate operation on the lower jaw, which they performed
on October 10 with the assistance of a Dr. Kray and a surgeon Dr.
Axmann.[5] The week's delay was evidently due to his desire to find
private lodgings which would be more comfortable for him with a
young child, especially if he had to look forward to a long convalescence. And it was well he did so since he had to undergo a
second operation on November 4, at which time the physicians removed four small pieces of the bone of the lower jaw that they at
first had hoped would slough off by themselves.

3 Julius Vincenz Edler von Kromholz (1782–1843) studied surgery in Prague and
Vienna. In 1814 he was appointed professor of surgery and in 1828 professor of
pathology and therapy at the Prague General Hospital.
4 Franz Willibald Nusshard (1785–1847), son of a village surgeon, was first on the
staff of the Prague General Hospital, then assistant in the surgical clinic under Fritz.
5 These two names have been taken from Paganini's notebook and are apparently
spelled phonetically, since they cannot be identified.

Paganini to Germi, Prague, October 20, 1828.

At Carlsbad I was utterly miserable, which explains why I didn't answer your letter of July 10. First of all, let me assure you once more of my deepest gratitude for your kindness and advice, which I immediately followed. All is off with Bianchi. At the magistrate's court in Vienna, to which I had recourse in order to get possession of my dear son Achilles, who has grown most adorable through the sensibility and soul that are now beginning to manifest themselves, I thought it well to accept Bianchi's proposal and paid her the sum of 2,000 Milanese scudi, whereupon she renounced all claims upon me, and my obligation to pay her an annuity of 100 scudi has been revoked. . . . The beginning of August she left Vienna for Milan and I for Carlsbad, where I gave only two concerts since more than a thousand guests had left, I having arrived too late. I started the cure with the waters,[6] but was seized with a fearful inflammation of the salivary glands caused by the ulcerated root of a left molar, the pus having destroyed the bone internally. Forty-eight poultices day and night for a month and a half were of no avail in reducing the inflammation. Meanwhile, I can never describe my suffering to you. The surgeons fixed me up so that I could come to consult the physicians here. I called in four of the most famous professors and upon their unanimous advice I placed myself in a chair, rigid as a statue, and they operated on me, armed with a huge needle, scalpels, and scissors. My intrepidity surprised the professors. For a few days now I've been feeling a little better and it's hoped that the decayed bone will slough off, or that they will be able to extract it so that I can recover quickly because the people here are wild to hear my violin and I hope to give a concert towards the end of November. . . . I have rooms in the house of a dear lady who cooks divinely and also *à la Genoese.*

When he crept into Prague on October 4, there is no doubt that he was a desperately ill man. Every fibre of his being was taut and his entire organism from head to foot one racking pain, his eyes, his jaws, his teeth, his throat, his chest, his stomach, his intestines— all quivering with agony for which no one could offer him relief. Moreover, he was now saddled with the sole care of a little child of three, a lively, fretful, restless little savage who most certainly had never been quelled by any parental discipline. "The poor child is bored! I don't know what to do with him [he sighed to Gordigiani]. I'm quite exhausted by playing with him. I've been

---

6 The Carlsbad springs are prescribed principally for dyspepsia, liver complaints, etc. Possibly Paganini's liver was also affected, as shown by his previous attacks of indigestion and jaundice.

fencing with him the whole morning. I've walked up and down with him, made chocolate for him, and now I really don't know what to do next!" Was this to be the end of his high hopes? Was it for this that he had left the suave climate of his own country, the sympathy of understanding friends, his mother's loving care? Concerts were for the time being quite out of the question. In his present physical state, even the thought of them was torture to him. So, when besieged with inquiries as to when Prague was to "have the pleasure of hearing him," he could only smile and "hope that it would not be long," that the "skilled surgeons" whose aid he had come here to seek would soon be able to find the root of the trouble, clear his system of the accumulated poisons and banish the pain that had been his constant companion for more than two months.

Prague, like Dresden and Vienna, had a large Italian colony, among whom he had the pleasure of finding his old friend Giovanni Battista Gordigiani,[7] who had been his companion at the turbulent Ferrara concert in 1812 and now helped him to secure accommodations at the "Pension" where he and Professor Schottky were also living.[8] With regard to the person of the Herr Professor, who was to go down in musical history as the Maestro's Boswell, we have little information. Then a man of thirty-four, he was reader in German at the University of Prague, played a certain role in academic circles, and after relinquishing this post settled in Munich, where he edited a newspaper for a time. Although he had literary ambitions, he seems to have written nothing of importance previous to his work on Paganini, but daily contact with the Maestro for three months, during which he "spent days at a time and sometimes half the night chatting with him," listening to his reminiscences, taking note of his opinions and points of view, would have kindled the flame of authorship even in one without a bent for it. "When I called on him for the first time [he wrote a friend], I found him wearing a black nightcap and fur-lined boots. He was without a waistcoat but a coat was flung round his shoulders like a hussar's dolman. He was sitting up in bed trying to help his black-eyed, black-haired youngster put on his red shoes." For nearly six

---

[7] Giovanni Battista Gorgigiani (1795–1871), teacher of singing at the conservatory.
[8] Julius Maximilian Schottky (1794–1849) was greatly interested in Germanic dialects and published a collection of folksongs.

months now the Maestro had been subjected to all the modalities of suffering, physical and mental, yet he evidently never refused to receive his visitors because of illness; no one must suspect that he was not his old intrepid self though, even so, it was still some weeks before he felt strong enough to step out before a public.

After the removal of the infected bones, his recovery was more rapid and by the end of November he was far enough along to announce a series of six concerts to take place between December 1 and December 20, in other words, an average of two a week, which represented a heavy strain even for a healthy person. Yet here, as in Carlsbad, the financial results were not all that he had anticipated. To begin with he quintupled the admission prices, which made the concerts too expensive for the general run of musicians, amateurs, and music students, with the result that the theatre was never entirely sold out, even for a charity concert on December 9 given for the benefit of the Municipal Almshouse, though for this and the remaining three recitals he sensibly reduced the prices almost 50 per cent, which still left them almost triple the customary rates.[9] True, the theatre was fairly small, which justified to some extent the higher prices; but Johann Stiepanek, the manager, realized after the second concert that the general reaction here was far more critical than in Vienna, so if further recitals were to be successful from the business point of view the prices would have to be considerably reduced. In Prague the theatre was owned by a group of Bohemian noblemen who engaged Stiepanek to run it for them and, while in such circumstances Paganini could count on no special favors, he was able to make his customary arrangement of two-thirds of the net receipts, which might still have proved quite satisfactory if the response had been a little warmer.[10] At all events, though the theatre "was long, narrow, and dark and (in Berlioz' opinion) also "bad for sound," the soloists were excellent[11] and the orchestra, under Friedrich Wilhelm Pixis,[12] was ex-

[9] The library of the Prämonstratensian Monastery in the Hradschin, Prague, has all the programs of the Prague concerts.

[10] The receipts in Prague were: 1,556.13 fl; 1,234.12 fl; 861.37 fl; 464.12; 556 fl; and 705 fl.

[11] One of his assisting artists was Katinka Podhorska (1807–89), nee Komelova, the leading Czech prima donna.

[12] Friedrich Wilhelm Pixis (1786–1842), pupil of Luigi and Franzel, who later worked with Viotti at Hamburg. He taught at the Prague Conservatory and was the

tremely efficient. Pixis, who succeeded Carl Maria von Weber in 1816, seems to have maintained Weber's level since a decade later Sir George Smart spoke of it in the highest terms, as did also Edward Holmes. Thus on this score, at least, Paganini's requirements were adequately filled.

At the first concert his share of the receipts amounted to 1556.13 florins but from then on it dropped to half and even a quarter of this sum, the concert of December 13 netting no more than 464.12 florins.[13] Yet the cause of this lack of interest was not traceable alone to the high prices. It sprang rather from the political situation which, being here a matter of blood rather than of boundaries, was always smouldering just beneath the surface.[14] The mere fact that the Viennese had engaged in emotional rhapsodies and had blown loud and long on their trumpets was sufficient to make Prague stifle any involuntary impulse toward enthusiasm, the more fervent disciples of Nicholas Chauvin being always on the alert to seize any opportunity of accentuating the divergencies between the two races.

Had Paganini sailed into the sky of Prague fresh from his Austrian triumphs before the local patriots and champions of Czech separatism had had time to weave him into the woof of their political platform, he might have sensed less covert enmity in the surrounding atmosphere. But in the two months' interval during which vague and disquieting reports were current regarding the vexing coil of illness in which he was involved many had decided that he must have deteriorated even from the "flippant, commonplace" standards prevailing in Vienna. So, besides branding him as an immoral and unregenerate sinner, they even questioned his artistic gifts, finding his performance "neither grandiose nor grace-

founder of the so-called Prague School of violin playing. The Prague orchestra numbered thirty players.

13 When Chopin visited Prague in August, 1829, he wrote his parents: "I'm only staying in Prague three days. Besides, I don't want to risk spoiling what I gained in Vienna. Even Paganini was badly received in Prague."

14 Edward Holmes wrote in 1827: "The situation which this city maintained fifty years since in the superiority of its musical taste over the rest of Germany is now usurped by Berlin—not that the Bohemians love the art less than formerly, or that they have imbibed the flippant, commonplace notions of music which prevail in Vienna. . . . There is a calm enthusiasm in all the Bohemians do; they acquire for the most part a greater skill in instrumental music than any other class of German, from their firmness of purpose and desire for the best."

ful; his embellishments and cadenzas in exceedingly bad taste, and his tone thin, without roundness or fullness." When his friends read these comments to him, he missed the familiar note of lyrical effusion; and this left him momentarily perplexed. A sinner he might be, he had never attempted to deny it. But to be despised and rejected as an artist could only be the work of secret enemies. "If you only knew how many enemies are inciting against me [he wrote Germi], you would never believe it. I never do anyone any harm and yet those who don't know me paint me as the most infamous creature, avaricious, egotistic, etc., and to avenge myself I've announced that I'm going to double the price of admission to my forthcoming concerts in the rest of Europe." "I've never found it worth my while to deny publicly all the silly nonsense circulated about me [he told Harrys]. If I please people as an artist, then they can believe all the romantic tales they like." But here in Prague he had failed to "please" even as an artist.[15]

On December 20, the day of his last concert, the literary supplement of the Hamburg *Börsenhalle* published a "Proclamation" by an anonymous Prague correspondent which purported to be a definitive appraisal of his art but was really intended (according to Schottky) to "sound his knell and bury his artistic reputation forever." Characteristically, the writer first took a pot shot at the Viennese:

O foolish world! O marvelous taste of the enthusiastic Viennese! Never have I fallen so suddenly from my heaven as through this . . . virtuoso. I cannot understand how people who have heard Romberg, Rode, Spohr, Lafont, etc. can lend an ear for a single moment to such harlequinades as these. I went to one of his concerts—but never again!

According to this caviler, from no angle of the horizon was there anything praiseworthy apparent, except "perhaps the Maestro's expertise in the left hand" which "anybody could learn with a little practice." As for his famous left hand pizzicato, "any fiddler could acquire it in six months if he ever wanted to learn anything so utterly useless." In the writer's opinion, "Paganini's compositions were beneath all criticism," his "bowing the most wretched imaginable," while there "wasn't a sign of expression or soul in his

15 Schottky, *op. cit.*, 327.

adagios." Indeed, it would never occur to any Prague musician "to smash his violin in despair," as some Viennese violinist allegedly had done. But never mind! such parlor tricks as these would never pull the wool over the eyes of the Berliners; they at once "would get his number" and put him in his place.

When Schottky translated to him this intemperate attack, he "merely smiled and shrugged his shoulders." "Would you ever believe it?" asked Schottky in surprise. However, even though the Maestro retained his outward composure and evidenced no resentment, it is easy to conjure up his feelings, since here the critic's scalpel touched his most sensitive spot—his artistic pride. Schottky gathered the impression that on the whole he paid little or no attention to the critics' personal reactions, or even to complimentary letters (if not written in Italian). Pulver, basing his hypothesis on Paganini's sanguine reception of the article and its "unutterable foolishness," suggests that it "might have been written by a friend in order to provoke discussion and increase his publicity." And here he may be right; for, while anonymous polemics of this kind were no rarity in Germany,[16] it is not impossible that Schottky indirectly had a hand in it since he seems to have known about it some time in advance and may even have inspired it so that he could provide the counter arguments—a suspicion supported by his subsequent treatment of the article in his book.

Unfortunately, at his last concert (the very day the article appeared) Paganini, through some capricious trick of fortune, played right into the hands of his detractors. The Vienna critics, as we have seen, had been very frank in condemning Panny's "dramatic sonata," but Paganini either still had faith in it or thought that because Prague "loved to applaud what Vienna censured" and was a much smaller place, the work might still have a success, particularly if served up with a little realistic theatre. During his convalescence he had frequently attended the performances at the Standestheater and had been commensurately impressed with the excellent *mise en scène,* so he decided to avail himself of the theatre's facilities and stage Panny's work to heighten the effect—*"un programme fort curieux* [wrote the correspondent of the *Re-*

16 Even Richard Wagner was frequently guilty of this practice. (Cf. Newman, *op. cit.,* I, 383).

vue Musicale] *avec décorations analogues."* For this, the concluding number on his program, he descended to the leader's desk in
the orchestra pit while the curtain rose on a scene representing (as
far as can be judged from the descriptions) the deck of a ship
engaged in a fierce battle with the elements, the eight movements
of the work being visually depicted by appropriate stage effects—
thunderbolts, lightning, cracking timbers, wind and storm ma-
chines, to the culminating apotheosis!

"The performance evoked laughter from some, while it angered
others [wrote one of the critics]. It was received in stony silence,
for it was entirely unworthy of a real artist to place himself in the
orchestra and from there accompany the madhouse on the stage.
With all the confusion, etc. on the stage and the wretched ma-
chinery, the performance ended in a real circus—it was like a
pantomime where someone seats himself behind a screen and
pounds out something on the piano. It was the worst part of Paganini's performance, and he could scarcely have chosen anything
more untoward with which to bid goodbye to Prague!"[17]

ii

During the following days he sensed his mounting unpopularity
and kept rolling over in his mind the most effective way to counter
it. The slander of his imprisonment, the rumor of the hulks must
surely be behind it. A provincial capital like Prague probably
ranked morals above art and was horrified that its irreproachable
ethics had been so grossly imposed upon. Not all the critics, of
course, were so drastic as the *Börsenhalle* correspondent; the Germans, especially, maintained their critical detachment, completely
free from the defects of prejudice. But the attitude of the Bohemians was deliberately tendentious (excused in part by the involved nature of the situation) and, since the "Proclamation" had
been copied in all the leading papers, Prague's reaction might have
a very deleterious effect on the remainder of his tour if no way were
quickly found to counteract the calumnies that were obviously behind it. But what was to be done? That was the burning question.
After the stormy farewell concert, while waiting for Rebizzo, many

---

[17] The Prague performance gave the coup de grâce to Panny's opus. Paganini
never played it again.

discussions took place at the daily table d'hôte till one day Schottky seems to have thrown out the suggestion that he be allowed to write the Maestro's biography, wherein he would not only subject the local situation to a searching analysis, for the benefit of posterity, but would "make every possible effort to paint the Maestro, both man and artist, with impartiality and truth," rejecting and denouncing all the slanders regarding his early life, which the foreigners were so ready to accept. Paganini, naturally, thought this a capital idea and at once dispatched a note to his friend Vacani in Vienna asking him to enlighten Schottky regarding the Durand-Duranowski episode (the most important in his eyes). At this late date, however, there was no time to attack the subject systematically even had the Maestro not been in an impatient, irritable mood. Fortunately, from the beginning of their acquaintance Schottky had been writing long letters about his famous house companion to several friends abroad who, knowing of their close association, had been plying him with questions. As an *aide mémoire* for these epistles he had been zealously taking notes and these, with Gordigiani's help, he felt would serve as the foundation for a work not fundamentally intended as an *Apologia di sua Vita* but inspired by a desire to present the Maestro to his contemporaries and posterity in a true light without either the hyperbole of the enthusiasts or the censoriousness of envious and unsympathetic colleagues.

The aim was admirable but the trouble was that, though constantly thrown with Paganini for four months, it was still not long enough for Schottky to sink himself into his subject, to enter deeply into the Maestro's mind, his opinions, enthusiasms, prejudices. He was also never able to persuade him to recall the early years of his career, with the result that, on the infrequent occasions when Schottky's observations are original, they betray a lack of profundity bordering on the superficial. During the progress of the work, while still engaged in collecting press notices of Paganini's German tour, DeLaphalèque's monograph appeared, which provided him with several useful hints that he at once took over and augmented by an assortment of anecdotes of little biographical value, garnered for the most part from casual acquaintances. It never seems to have occurred to him, any more than it did to Fétis, to appeal to Paganini's family, to Germi, to his old friends in Genoa, even for that matter to Morlacchi and Rebizzo. Which suggests that, despite his protestations, he was more interested in a romantic presentation of the virtuoso side of the Maestro's life and in surrounding him with an aura of the fabulous. As a result, the most valuable part of his haphazard opus is the anthology of press notices and the accounts of his several conversations with the Maestro. However, before criticizing him too severely it should be said in his defense that he had undertaken an extremely difficult task. He admitted that it was practically impossible to obtain printed material from Italy so that he had no other recourse than to present detached incidents and details—a "mosaic," as he called it. Still inexperienced as a writer and without authentic facts and a chronological sequence of events and, moreover, with a subject who never opened his heart freely and familiarly to anyone and was reluctant to lay bare the secrets of his life or even to put Schottky in the way of obtaining such information from others, the latter was obliged perforce to restrict his narrative to a brief period of which he himself had knowledge. In view of the numerous hindrances confronting him, it is surprising that he was able to gather together as much information as he did. As for Paganini, after his Berlin successes had obliterated any remaining memories of Prague, he seems to have lost all further interest in the enterprise, even its publication in 1830 inspired no comment in his letters. But by that time, of course, the pressing need for a champion in Germany had passed.

Whilst in the beginning Schottky, like Harrys later, was primarily attracted by Paganini's potentialities as journalistic material, he succumbed more and more during their two months' acquaintance to his charm and personal magnetism and regaled his friends abroad with long descriptions of the Maestro, his appearance, his habits, the trivia of his daily life.

True, at the first glance his appearance is repelling rather than attractive [he wrote]; in fact some jokers remarked that he was the living image of Old Nick, while others compared him with a fallen angel, and much more in the same strain. This, of course, is exaggerated, but in the theatre under the full glare of the lights—when one is sitting some distance away so that his features cannot be seen distinctly—the effect is nevertheless extraordinary. He couldn't possibly be any thinner! His clothes flop loosely about his limbs and when he bows he moves his body in such a singular way that every instant you expect the upper part to separate from the lower and both collapse in a heap of bones. When he plays he thrusts his right foot forward and in the rapid passages beats time with it in a most ludicrous manner. However, his face never loses its livid look, except in response to thunderous applause, when it breaks into a strange smile. Then his lips twitch nervously and his eye beams with self-complacency—though not ill-naturedly—as he glances from side to side. He is passion personified and it would have been a real blunder on Nature's part if she had made him any stouter.

The morning after the concert on December 4, their conversation turned to music.

I play more music at my concerts than many other artists [Paganini said], but it's a pleasure to do so and I should play even more were I not afraid that it might have a detrimental effect on my delicate health. The strain of playing is so great that it affects my chest and abdomen. I feel that very keenly today, having barely recovered from my serious illness. I've had three operations and believe I conducted myself like a Mutius Scaevola.[18] I'm very urgently in need of rest because the doctors were afraid that I might overstrain my nerves and lose the sight of my left eye.[19] Fortunately, the prognosis did not happen. You compliment me on my good memory. This I cannot deny because I play everything —even the works of others—from memory. Day before yesterday I had almost forgotten the Larghetto from Mozart's *Don Giovanni,* which you heard at yesterday's concert. But after running through it several times during the day, it all came back to me. Anyhow, when playing, the orchestra reminds me of what is coming next so that I never have to fear a slip in memory. But you are grossly misinformed if you think I'm always playing. In the entire three months of my illness, I never once touched the violin. Certain people therefore think I'm done for. But I hope to enhance my fame when I publish my compositions, which will be accompanied by instructions for those violinists who intend to adopt my method. This will give them a key to my playing, the purpose of which is to eliminate the difficulties of my method. . . . I received my musical training from Paer."[20]

In order to testify to the high regard in which he was held by his

[18] Mucius Scaevola was a young Roman who, during the siege of Rome by the Etruscans, penetrated into the camp of the enemy and, thinking that he was killing Porsenna, killed his secretary instead. Brought before the King, he placed his hand in a burning brazier to punish it for the offense.

[19] The left eye was obviously infected by the left molar.

[20] From a letter written by Schottky to a friend and published later in the *Archive für Geschichte* (Vienna), January 1829, and the London *Literary Gazette.*

countrymen, he left with Schottky several letters, among them one from his mother, probably because it bore witness to his continued generosity to his family, an all-important point if his Boswell were successfully to refute the scabrous charges that he was "an infamous creature, avaricious, egotistic." This letter would be of little interest to us now were it not that Mompellio, in his annotated edition of Conestabile's biography, throws doubts on its genuineness, scenting in it an element of fabrication and pointing out that it is the only letter from Teresa that has survived and in addition bears every indication of having been written for a purpose.

Teresa Paganini to Niccolò, Genoa, July 21, 1828.
At last, nearly seven months after I wrote to you at Milan, I had the joy of receiving through Signor Agnino your letter of the ninth instant, and was so happy to learn that you're in good health. I was also glad to hear that after your journey to Paris and London, it is your intention to return to Genoa to embrace me. I assure you that I pray God daily that He will keep me—and you—in health so that our hopes may be fulfilled. The dream has come true and what God promised me has come to pass. You've made a great name, and music, with God's help, has given you a comfortable living. Beloved and esteemed by your countrymen, in my arms and those of your friends, you will enjoy the repose your health requires. The pictures you sent me with your letter gave me great pleasure and I've already heard everything that our paper wrote about you. You can easily believe news of this kind is the greatest joy to a mother. Dear son, my one desire is to have frequent word from you. Buoyed by this hope I think I shall live longer and be certain of some day being blest with the happiness of embracing you. We're all well and I thank you in the name of the family for the money. Do everything you can to make your name immortal. Watch out for the bad weather in those big towns and remember that you have a mother who loves you tenderly and who never ceases to pray the Almighty to hold you in his keeping. Please embrace your most charming companion for me and also give a kiss to little Achilles.

Whilst the underlying nature of the projected biography might have recalled the letter to Paganini's mind and he forthwith extracted it from his packet of "unanswered letters" to add its quota to his glory, Mompellio's hypothesis gains some support from a later episode when Paganini wrote a letter, ostensibly to prove that certain slanders then in circulation had been concocted by his enemies. One suspicious detail is the pointed reference to the prophetic dream, which seems to have been brought in for an ulterior motive. For if we accept Codignola's contention that this was a figment of Paganini's imagination, he was here merely tightening —with his mother's aid—one of the fundamental rivets in his legend, to which he evidently attached great worth. With these two reservations, however, the letter is not incredible. It is couched in the characteristically stilted, high-flown style of the professional letter writer and is not unlike those he received regularly from his sisters, except for the more affectionate note. Moreover, the date would go far to establish its authenticity since, in July, Paganini was in the midst of his Vienna triumphs, his "charming companion" had not yet left for Italy, and up till then he had felt no pressing need "to confound his enemies."

iii

During the first year after Bianchi's departure, he allowed no one to care for Achilles but himself. There was no neat, beruffled, and beribboned *bonne* to tame this marmoset and pilot him safely through the day; but Paganini—ailing, worried, and resentful— had to be father, mother, nursemaid all in one. No matter how ill and exhausted he might be, when the new toys failed to please he would indulge in "high romps" with his little son, assume the role of playmate. Till he settled in Frankfort he never allowed the child out of his sight, taking him with him everywhere and "if the day was cold" even carrying him inside his voluminous fur coat "so that he might not take a chill." By now Achellino was a sturdy youngster of three and a half years, with "the brown eyes of a falcon and hair parted in the middle"—clever, wide awake and in every way (as Schottky tells us) "a most engaging little chap," who like all children picked up the new language like a parrot and was soon chattering fluent German to his daddy's great delight. "My son Achilles speaks German better than Italian," Paganini wrote Karl Fradel with becoming fatherly pride. "Are you going to make a musician of him?" asked Schottky. "Why not? If he wants to learn I shall teach him with pleasure. I love him very dearly and am almost jealous of him. If I should lose him, I should be lost myself, for I can't bear to be parted from him. And when I wake at night my first thought is of him." A year later he seems to have changed his mind. "As long as I live my son shall never take a violin in his hand [he told George Harrys]. I'll do everything to make him an excellent contrapuntist, but not a violinist." Was he perhaps thinking of another little boy who had "a violin in his hand from morn till night" and for this reason had missed many of the joys of his less gifted playmates? The bells of his own childhood years did not ring a pleasant tune, and with the memory still keen even after four decades, we may be sure that Achilles was never forced to do anything against his will, but was allowed to follow his own inclinations, shooting up unhampered like an Irish bramble rose.

Paganini to Germi, January 20, 1829.
I hear that a friend of mine in Berlin is holding 24,000 scudi at my disposal—money paid in advance by those who are eager to hear me in six concerts. But I shall give at least twelve. In two or three years I should be able to have about two million. My glory wishes it so. But what shall we do with so much money? Do you like fireworks? But no! I have a son and I pray Heaven to preserve him for me.

With a growing conviction that his own years were rapidly running out and that he must make haste, Achilles' patrimony soon became a fixed idea so that what began as Genoese economy was soon interpreted by an envious world as pinching parsimony.

The people should concern themselves with other things than my private life [he complained impatiently to Schottky]. Who can hold it against me that I practice the strictest economy? It is only within the last few years that I have known material comfort, and since then haven't I had a very serious illness that has cost me a lot of money? Can't this happen again and even incapacitate me for a long time so that I can't give any concerts? And then what am I to live on? Moreover, I must think of my son's future. Besides, my family is poor and I must also look after them in the years to come.[21]

That he was no real miser at heart is amply testified by many friends who in these middle years had an opportunity of observing at close range the conduct of his life. He was not only careless with his possessions—his jewels, for instance, and his ready cash—but

21 Schottky, *op. cit.*, 394.

to others less fortunate than himself, he was generous in numerous unobtrusive ways. But he always reacted violently to any imagined exploitation and never lived in state and luxury, never went about "trailing clouds of glory" in a practical sense so that he easily earned the reputation of stinginess and avarice, to which these circumstances were attributed.

iv

Although he intended after his last concert to leave Prague as soon as possible, he kept postponing his departure from day to day, always hoping that Rebizzo would finally tear himself away from the pleasures of Vienna and arrive in time to cross the frontier with him. But one week soon extended into three and there was still no sign of him. "I can't understand the reason for his delay [Niccolò wrote on January 10]. I pray Heaven that I may soon embrace him!"

Germi was equally anxious to have Rebizzo join him for he not only knew those doldrums of the spirit that overcame his friend when he felt himself alone in an uncomprehending universe, but he was equally aware of his knack of getting into trouble and of how the women fell to the fascination of this dark and amorous, this gifted and mysterious man. Since his warnings usually came too late, he looked to Rebizzo to keep a sharp lookout for that unchained beast that was roving in Paganini's blood and represented such a constant drain on his physique. *"Abbi cura alla tua salute"* (take care of your health—don't overdo things) was the ceaseless burden of his letters.

Schottky gathered the impression that Paganini really cared for Bianchi[22] and that the rupture touched him deeply. After four years of close companionship, he unquestionably missed her, while the manner of the break with its stormy preliminaries had jarred him to the center. Germi, too, may to some extent have been of the same opinion since, as soon as he learned of her departure, he urged his friend to move on to other scenes, to make a civilized use of his leisure, which would help to take his mind off his recent troubles.

"Rebizzo tells me that Morlacchi advises that it would be to your advantage to present yourself to the other German sovereigns and

22 Schottky, *op. cit.*, 346.

leave a desire in Vienna to hear you again [he wrote]; traveling, however, and deporting yourself like a gentleman. . . . My affection for you is unchanged and that day will ever be a happy one for me in which I can gain an advantage for you or keep you from harm."

Bearing this advice in mind and despairing of waiting any longer for Rebizzo, he and Achilles, on the night of January 12, set out for Dresden, where Morlacchi "was expecting him." Off in the distance lay the Prussian capital with two more influential backers, Meyerbeer and the still powerful Spontini—a comforting thought indeed, after his trying Bohemian experiences. So, tucking his little mascot in the enveloping warmth of his fur-lined ulster, he settled himself comfortably for the night and erased forever from his mind all bitterness of feeling engendered by any remaining painful memories of Prague.[23]

23 Lillian Day (*op. cit.*, 159) in referring to Stiepanek's letter to Schottky (Schottky, *op. cit.*, 402) states that "Paganini felt it necessary to publish it to prove his financial integrity." The letter was obviously written at Schottky's instigation:

"In pursuance of your suggestion with regard to your projected biography of Paganini, I can truthfully say, and with pleasure, that in all my business dealings with Paganini in connection with the six concerts given by this admirable virtuoso in our Standestheater, I found him to be an estimable person who honored me with the greatest confidence and frankness, far removed from any petty desire for gain. I shall always hold his memory dear and it would be a great personal satisfaction and pleasure if my voice could contribute to his recognition as a man of probity with whom—contrary to the general opinion, I don't know on what grounds—it is by no means difficult to get along."

XIII. *WANDERING STAR 1829*

La più grande ambizione dell'artista si è quella di essere ricevuto da' conoscitori con quell'espansione, esser salutato con quell'entusiasmo, che gl'insegnano i suoi sforzi non esser rimasti senza frutto.—PAGANINI.

THROUGH THE LONG political connections with northern Italy, as the Austrians came and went, as well as through Vienna's enthusiasm for everything Italian, Paganini could never have felt an alien there even though he did not speak the language. But the dark tower of Germany that now rose up before him was quite another thing. It was as though he were entering a dense forest with lurking dangers and hidden pitfalls on every side; and if he happened to be in a despondent mood, he more than once may have had a shiver of apprehension. True, he knew Spohr, Morlacchi,[1] Meyerbeer, Aiblinger, and several others, and there were a number of Italians in influential posts in nearly all the provincial capitals; but he was now crossing for the first time the frontiers of a largely non-Catholic country, a land with a different moral climate and intellectual tradition from his own—one in which the waves of Pietism following in the wake of the religious wars had not yet entirely receded. Not, of course, that religion ever loomed large in his life's scheme, but to one as sensitive as he, one reacting so keenly to his milieu, the change in atmosphere must have been immediately apparent and during his three months in Berlin probably more than one spiritual adjustment was necessary before he could accommodate himself to the Prussian order and formality, the coolness of a more prosaic attitude towards life. This explains, perhaps, why six months later he was content to settle in the south, where he found himself in more congenial surroundings, though certainly if his well-fitting legend, his personality, and appearance had been less charged with the properties of romanticism (which harmonized externally, at least, with the environment) he would have found it difficult even here to adapt himself with ease.

1 Francesco Morlacchi (1784–1841), pupil of Zingarelli and Padre Mattei (Bologna).

Either through a vein of laziness, a fundamental disinterest in fixing his history for posterity, or an innate indifference toward the order and the disciplines of life he left no chronicle of his movements during this grand tour; which represents a serious handicap for the biographer who desires to link together certain important episodes. "If it were a habit of mine to keep a journal [he told Schottky], if I had saved my press notices, or even if I carried with me a mere fraction of the numerous letters I've received—letters from more or less intimate friends—I should be able to tell you endless anecdotes of my youth and my professional career, which would not be without interest since my various peregrinations often resembled the wanderings of Ulysses."[2]

As it is, we have nothing but a few notebooks, for the most part limited to the financial details of his concerts. During Rebizzo's secretaryship the jottings are more explicit though, even so, there is little information that does not have to do, directly or indirectly, with financial matters. In the beginning, or rather, when setting forth on the German *étape* of his European tour, it was his evident intention to keep a detailed expense account, as shown by the memorandum covering the journey from Prague to Dresden with its itemized list of expenses for horses, drivers, toll fares, tips, etc., together with hours and dates of arrival and departure, mileage, and other related details.[3] Guided by these entries, we see that the

---

2 Schottky, *op. cit.*, 256.

3 The original *Libro Rosso,* which he used as a notebook on the first lap of his European tour, is not, as Mompellio states (Conestabile, *op. cit.,* 340), in Milan but in the Library of Congress, Washington, D. C. It was evidently given to him by Germi and consists of about eighty leaves bound in red cardboard and tied with a green cotton string. Written in ink on the cover are the words *"Versi, Storie / e / Sonetti,"* and on the back cover, *"Sonetti di / Germi,"* with Germi's name crossed out. The first owner had copied into it several sonnets and an Italian translation of the "Story of Mother Indiana; from an American Tale Book." The portion written in Paganini's hand has to do exclusively with his tour; a list of letters of introduction to persons in Vienna, Berlin, Warsaw, and Paris; drafts of several letters; a list of appropriate endings for letters and an *"Inventario dell'Archivio di Niccolò Paganini,"* covering seven packets of letters. A second notebook is headed *Giornale di Spese Durante il Viaggio da Genova a Parma* [1835] and was first used by George Harrys, who filled eight pages and then abandoned it. Two other little journals in the Library of Congress collection are for 1832 and 1834. These are bound in leather, and the one for 1832 has Paganini's name in gold on the cover. A notebook containing the financial accounts of his concerts is in the Liceo Niccolò Paganini, in Genoa, another small one is in the possession of the Paganini heirs in Milan.

buon legno purchased in Milan was still in navigable condition, and that his driver followed the main Prague-Dresden highway on the west side of the Elbe, taking first a northwesterly course to Laun via Serzedokluk, Schlau, and Jungfer-Teinitz, afterwards turning north to Teplitz by way of Moronitz. From there they proceeded to Peterswald, the customs barrier on the frontier, and then on to Pirna and Dresden, leaving well to the east the rugged and romantic scenery of Saxon Switzerland with its deep mantle of midwinter snow, and holding to the flat open country of the Elbe Valley.

The season was already well advanced and in his delicate condition, shaken by a constant cough, any travel in the heart of a northern winter must have been torture, especially in view of the deplorable state of the roads in this sparsely traveled corner of Europe, as so frequently attested by contemporary travelers. He seems to have averaged ten to twelve miles a day (about three and one-half leagues) and to have traveled continuously, the journey broken only by the long delays at the posting stations, where he always got out to exercise himself while the horses were being changed—a very leisurely operation in the Germany of that day.

Just when Rebizzo joined him, we do not know, but it was evidently in the week of February 7 since the financial accounts of the Dresden concerts are still all in Paganini's hand. Yet, even without a secretary, things in Dresden went a little more smoothly than in Prague for he not only had the influential backing of Morlacchi and the family of Antonio Rolla,[4] but he also found several old friends in Dresden's large Italian colony. Furthermore, the Italian influence here was even stronger than in Vienna, owing to the frequent intermarriages between the Saxon royal family and Italian royal houses, the former having been Roman Catholic in religion since the time of Augustus the Strong (1697–1733)—all of which combined to revive his flickering spirits after his recent disheartening experiences with the commoners of Prague.

King Anton of Saxony (1755–1836), who had ascended the throne in 1827 at the ripe age of seventy-two, was, like all the Wettin family, very keenly interested in music, both as composer and executant, his compositions filling no less than fifty large bound volumes. His nephew Prince Friedrich (who succeeded

[4] Antonio Rolla (1798–1837), first violin of the Italian Opera in Dresden.

him) and the latter's sister Princess Amalie[5] (whose Italian step-mother, Princess Louise of Etruria, was also a very cultivated singer) were both extremely musical, Prince Friedrich having an excellent, well-trained voice and Princess Amalie a pronounced creative gift in addition to her instrumental accomplishments, thirteen of her operas having been given at one time or another at the Royal Theatre. Furthermore, every member of the family played some instrument and all took part in the regular musical soirees of the court, forming as it were a family chamber orchestra. In his biography of his father, Max von Weber has left a charming picture of these musical evenings under the late King when the monarch, in his embroidered grey coat, black breeches, powdered wig, and buckled shoes, spent hours making music with his friends, performing the new composition of some member of the family, and even staging whole acts of opera, a practice continued in King Anton's reign. It is therefore easy to imagine how Paganini thawed in this cordial musical atmosphere where he could let himself go in the freedom of his liquid Italian speech and forget for a time the multifarious problems that beset him.

This gracious informality was, however, not restricted to the Saxon court. An equalitarianism in the familiar intercourse between classes was then characteristic of all rulers in the German states and Paganini was to enjoy it frequently in the next two years, in Stuttgart and Dessau, in Hanover and Darmstadt, in Karlsruhe, Rudolstadt, and Munich,[6] courts in which the social lines were less rigidly drawn than in other European countries so that, united by the common bond of music, it was no rare thing (to quote Max von Weber) to "find princesses singing at a social gathering and rulers who were proud to walk arm in arm with great artists," in those days a by no means universal practice, as Liszt and others often testified.

Morlacchi, having "invited him to come to Dresden," at once

---

[5] Maria Amalia Friederika, Princess of Saxony (1794–1870), wrote a number of comedies under the pseudonym of Amalie Heiter and composed thirteen operas. See Moritz Fürstenau: *Die musikalischen Beschäftigungen der Prinzessin Amalia* (Dresden, 1874).

[6] At some of the German courts the etiquette was a little stricter. In the semi-feudal Duchy of Weimar, for example, the nobility and the townspeople sat on different sides of the theatre.

assumed the role of impresario with the result that he was summoned to give a command performance for the royal family at Brühl Palace on Sunday evening, January 18, for which he was rewarded with a handsome snuffbox and 100 ducats.[7] The King then placed the Linkisches Bad Theater and orchestra at his disposition for four concerts, which took place on January 23, 28, 29, and February 6, Paganini donating one-fourth of the receipts of the last concert (216.18 thalers) to Dresden's public charities as a symbolic return for all the kingly courtesies extended to him.[8]

Paganini to Carlo Carli, March 1, 1829.
I gave a few concerts in Dresden, where I very keenly felt the absence of a splendid orchestra conductor, though I cannot find words to express my appreciation of the kindness shown me by Mme Rolla and her sister.[9] I shall never forget the courteous attentions they showered upon me. It was at their table that we drank to the accomplishment of our very ardent wishes, and to the health of Padre Rolla. We were in high spirits the entire time and I parted from those dear souls with the greatest desire and hope of seeing them again. Meanwhile, you are enjoying the company of both father and son. Oh how I envy all those who are privileged to attend their musical soirees! I think constantly of the delightful hours I spent with you all.

The concerts at the Royal Theatre[10] were usually directed by one of the older Kapellmeisters (at this time: Morlacchi, Carl Gottlieb Reissinger,[11] and Franz Morgenroth[12]) and, since Paganini was presumably not entirely satisfied, it is very likely that Reissinger or Morgenroth conducted, for had Morlacchi been at the helm, the Maestro's strong feeling of national solidarity would have prevented his voicing such frank criticism. Anyhow, quite

7 According to official records, he played *only* for the royal family; neither the court nor any outsiders were present, as stated by Pulver (*op. cit.,* 168).

8 A memorandum in Paganini's *Libro Rosso* lists the members of the orchestra for his concerts. See also Carse, *op. cit.,* 116ff., 486.

9 According to Ernest Newman, Germany at this time had neither orchestral players nor conductors "necessary for a thoroughly competent performance." (*Op. cit.,* I, 126ff.)

10 At his first Dresden concert, the assisting artists were Mathilde Palazzesi and Mlle Schiasetti of the Italian Opera.

11 Karl Gottlieb Reissiger (1798–1859) succeeded Carl Maria von Weber as conductor of the German Opera in 1827.

12 Franz Morgenroth (1780–1847), violinist-leader and assistant conductor, played under Weber. See Carse, *op. cit.,* 119.

apart from the person of the conductor, the playing of the Royal Orchestra was often criticized as "languid," which was probably his objection to it. He missed the lively quality to which he was accustomed with Italian bands.

Only the first concert was reviewed by the critics, as customary at that time; but the omission hardly mattered since in the shock of the first astonishment there was little left to say. The *Abend-zeitung* particularly called attention to his manner of "holding his right arm close to his side and guiding his bow with a sharply bent wrist and the palm of the hand turned upwards," while the *Merkur* felt that it must sound a warning note to any young violinists who might be tempted to imitate him—a situation deplored by Joachim many decades later as he watched the inclination of the younger generation to concentrate on virtuosity as an end rather than a means.[13] Both papers enthusiastically conceded that the Maestro's fame "was justified" (a little tilt at Prague) and being of the opinion that with such an artist, whose very genius should excuse his faults of showmanship, his little gestures to the footlights, it would be pedantry indeed to complain of crudities and imperfections, they passed them over in silence and forbore to raise any point that implied a tacit censure of the musical taste of the royal family or that might temper the pleasure of Dresden's music lovers.

ii

After a month in Dresden,[14] and with Rebizzo at his side, he was now ready to move on to Berlin, where Spontini and Meyerbeer, both good bell ringers, "were impatiently awaiting him." As for the strong anti-Italian sentiment resulting from Berlin's hostility towards Spontini and Rossini, he had heard (presumably from Morlacchi) that the wind of rebellion was blowing in these parts and therefore counted on some opposition from this quarter.[15] But

13 Joachim wrote Bachmann that a master of the true classical style may found a school and be taken as a model, but the virtuoso for whom supreme technique is mere child's play and who can get away with anything should *not* be followed, since his "is the lone, dangerous path of a comet."

14 During the Dresden visit, Kersting (1785–1847) painted the well-known portrait of him (on porcelain). It is now in the National Gallery, Dresden.

15 Codignola repudiates DeLaphalèque's statement of the "anti-Italian" sentiment in Berlin and the preconceived "aversion to Paganini" because of his "friendship

in a land with a network of petty courts and lingering feudal traditions nothing was more potent than a friend at court, so, with Spontini still in a key position, and with his own Cyclopean successes in Vienna behind him, he was no longer overly perturbed, that is, if his health did not suddenly go back on him in this raw, unfriendly climate.

Contemporaneous accounts differ regarding his Leipzig plans, some writers contending that it was his intention from the first to play there on his way to Berlin, others asserting that he was only persuaded to do so after his arrival. It is also very possible that the Saxon royal family, cognizant of Leipzig's pride in the quantity and quality of its music and the competition between its Gewandhaus Orchestra and Dresden's century-old court orchestra, may have suggested his playing there if he found sufficient interest. Some such motive must have guided him since the shortest and most direct route to Berlin was by way of Elsterwerda, while the detour to Leipzig represented an extra travel time of twenty-eight hours, though no doubt the road was better since it was a main commercial thoroughfare. Leaving Dresden on February 11 and traveling "via Meissen, Klappendorf, Oschatz, Luppa, and Wurzen," he arrived in Leipzig on the twelfth, and at a concert of the Gewandhaus Orchestra taking place that day Frederich Wieck (whose daughter Clara was to marry Schumann) learned of his presence in the city. As soon as the concert was over he and several of Leipzig's leading musicians called on the Maestro at the Hotel de Pologne and persuaded him to postpone his departure for several days and give Leipzig also an opportunity of hearing him. As a result of these impromptu negotiations a tentative date was set for February 16 in the Gewandhaus, with the regular orchestra of the subscription concerts under the permanent director, the "worthy but incompetent" Christian August Pohlenz.[16]

During the ensuing discussions with the business manager of the orchestra Paganini was unable to reach an agreement "regarding the size of the orchestra," his desire to reduce the number of

with Rossini" on the grounds of his enthusiastic reception there. As can be seen (on Paganini's own testimony) DeLaphalèque was here reliably informed.

[16] Christian August Pohlenz (1790–1847) in January, 1827, was appointed director of Gewandhaus concerts as successor to Johann Christian Schulz. He resigned in 1835 and was succeeded by Mendelssohn.

the players presumably clashing with the statutes of the orchestra. Thereupon he broke off negotiations and decided to give his concert in the theatre, where the orchestra was much smaller and the rulings more elastic. But here too he was confronted with an obstacle. From 1817 to May 1828 the theatre had been under the local management of Karl Theodore von Küstner, but when Küstner was called to the Ducal Theatre in Darmstadt the stock company was disbanded and the building leased to the touring company of Heinrich Edward Bethmann,[17] a crusty old specimen of the genus impresario, who was always hovering on the brink of bankruptcy. As he was then besieged by creditors, he evidently endeavored to recoup his fallen fortunes by demanding from Paganini 300 thalers rent, which the latter felt was unjustifiably high; so, viewing Leipzig as a den of organized robbers, he brusquely ordered his carriage and departed for Berlin. "And so [noted Wieck sadly in his diary] he left, and we gazed after him with long faces and yearning eyes; and then we all had to go to Berlin to hear him."

As the Leipzig *Abendzeitung* had already reported his willingness to reduce the price of admission to meet the wishes of the public, it now tried to explain the misunderstanding by placing the blame for his departure squarely on the directors of the Gewandhaus Orchestra.

Paganini was to play in the hall in which Catalani sang. At first he wanted to charge three thalers but then reduced the price to two. To begin with the directors demanded a very high rental for the hall; then they tripled the cost of the orchestra and in addition tried to force a singer on him. In the opinion of the directors and subscribers to the regular concert series, the programs should present a little of something for everybody. Paganini agreed to the tripled cost of the hall and accepted the artist, but he asked to have the orchestra reduced since it was too large for his purposes. This the directors declined to do. He then remarked, "Strange that others wish to dictate to me how many violins I need for my concert," and left. The members of the orchestra had nothing to do with the matter and said they would have been quite content with their ordinary fee; in fact, they would even have been willing to play for nothing just for the pleasure of hearing him.

17 Heinrich Edward Bethmann (1744–1857), a "curious old character" with a long career as theatrical director. See Friedrich Schulze, *Hundert Jahre Leipziger Stadttheater—ein geschichtlicher Rückblick.*

Since he returned to Leipzig later in the year, both sides seem to have been willing to forgive and forget; but Paganini's biographers, holding strictly to Schottky's unverified account (Schottky never made any attempt to control the information he collected) and feeling that the theatre director, as Pulver put it, "hoped to make his hay during one short spell of sunshine," placed all the onus of the incident on that individual and the directors of the orchestra. However, the dispute deserves a little fuller treatment than this cursory dismissal since it throws light on one of the main aspects of Paganini's character that dictated most of his actions at this stage of his career.

When Schottky's biography appeared, G. W. Finck, in reviewing the work for the *Allgemeine Musikalische Zeitung* (then the house organ of Breitkopf & Härtel), took sharp exception to Schottky's one-sided version of the episode. Paganini (he wrote) had been quite willing to reduce the admission from three to two thalers when the situation was explained to him, and up to this point had made no stipulations whatsoever, either with respect to the assisting artist or the size of the orchestra; but as soon as he was informed that "since he was doubling the regular price of admission, he would also have to double the orchestra's fee in accordance with municipal regulations," he immediately demanded "that the orchestra be reduced one half." Which, of course, still only represented the amount he originally wished to pay! "It is not true [continued Finck] that the managers demanded a higher rent from him than from other artists and, furthermore, no one tried to force any singer on him. Quite right—with the admission prices doubled, he was required to pay the orchestra double the ordinary honorarium. He was shown the law on the subject. Whoever demands more than the customary admission can let his colleagues enjoy part of the surplus."

According to Doerffel, the Gewandhaus Orchestra in 1831 consisted of sixteen violins, four violas, three cellos, three double basses, two flutes, two clarinets, two oboes, two bassoons, two horns, two trumpets, two trombones, and percussion—or approximately forty players. Paganini's request for only twenty was thus inspired more by financial considerations than artistic ones. It was the fee that mattered, not the "number of violins." Further, it is interesting to note that he never objected to the size of the orchestra when he was engaged for a stipulated fee or played under his customary two-thirds percentage. In Berlin, for the first three concerts he "insisted [Rellstab tells us] on having only twenty-five players at four thalers each, making a total of 100 thalers for the orchestra," which was not quite exact but was indicative of the gossip regarding his attitude on this point. For the first Berlin concert the orchestra cost him 121 thalers, some of the players receiving four, others five, thalers; for the second concert he had thirty-one players at a cost of 132 thalers, and for the third, twenty-nine at a cost of 125 thalers. When he played at the Royal Opera on a percentage basis, he accepted the full orchestra of seventy players without demur! In other cities of Germany he also raised no objection, the Darmstadt orchestra numbering sixty-three, Dessau forty-nine, Frankfort thirty-six, and Stuttgart forty-five, exclusive of percussion.

That the Leipzig incident did not rest quite lightly on his conscience is shown by his filing among his private papers Rebizzo's copy of a letter addressed to someone who at the last moment tried to persuade him to reconsider his decision.

Leipzig, February 13, 1829.
I'm distressed at not having spoken with you first, because we could have come to a perfect agreement on all the points brought up in your kind letter, which pleased me very much. From what you tell me regarding the musicians, it is clear that the demand for an increased fee did not originate with them. . . . The mutual respect customary between artists and my experience of many, many years enable me to judge the matter *ponderatamente*. For me it is important to have an orchestra in conformity to the size of the hall, and when Maestro Pohlenz made the arrangements with me regarding the number of players suitable for me, he deferred to the number I desired. . . . From what I hear of the prices charged here by Mme Catalani, it doesn't seem to me that my prices were too high, considering what is customary with artists of some reputation. I kept them at this low figure through a desire to favor the amateurs who are so numerous in this lovely city, and I regret that, owing to the misunderstanding, we have already withdrawn the announcements from the papers and I've made my arrangements to leave for Berlin, where they are expecting me. On another occasion I shall avail myself of the hall that you so courteously offer me and in the meantime please express to all those gentlemen my gratitude, together with my thanks for having called to see me at my hotel.

iii

Leaving Leipzig on Saturday, February 14, he arrived next day in Berlin and put up at the Hotel de Rome, the leading hotel in the city; then, four days later, in keeping with his regular practice he moved to private lodgings with a "Herr Neissen at Friedrichstrasse 80," evidently a hotel *garni,* which provided greater comfort for Achilles. He also wished to lose no time in announcing his first concert, but here he soon learned that the Prussians were far more formal than the Viennese. For neither Spontini, Meyerbeer, nor Count Redern, the intendant, could be of any assistance with respect to the Royal Theatre; for this he personally had to address a petition directly to the King. "My bad health forces me to take advantage of the time [he wrote in requesting a date during the first week of March] since my suffering leaves me only brief moments of respite." To which the King immediately replied by placing the Theater am Gendarmenmarkt (Schauspielhaus) at his disposition for six concerts to take place between March 4 and April 6 —no doubt on the urgent recommendation of his *Hofkomponist* and *Generalmusikdirector,* Gasparo Spontini.

Although feeling far from well, Paganini's debut proved an extremely brilliant and fashionable occasion, despite some scattered hisses from the anti-Italian ranks. The audience numbered approximately nine hundred, and included the "King and all the royal family as well as about eighty titled ladies and a large contingent from Leipzig" who joined with the Berliners in giving him an unprecedented ovation. Before considering the verdict of the leading critics, it is interesting to note the reaction of one of the most cultivated and prominent figures in the Berlin of that day, namely, Mme Rahel Varnhagen von Ense, whose salon was one of the intellectual centers of the capital.[18]

Rahel Varnhagen von Ense to her husband, March 7, 1829.
I heard Paganini on Wednesday. If you can, *do* read the article about him in yesterday's *Spener'schen Zeitung*—I can't figure out who wrote

18 Rahel Varnhagen von Ense, nee Rahel Levin (1771–1833), belonged to the Berlin "circle of literary Jewesses." She and Henriette Herz had the most famous "esthetic salons in Berlin, in which the cult of Goethe was fervently celebrated." See Tymms, *German Romantic Literature* (London, 1955), 130.

it, and that's one consolation.[19] I could in no way contradict this judgment—I could even endorse it in many respects, only I should say it all
quite differently. One important point escaped the author as it has all
the critics—a very outstanding and astonishing one! Paganini plays far
better on a single string than on all four. More correctly, surer, cleaner,
more Italian, more audaciously and therefore with more *élan* and dramatic accent. Whatever his past history may have been, one thing to
me is certain—he was for a long time in possession of a violin with only
one string. He really doesn't play the violin—he doesn't have the tone
(or tones) of Rode, of Durand, of Haack,[20] of Giornovichi[21]—but he
actually talks; he whimpers, imitates a thunderstorm, the stillness of
night, birds that descend from heaven but do not soar towards heaven
—in short, poetry. In the prayer from Rossini's *Moïse,* he plays the different voices as they enter one after the other, and then all together. . . .
I swear to you that again and again I was forced to repeat the words of
the harpist—*"Wer nie sein Brot mit Tränen ass"*[22]—to shudder, to weep.
It was the very embodiment of the poem. But enough of that. The stalls
were *not* inclined to applaud him, but they *simply had to!* I saw persons in front of me break out into applause who had hissed when he
was welcomed. The court, the whole audience, clapped. Everyone has
to admire him even though it may be only astonishment. He looks old,
worried, starved, and good-natured. The bows with which he acknowledges his applause date from the dark ages! Everybody laughed—he too.
Pantomime along with it—but modest on the whole.

Next day the two leading critics, A. B. Marx[23] and H. F. Rellstab,[24] men of experience and high standing in the world of music,
came out boldly for the Maestro, though Rellstab had always been
one of Spontini's bitterest and most implacable opponents and
had returned again and again to his attacks, even going so far as to
publish a virulent pamphlet against him that eventually landed
him (Rellstab) in jail. The reviews of these two men, unbiased
scholarly critics, are still interesting today, not because they differ

[19] The criticism to which she refers was written by Samuel Schmidt.

[20] Karl Haack (1751–1819), a pupil of Franz Benda and the teacher of Friedrich
Möser, (1774–1851), violinist-leader of the orchestra of the Royal Opera, Berlin.

[21] Giovanni Giornovichi (Jarnowick) (1745–1804), a pupil of Lolli. In Paris in 1770
he was all the rage. He was one of the most eminent violinists of the eighteenth
century.

[22] Goethe's *Lied des Harfners.*

[23] Adolph Bernhard Marx (1795–1866), editor of the *Berliner Allgemeine Musikalische Zeitung* and teacher of music theory and history at Berlin University.

[24] Heinrich Friedrich Rellstab (1799–1860), leading critic of the Berlin *Vossische
Zeitung.* His pamphlet was entitled: *Ueber mein Verhältnis zu Herrn Spontini* (1827).

essentially from a multitude of others, but because they furnish evidence of the tremendous impact of Paganini's personality on two distinguished musical specialists whose judgment was uncolored by prejudice and who both were famous in their day for their stiff-necked imperviousness to any kind of popular enthusiasm.

Marx, in the Berliner Musikalische Zeitung. (curtailed).
The man appeared to be bewitched and had a bewitching effect; not alone on me, or on this and that person—*but on everybody.* He came out on the stage and plunged at once into the Ritornelle, in which he conducted the orchestra and shot the orchestral texture with dispersed sparks of tone like shafts of lightning—then to pass into the most melting and daring melody ever heard from a violin. He sails nonchalantly, unconsciously, over all technical difficulties, interspersed with the most audacious flashes of a satirically destructive humor till his eyes take on the glow of a deeper, darker passion, the tones become more penetrating and onrushing so that it seems as though he were lashing the instrument. . . . Then he stamps his foot and the orchestra rushes in and fades away in the thunder of the unparalleled enthusiasm of the audience, which he scarcely notes, or acknowledges with a contemptuous glance or a smile in which his lips part in a strange way and show his teeth. He seems to be saying: you *must* applaud me, whoever or whatever I am, or whatever mood comes over me in my pain, or with whatever fetters my feet may have been burdened, which have lamed the happy, dauntless step of youth. But before these thoughts can pass through one's mind he has disappeared. . . . There is a queer thing about this man. The external elements of his playing, all the seemingly impossible tours de force, this combination of rapid arco and pizzicato runs, these octave passages on one string—all these things are merely vehicles, they really mean nothing to him. The inward poetry of his imagination, molding the creations before our eyes—this is what captivated the listeners. . . . This was not violin playing, this was not music— it was witchcraft—and yet *still* it was music, only not the kind to which we are accustomed.

Rellstab, in the Vossische Zeitung.
Paganini was welcomed with moderate applause, many faces revealing only too plainly an antipathy towards the Italian virtuoso whom the local heroes of declamatory singing despise in advance because he is a compatriot of their enemy Rossini. But in the end he also robbed the preoccupied of their composure before they themselves were aware of it. And after his first solo in a concerto of his own, a wild ovation broke out which put all "Sunday applause" in the shade. The audience was

in a state of exaltation the like of which I have seldom witnessed in a theatre, and never in a concert hall. . . . Never in my whole life have I heard an instrument weep like this. . . . I never knew that music contained such sounds! He spoke, he wept, he sang! . . . After the concluding trill, a wild ovation broke loose . . . the ladies leaned over the balustrade of the balcony to show they were applauding; men stood on the seats the better to see him and call out to him. I have never seen the Berliners in such a state! And this was the effect of a simple melody!

The general impression that he made upon me, including his personal appearance, is not a pleasing one. There is something demonic about him. Goethe's Mephisto would have played the violin like this. All the great violinists whom I have previously heard have their own personal style—one can follow them. Yet the mighty Spohr, the sweet Polledro, the fiery Lipinski, the elegant Lafont, merely aroused my admiration. Paganini is not himself; rather, he is the incarnation of desire, scorn, madness, and burning pain—first one and then the other. The tones are merely the instruments by which he expresses himself, and even the emotion he arouses is destroyed all of a sudden through harsh, unbeautiful bowing, through daring, tasteless capriccios. He often scratches and scrapes quite unexpectedly, as if he were ashamed of having just given way to a noble or tender emotion. Yet when you are about to turn away in disgust, he has recaptured your soul with a golden thread and threatens to draw it out of your body. . . . His compositions are neither accident nor design. They are the fruits of a ravaged, intemperate life—the external framework, the medium, by which he gives full vent to his feelings, after which he collapses, completely exhausted. After the first number they brought him a fur coat. He wrapped himself in it, pale as death, wiped the perspiration from his brow and sank down exhausted in a chair.

As for the Maestro himself, he was delighted.

Paganini to Germi.
I'm in Vienna again for the first time. I've found in frosty Berlin a theatre director, virtuosos, etc. who have behaved very decently and have been extremely obliging. I was surprised, and am deeply grateful. The enemies of Spontini and Meyerbeer were, of course, my enemies also from the very outset, even before they heard me. They even showed their hostility in the theatre. But after twenty-five bars they already began to applaud enthusiastically, quite without realizing it. The enthusiasm was so great that I could scarcely go on. As a surprise for the King, I'm now composing some variations on the national anthem. I'm enjoying myself hugely here, especially at the opera. No one who has not

seen it can have any conception of its excellence. Spontini and Meyerbeer have overwhelmed me with courtesies and have helped me in every
way they can.[25]

The Berlin reviews also pleased him tremendously since he
could see from them that he had made a deep impression, altogether a happy augury for his forthcoming tour. For as Edward
Holmes wrote, Berlin was one place in which "an artist might be
sure of having a liberal judgment passed upon his abilities with the
advantage that his fame spreads more rapidly from this part of Germany than any other." Paganini also had heard this from his
colleagues, in Prague, in Dresden, even in Vienna, so he was highly
gratified when he found himself the most talked-of person in the
place. "You'll have seen in the papers how I am received and acclaimed in this city [he wrote Galeazzo Fontana-Pino]. Modesty
forbids me going into details." Excellent, indeed, but there was
still one distressing circumstance. Marx, like his Vienna colleague
of the *Theaterzeitung,* had referred obliquely to the rumor of the
ex-galley slave, indicating that all the Maestro's efforts to counteract the slander had been futile. While in Prague, he had received
a letter from Fontana-Pino hinting of dark plots and intrigues in
Paris and of a report that he hesitated to measure swords with the
great French violinists. "If you're feeling better, as we all hope,
then *do* go at once to Paris in order to surprise and demolish all
those professors who don't believe a Paganini can exist . . . damned
asses! Hurry—rush and convince the incredulous of your unsur-
passable merit. This one laurel leaf is still wanting in your crown!"
At the time, he had been in no mood to answer, though gossip of
this nature rarely perturbed him—he needed only time and opportunity to establish his prestige. "The Paris canard is perhaps traceable to some charlatan making using of my name. . . . I shall divert
the Parisians in the late autumn—and there's no doubt but that
I'll divert them!" A week later, however, he began to brood on the
activities of his enemies. Marx's reference to some dark history of
sin and atonement, together with some idle gossip that may have

25 Germi did not share Paganini's enthusiasm for Spontini and Meyerbeer. "I
exult over your good fortune [he wrote on April 17] and I am tranquil now that
you're in the company of an honest man. I could tell you things about Spontini and
Meyerbeer. . . . I'm not fanatical over the first and I have little regard for the second."

come to Rebizzo's ears regarding what a Dresden music student called his "reputation for unbridled epicureanism," once more assumed formidable proportions in his mind, the anxiety, as usual, affecting his physical functions, something that just now he could very ill afford. Where was Schottky's promised biography and why hadn't he yet published it to put an end to all this stupid gossip?

Paganini to Schottky, March 7, 1829.
It's time that I let you have my news, and it's not bad. I'm suffering a little with my eyes[26]—my principal trouble at the moment. You'll have read the Dresden papers; in that city I found all the amenities[27] and the kindness of the royal family *y mit le comble*.[28] I also learned there that you've published an article announcing my biography,[29] but I've heard nothing further. I'm immensely curious. The relative of whom I told you joined me in Dresden and he too is impatient. Let me see some parts of your work. My honor is in your hands. How happy I am to have found an avenger whose name alone is enough to crush the calumnies. Your probity and talents will be the despair of my enemies and you'll be able to congratulate yourself upon having done a generous deed.

Paganini to a friend in Prague (Gordigiani?), Berlin, March 10, 1829.
I'm impatiently awaiting my biography—not just for my glorification but to silence evil tongues who, being unable, or not knowing how, to challenge my ability (whatever it may be), enjoy defaming my honor with false, the very falsest of allegations. What's Professor Schottky doing? I've already written him from here but have had no reply. Meanwhile, the rabble continues to narrate these fine tales and it's absolutely imperative that I choke off this gossip without further loss of time. I'd like to know what that comedy is that has been written about me. I believe the title is *Der falsche Virtuoso*. Please be good enough to tell me what it's about. I hope it hasn't been written to insult me because I

---

26 Besides his fundamental disorders, Paganini's ailments at this time resemble in many respects those of Giacomo Leopardi, as described by Iris Origo. (*Leopardi*, 250).

27 In 1827, Edward Holmes, a schoolfellow and friend of Keats, was music critic of the newspaper *Atlas*. He toured Germany and Austria and set down his impressions in his *A Ramble among the Musicians of Germany*.

28 Spohr wrote of the Gewandhaus concerts: "These concerts are got up by a society of shopkeepers. But they are not amateur concerts, for the orchestra is composed solely of professional musicians and is both numerous and excellent.

29 Schottky's announcement was dated Prague, January 15, 1829. It was also published in the Italian press, the *Eco* of Milan bringing a long comment as well as a translation of Schottky's communication. See Codignola, *op. cit.*, 278, n.

really believe I've never done anything to warrant it. Give my kindest regards to the professor and tell him that all my friends are impatient to see his work. Thus my honor will be known and vindicated and the truth will serve as a padlock on the lips of imposture.

The replies were evidently prompt and satisfactory, so, encouraged by Rebizzo's healthy, detached point of view, he was again ready to dismiss these silly worries as matters of no consequence. It never seems to have entered his mind to call on Rebizzo for testimony, which tempts one to believe that even though *Père* Antonio may have had some business dealings with the Rebizzo family, Lazzaro did not feel competent to issue any statement certifying to Niccolò's unblemished record during adolescence and early manhood.[30]

Paganini to Germi, April 3, 1829.
A friend like Rebizzo is a real treasure. The love he bears me is worthy of a great soul and I thank Heaven for having granted me his angelic company. I'm planning to postpone my journey to London because it would be a little late and, moreover, I can't decline the obliging invitations of the people here. . . . I've written some organic variations on the theme *Heil Dir in Siegerkranz* for my violin to convince the incredulous.[31]

Easily influenced, as always, by those he admired, Fontana-Pino's phrase rolled pleasantly on his tongue, yet "modesty forbade" his quoting it in its entirety. It was best to leave the logical conclusion to Germi's imagination.[32]

iv

On March 11, Mendelssohn conducted the historical first performance of Bach's St. Matthew Passion at the Singakademie, yet Paganini, strange to say, does not seem to have been present. "It would be interesting to know if he heard the Passion [wrote Sir George

[30] Paganini first mentions Rebizzo in a letter of June 18, 1823: "Rebizzo is a queer chap, and the others don't get him."

[31] On her German tour Catalani (1827) also chose this method of captivating the Prussian King.

[32] In criticizing the tendency of the world to condemn an artist's "impersonal egotism" on the score of immodesty, Jacques Barzun states very aptly, "And yet we know that the Lord looked upon his handiwork and found it good; but we fail to draw the inference." (*Op. cit.*)

Grove] and if, like Rossini some years later, he professed himself a convert to Bach." It would indeed, but all available records are silent on this point. A few nights after his debut he dined with Mendelssohn's parents in their hospitable home at Leipzigerstrasse 3, so that his attention must have been called to the forthcoming event, which was then engaging everyone's attention. Perhaps he expected young Felix to give him a complimentary ticket, a courtesy accorded him by all the theatres, but one that Zelter, the grouchy master of ceremonies, would have sharply frowned upon.[33] According to his contemporaries, Paganini was extremely fond of sacred music, so if he missed this memorable performance he must either have been feeling indisposed (extra-long intermissions were necessary at his concert on March 19, and the one announced for the twenty-eighth had to be postponed two days because of illness) or else Bach, like German opera, did not appeal to him.[34]

Up to April 18, Zelter was one of the few musicians in Berlin who had not heard the Maestro; not because he was disinterested but because he could not produce the requisite two thalers, and it would certainly never have occurred to Niccolò to send a complimentary ticket to a director of a choir! For the charity concert on April 29, however, when the distribution of press tickets, etc. was a matter of indifference to him, someone gave Zelter a ticket so that at long last he was able to satisfy his curiosity.

Zelter to Goethe, May 5, 1829.
Paganini is driving men and women mad with his cursed fiddling. The real misfortune of his coming here is that he's ruining all our young orchestral violinists. Last Tuesday he called on me at the Singakademie and heard our performance; then next day I finally heard him. It's extraordinary what the man can do and one must admit that his playing has in general the desired effect and is quite incomprehensible to

33 Among the Berlin journalists who requested tickets and was refused was the well-known Moritz Gottlieb Saphir, who, according to Marx, "exceeded in shamelessness and contemptuous disregard of others, anything that Berlin had yet experienced in the way of journalistic morality." Saphir was evidently in very bad odor with the Mendelssohn-Meyerbeer-Marx-Zelter clique in Berlin, which may have been the reason for Paganini's refusal.

34 In 1817, when Henry Matthews was in Italy, a German opera was being given at one of the Italian opera houses in a city where he happened to be stopping. "Musica tedesca," said his friend with a contemptuous shrug. "Non amiamo." Paganini (according to Harrys) felt the same way about it.

other virtuosos of his instrument. His nature is *more* than music, without being great music; and I shall probably remain of this opinion even after frequent hearings. I was so placed that I could watch all the movements of his hand and arm, which, with a rather slight figure, must be especially flexible, strong, and elastic; because in heightening his effects he can perform like clockwork the most fatiguing things of which a soul is capable. The hundred tricks of his bow and fingers, which are all individually thought out and drilled into him by practice, follow one another in tasteful sequence and prove him to be also a composer. In any case, however, he is to the highest degree a consummate master of his instrument, in that what won't go, even for him—with the best will in the world—comes off as a daring variation.

v

"I cannot fully enjoy the pleasure of being so greatly favored by this public [Paganini wrote Moscheles on April 2] because it delays the moment of making your personal acquaintance. I must reluctantly yield to the entreaties of the Intendant of the royal theatres, since the King wishes me to give some concerts in the Royal Opera. My fifth and last in the Schauspielhaus takes place next week;" which was only a half-truth.

Although the King had placed the Royal Theatre at his disposal for six concerts, he had been unable—owing to ill health—to give one a week as he originally intended. In any event, it is not likely that this failure to keep his schedule worried him to any great extent since he no doubt thought he could continue to give concerts in the theatre as long as he elected to remain. As Spontini or Meyerbeer now probably advised him not to request an extension of the privilege, he then suggested giving some "intermezzo" concerts at the Royal Opera (Königrätzertheater on Alexander Platz), where he would play one or two numbers between the acts or between the opera and the afterpiece for a stated percentage of the net receipts. Without being grossly unfair to him, it is a reasonable conjecture that, as his audiences began to dwindle towards the last,[35] he actually preferred this solution of the problem, though,

[35] After the concert of May 9, Rellstab wrote: "An unlooked-for, undesirable sight! Empty boxes! Stalls and third balcony fairly full. The reason? The fact that Paganini has repeatedly announced his 'farewell concert,' so that one felt sure of being able to hear him again." Another paper wrote that "his last concerts were fairly empty except for his more devoted admirers."

since it represented a marked departure from German theatrical usage, here too he must first have the permission of the King. When the monarch then accorded him the "royal permit," he impulsively donated to certain civic charities one half the receipts of the final concert of the series in expression of his gratitude.

In Central Europe no demands were ever made upon him for charity concerts, nor was there evidence of any deep-seated resentment (beyond some envious superpatriot now and then) at his "making millions and sending them out of the country," though whenever he stopped in a city for any length of time he usually gave a charity concert as a farewell gesture; hence, nothing more was asked or expected of him. Of course, the situation in Austria and Germany was a little different since the theatres were generally the property of the crown and were almost always placed at his disposition gratis by the music-loving prince by whom they were maintained, so he rather felt it incumbent on him to return the favor indirectly before he left the city.

Whilst the Berlin critics thought these "half concerts" (as Rellstab called them) an excellent idea inasmuch as they enabled many persons to hear him who previously had to forgo the pleasure, the attendance on the whole was not noticeably affected by this additional attraction. Even with the inevitable reduction in "audience appeal" he would still no doubt have remained in Berlin till June 20 for the wedding of the Crown Prince (later Wilhelm I) with Princess Augusta of Saxe-Weimar, had not two things occurred that immediately changed his plans. Spontini was exceedingly anxious for him to contribute his art to the coming celebrations, so, yielding to his friend's entreaties, he agreed to return to Berlin upon the completion of his Warsaw engagement, the Polish government having invited him to play at the coronation of Tsar Nicholas as King of Poland on May 24. These invitations from two powerful monarchs especially appealed to him, more perhaps from the idealistic than the financial side, for here he saw a prospect of receiving high Prussian and Russian orders to flank his papal Golden Spur—two distinctions that he very greatly coveted now that he was rising rapidly to affluence. And since it would be greatly to his advantage to have the Prussian order before he went to Poland, he was quite prepared to go all the way to make a spectacular bid for it, rather than to wait and take his chance of receiving it at the end of June as part of the royal wedding honors.

As Danzig had recently suffered from abnormal tide floods and numerous benefits were being sponsored by different national organizations, this seemed to him a ready-made occasion for a dramatic gesture that would appeal more strongly to the King than would generosity to some local, continuing charity. In addition, he had now finished his variations on the national anthem and, since the court would be in duty bound to attend such a charity affair, the work would prove a fitting climax and, if it did not woo an order from the King, it might at least inspire the civic authorities to have a medal struck in his honor. After deciding on this diplomatic move he transmitted (through Spontini) the regulation petition to the King and was delighted to receive again an immediate acknowledgment, placing the "large theatre, gratis" at his disposition for May 2.

The concert, which took place on April 29 (presumably for administrative reasons), netted the sum of 2000 thalers while Paganini had an unexampled triumph, even for Berlin. Although Rellstab thought the variations on the anthem required an orchestral accompaniment, no one seemed to find anything incongruous in the Maestro's delicate and sparkling arabesques any more than in Spontini's noisy orchestration of the work two years before, which had so shocked Edward Holmes.

The anthem was interlarded with long instrumental symphonies [he wrote], which were quite irrelevant to its style and character . . . this noisy parade of loyalty being intended by Spontini to please the King of Prussia, whose ear is obtuse except to an immense crash.

Perhaps this may explain why Paganini's treatment, while it touched off the patriotism of the audience, apparently made little impression on the King, who even accepted this obvious homage silently—another bitter drop indeed! Yet he still had another chance. Spontini, no doubt aware of his friend's ambition, then persuaded him to remain in Berlin till May 13 and play a "request program" at his Concert Spirituel which took place every year on Busstag (Day of Penitence) in aid of the Royal Orchestra's Pension Fund, which he had founded in 1826. Zelter, who heard him again on this occasion, now pronounced him "truly unique" but Rellstab could not resist a sarcastic comment when Paganini preluded his Concerto in B minor with the *Adagio Religioso* written in Vienna, "which would make the audience contrite." "Paganini [he wrote] composed an introduction stemming from the monastic forms and customs of his fatherland in the naïve belief that only such a prelude was appropriate for the Day of Penitence." Here the liberal north German was disturbed by the Maestro's sentimentality, while the latter, whose religious roots were in another soil, considered a mood of contrition as quite in keeping with the spirit of the day.

This time, however, he was not interested in the opinions of the Zelters and the Rellstabs. His ears were attuned only for the word of Caesar. Surely, after all these demonstrations, and within the short space of two weeks, King Friedrich Wilhelm would now do the unexpected thing! But alas, even Spontini had misjudged him. An hour or two before Paganini and Rebizzo set out for Frankfort on the Oder, the first lap of their Warsaw journey, Spontini hastened to his friend, bringing with him a cabinet order accompanied by the following communication in the King's hand:

J'ai résolu de vous donner avant Votre départ de ma capitale, une marque de la satisfaction que j'ai éprouvée en assistant à vos concerts. La nature Vous a departi un rare talent, que Vous avez cultivé avec un esprit original. Les sons que Vous tirez de quelques cordes vont à l'âme et excitent dans le coeur de vos auditeurs les émotions les plus rares. Je Vous ai nommé mon première Maître de concert honoraire et Vous autorise à porter ce titre.[36]

One can well imagine his dismay, but with his natural suspicion he probably attributed the disappointment to some envious bungling on Spontini's part. His bow had still one more, and indubitably better, string and he would make one final effort on his own behalf before abandoning the pursuit of another extravagant illusion.

[36] "Before your departure from my capital, I have decided to give you a token of the satisfaction that I have derived from attending your concerts. Nature has endowed you with a rare talent which you have cultivated with an original mind. The tones that you draw from a few strings touch the soul and arouse in the hearts of your auditors the rarest emotions. I have bestowed upon you the honorary title of First Kapellmeister, and grant you permission to use it."

Among the distinguished salons in Berlin where he was a frequent guest was that of Prince Anton Heinrich Radziwill,[37] member of an old Lithuanian family and at that time royal Prussian Statthalter, or governor, of the Grand Duchy of Posen, who was married to Princess Louise, only daughter of Prince Louis Ferdinand of Prussia, the King's brother. As Radziwill was a gifted cellist and composer, sang with taste and finish, and was a portrait painter of no mean order, he and the Maestro were soon fast friends and spent many charming evenings playing chamber music in the beautiful old Radziwill Palace on Wilhelm Platz, surrounded by the Prince's cultivated circle and the soul of music that permeated it. When Paganini received the invitation from the Polish government, Radziwill at once began to arrange recitals for him in Frankfort on the Oder and Posen, the only two towns along the way where a concert would repay him. Then at the conclusion of the Warsaw engagement he was to join the Radziwills for a week at their estate "Antonin," near Stzhizhevo, and return with them to Berlin for Prince Wilhelm's wedding. This was therefore a most promising connection, but with his Ligurian caution, he wished—before showing any further favors to the Prussian royal house—to make sure that his hopes would not again be disappointed. So he dropped a note from Warsaw to Princess Radziwill to enlist her interest and influence.

It is not vanity that prompts this request [he wrote], but I know the value of such a distinction coming from the hand of such a great monarch. And it seems to me to provide the best answer to those who never tire of inventing scandalous reports to calumniate me. My honor and peace of mind are therefore in your hands and your friendship alone can procure for me the greatest of all consolations.

The Princess acknowledged his letter with the polite evasion that she was referring it to her husband, "who would be joining him in Breslau within the week. . . . We've been expecting you every day for four weeks," she wrote, to recall his broken promise, and closed with cordial greetings. Since nothing more was heard

37 Anton Heinrich Radziwill (1775–1838) wrote a number of songs with piano accompaniment, as well as arrangements for guitar and cello. Goethe said of him that he was "the first and only real troubadour I have ever known." Paganini also played at a musical soiree given by Meyerbeer's parents on April 5.

of the matter and Paganini also never again referred to it, the Prince, who just then was slightly *persona non grata* with the Prussian authorities, probably filed it, knowing that the King kept such distinctions for military achievements or as homage to other reigning heads and was not disposed to establish a perhaps inconvenient precedent by extending the favor to executant artists—a point of view that he must have made perfectly clear to Paganini during their rendezvous in Breslau.

"*C'est hélas! l'effet naturel des injustices que de mettre à vif les vanités,*" wrote André Maurois with reference to Chateaubriand; yet, in Paganini's case, as "unjust" as were the rumors, he was clever enough to take advantage of them by camouflaging his tuft-hunting as a defensive measure, thus avoiding the ridicule usually meted out to the sycophant and climber. That he was here following a consistent line of conduct, a personal philosophy, which he had adopted very early in his life, long before such gossip troubled him, is shown by a letter he wrote about this time to his protégé, Ciandelli.

I'm enclosing herewith the letter of introduction to Ricordi in Milan, and will do everything possible to be of assistance to you. However, you should not think this is enough, but you must now proceed to help yourself. To trust in God without making any effort on your own part is dangerous, since God likes to see us zealous in our efforts. In our profession, a beginner must be very active and adroit, must procure introductions at the proper moment, climb many stairs and, when necessary, swallow many unpleasantnesses, if this can be done without stooping to vulgarity. One must foresee obstacles and be skilful in gauging them so as to avoid the snares of the many "gentlemen" with whom one always has to do. In short, playing is not enough. One must also be able to step out into the world—in other words, one must be an artist of life.

With respect to the Prussian order he may well have failed "to gauge his obstacles skilfully," but in keeping with his usual practice in such cases he rang down the curtain permanently on Berlin.[38]

[38] Dates of the Berlin concerts, assisting artists, and net receipts:

March 4	Schauspielhaus	Krüger, Schulz	1,463 thalers
March 13	Schauspielhaus	Binder, Hoffmann	1,775
March 19	Schauspielhaus	Stümer, Devrient	907
March 30	Schauspielhaus	Krüger, Schulz	?

April	6	Schauspielhaus	Schätzel, Bader	792
April	13	Royal Opera	Schulz, Devrient, Hermann	?
April	16	Royal Opera	Seidler, Milder, Laverenz, Pfaffe	1,223
April	25	Royal Opera	Milder, Stümer, Hauck, Griebel	1,014
April	29	Royal Opera	Milder, Bader, Griebel, Wörlitzer	2,000
May	5	Royal Opera	Bock, Hoffmann, Baganc, Devrient	1,365
May	9	Royal Opera	Wörlitzer, Gährich, Stümer, Hauck, Belcke	452

XIV. *WARSAW 1829*

La bataille horrible, incessante, que la médiocrité livre à l'homme superieur.—BALZAC.

THE JOURNEY from Berlin to Warsaw took from five to six days and lay for the most part through flat, monotonous, sparsely populated country with (as already said) only two towns en route where it would repay an artist of Paganini's standing to give a concert or where he would even find a proper auditorium and orchestra, namely, the little garrison town of Frankfort on the Oder (with a large colony of French Huguenots) and Posen, the capital of Pomerania, about thirty-six hours from Warsaw. Although Prince Radziwill, as circumstances proved, was powerless to help in the matter of the Prussian order, he did everything he could to make the concerts in these two places a resounding success and to ensure that the Maestro would be welcomed by an appreciative and representative audience. In Frankfort, he was guaranteed 100 friedrichsdor and was relieved of all expenses, a favor presumably accorded him (through Spontini's influence) by the Intendant of the royal Prussian theatres in Berlin, while in Posen, Prince Radziwill played host and assumed officially all expenses—also no doubt under directives from Berlin—not only placing a carriage and an apartment at his disposition (on this journey Paganini travelled *bourgeoisement* by diligence) but turning over to him the gross receipts of 807 florins.

Conestabile tells us that after the concert in Frankfort the Maestro was the guest of the young widow of Major General Karl Heinrich von Zielinski,[1] who, as he was on the point of starting out on the long night ride to Posen, personally tucked him up in his warm greatcoat to ensure that he would not take cold. Since Conestabile fails to cite his authority for this now popular little

[1] Wilhelmine (Minna) Wagner (1799–1875) married Major General von Zielinski (1772–1817) in Frankfort, March 7, 1816. In 1835 she married the retired officer and diplomat, Adolf Eduard von Treskow (1805–65), in Lossow, near Frankfort.

anecdote, which furthermore makes no mention of Achilles—the little toddler who would surely have been the principal object of Frau von Zielinski's motherly solicitude—one is inclined to question the authenticity though, as an enthusiastic music lover and an intimate friend of Rahel Varnhagen von Ense, Princess Agnes von Carolath, and the Radziwills in Berlin, it is not unlikely that she offered him the hospitality of her home for the few hours he spent in Frankfort. Born Wilhelmine Louise Antoinette Wagner in 1799 (presumably of Huguenot origin), she married in 1816 the distinguished Prussian officer Major General von Zielinski, twenty-seven years her senior, who died the year after their marriage. She was therefore a young woman of thirty at the time of Paganini's visit and was seemingly without any personal eccentricities, her interests in general being those of any young matron of her station. The point is stressed since Tibaldi-Chiesa *(op. cit.,* 215) adds the following gloss to Conestabile's account: "She was a great lady, practically the sovereign of the Silesian squireens. Her age was indefinable and she always dressed as a man; only in the evening she would change her brown wig for a white one and don a ceremonial waistcoat." She was not a "Princess," as Conestabile asserts, nor, judging by her maiden name and the absence in the Almanach de Gotha of any details regarding her origin and parentage, was she of distinguished lineage. As the "Frau Generalin" in a little garrison town, she no doubt played a certain role, particularly as a young and presumably attractive widow, added to the fact that a handsome dowry must have acted as the decoy that originally lured the Prussian aristocrat into this modest marriage.

Although Paganini remained in Frankfort less than twenty-four hours, it was here probably that he made the acquaintance also of his later manager, Paul David Curiol, a native of Frankfort who for some years—up to 1827—had been owner and director of the theatre. Thus it seems likely that Radziwill or the cognizant authorities in Berlin entrusted him with the arrangements which Paganini later found so excellent.

As Curiol signed a contract with the Maestro in Berlin on August 16, and for six months thereafter was associated with him as his personal manager, the initial negotiations may have taken place in Frankfort, where Curiol had many friends who could vouch for his integrity and fitness for the work. Since Rebizzo's six months were now almost up and he was anxious to return to Italy, it was imperative for Paganini to find a capable, honest, and experienced secretary-manager and Paul David Curiol seemed to possess all the necessary qualities, besides being warmly recommended by persons whose judgment Paganini esteemed.

Curiol (b. 1776) was then fifty-three years of age with behind him a career packed with adventure. He sprang from a well-known family of French Huguenots who had emigrated to Germany during the religious wars, his great-grandfather Michel having eventually settled in Frankfort, where there was a large and flourishing French colony and where he occupied the influential post of cantor and teacher. Although capable, thrifty, earnest, and industrious, the entire family seems, nevertheless, to have had the fatal knack of getting into trouble, Curiol's grandfather, a freethinker of Voltairian stamp, having been excommunicated in 1771 after one of his periodical feuds with the clergy. His son, Antoine Dominique (Curiol's father), in a desire to avenge this affront, then wrote an acid lampoon against the offending pastor which got him also into serious difficulties with the church, while Paul David in turn, after his father's death, made a false affidavit in his mother's name "in order to secure some rum and sugar," and for this youthful delinquency (he was still a minor) was sentenced by the magistrate to "twenty lashes of the cat-o'-nine-tails and six months in jail," which rounded out the record. The first Curiols were all teachers or professional musicians but Curiol's grandfather and father had descended slightly in the social scale and followed the trade of *patisseurs et confiseurs,* acting at the same time as local managers of the traveling theatrical companies that came to Frankfort during the annual commercial fairs, so that Paul David had the métier in his blood. As his mother, at the time of his conviction, was carrying on the bakery, she begged for clemency on the plea of his extreme youth and the fact that the business would suffer if it were known that she had "a son serving a prison term";[2] whereupon, the kindly judge commuted the sentence to two months with permission to serve the time in Berlin.

After this early misdemeanor Paul David mended his ways and,

[2] *Geschichte der Fransösische Kolonie in Frankfurt an der Oder* (1868).

since his mother (according to the municipal records) was "the highest taxpayer in the French colony," he enjoyed the educational advantages of a respected family of tradesmen in comfortable circumstances. Having no vocation for the trades, on his mother's death he sold the family business and after acquiring French citizenship and serving first as a French agent he enlisted in the French army and at one time was stationed (allegedly as commandant) in the Tenth Arrondissement in Paris. During the War of Liberation he then transferred his obedience to the German Volunteer Corps and rose to the rank of lieutenant, receiving several citations for "unselfish and disinterested conduct" and the Iron Cross "for personal bravery."[3]

In 1806 the French Huguenot Church in Frankfort had been made into a stable and hayloft and when finally put up to auction in August, 1816, it fell to Curiol as highest bidder for the sum of 3500 thalers. He then converted it into a theatre, founding at the same time a dramatic school at his own expense which provided him with the repertory company for his theatre, which he regularly took to Stettin and other towns in the vicinity. (In the history of the Frankfort theatre he holds an honored place for the high standard of the productions during his directorship.) However, through his Bohemianism and an ambition that outran his pocketbook he was constantly in debt and, having failed for seven years to meet the interest on the mortgage, he was declared bankrupt on September 13, 1827, and the church property returned to the French colony, while he "was relieved of costs because of his notorious poverty." For the next two years he seems to have divided his time between Frankfort and Berlin, engaged in sundry theatrical undertakings in an effort to eke out a living—till he became Paganini's manager in August, 1829. Several of his contemporaries have testified that he was extremely capable and likable, was well versed in the elaborate etiquette of official intercourse, highly thought of by his associates, well educated, an excellent linguist and musician, and thoroughly acquainted with theatrical routine even though, so far as his own ventures were concerned, he seemed to be a magnet for misfortune. His association with the Maestro

---

[3] His name was cited in the *Patriotische Wochenblatt* of March 5 and August 22, 1813, for "bravery in action."

was no exception; for, while his arrangements for the first German tour showed the careful, expert planning of a knowledgeable impresario with a wide acquaintance among theatre directors and court officials, Paganini's suspicious nature still "did not trust him," albeit as far as personal probity went he was surely as reliable as any of the fauna at that time. On the other hand, Paganini had always played as a "free artist" and, being by nature impatient of restraint, either could or would not accommodate himself to a rigidly charted course and was continually jumping the fence for a canter in the open and blithely defaulting on his contracts; which threatened serious penalties for his manager—an offering to genius that Curiol just then could ill afford. With a little less mistrust on Paganini's part, a little more indulgence on Curiol's, the association might have lasted longer and been more fruitful to both partners than either realized.

ii

Since he was directed to be in Warsaw by the twenty-first, he left Posen immediately after his concert, crossing the Russian frontier on the twentieth and arriving at his destination at half past eight on the morning of the twenty-first so that the director of the coronation music could go forward with arrangements. Two days later he gave his first concert at the National Theatre, which was attended by the Grand Duke and suite, the Polish Senate, the commandant of the city, and all the Polish aristocracy assembled in the capital for the coronation, the total receipts amounting to 10,953 florins, or a net intake of 8,975 florins after the deduction of expenses. Although the theatre (of which Karol Kurpinski was then director) could not compare in size or beauty with those in Vienna and Berlin, the audience on this occasion reflected the traditional splendor of the Russian court, while the orchestra, which had been especially organized for the month's festivities, was under the direction of Paganini's old admirer Karl Lipinski, who, as Poland's most eminent violinist, had come from Lemberg, where he was then engaged, to offer his personal contribution to the King.[4]

---

[4] In 1827, Lipinski had dedicated his Op. 10, *Tre Capricci per il violino* (Probst, Leipzig) to Paganini. (Schottky, *op. cit.*, 305.)

Despite Poland's long chronicle of political misfortune, life in Warsaw was very *mondaine,* so for the next eight weeks Paganini and Rebizzo lived in a constant whirl of social activity, one of the gay fringes of the Maestro's professional life that provided him with numerous pleasant diversions—amorous and otherwise—so long as his health did not give way under the persistent strain.[5]

Paganini to Germi, May 30, 1829.
At my twelfth concert in Berlin the public intimated a desire for me to return and I promised to do so for the wedding of the Prince, the King's son, on June 20. I'll soon write to you at greater length, also regarding Spontini, who loves me tenderly; and Meyerbeer, who has shown me every possible courtesy. At present he's on his way to Paris, saddened by the loss of his second son, having already lost his first-born. Rebizzo sends you kind regards and begs you to calm Morelli if he's angry;[6] because it really doesn't seem that he ever has time to write! My health is not too bad; I don't overdo. . . . On the twenty-fourth I played at court for the Emperor.[7] Yesterday I gave my second concert and this evening I'm giving the third. Tomorrow I shall rest since I have four more this coming week. I shall play in Breslau before returning to Berlin. His Majesty the Emperor of Russia gave me a diamond ring on the occasion of the coronation here.

It sounded very charming but it was not so simple as all that. True, his receipts maintained a gratifying level so that at the end of his visit he could send his banker 47,855 florins, which was not too bad for six weeks' work. But there were several other angles that were far less satisfactory. The political atmosphere in Warsaw, a factor always to be reckoned with in countries long oppressed by a powerful neighbor, was at this time especially tense and within a fortnight after Paganini's arrival rebounded on him in a manner not unlike his recent experiences in Prague. For once more he found himself the innocent bystander in a family brawl and,

---

5 Paganini listed only two of his social engagements, viz., one as "guest of Prince Xavier Lubecki," and the other "a dinner with Countess Zamoiska, one of the first families of Poland." That he was amusing himself along customary lines is indicated by a notice in the Vienna *Allgemeine Musikalische Anzeiger* of August 15, 1829, to the effect that he had married a young lady of twenty-one with a dowry of 130,000 francs who "had long been in love with him."

6 Gaetano Morelli was Rebizzo's lawyer in Genoa.

7 Codignola (*op. cit.,* 291) gives the date as May 14—obviously a typographical error.

through his fatal quality of pliancy more than through any deliberate impulsiveness, indirectly brought about, or at least did much
to further, a virulent controversy in the press that was fundamentally contrary to his character and principles. The controversy in
itself was no doubt inevitable, but without his intervention it
would not have taken place till after his departure and would not
have ruptured his old friendship with Lipinski.

Poland just then was on the threshold of the political developments that culminated a year later in a military revolt against the
Russian government, which was endeavoring to absorb the country into the Russian body politic, Russify its institutions, stifle
Polish nationalism, and even wipe out the native language. At first
weary and disillusioned after the crash of the Napoleonic empire,
the people were beginning to shake off this negative, fatalistic attitude and were turning an ever more receptive ear to the battle cry
of the Young Poles, who, incensed by the arrest, deportation, and
exile of many patriots and the enforced conversions to the Ortho-
dox Church, refused to compromise with despotism and seized
with eagerness any occasion that afforded them an opportunity of
reviving the dormant nationalism. Among the leaders of this militant front were Christian Lach-Szyrma,[8] professor of philosophy
and English literature at the university, and Maurycy Mochnacki,[9]
leading literary critic and writer who later led the anti-Russian revolt and whose writings contributed so greatly to the passionate
patriotism that led to the uprising.[10]

The refusal of the poet Adam Mickiewicz[11] to return to his

---

[8] Christian Lach-Szyrma (1790–1866). After the 1830 uprising he settled in England, where he was very active in *émigré* circles. When Paganini played at a benefit
for Polish exiles in London in the summer of 1833, the concert was disturbed by
rioters. One wonders if Lach-Szyrma was responsible in any way! He was described
as "very enterprising and ruthless."

[9] Maurycy Mochnacki was the greatest literary critic and writer of the Polish romantic age. His writings did much to further the revolt.

[10] During the coronation festivities there was an abortive Polish plot to assassinate
the Tsar. In his *Life and Death of Chopin* Casimir Wierzynski, in describing the
events of this summer, states that Prince Radziwill was a guest at the coronation and
"visited the Chopins afterwards." Since numerous statements in his work are open
to question (for instance, he writes that "Paganini did not visit Berlin"), this fact is
also quoted with reservations.

[11] Adam Mickiewicz (1798–1853), while attending the University of Wilno, was arrested and deported to St. Petersburg when the Philomats (a society to uphold Polish

native land (after five years of Russian exile) so long as it was under Russian yoke and his decision to take instead the road of exile to Germany and Italy added new and potent fuel to the patriotic fires. And the anger of the leaders reached incandescence when, on the heels of the saddening news that Mickiewicz had sailed from Kronstadt to Hamburg, a foreign artist received the signal honors at the coronation of the "King of Poland" to the admiring chorus of what they called "a group of sycophants and toadies" while a worthy Polish instrumentalist was allocated a supernumerary role and during the entire period of the Tsar's visit (for which Lipinski had come especially to Warsaw) was relegated, so to speak, to a back seat without a single influential person having the courage to raise a voice in protest.

Lipinski had come to Warsaw for the express purpose of leading the orchestra and among the coronation honors had been granted the title of "first violinist of the Tsar of Russia and King of Po-land"—the counterpart of Paganini's diamond ring. At three o'clock on May 24, after the coronation in the cathedral, it was Paginini who played at the royal palace (following a state banquet by the Tsar) to one hundred and thirty Polish guests.[12] So with the undercurrent of feeling in the capital the Chamberlain's selection of a foreign artist to entertain the Tsar's official guests while Po-land's "most distinguished instrumentalist and first violinist of the King of Poland" was relegated to a quasi-secondary role was in itself enough to inflame Lipinski's countrymen. The prime mover in the campaign and the one who, so to speak, fired the fatal shot was not, as Pulver stated, the Italian composer and singing teacher Carlo Soliva (an old friend of Paganini from his Milan days)[13] but Lach-Szyrma, seconded by Mochnacki, who, bending all their efforts to exalt Lipinski, brought about a violent clash between the Young Poles and the more moderate professional circles around Elsner,

culture and the language) were arrested and the university closed. In May 1829, after the publication of his *Konrad Wallenrod,* he was permitted to leave Russia and went first to Germany and Italy. See Mieczyslaw Jastrum, *Adam Mickiewicz* (Warsaw, 1949).

12 Some accounts say that Paganini played with Lipinski at the coronation cere-monies in the cathedral, but it has been impossible to verify the fact.

13 Carlo E. Soliva (b. 1792), pupil of Asioli and Federici of the Milan Conservatory, was called to the Warsaw Conservatory in 1821. During 1832–34 he served as conductor in St. Petersburg.

Countess Zamoiski, Kurpinski,[14] and others who regretted to see their young patriots sacrifice a distinguished guest on the altar of their political ideals.

Between his arrival and the first week of June, Paganini had given five concerts in a gathering crescendo of enthusiasm, Lipinski all this time modestly remaining in the background till he announced a solo concert to take place on June 5. As Paganini had given a recital on the third and was to give another on the sixth, Soliva (who was teaching at the conservatory) pointed out to him the unwisdom—given the present explosive atmosphere in the city—of having Lipinski sandwich a concert between two of his. In view of the existing tension, this could only lead to unpleasant polemics that would serve no useful purpose. Inasmuch as Paganini intended to leave within a week in order to be back in Berlin by the twentieth, why not go to Lipinski as an old friend and persuade him to postpone his concert till after his (Paganini's) departure, when he would then have the field entirely to himself?

Since Paganini was always wax in the hands of his strong-willed friends, it was not surprising that he lent a ready ear to Soliva's ill-advised suggestion. For first of all, they were old friends with many memories and interests in common. Then, too, Soliva had been residing in Poland for some years and Paganini could justifiably assume that he was acquainted with conditions and in a position to interpret the presumable reaction. However, the result was unfortunate in that he was actually tactless enough to approach Lipinski in this sense and naturally received a brusque refusal, Lipinski frankly saying that he felt that Soliva only made the suggestion in order to be able to say later that "Lipinski had not ventured to compete with him."[15] This unhappy tentative having failed, Paganini went ahead and gave his concert on June 3 to the usual crowded theatre, but on the fifth the rain came down in torrents, which naturally affected the attendance at Lipinski's concert, though he was still "greeted by a fair-sized audience and received a rousing ovation, Paganini also enthusiastically applauding." Next day the critics discussed the concert in a more or less per-

14 K. Kurpinski (1785–1857), director of the Warsaw Theatre, composer of many operas and editor of the first Polish musical magazine.

15 In a letter dated April 17, 1830, Chopin wrote regarding Soliva: "Perhaps he's a tricky Italian. I don't go near him when I can possibly help it."

functory manner, which was in marked contrast with the "indulgence" they had shown to Paganini and was even more conspicuous
after the latter's concerts on the sixth and tenth, which again were
lushly appreciated. The time (in the opinion of the Young Poles)
had clearly come to call a halt, so on the morning of the thirteenth
the *Dziennik Powszechy* (Universal Country Journal) published a
long article by Lach-Szyrma (signed L.S.) that immediately created a sensation.

Paganini is an extraordinary phenomenon in the world of music [he
wrote in part]. Guided only by his musical instinct without any actual
theoretical training, he has achieved a degree of perfection that would
scarcely have been possible for another artist with similar means. True,
the numerous rumors relative to his early life have been officially denied, but this much is certain—at times whole years went by without
anyone hearing anything about him. It was often thought he had died
in obscurity somewhere and had since been completely forgotten. But
during all this time he was living in some out-of-the-way place, cut off
from all the world. Left to himself, he neglected the musical side of his
art to concentrate exclusively on technique, in which he attained a
very high degree of proficiency. But this was of such a special nature
that few, if any, artists could follow in his footsteps for fear lest they
should be accused of charlatanism. Indeed, it seems as though he had
an entirely false idea of the true nature of his instrument, for he does
not try to reveal its natural beauties, but instead endeavors to imitate
the tones of other instruments, even the cries of animals. The same
tendency is evident in his compositions. They are not marked by any
particular style but are rather the product of a gloomy fantasy which,
guided by no canons of good taste, often wickedly destroys the most
beautiful passages. And yet it is only in his own works that he is brilliantly effective. The works of others confront him with difficulties that
he is unable to master, owing to the peculiar nature of his playing.
Where it is a question of a noble, powerful tone, of daring, passionate
bowing, of a pure cantabile—in short, wherever he should bring out all
the inherent beauties of the instrument, he merely displays technical
dexterity. . . . To this, Lipinski presents a striking contrast. This great
artist holds strictly to the canons of art. He never transgresses the standards of good taste and disdains all shimmering ornamentation. If one
can call Paganini a Romantic, Lipinski justly deserves the epithet
Classicist, in the finest sense of the word. . . . His bowing is far superior
to Paganini's and he is also his superior in power and fullness of tone,
in soulful cantabile playing and in harmonics. He is Paganini's peer in
rapid playing, but is inferior to him in light staccato playing, in the

less important transitions from the natural tones to harmonics, and finally in pizzicato with the left hand.[16]

This article launched the argument and very soon, despite the valiant efforts of Elsner and Kurpinski, patriotic feeling was running high and the discussion occupying increasing space in all the local papers. On the nineteenth the *Gazeta Korespondenta Warszwsjiego i Zagranicznego* brought a letter from Soliva in which he rushed to his countryman's defense and expressed his indignation over Lach-Szyrma's unfriendly criticism; then next day (probably in keeping with a concerted plan) the *Gazeta Warszawski* published a communication from Kurpinski, who took a similar attitude saying that "Paganini is self-taught—Lipinski, on the contrary, is the product of a master. After all, Lipinski should not forget that he studied with Paganini and only by admitting this fact openly can he now escape the suspicion that he inspired Lach-Szyrma's article."

Since Kurpinski evidently obtained his information from Paganini or Rebizzo—at least suspicion pointed very strongly to this source—Lipinski felt that he owed it to himself to enter the fray and thereupon addressed a letter to the press in which he categorically denied that he had ever studied with Paganini. "My own father taught me the rudiments of music and I'm not the product of a master nor of any conservatory. If I had studied with Paganini, I should be quite ready to admit it and should consider it a great honor. . . . I made Paganini's acquaintance in Italy in 1818, when he was good enough to call me a 'Valente Professore di Violine.' We gave two concerts together, but that was the extent of our association." He then expressed his deep regret that his compatriots should think him capable of disparaging a distinguished colleague. "Never before, at home or abroad, have false facts been used to humiliate me. No one has ever accused me of such things except the capital of my own country, which I am visiting for the second time. As much as I admire Paganini's great talent, I cannot, and never will, lay claim to a comparison with him since I have chosen

16 Everyone was anxious to learn Paganini's reaction to these polemics but he maintained his usual stoical silence, his only comment being: "I have been criticized on numerous occasions, but I have never yet encountered such a real connoisseur!" Was this tact, or real conviction? No doubt the former.

an entirely different genre, in which I am zealously striving to perfect myself so that some day I can call out to my countrymen—
anch'io son pittore."

As in all such discussions regarding the comparative merits of great artists of divergent styles and ideals, particularly when flag waving and patriotism are involved, the argument soon left the abstract plane and descended to personalities so that one is tempted to believe that Lipinski was not entirely blameless after all. If Paganini thought anything about Lipinski's letter, he did not say it, though there must have been more to the incident than chauvinistic fervor on the part of Lach-Szryma since it sounded the death knell of Paganini's friendship with Lipinski, a fact admitted by Fétis also, though his "well-informed" Polish friends gave him an entirely false idea of the real background of the argument. Pulver, following Fétis, also scoffed at the idea of there being professional rivalry involved, but Wagner's subsequent experience with Lipinski in Dresden and Lipinski's constant machinations against his rivals there provokes reflections and leads one to suspect that he was by no means as innocent as he pretended. In a letter to the Intendant, Wagner accused him of "insufferable vanity, of double-dealing and of being the fountainhead of the agitation in the theatre."[17]

Paganini was a bonny fighter where his personal reputation was at stake, but we have no record of his ever having flashed the bright sword of his irony against his colleagues in altercations of this kind. He was always quite content on such occasions to let the heathen rage and go quietly about his business with the contempt of a Brobdingnagian among the Lilliputians. Later on, the slightest innuendo regarding his past, his character, or actions moved him instantly to battle. But the testing fires of Paris and London were still some time in the future and he was not yet in a belligerent mood, though he was human enough to recognize what was going on around him and wise enough to listen to his own inner promptings and avoid all further connections in the future.

iii

Fortunately, the Warsaw sky was not always overcast and there

17 Newman, *op. cit.,* 371.

were many on whom his passing left an ineffaceable imprint, many whose hearts were big enough to harbor admiration for both artists without allowing politics and patriotism to dictate their prejudices. Prince Xavier Lubecki, the minister of finance, had shown him friendliness and hospitality, as had also Countess Zamoiska, Elsner, and Kurpinski. Among the many musicians who were enchanted with his music was the young pianist Maria Szymanowska,[18] who has been immortalized less through her music than through Goethe's infatuation for her. It was here, too, that he heard for the first time the gifted child Apollinaire de Kontzki[19] and (as he carefully noted in the Libro Rosso) met "M. Chopin, *giovine pianista,*" who in turn found the Maestro "absolute perfection." With Chopin the effect of Paganini's playing was more psychical than inspirational. It gave him renewed confidence in his own powers, though the experience had no visible effect on the manner of his playing or on his compositions, as it had with Liszt and Schumann, for his was not the heroic type that took fire from, or could absorb and transmute into another idiom, the molten flashing metal that was Paganini. Unlike his colleagues Liszt and Schumann, he did not attempt to transfer to his own instrument Paganini's achievements on the violin since the "diabolist atmosphere" (Sitwell's phrase) surrounding Paganini was emotionally and musically alien to one whose Muse dwelt rather with the intimate. Paganini himself seems to have enjoyed the piano merely as a cultivated listener, but without feeling any special sympathy for it. Probably he missed the subtler gradations of tone possible on bowed instruments (before Liszt charged it with electricity), so it seemed to him a little tame, like all the keyboard instruments. We know that he was intimately acquainted with Mendelssohn, Moscheles, and Cramer and was in Paris when the fame of Chopin,

18 Maria Szymanowska (1790–1831). Goethe had known her since 1821 and called her "an incredible player." She appears to have helped to inspire the *Trilogie der Leidenschaft,* and the third of its poems, *Aussöhnung,* contains a direct allusion to her. Paganini wrote her a little Albumblatt, which is now in the Adam Mickiewicz collection of the Polish Library in Paris. (Mickiewicz was her son-in-law). It consists of two lines of music with the dedication: *Omagio al distinto talento de Madama Scimanovski.*

19 Apollinaire de Kontzki (1825–79), a prodigy at four, in 1861 he became director of the Warsaw University. Paganini heard him in Paris in May, 1838. (Codignola, *op. cit.,* 543.)

Liszt, and Thalberg was sweeping Europe, yet there is no record of his having evinced any special interest in their art, nor that he noted the impact of his playing on their development, though Schumann's *Six Studies after the Capricci of Paganini* was published in 1833 and Liszt's *Grande Fantaisie sur la Clochette* was completed in 1834, both of which must have been brought to his attention.[20]

iv

Feeling intuitively that to return to Berlin for the wedding of the Crown Prince would prove only another blighted hope, he abandoned the idea and decided to stay on in Warsaw till Prince Radziwill's schedule enabled him to leave the pageant in Berlin and keep their belated rendezvous in Breslau. While waiting he repaid Kurpinski's favors and championship by giving a charity concert for the benefit of the widows and orphans of musicians of the National Theatre, and rounded out his Warsaw series by two final concerts early in July.[21]

His many friends, deeply regretting his departure and no doubt wishing to make amends for his recent castigation at the hands of their young patriots, arranged on the day of his departure (July

---

[20] See Kathleen Dale, *Nineteenth Century Piano Music* (Oxford, 1954), 190–95. The following table shows the Paganini *Capricci* selected by Schumann and Liszt for treatment:

Paganini	Schumann		Liszt	
1	—		4	
2	Op. 10, No.	5	—	
3	Op. 10,	6	—	
4	Op. 10,	4	—	
5	Op. 3,	1	1	Preludio
6	Op. 10,	2	Etude	
9	Op. 3,	2	5	La Chasse
10	Op. 10,	3	—	
11	Op. 3,	3	—	
12	Op. 10,	1	—	
13	Op. 3,	4	—	
16	Op. 3,	6	—	
17	—		2	
19	Op. 3,	5	—	
24	—		6	

[21] At these two concerts his share of the receipts dropped to a trifle over 3,000 florins, but this was owing to the departure of the coronation guests and not to any political prejudice.

19) a farewell banquet in his honor at a manor house on the main highway about two miles from Warsaw, on which occasion Dr. Elsner presented him with a gold snuffbox "on behalf of his admirers." Schottky, leaning on an anonymous report in Georg Lotz's popular *Originalien* (Hamburg), stated that Paganini was unaware of the intention of his friends—that they ambushed him as he was driving by. This statement is a little difficult to accept since various and more reliable accounts indicate that on this eastern journey, he, Rebizzo, and Achilles (who during the Warsaw visit was tenderly cared for by Signora Soliva) traveled by diligence, which would have precluded such an interruption of his journey. Since he was also congenitally addicted to sudden, unlooked-for changes in his plans, the engraved date (July 19) on Dr. Elsner's souvenir indicates that there must have been close collaboration between the guest of honor and his hosts. So he presumably drove out to the estate with friends and then caught the diligence when it passed along the highway later in the day. Be that as it may, this gracious way of speeding the parting guest, along with the many evidences of admiration and affection he received, proved extremely heart warming and surely eradicated any remaining memories of the friction that had gone before. It is only too bad that the pleasure could not have been more lasting, but the Saturnian goddess who forever trailed his footsteps left him little respite and was already preparing for him the only serious provocation he experienced during his whole two years in Germany, a provocation prompted, unfortunately, by more ignoble instincts than the national partisanship of which he had recently been the innocent victim in Bohemia and Poland.

XV. *FIRST GERMAN TOUR 1829*

*There are rascals in Germany as elsewhere but one must confess that there is in that country much more cordiality and a deeper feeling for art than in the rest of Europe. I have been treated with understanding, respect, and affection, which touches me to the bottom of my heart.—*BERLIOZ.

ARRIVING IN BRESLAU on July 23, he "engaged two rooms on the first floor of the best hotel in town at one thaler per day" and the next day gave his first recital in the Aula Leopoldina of the University.[1] On March 20, Baron von Eberstein, head of a distinguished Silesian family, had extended him an invitation to play in Breslau and on May 4 the Prussian minister, Baron von Stein, had placed the auditorium at his disposition for as many concerts as he cared to give, so he found everything in readiness, particularly since he must have advised Prince Radziwill of the prospective date of his arrival. While his letters give no hint of any unpleasantness at any of his concerts, the German and Austrian papers made no secret of the fact, the *Vossische Zeitung* of Berlin speaking of a "great ovation and even greater *Hitze*," and the *Allgemeiner Musikalischer Anzeiger* of Vienna going further and stating that "his visit could have left no pleasant memories on either side, no one in Breslau regretting his departure," thus giving the reader the impression that some serious clash had taken place between him and the public. Although Schottky, too, went into no details (perhaps intentionally), one still gathers from his brief account that despite the great ovation Paganini was in disfavor and therefore "gave only three concerts," whereas, in point of fact he actually gave four and remained in Breslau a whole fortnight. So we see that he did not allow the rowdyism and unwarranted demands of a distempered group of university students to disrupt his personal arrangements. A member of the orchestra now throws for us an illuminating beam on the hitherto mysterious occurrences.

1 The hall was given him "gratis," so to speak—that is, for the nominal sum of 25 thalers. The orchestra cost him 59 thalers, which included 5 thalers for a solo flutist.

Adolph Hesse to a friend, October 14, 1829.[2]

In Breslau the good Paganini almost came to grief. Just listen to this! The Senate of the University placed the wonderful auditorium, the Aula Leopoldina, at his disposition for his concert. This hall is really intended for the performance of oratorios only and was given him with the distinct understanding that at the rehearsal he should play at least *one* piece right straight through without interruption so that poor students who couldn't produce two thalers for this concert might have an opportunity of hearing him. I must also add that this hall is in the University and is consequently the property of the Senate and the students are all entitled to attend every concert rehearsal. The rehearsal was set for seven o'clock on Saturday morning. The whole orchestra was waiting in the hall, along with about 1500 students. Paganini appeared about eight o'clock; the orchestra played the first tutti of his Concerto in E flat with great precision and care. The hall was tense with expectation. All at once he began, played a couple of muffled, indefinite notes, and made a fool of the public and the orchestra in the basest way. Our dignified old Schnabel made no bones about expressing his disapproval, but that didn't help matters any.[3] Finally the students began to murmur, stamp, pound, shout, whistle, so that you couldn't even hear the Turkish music. Paganini laughed. All at once two angry students sprang into the orchestra, seized Paganini by the lapels of his coat and gave him the choice either of immediately playing a *pièce brilliante* or of being thrown out of the hall and down the stairs. Then he took fright. In addition, Schnabel and the orchestra were also making ready to leave so he had to play. He really acted very basely here. Therefore, he was allowed to give only two concerts in the hall.

The permit issued by the Prussian authorities in Berlin laid down no conditions, so that he probably was ignorant of the University's regulations or, if informed of them after his arrival, did not grasp their import, perhaps thinking it was a question of a handful of violin students whom he always readily admitted. At all events, when he refused to play for a nonpaying audience of 1500, his action was looked upon as trickery, a Machiavellian quality considered as inseparable from all Italians. Whereupon, the victims took justice into their own hands. It was no doubt because of this experience that from now onward he always expressly

2 Adolf Friedrich Hesse (1809–63), one of the most celebrated organists of his day. He heard Paganini first in Berlin and wrote at that time: "His facility is extraordinary and no one can explain his four part playing . . . but still his playing has something of the charlatan about it. In his Adagios he can't compare with Spohr."

3 Joseph Ignaz Schnabel (1767–1831), violinist in the Breslau Theatre Orchestra.

stipulated well in advance that "no one but the members of the orchestra or those whose presence was absolutely necessary" should be admitted to rehearsals and took particular pains to see, before entering the concert hall, that these instructions were followed to the letter. For he wished no repetition of such squalid brawls nor did he want to be forced, through rough mob violence motivated by spite, to capitulate and "give his art for nothing" like a helpless victim of brigands. Since both concerts in the University were disturbed by the student body and their sympathizers, the senate, to quell the rumpus, then revoked his permit—not because he declined to comply with the demands of the students but because his refusal to do so was seized on by the latter to stage a brawl that was as contemptible as it was odious. The times were such that the university authorities could not permit any "extraordinary circumstance to relax the nerves of discipline" and thus countenance the habit of revolt.

Finding the Aula Leopoldina closed to him, he then arranged to play two "intermezzo" concerts in the theatre (August 1 and 3), for which he received each time the sum of 600 thalers, making a total of 2845.18 thalers for his four appearances. Whether there was any attempt to disturb the last two concerts is not known, but it seems hardly likely that the students carried their war into the theatre, though they evidently managed to generate an extremely hostile atmosphere among the general public. In those days the *Korps* in the old universities were very powerful and, if ever bent on less harmless pursuits than fencing matches, duels, carousing and other activities of German student life, could stir up a riot that might easily get out of hand,[4] so the senate's action is therefore understandable. Pulver and other biographers who follow him state that the rector revoked the license because he objected to "the noisy ovations," but Hesse's letter makes it clear that it was not the ovations that disturbed the faculty, but the fact that Paganini's intransigeance (as they considered it) transgressed the University's traditions and thus led to a serious breach of discipline on the part of the student body.

4 The *Korps* was an exclusive club of students with distinct colors and emblems, where dueling was much encouraged. The *Burschenschaften* were associations of students professing national and liberal principles. The activities and interests here were more political in nature.

To continue the affront, the theatre chose this moment to revive a popular old farce by Adolf Bauerle entitled *Die falsche Primadonna in Krähwinkel,* which had been originally written as a take-off on the Catalani enthusiasm, but was now refabricated to apply to Paganini. The actor, W. A. Just, played the leading role in Paganini's mask and executed "a concerto *à la* Paganini to the accompaniment of the malicious laughter of the public;"[5] which called forth from one of the more dignified members of the community the justifiable rebuke that "things of this kind reflect little glory on the people of Breslau." Shortly after this the Bauerle farce was followed by *Niccolò Zaganini,* a musical comedy written by Wagner's old friend, Heinrich Laube,[6] under the pseudonym of W. Campo, which rapidly went the rounds of all the German theatres and finally caught up with Paganini in Frankfort. "All the world here [reported the Frankfort correspondent of the *Harmonicon*] has been to see the performance of an actor from the Breslau theatre who mimics the Italian virtuoso to a T. Paganini, instead of attempting to cut the poor mimic's throat, as most of your sensitive artists would have done, had the good taste, not to say good sense, to attend one of these performances and join in the general laugh with the best grace in the world." Whether he witnessed the performance of the same actor in Breslau in the Bauerle comedy and took it with equally good grace is not recorded.

As usual, in writing to his friends in Italy he was silent on this unpleasant episode, it being more "to his glory" to have them think he was going from triumph to triumph, quite apart from the fact that it was a little difficult in his laconic epistolary style to convey an idea of such matters without besmirching his own record, for once they became known they were always exaggerated beyond all recognition, so it was wiser, in his opinion, to concern himself with pleasant things.

Leaving Breslau on the night of August 5, he arrived in Berlin at ten o'clock on the morning of the tenth, after a nonstop journey of four and a half days,[7] his motive for returning no doubt being

---

5 Just also played the title role in Laube's musical comedy at the Breslau première on October 17, 1829.

6 Heinrich Laube was then editor of the *Zeitung für die Elegante Welt,* which for some years had kept Paganini's name before the German reading public.

to sign the contract with Curiol since all Berlin musical activities were suspended during August, the opera closed, and the orchestra away on holiday, though that probably mattered very little to him since by now he had beached the Prussian capital for good. His notebooks do not show the date of his departure but, as he arrived in Frankfort on the twenty-first, he could hardly have left later than the sixteenth since he traveled via Kassel, presumably for the purpose of seeing Spohr, who in the name of the Elector had sent him a pressing invitation to play there.

Spohr to Kühnel, September 26, 1829.
Paganini was here; he came to see me and then promised to return in four or five weeks and give some concerts. He asked me to make this fact known for the time being through the newspaper. We'll soon see if he keeps his promise. He has created a great sensation in Frankfort, Mainz, and Darmstadt so that I'm more than ever anxious to hear him.

But Paganini was still in no hurry to unroll his tricks for his illustrious colleague; he was not so sure that Spohr's judgments would be entirely free of prejudice, and preferred, no doubt, first to have his German tour behind him and his thalers safely in the bank before he ran the risk of condemnation from such an influential quarter.

After several days at the Hotel Schwann he moved as usual to more commodious quarters with a private family, and seems to have felt at home immediately in the picturesque old town, one reason probably being that Frankfort was still very French. "In patrician circles [wrote Bettina Strauss] the conversation was in French as at most of the German courts and, through the influence of French residents in Frankfort and of those German residents who had traveled in France, the use of French had become more and more general, even in bourgeois society." As Mme de Staël wrote: *"À Francfort tout le monde parle français."*[8] Then, too, the setting was not unfamiliar to him—the narrow crooked streets, the broad river, the surrounding fields and low blue hills recalled to him in many ways those Tuscan towns where he had spent his most

---

[7] Codignola (*op. cit.*, 649) lists a letter of Paganini's dated "Leipzig, 8 August 1829." This is a misreading of the abbreviation "8 bre," meaning October.

[8] Bettina Strauss: *La Culture française à Frankfort au XVIII siècle.* (Paris, 1911).

impressionable years. (Chateaubriand wrote of southern Germany that if it had not been for the porcelain stoves and the paler sky overhead the traveler could easily fancy himself in Italy.) Furthermore, Frankfort's situation on the cross-roads of Europe made it a busy commercial center with great merchant financiers of conspicuous wealth, while the music-loving population, many eminent musicians, an excellent theatre and orchestra, and even a good-sized Italian colony all conduced to his feeling of well-being.

After his opening concert the day after his arrival, he attended on the twenty-seventh a festival play in honor of Goethe's eighty-first anniversary and on the twenty-eighth was a guest at the annual Goethe banquet, three whirlwind engagements that successfully launched him in the artistic circles of the city that was to be his chief headquarters for the next year and a half. His second concert drew, as usual, an even greater crowd, while the reaction of the critics was similar to that of their colleagues in Berlin, that is, they were surprised "that this pale, sickly-looking man could overcome such colossal and seemingly insuperable difficulties," they were impressed "by his modesty and childlike nature," and astounded at the incredible dexterity "of a virtuoso who did not seem to realize [the words are Carl Guhr's] that he could rightly be considered as one of the greatest figures of the age."

Wilhelm Speyer to Louis Spohr, Offenbach, September 17, 1829.[9]
And now to give you my impressions of Paganini. I heard him first at rehearsal, then in several concerts, and last of all in a private company where he played Beethoven's F Major sonata with a lady. Although I was keyed up to the very highest expectations, the first impression in the rehearsal was that I had never heard anything like it in my life. Frey, from Mannheim, who sat alongside me swam in a sea of tears. The mysterious dusk of the stage, the remarkable personality of this man, the unusual enthusiasm of the orchestra, which broke out every minute in a stormy flourish of trumpets, all these things may very well have heightened the sensitivity of the nerves. But the main thing—his playing, his interpretation, even his musical tricks, the astounding ease and perfection with which he performed the difficulties (incomprehensible especially to a violinist) aroused the greatest admiration. The

9 Wilhelm Speyer (1790–1878) went to Paris in 1812, where he became a pupil of Baillot and derived many advantages from his friendship with Cherubini, Boieldieu, Méhul, etc.

cantabile passages and the Adagio he sings in a melancholy, deeply moving and albeit eloquent way such as I have never heard from any instrumentalist—about as I heard Crescentini sing fifteen years ago in Paris. This melancholy lament poured forth by a corpse grips the senses and one indulges in all kinds of romantic fancies. On the other hand, the noblest interpretation is often followed by some outlandish eccentricity and devices so obsolete that one seems to be listening to a violinist of past centuries, to a Lully or Tartini, perhaps. His performance of the Beethoven sonata was highly interesting and the most whimsical feature of it was that after the repetition of the first part of the Rondo, he played the theme in harmonics—double-stopped octaves! The theme of the Adagio he began each time with the upbow, proof that he does not follow traditional usage. In spite of his many thirty-second and sixty-fourth note embellishments, I have never in all my life heard anyone play so strictly in time! His compositions are very effective and though in part extremely old-fashioned, are still original. He played a wonderful Adagio in C minor. He speaks with great admiration of you. He sang to me the theme of *Liebe ist die zarte Bluete*,[10] which was sung at one of his Berlin concerts and assured me that he would never forget the impression made on him by this composition.[11]

ii

While Curiol was busy drawing up an itinerary, Paganini, finding himself at the focal point of a very fruitful pasturage, sent out feelers through Guhr and other friends to secure as many dates as possible within the immediate radius of Frankfort. One suspects, however, that success and flattery "in Vienna, Berlin, and Warsaw" had turned his head a little since the numerous invitations that came raining down upon him, coupled with the large sums he had received in certain places, led him at first to make exorbitant demands which sometimes defeated his own ends—an attitude that he wisely abandoned later. Among the promising places within convenient distance were Mainz, Mannheim, and Darmstadt, the latter with the "largest band in Germany," which was under the personal direction of Grand Duke Ludwig I, whose hobby it had

10 From Spohr's *Faust*. The aria was especially written for the tenor Schelble of the Frankfort Opera. The words were by George Döring, oboist of the orchestra. See Spohr, *op. cit.*, II, 59.

11 To this Spohr replied on September 20: "After your interesting letter regarding Paganini's playing, I can scarcely restrain my impatience to hear him. Should he have abandoned the idea of coming here, then—as unpleasant as it might be for me, and as difficult as it now is for me to get away—I would travel no matter where just to hear him." Frey (d. 1832) was conductor of the Mannheim orchestra.

been ever since his early manhood. "At Darmstadt all is quietly
and peaceably managed [wrote Edward Holmes], probably because the Grand Duke himself superintends the rehearsals. . . . The
road to promotion and court favor in this little state lies in musical
skill, for an aide de camp of the duke's gave the time to the choruses,
so that with this exalted assistance the Kapellmeister [Mangold]
had nearly a sinecure."[12] Paganini had already heard of the Grand
Duke's generosity, so, when no invitation reached him from this
famous theatre, he initiated the negotiations personally by writing
to the duke and then following up his letter by driving over to
Darmstadt for a performance of Spontini's *Nurmahal*[13] so that he
might have some idea of the auditorium and the capabilities of the
conductor, George Sebastian Thomas,[14] in the event his offer was
accepted.

Paganini to Grand Duke Ludwig I, September 2, 1829.
Fame never ceases to exalt the name of Your Royal Highness and for
a long time I have wished to present my homage to this princely pro-
tector of the fine arts who honors music with his genius and encourages
the artists with his great benevolence. The moment that I so greatly
desired has come. I expressly postponed my journey to England so as
to have the honor of submitting to the indulgent judgment of Your
Royal Highness a little sample of my compositions. I beg Your Royal
Highness to pardon my venturing to anticipate a favorable reply.

The Grand Duke immediately instructed Baron von Turkheim
to engage him for an "intermezzo" concert on September 8, for
which he received the entire receipts of 1,083 florins, in addition
to a gift from the Grand Duke of 100 friedrichsdor, and a further
gift of twenty Dutch ducats from his eldest son Prince Ludwig,
making a total of 2,195 florins, which was truly a kingly fee since
he only played three numbers.[15] Elated over his success and flat-

12 Wilhelm Mangold (1796–1875), a pupil of Cherubini's. He conducted all the
opera and orchestral concerts, while Thomas conducted the stage music.

13 The first performance of *Nurmahal* (libretto by Herklots) took place May 27,
1822, in Berlin in honor of the marriage of the Princess Alexandrina of Prussia.

14 George Sebastian Thomas, a pupil of Abt Vogler, played clarinet, viola, and
violin. He was in the service of the Grand Duke for twenty-nine years.

15 The program was:
> Overture to *Oberon* (first time in Darmstadt).
> Grand Concerto in E flat Major. Paganini.
> *Das Rätsel* (The Puzzle). Comedy in one act by Contessa.

tered by the attentions of the orchestra, which had serenaded him outside his hotel (the first homage of this kind in Germany), he at once dispatched a note to the conductor thanking him in cordial terms for the orchestra's efficient support.

Paganini to George Thomas, September 9, 1829.
I already knew by report how perfectly this orchestra played the most difficult compositions but the marvelous way in which it performed Spontini's wonderful opera last Sunday aroused my greatest admiration. So yesterday evening, pleasure was paired with gratitude for the precision and mastery with which my concerto was accompanied. I have to thank you and the first violin in particular, as well as all the members of His Royal Highness's orchestra. I must also thank you for honoring me with the serenade, which gave me such great pleasure. I shall always preserve the most lively memory of it.[16]

In writing Germi later, he spoke of his Darmstadt appearance in the plural and Karl Theodore von Küstner (the intendant) in his memoirs also referred to "several appearances in the theatre," but the official Darmstadt archives record only this one concert, though it is possible that his "musical skill" procured him a private engagement at the royal residence before members of the court, which might account for the two generous gifts.[17]

Meanwhile he proceeded with his Frankfort schedule, playing there on September fourth and seventh and again on the fourteenth and the twenty-first, making six appearances in all. In between these two latter dates he gave the first of two concerts in the large Reithalle of the Golden Horse Garrison in Mainz (which from 1793 till 1833 served as theatre and concert hall); then a few days later the *Mainzer Zeitung* brought the report of an interview which a member of the staff had had with the Maestro during his visit, the author stating that Paganini had gone through the article

Sonata Militaire. Paganini.
Der Strauss (The Ostrich). Comedy in one act.
Variations on *Nel cor più non mi sento*. Paganini.

16 In 1825 the orchestra numbered sixty-three, exclusive of percussion, piccolo, and extra wind instruments. "No orchestra in the world is so harassed as this [wrote Spohr], for the players (without a single exception) must be present every blessed evening in the theatre from six to nine or ten o'clock."

17 The reason why Paganini did not play in Darmstadt again was probably owing to the death of the Grand Duchess Louise on October 24, 1829, after which the theatre was closed for a month.

very carefully before publication and had "made no alterations or corrections in it." After discussing his playing and disposing once for all of the rumors regarding his incarceration in Italy, the author summed up his personal impressions as follows:

Among the many portraits we have of Paganini, lithographs stemming from Vienna and Berlin, those from Berlin are a far more authentic likeness. The Vienna pictures give the impression of a much older person. From the expression of his face one would take him for a misanthrope—which he is not. Although still showing the effects of his recent illness, he is still much younger in appearance than the pictures would lead one to suppose; and he also looks much younger (especially for an Italian) than he actually is. He looks like a person in the middle thirties, though he is already forty-five. His manner is very modest, almost shy. He has little to say and speaks in a low voice without gesticulations; but everything he says is definite and strictly to the point. . . . Altogether he is a simple, modest person and, though little conversant with present social usages, he never offends the laws of politeness and in ordinary informal intercourse is good-natured and affable, which qualities are reflected in his features and his eyes as well as in the tone of his voice. He speaks French brokenly, but in developing an idea he usually finds the right expression. In conversing in his own language he shows wit and *esprit*. He is fairly conversant with the classical literature of his own country but has not pursued the subject very deeply since he seems to lack the ability for a scientific study of it, all his spiritual forces being concentrated on his music, though in his early years he appears to have taken a very active part in politics. He tells us that it was only after great effort that he could be persuaded to demonstrate his talent abroad; through a lack of self-confidence, so to speak, it was very difficult for him to decide to take the step. He is a simple, *gemütlicher* man, a sincere friend and a very tender father to his little four-year-old son, to whom he is devoted and whom he takes with him everywhere. He leads a very simple life in keeping with his delicate constitution. He never goes to bed later than nine or ten o'clock, except when he has a concert. He sleeps late and when the weather is fairly good he takes a bath before breakfast. He lunches at three o'clock *modicum et bonum* and then takes a siesta. He does not bother himself about the business details of his concerts, leaving all this to his manager, Lieut. Curiol, Ret., who through knowledge of the field, the world, and mankind is the predestined guide and friend of this great artist and able, with respect to outward form, to supply that which Paganini lacks and which, for a roving artist who desires to garner money and renown, is almost as essential as talent. Artists who started or pursued their careers under Curiol's guidance praise his judgment and discernment and his humane and honest dealings. In all circumstances he shows consideration, ability, and *savoir-faire*—three qualities that are of inestimable value to Paganini.[18]

It was his original intention to give two concerts (a week apart) in Mannheim but, since his two-thirds share of the receipts of the first concert amounted to only 805 florins, he decided that a return date would not be worth the trouble. The Mannheim orchestra still ranked as one of the better smaller bands,[19] but the Elector having moved his court to Munich in 1778 the theatre now lacked the resources of a royal institute, so there was no hope of a substantial gift should the receipts fall short of expectations. Therefore, after a second concert in Mainz (also financially disappointing)[20] the long drive down to Mannheim seemed hardly worth the effort and fatigue.

Leaving Frankfort on the twenty-seventh, he spent the first night at Fulda, on the main highway, then proceeding leisurely arrived at Gotha the next evening and put up at the Gasthof zum Mohren,[21] where he was immediately visited by a delegation of leading citizens who tried in every way to persuade him to give a concert. But he either did not consider the prospects as promising enough, or else the hall and band did not meet his minimum requirements since he declined the invitation and did not reverse his decision when he passed through Gotha on his return journey. The court there had been broken up in 1825 when the duchies of Coburg and Gotha were united in Saxe-Coburg-Gotha and the orchestral players had been pensioned off, so that there was now no regular orchestra. Since (with few exceptions) he never played with piano-

18 The article closed with the statement: "Paganini has never been in Paris, as erroneously claimed by many French papers. But he is impatiently awaited there as we have been assured by Lafont, who rushed to Frankfort to hear Paganini's concerts and also attended last night's concert in Mainz. He is in raptures over Paganini's playing." At that time Lafont was taking the waters at Baden-Baden. Paganini does not seem to have been aware that Lafont was in the audience.

19 See *Harmonicon*, December, 1824, p. 230, and *Allgemeine Musikalische Zeitung*, Vol. XXVI, 506.

20 Spohr described the orchestras in Mainz, Bremen, and Nuremberg as "remarkably bad."

21 Paganini's name appears in the old *Trinkgeldverzeichniss* of the Hotel zum Mohren. This was formerly in the Ducal Library and is now in the Landesbibliothek.

forte accompaniment till he went to England, the fact that there was no adequate band was sufficient reason for his action. (Schottky's statement [p. 203] that he played in Gotha is therefore demonstrably wrong.)

Next day, late in the afternoon, the little cavalcade rolled into Weimar and after depositing their luggage at the Hotel Riesen and having some refreshment the Maestro, accompanied by Achilles and Curiol, went to call on Goethe despite the lateness of the hour. (Before leaving Frankfort he had announced his intention of paying his respects to the poet.) "Late in the evening Paganini called with his companion and little boy [Goethe noted in his diary on September 29]. A wonderful apparition—for the moment. He intends to return." The Maestro was completely silent on the subject of this visit and even Goethe did not enlarge on this laconic comment, so they may both have looked upon it as a perfunctory exchange of courtesies. However, the writer Friedrich von Matthieson (1761–1831), who also happened to be stopping at the Hotel Riesen, thought the meeting sufficiently interesting to record it in his journal.

September 30, 1829.
Paganini spent the night here and called on Goethe yesterday. I've just seen him getting into his carriage—pale as a ghost, stooped, fearfully thin, with a Jewish cast of features. His little son, about three years of age, looks just like him. He was carrying a tiny toy violin. Paganini's companion and business manager, on the other hand, looks like the Abbot of St. Gall in Bürger's tale. My landlord said: "If I ever encountered him in the forest, I should take to my heels at once."[22]

After another night's stop along the way they arrived in Leipzig on the evening of the thirtieth, which gave Paganini an opportunity of refreshing himself before his opening concert. Whatever his personal frailties, it must be said for Curiol that as a manager he was as enterprising as they come. For the month of October he had twelve or thirteen fixed engagements for his client—making an average of three concerts a week. So the Maestro must have been feeling uncommonly fit or he could never have kept up the pace.

---

[22] He is here referring to Gottfried Bürger's poem of this name in which the Abbot, formerly a very corpulent friar, had been reduced to a shadow through his inability to solve a riddle put to him by the king.

After eight months of remorse, Leipzig was now ready to make amends and this time the negotiations went through rapidly and without argument of any kind. As already stated, the theatre had reopened in August as a Saxon court theatre, so, in view of the admiration and interest of the royal family,[23] Curiol now had no trouble in arriving at an arrangement with the local manager whereby Paganini received two-thirds of the receipts, the balance going to the theatre. Pulver wrote that for the "third concert" the management turned over to him the entire receipts "without deductions, as a matter of esteem, which redounded to the eternal glory of the management"; but there is no foundation whatsoever for such a statement. As shown by Curiol's meticulous accounts, all the Leipzig concerts were on a strictly business basis, Paganini's share of the receipts of the four concerts amounting to 3391.13 thalers.[24]

Not long after his arrival he received a visit from Friedrich Wieck and his little daughter Clara.[25]

I had to play my Polonaise in E flat on a horrid old pianoforte with black keys that some student had left behind [she wrote]. Paganini was immensely pleased, father telling him meanwhile that I have a bent for music because I have feeling, sensitivity. He at once gave us permission to attend all his rehearsals, which we did.

While the first concert was taking place Wieck saw to it that a new instrument was installed in Paganini's rooms so that Clara, on her second visit, could do herself a little greater justice. This time she and her father "played a still uncompleted Rondo on four Paganini themes" written by Wieck's friend, the Saxon court pianist Kragen (d. 1879), and Hünten's Rondo from *Elizabetta,* both in an arrangement for four hands.

He complimented me but said that I shouldn't be so fidgety—I shouldn't move my body so much when I play. As he was just then having his

23 Prince August of Saxony attended the second and third concerts, paying an admission of twelve ducats.

24 One of his assisting artists in Leipzig was Marie Loewe, mother of Lilly Lehmann.

25 Friedrich Wieck (1785–1873), noted teacher of the pianoforte. At the time of Paganini's visit he was also director of a piano factory.

dinner, he made me eat some English pudding with him and drink some wine. On the twelfth I went to the rehearsal again and he introduced me to Herr Rellstab and Herr Elsholz from Berlin.

For the last concert he sent Clara and her father seats on the stage,[26] and on the eve of his departure rejoiced Clara's heart by writing in her autograph album "four bars of a scherzo and the chromatic scale harmonized in contrary motion, which she treasured as "a souvenir of the greatest artist that has ever been in Leipzig."

I gave the little four-year-old Paganini two bunches of grapes for the journey—one purple and one white. Paganini kissed father twice and shook hands with me, and thus we parted. He left at four o'clock for Magdeburg.[27]

Three years later they were to meet again but Paganini, either through design or accident, failed to play the grateful host with the perfect courtesy Wieck was surely entitled to expect. Memories of Leipzig had by then already slipped into obscurity.

Paganini to Germi, Leipzig, October 16, 1829.
My heart danced for sheer joy on seeing your writing in your dear letter of the twenty-second from Sarzana. It's not true. I'm still a bachelor and haven't touched a woman, nor taken any medicine, for more than two years.[28] I'm delighted over my good luck in having you for a real friend and the custodian of my little capital. Having been invited by these German princes, I must let them hear my music and my violin, not so much for the money that I'm going to take in, but for the glory. . . . They write me from Paris that M. Lafont, upon learning that I'm about to arrive there, is leaving to spend the winter in Russia. To which I replied that I shall forgo the pleasure of seeing him for his good, knowing how virtue is rewarded there. . . . I gave some concerts in Darmstadt and was overwhelmed with honors by the prince and also by the people. A huge crowd continually followed me about just to gaze at the windows of my rooms, serenade me, etc. . . . The house is full of people clamoring for souvenirs, some for a piece of violin string, others for a kiss. My son Achilles, who speaks perfect German, acts as my interpreter. . . . I've written the first movement of a Concerto in D

26 For the first concert, 69 seats were installed on the stage; for the second, 101; for the third, 47; and for the last, 4.

27 From Clara Schumann's Journal, now in the Schumann Museum in Zwickau, Germany.

28 He is referring to the Warsaw report of his marriage.

minor[29] and an Adagio in E flat minor with a *colpo di tatan* at the end. But these blessed concerts give me no time to write the rondo, though I've settled on the theme. *Addio*. Your exhausted friend.

It was during this Leipzig visit that he made the acquaintance of his second German biographer, Friedrich Karl Julius Schütz,[30] son of Professor Christian Gottfried Schütz, the eminent philologian and humanist of the University of Halle. Schütz, who gave up his pedagogical career as a result of some differences with the student body, had married the famous actress Henriette Hendel (known professionally as Hendel-Schütz) in 1811 and from then on accompanied her on her tours and from time to time even acted in her company.[31] In 1827 this marriage, like his first, was dissolved, his wife remaining in Halle with his father while he settled in Leipzig, where he devoted himself to writing biographies of historical figures, which he turned out with great rapidity though without any of the more solid literary merits that would have lent them permanent worth. His brief spurt of literary fame therefore tailed off into obscurity even during his lifetime, and though endowed by nature with excellent abilities as a scholar he was unable to apply them properly and died in Leipzig in 1844 completely broken in health and in abject penury. While his little monograph on Paganini could not compete with Schottky's work, it was much less discursive and furnished some additional details regarding the second Leipzig visit that contributed to its interest.

29 The history of the Fourth Concerto is now well known. The manuscript was contained in a packet of old music in the possession of Signora Edina Bonatti Paganini, widow of Achilles' son Giovanni. In 1936 she sold it to Anacleto Focht, a Parma shoemaker and old-book dealer. In looking through the music he discovered Achilles' certification and at once took it to the Parma Conservatory where its authenticity was established and the manuscript temporarily sequestrated, Focht being given a receipt certifying to his ownership. The work was later sold to Gallini, the Milan publisher, and the proceeds divided between Focht and the Paganini heirs. When Gallini acquired the manuscript, the solo violin was missing but he claims to have discovered it later among the papers of Giovanni Bottesini, a double-bass player on the faculty of the conservatory. Signora Giovanni Paganini is now living in great poverty in Felino, near Parma. She states that her husband sold a collection of Paganini relics to Mussolini for 500,000 lire. She still has some pictures, letters, and official documents in her possession.

30 Karl Julius Schütz (1779–1844) studied at the universities of Jena, Erlangen, and Göttingen, graduating from Jena in 1800.

31 Johanna Henriette Hendel Schütz (1772–1849). Goethe called her "the dear, incomparable feminine Proteus"; Schiller immortalized her, and other poets paid her similar tributes. Marx draws a very sympathetic picture of her in his memoirs.

Between the third and fourth Leipzig concerts, Paganini played in Halle and at the termination of his Leipzig engagement went on to Magdeburg, where he remained an entire week, with the exception of one concert in nearby Halberstadt. Magdeburg was one of the first cities to extend him an invitation and had even sent a special delegation to Berlin before he left for Warsaw, so here he found a very cordial, interested, and enthusiastic public awaiting him.[32] In fact, there was such a demand to hear him that though he had intended to give only two concerts there he was easily persuaded to prolong his stay and give another on October 24, despite his having signed an agreement to play at the Ducal Theatre in Dessau on the twenty-third. But as we have already said, he never permitted such minor matters to influence his decisions. Indifferent to the financial interests of others, and following his sudden whimsies like an extremely lively flea, he was temperamentally unable to consider any contract as binding till the sad school of experience taught him that in some matters it was dangerous to succumb to a caprice. "Having now given my word, if I failed to keep it, they'd sue me, which would cost me dear, according to the blessed laws of this world," he wrote in 1833 after he had learned his lesson.

Fortunately, Duke Friedrich of Anhalt-Dessau was very understanding of such outbursts of genius so that, despite the disappointment of a large public and much inconvenience resulting from the Maestro's change of plans, the concert on the twenty-sixth was a very great success, the Duke turning over to him the entire receipts free of all expenses.[33] Two days later he played in the new theatre in Bernburg, where the little town of four thousand inhabitants had guaranteed him sixty friedrichsdor and where he was assisted by the court orchestra from Ballenstedt, the elder von Bosse conducting. It was also hoped that he would play in Köthen, the third capital in Anhalt, which he had to pass through to reach Weimar, but the idea was abandoned, owing to the lack of a suitable hall and orchestra.

Turning southward to Weimar,[34] where the Grand Duke had

---

[32] A severe electric storm took place during one of the Magdeburg concerts, which apparently added greatly to the effect of Paganini's music! The violent thunderstorms in Germany are said to have made him very nervous, probably because of his sensitiveness to noise.

[33] The orchestra was conducted by Friedrich Schneider (1786–1853).

also guaranteed him one hundred friedrichsdor, he played in the court theatre on October 30 with Johann Nepomuk Hummel, the "Apollo of Weimar," conducting. During the recent Leipzig engagement, Friedrich Rochlitz wrote Goethe and advised him "very urgently—whether or not he liked the violin—to hear Paganini play—*and see him play*—but in public!" This advice Goethe evidently took to heart since in sending some tickets to a friend he wrote: "it will be well to sit as near as possible to the performer, because they say it is as interesting to watch him as to hear him. In my box I must forgo this double pleasure." Goethe occupied a parterre box near the center entrance, but he still heard and saw enough to report his impressions to his friend Zelter in Berlin.

Goethe to Zelter, November 9, 1829.
Now I too have heard Paganini and straightway that same evening got out your letter so that I might arrive at an intelligent estimate of all these wonders. For this pillar of flame and cloud, I lacked a base for what one calls enjoyment, which with me always hovers somewhere between the sensuous and the intellectual. I only heard something meteoric and then couldn't account for it. Yet it is curious to hear people, especially women, talk about it. Without any hesitation they give utterance to what are in fact confessions.[35]

From 1816 till his death Goethe was more and more preoccupied with the demonic element in the universe, something of which Paganini, in his opinion, was the supreme embodiment. "The demonic is that which cannot be explained in a cerebral and a rational manner [*mit Verstand und mit Vernunft*]," he said to Eckermann. "It is not peculiar to my nature but I am subject to its spell. Napoleon possessed the quality to the highest degree. Amongst artists one encounters it more often with musicians than

34 The Weimar orchestra numbered twenty-eight, exclusive of percussion. Lobe was a member of the orchestra from 1811 till 1842, first as principal flute, and then as viola player. The theatre had been fairly new, having been erected in 1826 to replace the old one, which had been destroyed by fire. Johann Nepomuk Hummel (1778–1837) had studied with Mozart for two years and was a noted piano virtuoso of his day.

35 To which Zelter replied: "What arrests the attention so much in this virtuoso may be a mixture of the whimsical and a longing for freedom. It's a style that is nevertheless without style since—like a thread that grows thinner and thinner—it leads to nothing. It smacks of music and is gulped down like a peppered and marinated imitation oyster."

with painters. Paganini is imbued with it to a remarkable degree and it is through this that he produces such a great effect."

But was this quality alone the secret of his power on the platform? Perhaps it lay rather in his "ability to make others feel," for as has been said, "every genius is a magician in his way." Be that as it may, if Goethe could not account for this supersensual, supernatural impression, Johann Christian Lobe, violist in the Weimar orchestra, tried, in a long article in André's *Hesperus,* to describe the emotions of the audience as they listened, in a tense hypnotic hush, to the Italian's music—"the greatest, the most consummate technique the human ear has ever heard." There is no doubt that Paganini had the same effect on everyone, but astonishment and the effort to climb higher and higher on the ladder of superlative impeded for the most part the sure-footed value judgment that instinctively finds the pregnant word, the trenchant phrase. Therefore, after reading one or two of the criticisms, one has practically read them all. The most interesting thing about them is the writer's psychological reaction; on some points almost everyone agreed, and on others the impression was totally divergent. Perhaps those who first accused him of some dark traffic with the devil were merely giving expression to a feeling of something sinister in his personality. In their eyes some "unlawful sacrifice" must have been made to acquire such dazzling proficiency, such obvious power over others. And since this was related in a way with his outward appearance, with "seeing him play" (in the words of Rochlitz), some of the critics provided a more sympathetic study of him than the lithographers, who captured little but the obvious, external peculiarities.

Lobe: Never in all my life have I seen a man whose aspect so made my heart ache and who filled me with such a feeling of compassion and commiseration. An emaciated figure in old-fashioned evening clothes and long black trousers falling to his heels and flapping about his bony limbs as though he were a skeleton. Between the long wavy locks and the curly black whiskers emerged a thin and bloodless face with a long aquiline nose.

Schütz: A man of little more than moderate height, of slender build. His gait, like all his movements, is awkward, his figure stooping and expressive of anything but nobility of spirit, quite apart from that of pride. His features undeniably betray a soul lacerated by painful experiences and strong passions, but the moment he begins to play they become attractive, spectral, almost ecstatic.

Finck: He looks pale and ill, but by no means melancholy. Only when he is not emotionally excited does the slightest trace of melancholy show in his expression. His dark eyes indicate great affability. In conversation he is very vivacious, though controlled by manly restraint. His manners are courtly and polite without undue concern with outward formalities. His behavior is marked by a sort of free and easy sincerity and modesty combined with that seriousness and consciousness of achievement that is an indisputable quality of every real man. He loves to praise others, even untalented dilettantes who would do well not to believe all he tells them. He also knows how to dine well—and he likes the ladies.

Leigh Hunt: He does not look so old as he is said to be. . . . His face at the same time has much less expression than might be looked for. It first seemed little better than a mask, with a fastidious, dreary expression, as if inclined to despise his music and go to sleep. His fervor was in his hands and bow. Occasionally he put back his hair. When he makes his acknowledgments he bows like a camel, and grins like a goblin or a mountain goat.

Whilst all the descriptions stressed certain details of his physiognomy, a few observers looked beneath the surface and in some telling phrase passed on to later generations a more vivid picture of him in these hectic middle years. For rich and satisfying though they were, they had already begun to tick away his life, each one in turn demanding an increasing toll in strength, in courage, and in suffering. Yet at this time he was by no means depressed. Indeed, nearly everyone who came in contact with him spoke of his gay, lighthearted manner, his sunny mood, even the knockabout humor that so startled Spohr—an indication that his nerves were far less tense than usual. True, his energetic factotum left him little time to ponder things; but on the travel days he could relax and rest as they drove through the lovely Thuringian countryside with its sombre firs and fragrant pines spreading like a dark-green velvet carpet as far as eye could see and lighted here and there with some red-roofed village nestling like a scarlet poppy amidst the rolling hills.

iii

After concerts in rapid succession in Erfurt, Rudolstadt, Coburg, and Bamburg, his next stop was Nuremberg, where he received a welcome worthy of the city of the Mastersingers. Although throughout his stay the weather left much to be desired, with frequent heavy rains, his two concerts still attracted enormous crowds and brought his net receipts to 1,677 florins. Schottky tells us that Achilles possessed a bewildering array of toys, his father buying him anything that chanced to catch his fancy, so we may hazard a safe guess that a goodly portion of the receipts was diverted from his Vienna bank to tiny Nuremberg toys which could be stowed away so easily in the wayworn leather trunk. Indeed, one can easily picture the two, weaving their desultory way through the medieval streets, to pause enraptured before the window of some toyshop or gaze with fascinated eyes at the parading figurines in the belfry of the Lorenz Kirche when the old clock struck the hours. However, not all the witchery of Nuremberg was reserved for Achellino. For after the first concert Paganini was presented to Baron Ludwig Friedrich von Dobeneck and his pretty wife Helene (she was christened Rebekka Magdalena), daughter of the great jurist and writer on criminal law, Paul Anselm Feuerbach[36]—a fateful meeting that bore tragic and bitter fruit for the susceptible Helene, who was not emotionally geared to take the shock of such a galvanic encounter. Young, impressionable, highly sentimental, and married without love, one meeting with the baffling personality of the amazing Italian and his incandescent music swept her completely off her feet—an infatuation from which she never more recovered.

As the Dobenecks resided in Ansbach and had driven over for the concert, it is presumed that the Baroness prevailed on her husband to remain in Nuremberg for the second concert and thus during the week had more than one opportunity of meeting the Maestro and of making plain her *engouement,* since the friendship seems to have developed very quickly, Paganini entering with equivalent zest—albeit, one imagines, with fictitious ardor—into an adventure that was a flattering tribute to his undiminished

---

[36] Feuerbach occupied a prominent place in the history of criminal science and was responsible for the reform of penal legislation in Bavaria and the abolition of torture.

power as a weaver of spells. For in spite of "two years of abstemious-ness" his technique with the ladies had all the old bravura and he even for a time considered a more permanent relationship. Although there is no indication that the spell-caught Helene ever appealed very strongly to his sensual side, he at least weighed from the practical angle the pros and cons of such a union, finally to abandon the idea, no doubt for that reason. Conscious in his calmer moments of his own nature, he perhaps could not bring himself to impose a burden of this kind on a woman who loved him in this way. If their meeting represented only another amorous adventure, there would be little need for the biographer to mention it other than to note that he was extremely flattered by this conquest. But as we shall see, its effects were revolutionary in the life of a young woman whose beauty, varied gifts and versatility, and the prominence of whose family made the encounter one of the most romantic episodes of Paganini's life.

As for Paganini there is no hint of his being consumed *dall'-amore e dallo spasimo,* as with his Neapolitan flame. Instead, he calmly checked off Helene's good points as though trying to convince himself. She was young, she was musical, she was beautiful, she was madly in love with him, and she was the daughter of a famous man—all something to consider, seeing that he was no longer "young and handsome." Obviously the special circumstances—Helene's family, her title, the bulwark of strict German etiquette behind which she was enclosed—added a fillip to the mixture so that he enjoyed weaving round her his disturbing emotional atmosphere and tasting the fruit of his endeavors. But it was never a completely absorbing episode. One feels that La Bianchi had withered some chord in this Dionysiac soul and increased his natural antipathy to woman as a permanent possession, since all his *affaires de coeur* after 1828—if he ever really had any—had manifestly lost the effervescent quality of his early years.

iv

After a concert in Regensburg on November 18, for which the Prince of Thurn and Taxis had advanced twelve ducats as initial guarantee, he went on to Munich the same night, arriving shortly before midnight and putting up at the Bayerischer Hof, where he snatched a few hours rest before the morning rehearsal for his concert, which took place on the seventeenth. Besides his old friend Aiblinger, he found several other acquaintances in the Bavarian capital, in particular Joseph Hartmann Stuntz,[37] conductor of the orchestra, who had written several operas for Venice and Milan during the years when Paganini was an assiduous frequenter of those opera houses. The Munich orchestra was also a more proficient instrument than those with which he had recently been playing, and indeed prided itself "on being superior to Berlin,"[38] an opinion shared by Edward Holmes. Another reason for gratification was that since the theatre was crown property he could triple the price of admission, which raised a little rumble of protest in some quarters, though here—unlike the situation in England later —the malcontents could find no sympathizers; in fact, after the second concert the *Münchener Politische Zeitung* could not resist a mild reproof leveled at those who from necessity or parsimoniousness had remained away.

Between the second and third concerts, he was summoned to give a command performance before the Queen Mother at her castle in Tegernsee, in the Bavarian Highlands, for which pleasant excursion he was rewarded with a "beautiful emerald and diamond pin."[39] Fantastic tales of his magic violin had, of course, seeped through to the Bavarian peasantry, so as soon as they learned that he was in their midst, they converged on Tegernsee from all directions in the hope of seeing him. Lined up along the highway leading to the royal estate, the moment his high-hung phaeton passed through the gates,[40] they closed in behind and with the connivance of the servants congregated round the entrance of the castle in order to catch some strains of that mysterious music that reputedly could arrest a lark in flight. "While Paganini was playing [wrote

37 Joseph Hartmann Strunz (1793–1859), Swiss composer and conductor who studied with Peter von Winter. He spent some time in Italy, and was appointed conductor in Munich in 1826.

38 At the time of Paganini's visit, the total strength of the Munich orchestra was about eighty-seven, with twenty-four first and second violins.

39 Fredericke Wilhelmine Caroline of Baden, widow of Maximilian Joseph and mother of King Ludwig I.

40 Paganini was accompanied by Antonio Brizzi, an Italian luthier of Munich, who wrote him on February 22, 1836, recalling "the beautiful days they spent together in Tegernsee."

Schottky, quoting an eyewitness] a subdued murmuring could be heard and Her Majesty, upon sending out to learn the cause of the disturbance, was told that about a hundred villagers were extremely eager to hear the violinist and begged that the doors might be left open so that they too could enjoy the concert. With that the Queen immediately ordered them to be admitted to the concert hall, where they showed themselves worthy of her gracious act by behaving decently and quietly." Probably Paganini never had a more appreciative audience than these simple, superstitious folk of the Bavarian countryside, living daily in a land of faery.

His farewell concert on the twenty-fifth proved for him another memorable occasion since for the first time he was "crowned with laurel" on the stage. "As he bowed to the box of Prince Karl, who was applauding vigorously [wrote a Munich journalist] Strunz stole up behind him and placed a large laurel wreath on his head. The strange man looked like a Roman emperor! The excitement was really indescribable. Poems fluttered down from all over the house, tears stood in the eyes of many. Paganini embraced Strunz and several others who had crowded round him; then weeping and trembling with excitement, he bowed again and again. Deeply moved and so excited that he could scarcely contain himself, he passed through the crowd—and was gone!"

Yet delightful as it was, the Munich visit was still clouded a little by a legal altercation with a certain Günther, the circumstances of which are veiled in obscurity. A tenor by this name was his assisting artist in Mainz and he may have arranged to have him appear with him elsewhere and then forgot about it, or it might be that Günther was some local manager with whom Curiol had signed a contract which Paganini capriciously disregarded. In Italy he had always arranged his concerts after his arrival in a town and was therefore unable to grasp the fact that the German theatres worked on schedule so that if he skipped a date or dropped a singer, it might easily lead to legal arguments, a realm of dialectics in which he was invariably worsted. When the aforesaid Günther bore down on him in Munich, Curiol, with an eye to the future, appealed to Aiblinger to act as intermediary and obtained from Paganini a written agreement "to respect his dates in future" (an illuminating phrase!), the only concession being a still open engagement in Stettin[41] which now, of course, was no longer practicable. Although momentarily outmanoeuvred, Niccolò was by no means convinced and continued to struggle against his chains till a few weeks later he gave his "companion" the inevitable *coup de grace*—in his eyes, no doubt, a justifiable revenge for having to run counter to his inclinations.

After two concerts in Augsburg, for which he distributed an unusual number of free tickets,[42] he left for Stuttgart, where the court theatre and orchestra under Lindpainter had been placed at his disposition gratis.[43] Pulver (without citing his authority) wrote that he had a serious accident en route—that "his carriage had overturned," throwing him and Achilles into the road in the velvet blackness of an icy cold Bavarian night. But neither Schottky nor the Stuttgart papers mention such a contretemps, though the papers spoke of his arriving "at three in the morning" and of his prompt appearance at the ten o'clock rehearsal; which, even without an accident, was sufficient ordeal for a person who had traveled most of the night. Pulver then quotes him as "confessing that he bungled his playing very badly," adding that the usual electricity was lacking and "for the first time in his career his concert failed to produce any effect."

In a contemporary lithograph showing him at the rehearsal for his second concert, he and the members of the orchestra are swathed to the ears in Siberian furs—a good indication of the temperature in the building. Thus, after a night's journey with a tired and petulant child, he may well have felt exhausted and therefore not entirely satisfied with his performance, though in a letter to Germi

41 The document signed by Paganini read: "In accordance with my contract with M. Curiol, I declare in the presence of Music Director Aiblinger my readiness to follow the itinerary designated in aforesaid contract of August 16, without exception. M. Curiol also accedes to the wishes of M. Paganini and will cancel the Stettin date even though it would guarantee him a sum of two thousand thalers for two concerts in said city."

42 For the first concert, Paganini gave away twenty-six tickets (149 florins), and for the second, eight or ten (40 florins).

43 Peter Joseph von Lindpainter (1791–1856) was appointed conductor at Stuttgart in 1819 and held the post until his death. He had a very notable career. Mendelssohn considered him "the best conductor in Germany." Paganini showed his manuscripts to Lindpainter, who was responsible for the statement that "while in Germany he wrote twelve concertos." Schottky quoted Lindpainter in the preface to his work and Conestabile (n. to page 226) in turn took the information from Schottky. Possibly Paganini gave Lindpainter this erroneous impression for reasons of his own.

he gives no hint of it and the reviews next day were also one long-drawn-out hyperbole: "There was only one verdict in all Stuttgart —no one had ever heard anything to equal it—it surpassed all expectations." This would therefore seem to be another case in which an unfounded assumption has been raised, through a biographer's unruly imagination, to the dignity of fact, which can now be discarded as embellishment, granting, of course, that some hitherto unpublished letter of the Maestro does not supply the missing details.

Leaving Stuttgart on the eighth, he played next day at the court theatre in Karlsruhe, where the Grand Duke had guaranteed him 150 friedrichsdor, and where he also made the acquaintance of Anton Haizinger and his gifted wife Amalie Naumann, stars of the Karlsruhe theatre, who later became great friends of his.[44] Although the local papers, for some reason, did not review the concert, Paganini sent Germi a brief account of his success—as artist and as charmer.

Paganini to Germi, December 12, 1829.
For your information here's a little memorandum of my transfers to Arnstein & Eskeles in Vienna, amounting in all to 99,979 florins.[45] The day before yesterday I gave a concert at the theatre here, guaranteed by His Royal Highness, the Grand Duke, with 150 friedrichsdor. My music has such a magical effect that it goes to the head of the most exalted and highly cultivated people. I don't dare tell you what was told me of a queen by one of her intimate counselors. You'd be astonished if you could see the letters of a most beautiful lady, twenty years old, wife of a baron, who would like to abandon her family and join me for life. But being the daughter of a most illustrious man in Germany—the intimate councilor of His Majesty—I must relinquish the joy of possessing her for religion and my glory. Some day you'll read her letters, which will make you weep. . . . Tomorrow I'm going to Mannheim to give a second concert[46]—I don't plan to play in Frankfort again.

44 Anton Haizinger (1796–1869), famous tenor of his day and pupil of Salieri. When Paganini was in Paris, he sang there in a German company under the management of Roeckel & Fischer.

45 In Codignola (*op. cit.*, 298) the list of transfers is itemized, but Codignola has indicated "francs" instead of "florins." During the first tour, all of Paganini's accounts were estimated in florins and the total then reduced to thalers.

46 This concert also did not take place. The Mannheim "incident" may have been the cause of the Munich dispute. Paganini originally agreed to play two concerts in Mannheim, the first on September 19, the second on the twenty-sixth. The posters

On leaving Frankfort in the autumn he had given everyone to understand that he had bidden them farewell, but Achilles had recently contracted a very severe cold which required care and medical attendance, so at the close of his tour he decided to return to Frankfort till the youngster had recovered, and perhaps wait until the spring, which would also give him a much needed rest. Meanwhile, he talked constantly of "leaving soon for Paris" and made no secret of the fact that "he was looking for another manager." This, naturally, did not fail to reach the ears of Curiol, who not only confidently expected, on the basis of Paganini's reiterated assurances, to accompany him to France and England, but when the political situation in Paris commenced to take ominous forms and Paganini received word that the theatres there were empty and that in Belgium and Holland all concerts were temporarily suspended, he had also begun to draft an itinerary for a two months' tour in western Germany immediately after Easter, hoping that by then the threatened Paris "revolution" would be over. However, long before the time came round to set forth on the tour, the working partnership between him and his illustrious client was for some reason abruptly terminated, Curiol retiring with a moral victory, Paganini marching forward, unconcerned, to gather in the spoils.

---

and programs were all printed for the second concert and many persons had come to Mannheim from neighboring towns, only to be greeted with the announcement a few hours before the concert that he had cancelled the Mannheim date. Since the theatre was subjected to considerable expense and inconvenience, Count Luxberg may have exerted some pressure on Curiol so that Paganini agreed to play the missing concert on his return to Frankfort. The idea, however, seems to have been abandoned.

*Die Grösse und Vollkommenheit der Kunst
hängt nicht von der Grösse und Vollkommenheit
der Mittel, sondern von der des Künstlers ab.*
—HANS PFITZNER.

ONE OF FRANKFORT'S musicians with whom the Maestro, for the next five months, was most intimately associated was the violinist and conductor Carl Guhr,[1] Kapellmeister at the theatre and director of the concerts of the Museum Gesellschaft. Through rigid discipline at rehearsals and his own excellent musicianship, he had given the orchestra, during the nine years of his incumbency, a high degree of finish even if the material, individually, was not so distinguished as in Berlin, Stuttgart, Darmstadt, Munich, and other places enjoying the patronage of a court. For in Frankfort, one of Germany's four free cities,[2] the support of the Komödienhaus, dedicated like all provincial theatres to drama and opera, devolved on a syndicate or group of subscribers who guaranteed the running expenses and then appointed a manager to operate it for them along paying lines.[3] Spohr had been appointed conductor here in 1817 on his return from Italy but, owing to his temperamental inability to trim his art to the more practical requirements of a manager who was expected to operate the theatre without a deficit, he held the post only two years; then in 1821 after the ad interim direction of the leader, Heinrich Anton Hoffmann, Guhr was appointed permanent conductor and, having a more open mind than his famous colleague regarding the practical realities of art, let the Intendant run the theatre to suit the taste of the subscribers and gave his full attention to the orchestra, with the above results. According to Wagner, Guhr was "sure of his business,

---

1 Carl Guhr (1787–1848), pupil of Schnabel and Janitschek in Breslau, held various posts before coming to Frankfort in 1821, where he remained till his death.

2 Frankfort, Lübeck, Bremen, and Hamburg.

3 O. Bacher: *Die Geschichte der Frankfurter Oper im 18ten Jahrhundert* (Frankfort, 1926); A. Carse, *op. cit.*, 144–146.

despotic, and by no means polite," all admirable qualities in training an orchestra, so by regularly attending Guhr's rehearsals Paganini no doubt picked up many of the valuable ideas that seven years later he tried to turn to good account in Parma.

During his first six weeks in Frankfort in the early autumn his association with Guhr had grown from formal professional contact to intimate friendship, a relationship that was immediately resumed on his return. When his health permitted, he attended the rehearsals, made music frequently with Guhr's quartet, took the Herr Kapellmeister along with him to Darmstadt and turned to him for advice in numerous ways. In fact, during his entire residence in Frankfort, Guhr's staunch friendship must in many ways have been a tower of strength to him.

Further, he presumably derived much pleasure from Guhr's acquaintance and the opportunity it afforded him of indulging his predilection for quartet playing and his passion for the theatre, besides participating in the other musical activities that revolved round the figure of the music director of the theatre; though it seems likely that Guhr, flattered by his friendship, sought (at least in the beginning) these occasions more frequently than he, especially since his curiosity was aroused by the amazing performances of the Italian. While too sane a person and too sterling a musician to swallow the current prattle of necromancy and other hard-dying myths, he had heard it said that Paganini possessed "a secret," some technical short cut, and was quite ready to believe that this might possibly explain those paranormal powers that had hitherto eluded any equivalent combination of talent and hard work and were dismissed by the envious as trickery. So he was determined to penetrate the mystery if close observation, or even ruse, could bring him to his goal.

Quantities of ink have been spilled on this perplexing subject and numerous "definitive solutions" of the riddle have gone forth under the banner of imposing names without either writers or virtuosos coming any nearer to the truth. "It is very much to be doubted [wrote Pulver] if Paganini's extraordinary facility was to as great an extent as is generally supposed the result only of frantic practicing. . . . We know that he experimented with certain passages with a patience that is scarcely believable; but the potentiality for the eventual conquest of the most difficult of his problems on the fingerboard lay already in the peculiar adaptability of his body, the suitability of his organs, and the ease with which his mental processes and his physical reactions collaborated";[4] or as Fétis put it, in *une exquise sensibilité nerveuse et d'un grand sentiment musical."*

"How did the legend of Paganini's secret ever arise? [asked Federico Mompellio]. Probably through two circumstances. First of all, because anyone who heard him—even expert violinists—could not understand how he could perform such hitherto unimaginable difficulties. Then because he himself helped voluntarily or involuntarily (very likely the first) to surround with mystery his own performance."[5] "For he often said [wrote Fétis] that his talent was the result of a secret that he had discovered and that would astound the violinists when he revealed it. Was he not mistaken? Was this not just an illusion? Is there any other secret than the one that Nature has placed in the heart of the artist—in systematic and persevering study? I do not believe it.[6] Yet I must admit that there was something extraordinary and mysterious in his ability to execute infallibly the most unheard of difficulties."[7]

"My secret [said Paganini in turn]—*if I can call it such*—will point the way to a better understanding of the instrument, which is far richer than is commonly supposed. I owe that discovery not to chance but to profound study. By applying it, it will no longer be necessary to practice four or five hours a day. It should supplant present teaching methods, which seem to strive to make things difficult (for the student) rather than to teach him how to play. Take Gaetano Ciandelli for instance. He had played the cello a long time in a mediocre way so that his playing never aroused the slightest interest. I then revealed my discovery to him, which had such a magical effect that in three days he was completely transformed and everyone said that such a sudden change was astounding. At first his tone was an offense to the ear, while he used the bow like a beginner. After three lessons the tone was full, pure, and graceful, and he had complete control of the bow. I swear that I am

4 Pulver, *op. cit.,* 315 f.
5 Conestabile-Mompellio, *op. cit.,* 390 ff.
6 Fétis, *Biographie universelle,* 1st ed., 128.
7 Fétis, *Notice biographique sur Nicolo Paganini,* 79.

telling the truth. Only one single solitary person [Ciandelli] knows my secret."[8]

"Over a long period [said Guhr] I was fortunate enough to hear this great master constantly and to discuss with him the manner of his playing. As he discreetly tried to evade anything touching the 'secret' of his art (if I may call it so), I was at some pains to observe him studiously and note the things he did differently from other violinists so as to imitate such differences on my own instrument, of course in an imperfect manner."[9]

With Guhr's blunt directness he perhaps began by requesting Paganini to explain certain technical procedures and when that method proved abortive, asked to see his manuscripts—an equally delicate question. For the Maestro was never very anxious to convey his knowledge to others. In fact, it may have been this psychological inhibition and the desire to protect himself by a delicate lacquerwork of myth that caused him to guard his compositions so zealously from profane hands, to create the suppositious "secret." At all events, Guhr, with German thoroughness, went systematically to work to analyze his method—an aim in which Gottfried Weber heartily seconded him,[10] since up till then the Maestro's playing had never been subjected to a careful technical analysis by a trained musician.[11]

For the rest, in how far was Guhr eventually successful? To what extent are the statements in his book his personal assumptions, or Paganini's own disclosures? Working always to exigent standards, with great care for detail, a disciplined, experienced, and intelligent musician, quick to take note, he was indisputably in a position to "discover" much, if there was anything tangible to be discovered. But in this brave endeavor it is not likely (as he intimated)

[8] Schottky, *op. cit.*, 281. Ciandelli was a pupil of Vincenzo Fenzi.

[9] After contributing several articles to the Frankfort papers, Guhr wrote an essay for Weber's *Caecilia*, giving a general outline of his ideas on Paganini's playing.

[10] Gottfried Weber (1779–1839) founded the *Caecilia* in 1824. He was one of the first to defend the authenticity of Mozart's Requiem.

[11] "The essay [wrote Weber of Guhr's article] made no pretension to solve or elucidate Paganini's accomplishments but merely intended to point out to the musical reader the extraordinary, the exceptional, in Paganini's playing—information that is anything but superfluous since I, among others, have heard more than one sublime music critic marvel over this or that in Paganini's playing, which every other violin virtuoso does just as well, and just as effortlessly, every day in the week."

that the Maestro assisted him in any way. If he chanced to stumble on any little technical "trick" (and what executant musician is without them?), Paganini was quite capable of vigorously denying it, and again, if Guhr erred in his assumptions, Paganini with his astute instincts and innate Machiavellian strain would no doubt have allowed him to bask in the illusion that he at last had found the touchstone.

The work selected by Guhr for his experiment was Paganini's variations on Rossini's aria *Non più mesta,* and after "some twenty or thirty hearings" he actually performed the feat of writing it out from memory, yet long before this time he had convinced himself that there was no trickery in Paganini's playing; though "fabulous," it was legitimate virtuosity, capable of logical explanation. And having arrived at this conclusion, he set down his observations in a series of articles for Gottfried Weber's *Caecilia* in which he by no means presumed to imply that he had cracked the nut or that he had, in fact, made any sensational discoveries. He was merely calling attention to certain details that departed from the traditional and would not be perceptible to the ordinary listener who had not, like himself, heard them "twenty or thirty times."

In his opinion six particular points distinguished Paganini's playing from that of other violinists. First, his peculiar method of tuning his instrument, wherein he "went back to a system that was employed in the last half of the seventeenth century to produce particular effects and enable the player to execute passages with ease that would have been frankly impossible in the original key.... Herein lies the secret of many of his effects, of his succession of chords, etc., that ordinarily appear impossible."[12] "One will admit [wrote DeLaphalèque in derision] that it does not require any great perspicacity to discover secrets of this nature. Unfortunately,

---

12 The *scordatura* originated in the lute and viol, which were tuned in various ways to suit the key of the music. The six strings were commonly tuned by fourths, with one third in the middle; the third was shifted as occasion required and an additional third or a fifth was introduced elsewhere so as to yield on open strings as many harmonies as possible. Guhr admitted that even with the closest observation he had never been able to ascertain if Paganini ever changed the tuning of his instrument during actual performance. In the prayer from Rossini's *Moïse,* Paganini mounted the G string alongside the E string, instead of the A string—a practice imitated by Sivori. In these works the violin was generally tuned a third higher, major or minor.

Guhr's work will prove to the public that he has discovered—just nothing!" However, it should be said for Guhr that before he unrolled the question of Paganini's tuning, the subject had never been broached, either in Italy or in Germany. True, some anecdotes were in circulation later that had a bearing on the point, but they were *inventées après coup* and were no doubt traceable to Guhr's elucidations.[13]

The second point, in Guhr's opinion, was his "bowing which distinctly differs from that of other violinists."

Reversing the rules, he takes offbeats with a down bow, downbeats with the reverse. He holds the right arm close to his body while his wrist moves with the greatest flexibility and rapidity as it guides the elastic movements of the bow.[14] In strongly accented chords, in which the lower part of the bow is used close to the bridge, he raises the hand and forearm a trifle higher and the elbow from the body. In his *Perpetuum Mobile* he plays whole passages with one bow stroke and the staccato with incredible perfection. In general he does not accent the notes by a stroke of the arm muscles, but the bow bounds lightly on the strings during the continuous movement of the arm—to a certain extent through its own elasticity or that of the string, like a stone sent spinning over the surface of the water. . . . He rarely plays a staccato with the tip of the bow, like Rode, Spohr, and others, but presses it firmly on the string. One often hears a peculiar staccato tone, which he produces by throwing the bow on the strings and letting it rebound, running through the scales with incredible rapidity, the notes of which roll off like pearls.

I've never heard the weak beats (in the most rapid passage work) come out so clearly and without any change in tempo. He is a perfect master of long, sustained bowing, which gives his cantabile passages an indescribable softness,[15] an extraordinary range and delicacy of nuance. For soft passages, he gives the bow a springing or whipping action,

13 Schottky, *op. cit.*, 282 n.

14 Fétis: "His attitude while playing, the position of his right arm, and the manner in which he holds the bow would lead one to believe that it would be awkward, but it was soon seen that this position had been very carefully calculated to facilitate the desired effects. His bow did not exceed normal dimensions but, having a higher tension than usual, the stick was a little less convex, which he probably had adopted to facilitate the rebound of the bow in the staccato, which he played quite differently. His tone is thin, but he is able to give it the quality of the human voice, incomparably rich in dynamic shading, in the contrasts of light and shade."

15 Albert Jarosy: "For the secret of the magic tone of his cantilene, we must seek a solution in his complete understanding of the Italian *bel canto* (following Tartini's maxim: *"Per ben suonare, bisogna ben cantare"*) so admired in his time."

using it near the middle—a technique in which much depends upon the wrist.[16]

Third, the combination of left-hand pizzicato with bowing. The German and French schools have forgotten this technique. To perform it well it is necessary that the second, third, and fourth fingers of the left hand pluck the strings clearly and exactly, which is difficult on the third and fourth strings, particularly when the finger that presses the string to the fingerboard is close to the finger plucking the string.

He next called attention to the bridge, which "was lower than usual, making the highest positions easier to the hand and enabling him to finger three strings at once.[17] The strings are rather high from the fingerboard, which enables him to play forte passages without the rattling that usually accompanies force applied to strings close to the fingerboard."

Fourth, his use of harmonics; fifth, his performance on the G string; and sixth, his extraordinary tours de force.[18]

The fact that Paganini's tone was less full than that of other eminent violinists, Guhr attributed to his preference for thin strings,[19] the reason for this being that "he constantly employed the highest tones, which were seldom used by other violinists; and

[16] Fétis: "Another novelty is the vibrato, which he uses in melodic passages, and in effect is very like the human voice, especially on the last three strings. Unfortunately, this is frequently combined with a sliding movement of the hand, similar to the portamento in singing, which in singers is justly condemned as wanting in taste. His fingering also differs from the ordinary method and he rarely terminates his trills. He also plays a trill in various positions with the little finger—a technique unknown to other violinists."

[17] David Laurie described the bridge as follows: "The bridge is low and the band is almost straight from the body to the head, with little backset, which prevented the use of a higher bridge. The upper line of the bridge is very narrow and straight, with small droopings at each side. Both the straightness and narrowness of this top line combined to bring the strings closer together and would therefore greatly facilitate the playing of the chords to which he was much given, and by means of which he produced some of his finest effects. This close grouping of strings both on bridge and fingerboard would entirely prevent its use by players in these days." Ole Bull also used a low bridge. See Spohr, *op. cit.*, II, 223.

[18] Various artists have written on the subject (Flesch, Salzedo, etc.). Emil Urbschat published a brochure in 1951 in which he advanced the theory that Paganini's "secret" lay in the way he held the violin and in the position of his left hand, offering as evidence the groove made by his thumb on the back of the neck and the long groove down the side of the fingerboard.

[19] When Paganini was in Breslau, he wrote a letter to a luthier in Naples, directing him to send him some E strings, which "must be very thin." "The E strings from Naples, even when made to order, were never very satisfactory." (Letter in the collection of Professor Leo Krassner, Syracuse, New York.)

he could produce the harmonics more easily in the higher positions with thin strings. In addition he sometimes tuned all four strings a semitone higher (the G string a minor third or more) and thicker strings would not have stood the strain. As for harmonics, he has such an incredible command of this technique that he never misses a note no matter how rapid the passage. . . .[20] His attitude is relaxed, though not so dignified as that of Baillot, Rode, and Spohr since he throws the weight of his body on the left side, bending the left shoulder forward. Before Paganini, nobody ever dreamed that it would be possible to play not only simple harmonics but also harmonics in thirds, fifths, and sixths, and that normal tones could be combined with harmonics in octave passages. But he does all these things—in all positions—and with bewildering ease."

As to his fingering, the most that Guhr could say was that it was "individual." This was one secret that no one penetrated and to which the Maestro left no key, the only one of his compositions to which he appended his fingering being the *Cantabile e Valzer* dedicated to Sivori, which is now in the Reuther collection.[21] "His fingering [wrote Gottfried Weber] which is sometimes unorthodox or, rather, is independent of the laws of fingering, is the result of a deeply reasoned method, and is not a mere caprice," a statement that he probably derived from his personal conversations with Paganini. Fétis' reaction was the same: "His fingering bears no resemblance to that which is usually taught. He will, at times, employ one finger instead of another, but more often he uses one and the same finger for several notes." According to one recent writer on the subject,[22] he "probably discovered his fingering through his playing of the guitar, on which slides of semitones are rendered impossible because of the frets on the fingerboard, necessitating a

[20] Conestabile wrote that in practicing Paganini used a large violin strung with cello strings; then he let a day or two intervene before he resumed his regular instrument.

[21] "The fingerings used by Paganini in his Caprices are totally unknown, or at best, merely a matter of individual guess work. . . . In the light of present notions, the fingerings on the Sivori manuscript, which in this case are quite authentic, would be regarded as singularly unusual. . . . In Caprice No. 21 the chromatic scale covers three whole octaves in the Guhr version, instead of only two in the published editions of the Caprices. How many present-day violinists would select the Paganini fingering to play this scale?" (A. Rizo-Rangabé in *The Musical Times* [London, 1953].)

[22] André Mangeot in *The Musical Times*, (February–March, 1953).

different finger for each semitone."[23] However, since this is one
question that Paganini evidently never discussed, and since he left
us (with the exception of this one work) no evidence of his own
practice, any theory that might be advanced cannot, by very force
of circumstance, be other than hypothetical.

One point on which Guhr and Fétis disagreed was the size of
Paganini's hands. To Guhr they seemed rather "small and thin, but
so flexible that he could easily span three octaves"; and to Fétis,
"grandes, sèches et nerveuses." When Paganini was in Marseilles
in 1839, a physician—Dr. Sirus Pirondi, pupil of Lisfranc and
Delpech—who was a friend of Paganini's host, had many occasions
to observe him closely.

The fingers of the left hand [he wrote] are more than a centimeter
longer than those of the right hand and, as a result, no doubt, of a particular disposition of the right shoulder muscles, he does not place the
bow on the violin till he has described a wide circle with his extended
arm. The collarbone is formed in such a way that he can hold his violin
firmly in position with his chin without the support of his left hand,
which gives him perfect technical freedom. The shape and suppleness
of his left hand are really unique; for instance, he can bend his thumb
back to an extraordinary degree, and without the slightest effort. It was
once thought that his fingers were unusually long, but this is a great
mistake. They are of normal length in repose, but very thin and slender. In playing he can extend his reach in a manner that only the
savants can explain.[24]

In the opinion of both Guhr and Fétis, he was less the great, exceptional artist in the works of other composers, Guhr's contention
being that "he was unable to free himself of Paganini, the com-

[23] The Hungarian-American violinist, Arthur Hartmann, also maintained that
"Paganini's study of the guitar with its large frets developed his reach and the strength
of his fingers." (Day, *op. cit.,* 301.)

[24] In 1925 and 1926 a long correspondence was conducted in *The Strad* on the
subject of the size of Paganini's hands, in the course of which Mr. John Dunn published a letter from one of Paganini's grandsons stating that, according to his father
(Achilles Paganini), Niccolò's hand "was very similar to his own for length, strength,
and structure." In the sketch furnished Mr. Dunn, "the fingers were half an inch
longer than a medium-size large hand." The museum of the Paris Conservatoire
owned at one time a cast of Paganini's right hand, allegedly made by Dantan. It is
listed in an old catalogue of 1884, but there is no record of its origin, its acquisition,
or its subsequent fate.

poser. . . .[25] His imagination is so active, so ardent, when expressing his own passions and emotions that when he tries to escape from himself and project himself into, and give expression to, the passions and emotions of others, he feels hampered. When he plays the quartets of Mozart and Beethoven, though enthralled by their genius, he still cannot shake off his own personality—his own ideas come through those of the masters and, carried away by his prodigious dexterity, he has to watch himself to keep from injecting into these works some of his own tours de force . . . so that he often passes without transition from the role of an incomparable artist to that of a musical prestidigator performing tricks of surprising mastery but of questionable taste." Fétis was even harsher. In the works of others *"il ne s'y éleva point au-dessus du médiocre. L'art de Paganini ne s'appliquait pas à toute musique quelconque; c'était un art tout spécial dont il était le seul interprète; art né avec lui et dont il a emporté le secret dans la tombe."*[26]

"Those who imagine that they will find the key of my secret—the application of which requires brains—in my tuning of the instrument or in my bowing, are very greatly mistaken," said Paganini with obvious reference to Guhr.[27] Was this sharp retort anger at finding himself misrepresented, or annoyance that Guhr had discovered and revealed something that he wished to remain a mystery? The question is one for the psychologist rather than the biographer and, since one must forgo the impossible task of attempting to demonstrate the correctness of Guhr's expositions, the "secret" will no doubt continue to remain a favorite tilting ground for theorists. However, to deny Guhr all real authority, as is now the tendency, would be as wrong as to accept his theories and explanations as ex cathedra pronouncements, as was the practice in the past. He surely did not claim to be other than "a good guesser and a persistent man," but in the course of several months of uninterrupted intercourse, centering exclusively on music, added to his curiosity, his trained ear for detail, his tenacity of

[25] According to Professor Edward Dent in Grove's Dictionary (3rd ed.) "it was admitted that Chopin did not excel in the interpretation of music other than his own," so this circumstance, upon which Fétis laid so much weight, was not peculiar to Paganini.

[26] Fétis, *Notice biographique,* 79.

[27] Schottky, *op. cit.,* 282.

purpose, and his analytical German mind, he could not help seeing more than men like Fétis, Chorley, and others who judged
Paganini solely from the concert platform. To what extent Paganini's own disclosures furthered or baffled his designs is of course
another question. The Maestro's character, as we know, was exceedingly complex and all his acts—even his most impulsive—were
influenced by the darker, secretive motions of his irrational passions. If he regarded Guhr's doctrine as heretical, he perhaps felt
that he was not answerable for ideas that had been misunderstood,
and so was not called upon to set the public straight. Sivori, the
only person who could have passed valid judgment on the theories
expounded in "Paganini's Art of Playing the Violin," seems to
have accepted them; at all events, so far as can be ascertained, there
is no record of his ever having questioned or rejected them.[28]

To Dr. Bennati, the physician, the secret lay in the fact that
"Nature or work, or both together, had formed his body to meet
the specific requirements of his chosen instrument and in a manner
that another cannot imitate at will."

Just note how he picks up his violin and places it in position—note the
occasional position of his arm, and then tell me an artist who can imitate it! Who, for instance, in order to produce certain effects can almost
cross one elbow over another on his breast? Would this have been
possible if instead of being thin he were as stout as Rossini? Then another thing that greatly facilitates his playing is that his left shoulder
is more than an inch higher than the right, which, when he is standing
with his arms hanging at his sides, makes the right arm appear much
longer than the other. In addition, there is the elasticity of the shoulder
tendons and the ligaments uniting the hand with the forearm, the
carpus with the metacarpus and the phalanges with each other. His
hand is of normal size but it is so flexible that he can double the natural
span. Then without altering the position of the hand, he can bend the
upper joints of the fingers of the left hand (that touch the strings) in a
lateral direction (i.e., laterally to their natural flexion) with the great-

28 After Paganini's departure and while working on his book, Guhr composed a
work based on some Paganini themes, wherein he applied his theories of the Maestro's method. (*Erinnerung an Paganini.*) After the latter's return, Guhr performed
the work at a concert. "Paganini [wrote the Frankfort paper] heard this unusually
artistic work and was astonished. He told us that Guhr had very skilfully applied
all the distinctive characteristics of his method." Guhr then asked Paganini to play
a duet with him at a forthcoming concert so that he could demonstrate his achievements, but Paganini graciously declined.

est ease, precision, and rapidity. . . . It is also impossible to find a more sensitive hearing. He understands what one says—even in a low voice—at a very great distance, and the tympanum is so sensitive that he experiences real pain if anyone speaks loudly near him and from the side. He is therefore obliged to stand directly in front of his interlocutor. The sensation is much stronger on the left side, which is nearer the violin. No ear is more adapted for the reception of sound waves.[29]

Goethe, for one, was extremely impressed with Bennati's theory.

Goethe to Zelter, June 9, 1831.
He sets out in a very clever way how the musical talent of this extraordinary man, through the conformation of his body, through the proportions of his members, was predetermined, favored, in fact compelled, to bring forth the incredible, the impossible. He leads us back to the conviction that the oganism in its determinations produces the most singular manifestations in the living creature. Since I have still a little space, I will jot down one of the most profound sayings left us by our forefathers: *Animals are taught by their organs.* Now if we consider how much of the animal still remains in man and that the latter has the faculty of teaching his organs, one returns again and again to this intriguing train of thought.

Modern opinion, however, is less ready to accept Bennati's theories. Dr. Géza Révész, former professor of musical psychology at the University of Amsterdam and an acknowledged expert in the field, and Professor Pietro Berri of Rapallo subject this famous *diagnostique* to a searching appraisal in the light of their own specialized experience.

Bennati's statements [wrote Révész] regarding the relationship between the physical conformation of the body and musical capacity are without the slightest scientific foundation. Furthermore, they are directly contradictory to the findings of experience. There is no perceptible physical characteristic that would correlate with talent and much less with certain distinct types of talent. Bennati would first have had to produce evidence that certain physical characteristics were present in all great executant musicians and that these same characteristics were lacking in the musically untalented. Only when he could have

[29] The Italian violinist, Francesco Sfilio, and the Calabrian phrenologist, Biago Miraglia, also stressed the importance of Paganini's tactile sensitivity in the development of his gifts. Cf. "L'opinione del frenologo Biago Miraglia sul talento della Musica," *Revista Italiana Musicale,* Vol. 40, No. 5/6 (1936), 500.

demonstrated such a relationship would he have had the right to apply this procedure to Paganini also. However, this in no way contravenes the fact that we occasionally perceive special physiognomical traits in outstandingly gifted men and women. These psychosomatic manifestations, nevertheless, are not congenital. They are not inherent in the physical constitution but have gradually developed as the result of intensive intellectual activity. In the history of human intellect, one finds far more cases in which these traits are lacking than cases (Haydn, for instance) where they are found. Yet even when existent, these perceptible signs by no means point to a specific talent (music, representational art, science, etc.) but only to talent as such, or more correctly, to the presence of inner concentration and the capacity for labor in the pursuit of high intellectual aims. Race also seems to play a role in this. One finds personalities with interesting features and external traits more often among the Romance people than among the Germanic races. A type like Paganini could only have been an Italian or a Spaniard. Bennati's ideas are a wholly outmoded anthropological prejudice—a point of view that is completely out of date today. False assumptions and theories, strange to say, are very difficult to eradicate —for example, Lombroso's theory that a causal nexus exists between insanity and genius. This nonsense lasted fifty years in spite of all evidence to the contrary, and one still finds it among the laity when one encounters an exceptional person with certain abnormal traits.

Today Bennati's arguments [wrote Professor Berri] are of merely historical interest. But he has very intelligently grasped the nexus between the physical organism and the violinist's posture, the first either favoring the second, or the second favored by an exceptionally inventive faculty that effects changes in the physical constitution and adapts it to the violinist's requirements. In Bennati's opinion physical constitution and intensive training were the basis of Paganini's great expertise, enabling him to wander with rare ease in the ambit of transcendental technique. Posture in playing and other nonscholastic procedures, the method of achieving amazing effects with a minimum of fatigue, little secrets of the great secret, are perhaps nothing other than intuitions in the pure and simple field of physiology.[30] (That is, the harmonious application of the most elementary laws of neuromuscular physiology.)

All these efforts to seek the "riddle of Paganini," the "secret of his mastery," in his fingering, the position of his left hand, the flexibility of his muscles and ligatures, his tuning, his bowing, his "fury of unconscionable labor," and other material resources of

[30] Berri, *op. cit.*, 75.

his art, miss the real point of the argument. His emulators and admirers forget that he was a historical phenomenon like Leonardo da Vinci, Michelangelo, Shakespeare, Dante, and the rest of that "illustrious company irrevocably destined to superb consummations." Would knowledge of how Leonardo mixed and applied his colors produce another Leonardo? Would awareness of how the poets wrought their magic lines produce another Dante, another Shakespeare, or has the most thorough acquaintance with Beethoven's compositional technique ever produced another Beethoven? The continuing effort down the years (usually on the part of moderate talents) to reduce Paganini to the stature of a practiced artificer whose dexterity is of the tangible, earthy order capable of imitation by any industrious disciple runs close on the pathetic. For as Codignola says, *egli nacque sommo,* like the other great ones of this earth, and no amount of study of his presumable devices, of his tricks of technique, his fingering (should the mystery ever come to light) will produce another Paganini till Nature, with the help of some cryptic star, "elaborates another of the species." One must continually keep in mind that "there are magical names in the history of humanity—names that are like shaken lights or sudden chords of music. They are properly to be called magical because they make an indescribable stir in the mind and provoke excited responses, and awake the sense of wonder.... They are the names of the beautiful, the strange, *the kindred of the gods* [Italics added], of the people who pass easily into legend because we do not question them as to what they achieved while we ponder what they were."[31] Therefore, all attempts on the part of the less gifted to capture his mind, his spirit, his imagination in the material form of some slick technical device are inevitably doomed to failure for "genius must be born [as Dryden said]—and never can be taught."

In Germany there was no tendency to engage in pedantic criticism—the critics intuitively accepted him as a comet or other interstellar phenomenon and limited their comments to the enchantment of his playing, trying only to convey an idea of a music so stirring, so magnetic, so moving in its effect as to bewilder them. It was reserved to certain disciples of the French school to launch the esthetic controversy, though this remained for the most part in

[31] Rachel A. Taylor, *Leonardo the Florentine,* xv.

the realm of pure polemics and did not touch the general public, which was too overwhelmed by what they heard to indulge in technical discussions so obviously outside the sphere of the ordinary concertgoer's comprehension.

ii

It is now time to return again to the Maestro's daily round, his plans, his problems, and his pleasures. Although it is unwise to indulge in vain conjecture, a study of existing documents still leads one to surmise that between the concerts in Bamberg and Nuremberg, he canceled for some reason a date in Würzburg, to which the manager took vigorous exception. After the little Munich argument when he agreed "to respect his dates in future," he evidently consented to reconsider his impulsive action and on January 14 signed a contract for a concert there on February 19 at a guarantee of 1,000 florins, which was sufficiently enticing to persuade him to put business before pleasure.

Paganini to Marquard George Seufferheld, February 15, 1830.
An agent from Würzburg came to see me and since I was not in a position to refuse to give a concert in that city inasmuch as I had practically promised to do so, I must leave the day after tomorrow and shall therefore be unable to dine with you tomorrow as arranged.

Another date that was evidently hanging fire from the original itinerary was Aschaffenburg, but here, despite the Munich agreement, he again ignored his obligations and the morning after his Würzburg concert, instead of going on to Aschaffenburg, where he was due to play next day, he returned "by express diligence" to Frankfort, thus disappointing another public that was all prepared to hear him. "Some interest must be holding him in Frankfort [read the cancellation notice], which is of greater importance to him than the exploitation of his rare talent."[32]

Paganini to Germi, February 11 and 15, 1830.
I've finished the concerto in D minor and have begun another in F minor, which is going to be my favorite; but I've no time to finish it since I must still orchestrate the other, and I have to go to Paris, leaving

[32] The letter to Seufferheld was one of the exhibits in the Paganini-Curiol suit.

here the first of next month. I've also written for the G string a sonata in B flat with variations, which I still have to orchestrate. I'm lazy, but the cold weather is letting up. Tomorrow I absolutely must go to a ball to which I've been invited by His Excellency, the Austrian Minister, and I plan to dance a waltz with the most charming of the ladies. These beauties are stirred by romantic sentiments. . . . How's my mother? I hope to hear that she's recovered. . . . (Later). This is to let you know that I went to the aforesaid ball but didn't dance. However, I shall surely dance at the Russian Minister's fete next Monday. On Wednesday, the twenty-fourth,[33] I'm giving a concert in the theatre to satisfy all these ladies who are crazy to hear me before I leave for Paris. I shall leave the beginning of next month after I have orchestrated the aforesaid grand concerto, I hope, and the sonata for the G string with variations on a theme of Rossini's. I'm going to engage a good Italian servant, who is reputedly honest and speaks French and German very well. For Paris I shall have with me a certain M. Curiol with whom I made a tour of Germany. But I don't trust him, which is why I should like to get rid of him. Scatizzi is said to be very honest, capable, and energetic in my interests.[34] It will be well to write to me to Paris at the Hotel Princes, rue de Richelieu, No. 109. All the important people go there and the Meyerbeers are now stopping there. All the Paris papers are saying beautiful things about me. . . . My adorable Achilles is now almost over his cold and sends you a tender kiss.

Although his statement that he "was leaving for Paris" had no more factual basis than similar pronouncements in the past, this time there was undoubtedly method in it—in short, it was one way of ridding himself of Curiol. But the latter had done all the necessary spadework for the tour in western Germany and he had no intention of allowing the Maestro to drop him overboard and take on an outsider; nor was he disposed to let him disregard these obligations since this might react unfavorably on himself. Poor, frustrated, and depressed, he therefore turned the case over to a law-

[33] *Paganini to the Intendant:* "I have the honor to inform you that I agree to the conditions that you have had the kindness to propose to my business agent, M. Curiol, with regard to the concert I am planning to give. The receipts will be divided as follows:—I am to receive three-fifths of the total proceeds, the remaining two-fifths going to the theatre, which agrees to defray therefrom all the necessary expenses of said concert. After M. Leerse has stated that the projected ball will not take place on Wednesday, the twenty-fourth, there is no longer any obstacle to my concert on that date. Will you therefore be kind enough to notify the daily papers as soon as possible?"

This letter formed one of the exhibits in the Curiol suit.

[34] Scatizzi was acquainted with Rebizzo.

yer, Paganini on his part engaging as his counsel a Dr. Reinganum, to whom he gave a power of attorney on March 9, so for the time being there could be no question of his leaving Frankfort.

No information is available regarding the exact nature of the argument, or the outcome of the litigation, except that since Paganini's luck always deserted him when in contact with the law, once more he apparently lost the case, with the result that he was again without a manager. The incident was evidently common gossip in Frankfort, where the sympathy of the public was unanimously with Curiol, so that an increasing number of persons absented themselves from the Maestro's concerts till at the concert of April 26 (his ninth in Frankfort) his two-thirds share of the receipts amounted to only 225 thalers.[35] Of this unfortunate occurrence, the Frankfort correspondent of the *Allgemeiner Musikalischer Anzeiger* (Vienna) had the following to say:

One of the contributory causes of this fiasco was perhaps a legal suit which Paganini's former traveling companion and business manager was forced to bring against him in the local courts and in which the plaintiff had public opinion on his side, the public being well acquainted with the case. One point worth mentioning is that the presence of this artist in Frankfort has caused the authorities to prohibit local journalists from engaging in any controversy, especially regarding local incidents. At the time of Paganini's debut, someone protested in the newspaper against the fantastic statements of a panegyrist, which the latter sharply rebutted. This resulted in the aforesaid interdict.

Throughout the rest of Lent, Paganini remained quietly in Frankfort, carrying on "his gallant affairs" and working intermittently on his new compositions till it came time to set out on the projected tour. Guhr usually gave his annual benefit concert on Good Friday but this year postponed it till Easter (April 11) since the Maestro "as a special favor" had consented to play two numbers in return for "half the receipts," so in these circumstances Easter Sunday was, of course, the more propitious date. This was the concert at which Schumann heard him for the first time. He was then studying law at Heidelberg University and as soon as he

35 Paganini played his Fourth Concerto for the first time at this concert (April 26, 1830). He played it also in Kassel and Hamburg.

learned that Paganini was to play, he and his friends Theodore Toepken, Weber, and Hille, taking advantage of the long Easter holiday, hired a one-horse carriage and drove over to Frankfort to hear the artist of whom his future father-in-law had so often spoken. "Easter Sunday! [he noted in his diary]. In the evening Paganini; was it not ecstatic? Under his hands the driest exercises flame up like Pythian pronouncements!" Besides the thrill of the Maestro's playing—long anticipated and magnificently realized—the excursion eventually proved for him a very fruitful one since it led to his transcriptions of a number of the Capricci—his Op. 3 and 10.[36]

At the end of a fairly quiet winter, Paganini may have welcomed the two months' tour as a pleasant change of scene, but nonetheless he could not have been in a very conciliatory mood, though he must have seen that his late "agent" had arranged a very satisfactory itinerary. Proceeding from the numerous invitations received from different theatres, Curiol first followed the Rhine and then the principal trunk roads so that the Maestro could travel by water and by diligence without the need of covering long, unprofitable distances or of extending the tour beyond eight weeks, which made it possible to leave Achilles behind with his housekeeper rather than to subject the lad to the discomforts of travel, which had resulted the previous autumn in a protracted and serious illness.

In the preliminary negotiations Curiol seems to have tried to obtain a minimum guarantee, it having come to Paganini's ears that Lafont's net receipts in Cologne amounted to only five francs. When the time came, however, and he no longer had the support of an experienced agent, he was willing to gamble on his reputation, and as a result came out surprisingly well by taking almost everywhere two-thirds of the net receipts.

iii

The tour opened in Coblenz on May 12 and on the fourteenth he played in Bonn, in the old theatre on Vierreckplatz, where he had the assistance of Professor Breidenstein and a modest orchestra, the receipts in both places amply meeting his demands.[37] Although

---

[36] De Saussine (*op. cit.*, 126) writes that "Vieuxtemps heard him in Frankfort." This is incorrect. Vieuxtemps states quite clearly in his autobiography that he heard Paganini for the first time in London in 1834. He was then a boy of eleven.

these small Rhenish towns could have contributed very little to his glory, or even to his wealth, they frequently provided some memorable encounter or experience that figured later in the memoirs of the period and have left us a picture of the highly romantic atmosphere within which he moved, and the ardent adulation he inspired in the most unexpected quarters. (cf. *Memoirs* of Wilhelm Smets as a typical example.)[38]

After two concerts in Cologne (May 16 and 18)[39] and one in Düsseldorf (May 19) he played in Elberfeld on the twentieth, which left him plenty of time to reach Kassel by the twenty-fourth, the day before his scheduled concert. However, he had such an enthusiastic reception in Elberfeld that he decided to give another on the twenty-second, which left him barely thirty-six hours for the journey to Kassel, one place where it was imperative for him to be in perfect physical trim.

In January when several of the papers announced his imminent departure for Paris, Spohr wrote (January 16) to express his great regret that Kassel was not to have the pleasure after all of hearing him. Could one not induce him to honor his recent promise and still visit them before he left Germany for good? Paganini let three months go by before replying and then on April 25 dropped Spohr a note saying that they might expect him "within the month" and

[37] Carl Heinrich Breidenstein (1796–1886), music director of the University of Bonn.

[38] Wilhelm Smets (1796–1848), only son of Sophie Schröder by her first husband, Johann Nikolaus Smets, an actor whose stage name was Stollmers. Smets was then priest in the little town of Hersel, not far from Bonn, and had heard much of Paganini from his mother and half sister, Wilhelmine Schröder-Devrient. In describing the effect of Paganini's playing, he wrote that he was seized with a great desire "to break out into loud sobs," yet could not bring "forth a single tear." Several months later, he was chatting with Guhr in the Hotel Weidenbusch in Frankfort, when Paganini came to call on his sister. When he was announced, the three went out into the lobby to greet him, and Smets, to everyone's surprise, "broke out into uncontrollable sobs, which greatly astonished Paganini. . . . He could not understand that upon Smets' suddenly coming face to face with the man whose magic playing had so shaken his nerves six months before, the pent-up tears finally gushed forth." Smets was well known as a writer and at the time of his death was canon of Cologne Cathedral.

[39] Franz Hartmann (1807–57), a pupil of Friedrich Schneider in Dessau and of Spohr in Kassel, was a member of the Cologne orchestra at the time of Paganini's visit. He later told a story to the effect that during the rehearsal Paganini filled the snuffbox of one of the older members of the band "with real Parisian snuff," which the old fellow surreptitiously threw away, "thinking it might hold some satanic spell!"

asking if he might give his concert in the theatre. Since this was a matter for the theatre directorate, Spohr referred his letter to the Intendant, who at once requested instructions from the Elector. (It is very likely that initial arrangements were conducted by Curiol, but it is now impossible to verify the fact since the archives of the theatre were destroyed by enemy action during the late war.)

Intendant Feige to the Elector, April 28, 1830.
After repeated invitations extended to the well-known violin virtuoso Niccolò Paganini, he has now sent word that he will arrive in Kassel within the month and inquires, at the same time, if he may give his concert in the Court Theatre. In asking if Your Royal Highness will accord him this permission, I beg to be instructed whether I should draw up an agreement with him along the following lines: at his first concert on May 25 he will receive the total receipts, but at the second, which falls on the first Whitsun holiday when as usual the concert is for the benefit of the theatre, he will receive only one half. As he will attract a large public, the theatre treasury will not suffer any loss.[40]

When the Elector returned the communication marked "Approved," Spohr wrote Paganini on the thirtieth to inform him that the Elector had graciously accorded him the theatre for two concerts (May 25 and 30) on the aforesaid terms, which makes it very clear that he was not "guaranteed" any stipulated sum, though in his original invitation Spohr may have held out to him the expectation that he might safely count on 1,500 florins. Be that as it may, Paganini promptly accepted both the terms and dates, very probably anticipating an amount similar to that he had received at other court theatres, plus a generous gift from the Elector. But by extending his stay in Elberfeld, he did not arrive in Kassel till a few hours before the scheduled concert on the twenty-fifth and since, furthermore, he had failed to communicate with the directorate after leaving Frankfort, the Intendant had to inform the Elector on the twenty-fourth that "after signing the agreement for the twenty-fifth Paganini had not yet arrived in Kassel, so that it was uncertain whether the recital would take place next day or the Thursday following."

Caught in this predicament, which was entirely Paganini's fault,

---

[40] While in Kassel, Paganini sat to the painter, Ludwig Emil Grimm, youngest brother of Jakob and Wilhelm Grimm of fairy-tale fame.

the directorate was unable to announce the concert, with the result that the general public was unaware that he had arrived in Kassel, so that at the first concert the audience was relatively small, the total receipts amounting only to 351 florins (about 200 thalers), which was appreciably less than he had received at other places on his tour. (Several writers have recently stated that he was greeted at both concerts by tremendous crowds, but Paganini's own notations in his diary and the ensuing correspondence with Spohr conclusively show that for the first concert the theatre was scarcely half filled.)

Leaving early the next morning for Göttingen, where he had a concert on the twenty-eighth and an appointment with the physician Dr. Himly, to whom Spohr had recommended him, he had ample time during the eight hours' ride by diligence to think over his experience and, failing to appreciate that it was entirely his own fault, he decided that it was not worth his while to return for another concert if his half-share of the receipts might be less than 300 florins. So, irrespective of his agreement, he dropped a note to Spohr informing him that he had changed his mind; he would not be returning to Kassel after all.

Paganini to Spohr, Göttingen, May 26, 1830.
Since the receipts of last night's concert did not amount to half the 1,500 florins guaranteed me in the letter of invitation addressed to me in Frankfort, I therefore beg to be excused from the second concert, which was to take place on Sunday next, the thirtieth, since it seems that the city is not interested in foreign artists. I should greatly appreciate a souvenir from His Royal Highness, if he would accord me such an honor, and I shall always be grateful for the privilege and honor of having been able to play in Kassel.[41]

To this, Spohr, as liaison officer, immediately replied, offering his sincere apologies for Kassel's poor showing on the twenty-fifth and promising him the entire receipts of the second concert as well as a "souvenir" from the Elector, who "was looking forward to the

---

[41] It was the custom of the German princes (who prided themselves on being generous patrons of art) to give a "present" to any visiting artist of Paganini's eminence who appeared in any of the court theatres, particularly if the receipts fell short of a reasonable figure. It is evidently to this that he was referring in his letter to Spohr and not to an honorary title, as assumed by Pulver, who accuses him of "tuft hunting."

pleasure of hearing him again."[42] For this reason he urged him to reconsider his decision and respect his original agreement.

Paganini to Spohr, May 28, 1830.
Appreciating the contents of your dear letter, your nobility of soul, the kind favors of the Directorate, the reception of such an indulgent public, and finally the great honor of being favored by His Royal Highness, I shall have the pleasure of once more seeing the fortunate city of Kassel. The concert here takes place this evening and with the diligence I shall be there tomorrow in good time for the rehearsal, as indicated. I shall be better able in person to thank you for the great kindness you have shown to your very obedient servant, etc. Pardon the haste—I'm off to rehearsal.

It is quite possible that when inviting him to play in Kassel, Spohr had held out hopes that had failed to materialize, which may explain his eagerness to adjust the matter and urge reconsideration of a decision which, had Paganini upheld it, might easily have been interpreted to his (Spohr's) disadvantage.[43] As for his personal reaction to the Maestro's playing, one can read it easily between the lines.

Spohr to Wilhelm Speyer, June 5, 1830.
I heard Paganini with the greatest interest in the two concerts he gave in Kassel. His left hand, the purity of his intonation, and his G string are admirable. In his compositions and his style of interpretation there is a strange mixture of consummate genius, childishness, and lack of taste, so that one is alternately charmed and repelled. In my own case the total impression, especially after frequent hearings, was by no means satisfying and I've no desire to hear him again. On the second Whitsun holiday he was my guest in Wilhelmshöhe and was in very gay spirits, in fact quite boisterously so. My *Faust* was given in the evening; he heard it for the first time and it seemed to interest him greatly.

As Spohr had foretold, the second concert attracted such a crowd that "the musical critic of the leading paper was unable to get in-

---

[42] The Kassel orchestra was composed of civilian and military musicians, all holding life appointments.

[43] De Saussine's statement (*op. cit.*, 130) that *"son ancien rival Spohr fait perfidement manquer un concert"* is without the slightest foundation. In a recently published English translation of Paganini's letter to Spohr, the phrase: *"alle grazie della direzione"* has been mistranslated as referring to Spohr's conducting. Paganini was acknowledging the generosity of the Directorate in according him the full receipts at the second concert. He was paying no compliments to Spohr.

side the building," the total receipts amounting to 857.16 florins. In addition, the Elector's "souvenir" of 250 thalers brought up the grand total to a little over 1,600 florins, or approximately the amount he had originally counted on.[44] And the stormy episode was over!

iv

Leaving Kassel on June 1, Paganini arrived in Hanover on the afternoon of the second in ample time to arrange his rehearsal for the following day and avoid a repetition of the Kassel contretemps. As this time he had taken the precaution of notifying Count Platen, court intendant, of the hour of his arrival, a large crowd was awaiting him at the diligence station, among them the retired "Inspector of Military Hospitals" George Harrys, who, upon learning of the Maestro's recent difficulties (which he attributed solely to the lack of a proper business manager), offered forthwith to accompany him to Hamburg and Bremen and relieve him of the task of dealing with the theatres. Probably not even Harrys would have pretended that this was pure kindness on his part, for as he was now earning his living by his pen, he scented here a splendid opportunity of gathering firsthand information of palpitating interest, something that, with his experienced journalistic touch and his previous military training in throwing an illuminating beam on insignificant detail, might easily supplant Schottky's biography, which was already selling briskly. Still smarting from the little Kassel tilt, the Maestro, after making inquiries regarding the person of this unexpected and welcome coadjutor and upon learning that he was staunchly supported by the Viceroy, at once dispatched a note to him, its style revealing clearly that he viewed the officious *Herr Inspektor* solely as an employee and of inferior social standing.[45]

Paganini to George Harrys, June 2, 1830.
I beg you and your son to give me the pleasure of attending my rehear-

[44] The order to the treasurer for the payment of 250 thalers was written personally by the Elector.

[45] Harrys' autograph collection contained only three autographs of Paganini: the letter to Harrys, a memorandum for a Hamburg concert on June 16, and his musical setting of Harrys' *Patriotisches Lied*.

sal and concert tomorrow evening because I have something to communicate to you. Hoping that you will accord me this favor, I remain, Your obedient servant, etc.

Informing Harrys that he was ready to accept his offer of assistance on the basis of his traveling expenses plus 2 per cent of the net receipts of all concerts during the term of their agreement, they signed a formal contract for the duration of three weeks, viz., from June 7 to July 1, Paganini thereby acquiring a temporary "secretary-manager," Harrys—the most exciting "copy" the country had to offer.[46]

v

The Viceroy (Adolph Frederick, Duke of Cambridge, brother of the Duke of Sussex, who in London was to prove a veritable friend in need during Paganini's preliminary skirmish with the British press) had been eager to welcome him to Hanover ever since his arrival in Germany,[47] so here, at any rate, he found everything in readiness. True, the orchestra could not compare with that in Kassel nor was the conductor, Heinrich Aloys Praeger (1783–1854), a second Spohr. But he found an excellent leader in Ludwig Maurer, while three other players, who also came in for a share of his *"Bravissimo! Siete tutti virtuosi"* were the cellist August Prell, the flutist Raphael Dressler, and the oboist August Kiel.

In addition to two concerts at the theatre, which were attended by enormous crowds from all the surrounding towns, he also played at the Viceroy's residence *Montbrilliant* and after the formal concert "did not disdain to play a simple Mozart quartet with the Duke, who, excellent violinist though he was, found it a little difficult to play second fiddle to Paganini's first since he played so fast that he did not keep the proper beat." However, the Duke's orchestra must have also found it "a little difficult" to keep up with such a spirited steed, since Harrys tells us that more than once he had to urge them on with a "Courage, Messieurs!" While Paga-

46 In his annotations to Conestabile's biography, Mompellio wrote that "Harrys followed Paganini across Germany for almost two years, probably from January 1829 till the summer of 1830." Harrys' Preface distinctly states that he was with the Maestro for three weeks and gives the exact dates.

47 Adolphus Frederick (1774–1850) was appointed to the viceroyalty of Hanover in November, 1816.

nini was undoubtedly aware that his new employee was systematically Boswellizing him and recording all his comments for posterity, he presumably looked upon it as an advantage, and in this respect Harrys did not disappoint him for, though he made no attempt to write a biography or even delve into the Maestro's past, he presented a charming close-up in which he described his habits, daily routine, and the myriad trivia that interested the general public, avid for any information that would throw light on such an enigmatic character.[48]

Born January 19, 1780, in Hanover, the son of Solomon Harrys, a Jewish banker of that city, Harrys lost his parents when he was still a boy and was sent by his guardian to Nantes, where he received his schooling and passed his apprenticeship. On his return to Germany in his early twenties he was baptized and in 1805 married Wilhelmine Kessler, daughter of George Albrecht Kessler, surgeon to the Hanoverian Court. There were eight children from this marriage, but only one son (Hermann) and three daughters reached maturity. Entering the army, Harrys rose to the rank of Inspector of Military Hospitals and in 1814 accompanied the Hanoverian troops to Brabant and Paris. Two years later when the hospital to which he was attached was closed,[49] he was retired at the age of thirty-six on a monthly pension of six thalers. From then on he devoted himself to literary work of a miscellaneous character (comedies, farces, poetry, short stories, etc.) till in 1831 he founded the newspaper *Die Posaune*, which was continued later by his son as the *Hannoverische Morgenzeitung*.[50]

He was therefore neither an "Englishman" nor a "polished diplomatic attaché who looked after the English interests at the Hanoverian Court," as Paganini's biographers have hitherto as-

48 Harrys' book was published by Fr. Vierweg and went on sale in December, 1830. It was "printed on fine vellum" and sold for 45 kreutzer.

49 *Communication from Adolphus Frederick, Hanover, January 22, 1816.* "In reply to the application submitted to us by Hospital Inspector Harrys, we have to state that since the hospital to which he has hitherto been attached is to be closed in the near future, his return to the same is not necessary; on the contrary, his services as Hospital Inspector and the emoluments that went with such service will cease the end of February of this year."

50 Among his published works were a Handbook of Military Songs, dedicated to the "brave Hanoverian Army"; *Das Kaiserbuch* (reminiscences of the Grand Army), published in Weimar the year of his death (1837); three comedies based on Scribe and Melesville.

serted; but nonetheless he was well equipped by talent and by temperament to acquit himself of the duties he had assumed, the rewards of which (for a person with his interests) far outweighed the disadvantages of a supernumerary position. He was not interested in the Maestro's famous "secret," as so frequently claimed, for he was neither an executant musician nor a professional critic. He was bent solely on journalistic plunder—in other words, he set out deliberately to obtain material for a book.

Leaving Hanover on June 7, they arrived, after a rough journey of eight hours, in the pretty little garrison town of Celle, where Paganini hoped to have a good night's rest. But his fame had either preceded him, or his companion, scenting the possibility of a lucrative concert, had passed the word along for he had hardly settled himself at a table underneath the trees in the garden of the pleasant little inn when he was visited by a local physician (Dr. Koehler) who "after long negotiations" finally persuaded him to give a concert next day, which, though the town was small, still enriched him to the extent of 275 florins, enough to cover the incidental expenses of his secretary and himself.[51]

After two more nights along the way, they arrived in Hamburg on the eleventh and that same evening Paganini attended a performance of Weber's *Oberon* at the Stadttheater, where his old friend Fräulein von Schaetzell of the Berlin Royal Opera was filling an extended guest engagement.[52] At his own concert next day he was assisted by an excellent orchestra of forty players and was stormily welcomed by such a crowd that Heine, on his own testimony, "could scarcely fight his way to a seat." For the Maestro's renown in southern Germany, together with the spate of articles and anecdotes that had been appearing in all the provincial papers, had whetted an already eager curiosity to hear this mysterious conjuror who (as Heine put it) "looked as though he had risen from the underworld. . . . Is that a living being who wishes to delight the audience at the moment of his dissolution, or is it a corpse that has arisen from the grave, a vampire with a violin who sucks, if not

---

[51] The contemporary accounts of this concert stated that since the town organist could not read from score, Paganini "hastily wrote out a piano accompaniment for his three works, but upon rehearsing them next morning, one of them did not suit him, so he interrupted the rehearsal long enough to rewrite it."

[52] The new Stadttheater in Hamburg had only been opened in 1827.

the blood from our hearts, at any rate the money from our pockets?"
But Hamburg left such speculations to the poets and flocked in
equal numbers to his two following concerts, thereby increasing
his bank roll by approximately 5,000 florins, not counting what he
garnered at some private engagements. As Heine said, all doubts
and mystification ceased as soon as "the wonderful master raised
his violin and drew the bow across the strings—"such music as the
ear has never heard—such music as the heart alone can dream when
one rests at night in the arms of the beloved;" which undoubtedly
came nearer to penetrating the enigmatic secret than all Guhr's
learned disquisitions.

After two years spent in inland cities, to be once more in a large
and busy seaport acted like a tonic and though, as Harrys testified,
he had not arrived in the most golden of moods, owing to the uncertain weather, he soon threw off his depression and made the
rounds of all the theatrical entertainment the city had to offer,
from Weber's *Oberon* and *Freischütz* and Winter's *Opferfest* at
the Stadttheater to the magician and prestidigitator Olivo,[53] who
was exhibiting his *magischen und equilibrischen Künsten* in a
booth outside the Altona Gate. At this season of the year the Hamburg weather was as usual frequently overcast, but nonetheless he
enjoyed his daily *"passeggiata* under the green trees of the Jungfernstieg."

He wore a dark grey ulster [Heine tells us] which, reaching to his feet,
makes him look very tall. His long black hair fell in tangled locks about
his shoulders and formed a dark frame for the pale corpselike face in
which care, genius, and hell had engraved their indelible marks. Alongside him tripped a tubby little man, quaintly prosaic, with shriveled
ruddy cheeks and wearing a light greatcoat with steel buttons—his manner insufferably friendly, bowing in all directions, meanwhile casting
furtive, anxious glances at the mournful figure walking solemnly by his
side, lost in meditation.

In addition to these activities, Paganini took great pleasure in
the company of Joseph Rudersdorff,[54] leader of the orchestra, and

---

[53] Harrys wrote that the magician was Bartholomäus Bosco (a famous magician
of that day) but this was evidently a slip in memory. There is no record of Bosco's
appearance at this time, while Olivo's announcements were in all the papers.

[54] Rudersdorff's daughter Hermine was a famous singer in her day. Born in 1822,
she was only eight years old at the time of Paganini's visit.

also "patiently gave up two hours a day for three consecutive days to sit to the painter, Heinrich Gottfried Krug,[55] and later to Peter Lyser,[56] who was bound on the same errand and who, according to his own testimony, "executed such a satisfactory portrait that Paganini kissed him in sheer delight, declaring the likeness to be the best that he had ever seen."[57] In view of Lyser's notorious reputation for prevarication, this statement must be accepted *cum grano salis* despite the fact that Heine (at that time Lyser's boon companion) felt that he was the "only man who really succeeded in transferring Paganini's features to paper."[58] It is a little difficult to share Heine's enthusiasm, though Lyser undoubtedly had a natural gift as a cartoonist and illustrator, in which field his artistic activities predominantly lay. He had taken a few drawing lessons from L. Fischer in Schwerin but on the whole he was self taught, both in drawing and in music, and so was incapable of producing more than the sketchy improvisations of the cartoonist.

Ludwig Peter August Lyser was born in Flensburg (then belonging to Denmark) in 1803, son of the actor Friedrich Burmeister. Two years after Peter's birth, his mother obtained a divorce and married Friedrich von Mertens, member of a distinguished family in Cleve, who, after serving for some years as a Prussian officer, had the misfortune to kill his opponent in a duel and had to leave the army, after which he assumed the name of

55 Heinrich Gottfried Krug (d. 1847) was not only a well-known painter, but a sculptor, architect, and lithographer. Singer lists two Paganini portraits by him, one engraved by C. Pabst, the other by A. Bucheister.

56 "This painter [wrote Heine] was always a queer chap. In spite of being deaf he was an enthusiastic music lover and if he were close enough to the orchestra he could apparently read the music from the faces of the musicians and judge the quality of the performance from the movements of their fingers."

57 After Paganini's appearance in Hamburg, the publisher Campe commissioned Ludolf Christian Wienbarg (1802–72), who wrote under the pseudonym of Ludolf Vineta, to write a short biography of the Italian artist. Since he was not a musician, Wienbarg avoided any discussion of Paganini's art, which did not satisfy his publisher. "Campe [wrote Lyser] then fetched me from the Alster Pavilion on the Jungfernstieg, where I was drinking punch with Paganini and Heine, and commissioned me to write the musical notes to the work." Lyser's contribution appeared in Part II under the title *"Fantasien aus B moll."*

58 Lyser made two drawings of Paganini, one a profile, and one full length, one of the originals bearing the annotation: "Drawn by Lyser, with pen, in three minutes, on June 16, at K's—standing." The "K" is of course Krug. The present whereabouts of the Lyser drawings is unknown.

Lyser and devoted himself from then on to a theatrical career, first as actor and later as manager of the Altona National Theater.

Young Lyser was extremely versatile, showing from his very early years a decided musical, artistic, and literary bent, all three gifts being furthered and encouraged by his stepfather, who had him taught the violin, flute, and piano, and the English, Italian, and French languages, which he later spoke with ease and fluency. At the age of sixteen, he unfortunately lost his hearing as the result of a severe attack of grippe, which put an end to his musical and stage career and tended eventually—along with a restless, unsettled disposition—to scatter his abilities so that, while a prolific writer in several genres, he never achieved the standing that might have been expected from his versatility and native gifts. After a short period at sea as cabin boy, he was employed at various times as scene painter, actor, and free-lance writer, and after settling in Hamburg in 1827 served as musical critic on the Hamburg *Freischütz,* a local scandal sheet that largely owed its popularity to his criticisms. In the opinion of his biographer, Friedrich Hirth, his reviews, as well as the articles on music he contributed to Pappe's *Lesefrüchte* and Georg Lutz's *Originalen,* all showed "considerable originality," though "by nature and by talent he was more of a clever copyist than an original thinker." In 1836 he married the well-known improviser, Caroline Leonhardt, by whom he had two daughters and a son,[59] but after their divorce in 1844 his life suddenly seemed to have lost its moral prop so that from then on he constantly played a losing game with fate. Reduced at last to living in a miserable cellar room, he managed to eke out a wretched existence as a public amanuensis and writer of shoddy farces for obscure suburban theatres till, sinking more and more into hopeless penury, he died in the Hamburg hospital at the age of sixty-seven (1870), the Municipal Almshouse having to defray the expenses of his funeral.[60]

Through his connections with the publisher Campe at the

[59] Lyser's son Gustave was first an actor at the Carl Schulze Theater in Hamburg. He was also one of the founders of the German Social Democratic party.

[60] Lyser's biographer Hirth gives a list of his works, which fills forty-five pages and includes romances, novels, fairy tales, travel diaries, poetry, dramatic works, essays, memoirs, musical criticisms, political articles, etc.

height of his career, he was commissioned to illustrate a number of books but his work was all more or less in cartoon style (like his well-known sketch of Beethoven). On one occasion, for example, he received an order to illustrate a new work of Immermann's, but the author rejected his drawings as unacceptable and transferred the commission to Wilhelm von Schadow and his pupils,[61] one of whom was indubitably the author of the famous pen sketches auctioned by Meyer & Ernst in Berlin in December, 1931, and since erroneously attributed to Lyser.[62] In addition to the fact that all his drawings and sketches were destroyed in the great Hamburg fire of 1842,[63] and that these particular pen sketches indubitably were the work of a superbly trained artist (who first saw the figure unclothed), one shows Paganini with Rebizzo, while in another he is astride Achilles' rocking horse, indicating quite clearly that they were made in Berlin in the spring of 1829 since Rebizzo returned to Italy in August and in the summer of 1830 Achilles did not accompany his father to Hamburg. The main reason for associating them with Lyser is that when the collection (which belonged to the Hamburg violinist Heinrich Bandler, leader of the Hamburg Philharmonic Orchestra and the Bandler quartet) was put up for sale after Bandler's death, the Berlin dealer published a catalogue in which each sketch was accompanied by an appropriate citation from Heine's *Florentine Nights,* thus giving the impression that they were made in Hamburg.

vi

While Harrys was less of a poet than his colleague Heine, his recordings—though on a lower literary level—are more factual and detailed and therefore of greater value to the serious biographer. On the whole he seems to have been a loyal and faithful chronicler, drifting into exaggeration only once or twice at most, as when he

[61] Among some of the leading artists of the Berlin school were Wilhelm von Schadow, Karl Wachs, Karl Jolbe, Adolf Henning, and Begas.

[62] Sketch No. 10 has the word "Schadow" in the left-hand corner, not as artist's signature, but evidently an annotation, which would indicate some connection with the artist. This collection consisted of twenty-seven sketches. Twelve of the original sketches (Nos. 1, 2, 3, 5, 6, 10, 11, 17, 18, 23, 24, and 26) are now in the Library of Congress, Washington, D. C. The whereabouts of the other fifteen is unknown.

[63] Friedrich Hirth, *Johann Peter Lyser,* 105.

quoted the amount of Paganini's earnings (for which Codignola, for example, censures him). But he no doubt derived this information from the Maestro, who was never averse to adding something to the brew if he felt that he might thereby heighten the effect and contribute "to his glory." The reason why he never referred to Harrys' book (so far as can be learned) is probably because Harrys carefully eschewed all hyperbole though he was by nature a born toadier and lion hunter, as shown by his autograph collection (now in the Kestner Museum, Hanover) which consists almost exclusively of the ruling heads of European royal houses. Pandering to this ingrained quality, he persuaded the Maestro to set to music a poem, *Quel jour heureux,* which he wrote in honor of William IV's accession to the throne as King of Hanover, probably anticipating some special recognition from the Viceroy. The work (scored for solo voice, chorus, and piano) was published by Bachmann & Nagel in Hanover in 1830, presumably without Paganini's knowledge, since he never mentioned it, though he may have viewed it as an autograph and of no particular importance. As a further indication of Harrys' pretentiousness, in receipting for his fee on the termination of their association (to which Paganini added in the margin *"Graziosa quietanza"*), he used a sheet of his old official stationery as "Hospital Inspector," thus giving his employer the impression that he was still "in the service of His Britannic Majesty."[64] However, from Paganini's complete silence on the subject of their association, we can assume that despite all these efforts he still regarded Harrys as a parvenu and not as a person "worthy of his friendship."

Nevertheless, whatever Harrys' little foibles may have been, later generations can be grateful to him for a profile of the artist caught from a side usually hidden from the public. With the sharp eye of the trained inspector, he observed every mood and action, saw him in full dress and *en pantoufles,* drew him out like a skill-

64 *Harrys to Paganini, Braunschweig, July 2, 1830.* "The undersigned Inspector of Military Hospitals in the service of His Britannic Majesty is very deeply grateful to Cavaliere Paganini for his kindness in entrusting to him the direction of his affairs in connection with his concerts between June 7 and July 2, 1830, in the cities of Celle, Hamburg, Bremen, and Braunschweig, for which he paid me 200,000 per cent in pleasure and 2 per cent in cash. I hereby state that I have not only been paid in full by the divinely melodious music of the distinguished artist, but that he has satisfied all claims that I might make upon him. . . ."

ful catechist, seized on every little trifle capable of further treatment in the practiced writer's crucible. Yet his gleanings, like his
guesses, were handled with due reverence, with the sympathy and
admiration of one who had succumbed to the fascination of the
Maestro's personality and who kept strictly within the unpreten-
tious framework he had set himself, with only here and there a
sally into a little broader field as Paganini warmed to his subject
and grew more communicative.

While traveling by hired carriage, post chaise, or diligence, as
the case might be, there could have been few moments favorable
for conversation, which probably pleased Paganini, who at this
time was not in a particularly expansive mood. Harrys, averse perhaps to admitting any aloofness on the part of his employer, attributed this seeming taciturnity to his anxiety for his health,
offering as evidence that he wrapped himself in his heavy fur-lined
coat even at that season and hermetically closed the carriage so that
no chance draft could reach him. In fact he had "such a mortal
terror of taking cold that he even wore a *beretta* in the house," no
matter what the temperature might be.[65]

After the first day, when his zeal was at white heat, Harrys seems
to have abandoned any serious attempt at conversation while en
route, since Paganini, in this unavoidable tête-à-tête with an inquisitive companion, replied mostly in monosyllables except when
the carriage chanced to strike a strip of sandy road[66] where he could
make himself heard without the strain of shouting. "I like to rest
when traveling," he said in explanation of his silence. "I get enough
noise in the cities." In Hanover, Hamburg, and Bremen, however,
he knew very little peace, for the moment word got abroad that he
was in the city, he was besieged from morn till night with callers;
some to pay their respects, others in idle curiosity; souvenir and
autograph hunters, indigent Italians, violin dealers, young prodigies, and all the host of the inquisitive who were accustomed to
swarm round such spectacular celebrities. "On some days [wrote
Harrys] fifty to eighty persons called at his hotel, while he was

65 Among Paganini's effects at the time of his death was such a little cap, "made
from his mother's wedding dress."

66 In northern Germany, particularly in the district between Hamburg and Bremen, bricks were used from very early times for constructing houses and paving roads
in this famous "sand pile of the Holy Roman Empire."

inundated with invitations to dinner, banquets, soirees, etc.," none
of which really interested him since his delicate health and lack of
teeth required him to follow a strict regimen and eat and drink
with moderation. For this reason he preferred to dine quietly in
his room, where he could slip into an old dressing gown, make himself comfortable in his own way, and escape, if only for an hour or
two, from the tension of spirit of the mortally diseased. Harrys
found him of a "strongly meditative turn"—he "would often spend
long hours alone in his room, sitting in an easy chair," harrassed
like Cervantes "by endless imaginings." (*"Son tantas las imagi-
naciones que me fatigen."*) Many times Harrys walked in on him
unawares to find him sitting in the twilight in a trancelike absorp-
tion, lost in melancholy broodings over his rapidly declining health
and the brief time still before him. If in physical pain, he never
showed it in the presence of outsiders, though the struggle to hide
his suffering from the eyes of strangers may well have accounted for
much of his irritability and impatience; for people are not inclined
to be benign when in acute physical pain. He longed for security
in his old age, were he fortunate enough to attain it, and to be able
"to sleep sound and breathe easy" when his earning days were over.
And this, rather than cold avarice, may explain his blistering irony
when any imposition threatened to delay or frustrate the achievement of his aims. Harrys, who obviously had a weakness for ceremonial effects, was naturally "astounded" that a "virtuoso of his
rank had neither a carriage of his own nor a personal valet" and
was, moreover, satisfied with the most modest appointments, re-
quiring only that "his room be so situated as to guarantee him
perfect quiet." According to Harrys' ethics, a person of the Maestro's standing should not economize too greatly; his fame demanded a more luxuriant setting than ordinary mortals. Although
Paganini was by nature never *amantissimo del lusso,* his secretary
was evidently able to impress him with the fact that certain ap-
purtenances were necessary for a person in his station, since upon
his return to Frankfort he at once turned his attention to the
acquisition of a valet and was never more without one. At best,
Harrys never found him very talkative, but "he was more so with
men than with women," though with the latter he was "always very
gallant," just as he was infinitely lovable and charming with little

children, like all his countrymen.[67] However, he absolutely refused
to put up with tiresome people, so if his callers stayed too long, he
dropped his surface affability and replied curtly to their sallies,
making no effort to conceal his boredom. If they still refused to
take the hint, he would rise abruptly and retire to his own room,
leaving Harrys to make the necessary excuses on the score of his
ill-health.

vii

The society of Hamburg and Bremen, like that of Frankfort, was
composed of wealthy merchants—a "whole Olympus of bankers
and other millionaires, of coffee and sugar gods" (as Heine put it)
—who supported very liberally the city's musical activities and if
they could not offer their famous guest the social background of a
court, they more than made it up to him by their enthusiasm and
"overwhelming hospitality." "If he had even attempted to accept
the invitations for dinners, banquets, etc. he received [wrote
Harrys], he would have had to have dined six times a day. . . .[68]
Luncheon engagements were especially distasteful to him" because
they deprived him of his regular siesta, so if for tactical reasons he
was unable to decline, "he merely nibbled at his food and as soon
as the repast was over tried to slip quietly away," since conversation
tired his throat and several hours in close, smoke-filled rooms were
apt to bring on a severe coughing spell. However, if he were in the
company of his compatriots or professional musicians, where he
could let himself go informally, his "secretary" noticed that he
dropped his customary reserve and took an active part in the conversation, spinning amusing yarns from his experience or drawing
on his imagination with far-fetched anecdotes. Here it may be said
for Harrys that he was far less gullible than Schottky and did not
attempt to perpetuate these gallant tales within the covers of a
book since, even with his much shorter acquaintance, he was quick

67 When Paganini was in Glasgow in 1831, he visited the dancing academy of a
M. Dupuis (who claimed to have been a former pupil of his). "To those who sought
the honor of addressing him [reported the *Glasgow Courier*] he was affable and
courteous and many of the ladies were gratified by the attention and caresses which
he lavished on their little offspring."

68 Moscheles' wife was a native of Hamburg, where her father, Adolf Embden, was
prominent in the cultural and social life of the city and seems to have secured for
Paganini "a lucrative engagement" that was immensely gratifying to him.

to recognize the egotist and *farceur*. If, on the other hand, anyone turned the talk to music, either in the desire to flatter him or draw him out, he at once withdrew into his shell and brought the conversation to a standstill. He enjoyed the vivid interchange of musical minds pooling their common knowledge, but he had no taste for conversation of the workshop with amateurs, and had an understandable horror of being forced to listen to dilettante performances, arranged either in the mistaken idea of paying him a compliment or in the hope of getting his verdict on the talents of some local prodigy. He was invariably kind and gracious if anyone sought his judgment or advice, showed him some composition, or asked his opinion of an instrument; but this in his eyes was straightforward dealing and not a wily stratagem.

As for diversions, Harrys could see that "the theatre was his favorite form of entertainment"; sacred music, too, exerted a very strong appeal. But he very frankly admitted that "he did not like German opera," probably because the language made it difficult for him to follow, and the subject matter and its form, as exemplified in Marschner, Spohr, Weber, and the *Singspiele* that were then the fashion, lacked the accustomed magnificence of the dialogueless aria-opera in the manner of the Italians. The work from which he derived most pleasure, among the current operatic fare, was Auber's *Masaniello* (an opera that Wagner also greatly admired) —perhaps because the theme, the struggle to throw off foreign rule, appealed to him subconsciously.[69]

Be that as it may, Harrys was firmly convinced that political events held little interest for him; indeed, he deliberately avoided the subject as though it were better left alone. The papers were then full of the unrest in Paris and its possible reverberations on the Continent; but under direct or indirect attack, he maintained an impenetrable reserve, which, as has already been suggested, may have been the result of some unfortunate experience in his youth, so that he was careful not to commit himself to strangers. Whatever may have been his early equalitarian enthusiasms when, like the other Genoese, he fell under the sway, and adopted the ideals, of

---

[69] Masaniello is the traditional name of the boy who struck the spark of rebellion against the Austrians in Genoa in 1746. In Prague, Paganini taught Achilles to sing some of the melodies.

the French Revolution, one feels that at this late phase of his career, if he were partial to any political structure, it was to a monarchy, though on the whole he sought the wine of life in neither politics nor religion. *L'esprit national* was not part of his spiritual inheritance, as witnessed by his attitude towards Metternich, though this, too, was perhaps traceable to other motives since it would be strange indeed if anyone in whom the spark of independence burned so brightly did not at heart desire it for his country.

The journalist in Harrys was immensely surprised to find "that mundane affairs in general did not interest him" and that he was seemingly indifferent to everything extramusical, whether politics, the public, or the picturesque. "He took no pleasure in the scenery round him, no matter how beautiful it was![70] If I called his attention to some lovely landscape, some fine old building, he would reply a little condescendingly: 'Yes, yes—very charming,' though he hardly deigned to glance at it." In his efforts to draw him out, Harrys failed to consider that a man like Paganini, marked by destiny to be a lifelong martyr to physical pain, was hardly in a condition to react with pleasurable interest to external things, especially if battling with the discomforts of a stuffy carriage or weary from a concert that had sapped all his vitality. During the twenty-five days of their association, he gave a public concert every third day (not including his private engagements), which kept him under constant strain. "On the day of a concert [Harrys wrote] he always took a long rest, usually lying on his bed in a darkened room, napping, or lost in thought, meanwhile consuming vast quantities of snuff.[71] Then as the concert hour drew near, he would quickly dress, take his violin from the case, tune it, and then carefully replace it. After this he would get his scores in order, his extreme nervousness manifesting itself in his counting and recounting the orchestral parts."

Harrys found him "almost always courteous"[72] but had a feeling

---

[70] In his copy of Conestabile's biography, Achilles Paganini added a marginal note with reference to Harrys' assertion that his father was indifferent to the beauties of nature: "An absolutely incorrect assertion. It's extraordinary how one can write such twaddle!"

[71] Codignola (*op. cit.,* 58) attributes the description of Paganini's actions before a concert to Fétis. Fétis, of course, took the passage over verbatim from Harrys, via Conestabile.

that he despised the common herd (as when he reacted with an impatient *"Que me veut cet animal?"* when someone in this stratum of society accosted him in German), though on the whole he took care to key his courtesies to his public.[73] Harrys also had much to tell of his personal vagaries, his diffidence, the absence of all fuss and glitter in the conduct of his life, a trait that was supremely characterized, in Harrys' eyes, by his very modest luggage, which "consisted solely of his violin case and a small dilapidated trunk" containing his few belongings, his jewels, manuscripts, and personal linen—as though he were a strolling player or some penniless *Stadtmusikus*. Having started out on life's pilgrimage with little impedimenta of property and therefore accustomed to "travel light," his tastes and needs had been fashioned by long habit and it was now too late to alter them, though even in the present day a virtuoso would hardly burden himself with more than two or three pieces of hand luggage for a six weeks' tour in western Germany. Harrys, however, evidently expected this opulent King of Fiddlers to travel, like all the local princelings, with a baggage train.

He was also singularly struck with Paganini's abstemiousness. If "they set out on their journey in the very early morning, he frequently fasted nearly the whole day, while at other times a bowl of porridge or a cup of chocolate constituted his breakfast, his supper consisting usually of a cup of camomile tea."

Many regard it as a crime [wrote Schottky on the same subject] that he eats so little, that in the morning he makes a cup of chocolate for himself in his room and goes so seldom to the table d'hôte. One gets the impression that he nourishes himself like Don Quixote, solely with pleasing thoughts, contenting himself with two small portions, which have to do for himself and Achillino. He never eats meat and in the evening limits himself to a simple soup without bread; but one must not forget that he has only just recovered from a long and dangerous

[72] According to Berlioz, Paganini once smashed a mirror in the foyer of a theatre on learning that the auditorium was not well filled.

[73] Paganini's Irish manager told the following anecdote, which illustrates this side of his character. When the aide-de-camp of the Lord Lieutenant of Ireland called on him to extend an invitation to dinner, he said: "This is a great honor; but am I expected to bring my instrument?" "Oh, yes!" said the delighted emissary. "As a matter of fact the Lord Lieutenant's family wish very much to hear you in private." "Caro amico," retorted Paganini with petrifying composure, *"Paganini con violino e Paganini senza violino—eccò due animali distinti!"*

illness. . . . If he were as miserly as people say, he would never engage two rooms at a hotel, drink wine, etc.[74]

Another "legend" laid at Harrys' door is the statement that "he never practiced"—a theory refuted by dozens of passages in his letters at all stages of his career. True, he heartily disliked the idea of anyone listening to him surreptitiously and, even when his public career was over, he habitually used the mute when playing in his room. But in the present instance he was no doubt well aware that his temporary secretary intended to put him in a book, so he deliberately gave him this impression "out of vanity," wishing to have the world believe (as De Ghetaldi observed in 1824) that "he never touched his violin except at his concerts and rehearsals."[75]

At rehearsals Harrys found him very "exacting" and impatient. If things did not go to suit him, he did not hesitate to indulge in a little robust invective, yet if the accompaniment only halfway met his requirements, he could be just as effusive with his praise. He always made a point of distributing and collecting the orchestral parts himself and, like every artist the world over, was immensely interested in the size of his audience, his first question on arriving at the theatre being, "Is there a large crowd?" If the answer were in the affirmative he would evidence his satisfaction, but should the contrary be true, he could easily fly into a passion or would cut short any intercourse with an abruptness and a harshness that revealed his nervous tension. Was this to be attributed to avarice? Not altogether. As has been said, the proud suffer as much from indifference as from injury and disgrace, so—though indubitably interested in the receipts—his pride and vanity may often have been the real offenders.

Like the rest of his countrymen, he had an immense liking for bells and tempests of noise, so that the forte passages could never be played loud enough to suit him.

In some places I've been criticized for employing too much *musica turca* [he told Schottky]; but I don't believe that I deserve this criticism. I only use it to fill in the gaps between my solo passages so that I can get my breath. . . . When I step out on the stage, I'm an entirely

[74] Schottky, *op. cit.*, 396.
[75] Fétis, *Notice biographique*, 79.

different person; an uncontrollable seriousness comes over me till the music carries me away and I follow whither it leads me, having no will of my own.[76]

But when the concert was over, he presented all the symptoms of a person recovering from an epileptic attack. He grew deathly pale, broke out in a cold sweat, and manifested hardly any pulse, while his eyes stared vacantly into space as though distracted. Quite naturally, like any sensitive artist, he was not always at concert pitch and was the very first to realize it. "If I were in Paris or London today [he would say to Harrys] I should never play." But the phase was only momentary. Once he was in contact with the public the required "electricity" returned as though by magic.

Harrys, like Anders in Paris, tried to defend him against the charge of avarice and meanness in his financial dealings, basing his judgment on his own personal relations, though statements of this nature carried very little weight with those determined to find a flaw in the Maestro's life or character to satisfy their personal envy. As De Ghetaldi wrote, "He is unbelievably avaricious, coldhearted, and sordid. He thinks only of himself. He despises mankind. He plays a part—and is delighted when he takes people in." "I told Professor Schottky many details of my life and he came nearer the truth than all the others," Paganini used to say, but Schottky readily admitted that he "by no means found him blameless—all the allegations of his enemies were true to some extent. A faulty upbringing, added to bitter experiences and fear of new disillusionments, often made him act in a tactless manner." Harrys, on the other hand, applied his colors with a kindlier touch. As far as he could see, the Maestro was a man of kindly disposition, simple and unassuming in his tastes, and possessing to a high degree the cardinal virtues of justice and fortitude—glad of heart, patient in suffering, generous towards those he cared for, stooping at times to a suppliant gesture but never a groveling one, instant in his sympathies yet never flaunting his generosities before men. That he evidently failed to appreciate the value of such testimony is probably due to the age in which he lived, which in general had a failing for more spectacular virtues.

[76] Schottky, *op. cit.*, 272, 275.

409

viii

Leaving Hamburg on the twenty-first, they arrived in Bremen on the twenty-third and put up at the Hotel Stadt Frankfurt, a popular hostelry in the vicinity of the Lindenwall. It was his original intention to give only one concert here since his time was running short; he had arranged to be away for only eight weeks and, besides, his contract with Harrys expired on the thirtieth. Further, having heard from Spohr of the excellent orchestra in Braunschweig and of the four famous Müller brothers,[77] whose father was *Hofmusikus,* he wished very much to play there, and all the more so since Harrys was an old friend of the theatre director, to whom he later dedicated his book. Next morning, however, it looked as though even one concert in Bremen was going to be impossible since in spite of Harrys' efforts he was unable to find a proper hall. The Stadttheater was then in process of renovation and one outer wall had been removed, but as one of life's amusing little ironies, who should Paganini find as the lessee of the building but his old friend from Leipzig, Bethmann, who again saw a fine chance to turn an unexpected penny by offering him the building, as it stood, for a rental of twenty louis d'or. This time the offer was accepted without argument, and extended to cover a second concert, the two appearances netting approximately 1,100 florins, which more than justified the outlay.[78]

Early on the twenty-ninth they then set off for Braunschweig, where the Maestro gave two concerts in the Ducal Theatre, though Duke Karl does not seem to have shown him any special favors, probably because of the political unrest, Braunschweig being one of the few places in Germany where the revolts took a more serious turn.[79] But he enjoyed himself, even without the anticipated "souvenir," and remained over a week, resting and recuperating after a strenuous three weeks with his extremely energetic manager. When he was about ready to board the diligence, he was fortunate-

[77] The four brothers (Karl Friedrich, Theodore, August, and Franz Friedrich) were all leaders of their sections in the orchestra.

[78] Since the theatre was temporarily closed, all the diversion that Bremen offered him was a sacred concert in the Reformation Kirche.

[79] Reverberations of the French July Revolution were felt in several German states and some additional local constitutions were granted, but autocratic rule remained untouched.

ly offered a place in the comfortable traveling carriage of a Braunschweig friend who had business in Wiesbaden,[80] and five days later
was home again in Frankfort after an absence of two months, during which he had played twenty-one concerts and added approximately 21,000 florins to his rapidly swelling bank account.

[80] Adolf von Scaden described contemporaneous traveling conditions as follows in
his *Berlin's Licht und Schattenseiten:* "We would advise anyone who does not have a
chest of iron, intestines of copper, and buttocks of platinum not to undertake a journey in the ordinary post chaise. . . ."

XVII. *HELENE 1830*

E molto difficile di trovare una donna che ami quanto Elena.
—PAGANINI.

IN GÖTTINGEN, Dr. Karl Himly,[1] the famous ophthalmologist, had advised his taking the "baths and waters at Baden-Baden" upon the conclusion of his tour and he probably would have gone south at once had not Baron von Eberstein (his Breslau friend) effectively convinced him of the virtues of Bad Ems for laryngeal and kindred ailments.[2] As Eberstein and his daughter Pauline were then in Ems, they may have invited him to join them and give a concert in this fashionable resort, which would afford him an opportunity of trying out the waters for himself and at the same time would give Achilles a little excursion down the Rhine. For after his long illness the previous winter, followed by a lonely spring when he had to be left behind with strangers, the youngster deserved a little treat—his first adventure on the water since he was old enough to notice things.

After a day or two in Frankfort, he took the steamer down to Coblenz and from there went by diligence to Ems, where he played in the Casino on July 24.[3] However, whether the waters disagreed with him or the resort was too quiet for his restless temperament, he remained only five days.[4] By the twenty-seventh he was already back again in Frankfort, after a concert in Wiesbaden en route. Then as soon as he had engaged a valet (one of Harrys' unacknowl-

1 Karl Himly (1772–1837) was one of the first German advocates of vaccination.

2 The hot alkaline springs at Ems, with their high percentage of bicarbonate chloride, were especially recommended for maladies of the respiratory organs, larynx, etc. Paganini's eyes were evidently giving him more trouble at this time than his larynx and related ailments.

3 Paganini's arrival was noted in the Ems *Kurliste*, No. 17, for the period July 21–25. While there one of the papers wrote that "the mere magic of his presence was sufficient to provide a fairly sizable audience for a traveling musician, when it became known that he intended to be present at the concert."

4 Codignola (*op. cit.*, 309, n.1) states that he "spent several weeks in Ems," where he "arrived the end of February after a tour of northern Germany," though he lists the correct dates of the tour on page 43.

edged services), he set off for Baden-Baden, where he arrived *felicemente dopo pranzo* on Sunday, August 1.

Paganini to Germi, Baden-Baden, August 4, 1830.
I've recently remitted the following sums to Arnstein and Eckeles, which represent the proceeds of various concerts over a period of about a month and a half in different cities, among them: Kassel, Hanover, Hamburg, Bremen, Braunschweig, etc.

Florins:	7,301.00	June 28
	8,200.00	August 21
	1,586.13	August 19
(*circa*)	2,104.00	August 20–29
	1,549.22	September 3
	20,740.35[5]	

I'm now here to take the waters and baths on the advice of the famous Professor Himly of Göttingen, and shall remain here all through September. Then I'm going to Holland on my way to Paris, where I shall pass the winter, hoping that by then the disturbances will be over. . . . I'm going to direct the Vienna bankers to transfer my funds to you and hope that you will have received them by the middle of September—if they don't lose any time. Therefore, please notify me in due course for my peace of mind, addressing your letter to me care of Signor Geronimo Panatti in Frankfort.[6] I would appreciate a line regarding the *Delizia* you're planning to acquire for me, or us;[7] and I already approve in advance anything that you advise in the matter. Lafont is here and came to see me and embrace me, but he evidently doesn't intend to play, as was hoped. Sunday at five o'clock I'm giving a concert with pianoforte in the reception rooms, the theatre being too small. Even when I appear in cities where I've never been before, the people recognize me and swarm round me as though I were the Befana.[8] It would be impossible for me to travel incognito unless I wore a mask. I shall write you later of my gallant affairs.

5 Paganini evidently took these figures and dates from scattered jottings in his notebook, which will account for the confusion.

6 Panatti was evidently a local banker who had business relations with Paganini's Genoa banker, Luigi Migone.

7 Germi was already negotiating with Count Castellinard for the Villa Gaione in Parma, though the deal was not terminated till April 9, 1833.

8 The Befana, according to an Italian folk legend, is an old witch who makes her appearance from January 1–6. On the last night, the eve of the Epiphany, wonders of all kinds take place—the trees are covered with fruit, animals bear young, rivers and fountains turn to gold, etc.

At this popular international resort and at the height of the season, there was no lack of diversion for a person whose nature demanded a certain quota of self-indulgence, so it was naturally more to his taste than quiet little Ems. In addition to the famous gaming casino,[9] there was a continual round of concerts, fetes, and other entertainment to occupy his leisure hours, though to his marked disappointment he found that "most of the French visitors had already left," owing to the recent tumults in Paris.

Paganini to Germi, August 30, 1830.
Your letter of the eleventh influenced my recovery from a terrific cold, for which reason I had to break off my cure of the waters and baths; and now it's too late and I must abandon the idea. Rebizzo! The name of Rebizzo is dear to me and Achilles is always talking of him. He lost the most beautiful moments of his life when he left me. The German beauties, who are over head and ears in love with me, would have delighted him also. His name is still remembered in Berlin, Warsaw, and elsewhere, and not a few young ladies ask after him, which is why I beg you to let me know where he is at present. . . . As for myself, I often think of marrying! In Frankfort, I asked the most charming girl to marry me. She's the daughter of a businessman, not rich, yet well off. However, upon reflecting that she is too young and too beautiful, and doesn't love music—or rather, has no music in her soul—so that she wouldn't be able to dedicate herself to me except under false pretences, I'm beginning to abandon the idea.

It would be far more fitting if I should marry another. This is the daughter of a famous (or rather *the* most famous) writer on jurisprudence in Germany (M. de Feuerbach), a knight of many orders, the intimate counselor of the King of Bavaria, and president of the city of Ansbach. His daughter, whose name is Helene, is a baroness, having married a baron three years ago—but not for love. She is passionately fond of music and sings extremely well. She came to Nuremberg to hear me and begged her husband to bring her again to my second concert. After having heard, seen, and spoken to me, she fell so much in love with me that she no longer knows any peace of mind and will die if she doesn't eventually get me. I've had the pleasure of knowing her nine months now. She has a nice appearance and a most excellent education. Her letters, of which I have more than twenty-four, are worthy of being printed and are inspired by a sentiment far surpassing that of Heloise and Abelard. I have them all in Frankfort and if you'd like to see them,

---

[9] The director of the Casino was Lieutenant Colonel Jacob Benazet, of the French National Guard.

I'll send you copies. In this young woman I should have a fine wife, Achilles an excellent mother. Meanwhile, read the enclosed letter.[10]

Upon its receipt I went to Ansbach, where, in order not to be recognized, I arrived at midnight and didn't go to the posting station but got out in the middle of the road, and under the assumed name of an architect of His Majesty, the King of Prussia, stayed three days at an inn without anyone remarking me, strange to say. The Baroness visited me there and I left again at night to return to Baden. I am so impressed by the sentiments of this lady that I must respect and love her. She has persuaded her father to get her a divorce in the hope of becoming my wife, and declares that she is ready to renounce all my wealth and wants only my hand! What do you say to that! It's very hard to find a woman capable—like Helene—of such love! True, when they hear the language of my music, the lilting cadence of my notes makes them weep. But I'm no longer young, no longer handsome. In fact, I've grown very ugly. Think it over and tell me what you think. She reasons like she writes. Her speech, her voice, are insinuating. She knows geography like I know the violin.

Before I forget, give my tender greetings to my mother. As for that fool brother of mine, give him similar greetings and in the way you think best. How's your violin? When I see you again I'll explain the *suonare parlante* to you. Lafont and his family came to my concert on the eighth and paid admission. Then he left and went back to France without playing here. He's not going to Russia this year so as to be able to enjoy my sojourn in Paris. That's what he told me.

Whatever may have been his reaction in the beginning, his ultimate handling of, and his future silence on, this passionate episode indubitably sprang from the same idealistic strain that found similar expression in his relations with his boyhood sweetheart, Eleanora Quilici. In none of his numerous affairs had he ever "offered homage to any of the great professional beauties" of the day, nor till he met the lovely Helene had he ever made a deep impression on anyone of a higher station. For she had all the advantages of education, birth, and breeding that his previous flames had lacked; which in itself excused his little spurt of vanity. However, when faced with a decision and the thought of having to maintain a standard far above his natural background and his own uninhibited instincts, his intuition warned him that he could not keep up the pace, especially since he sensed at once that he had evoked something deeper and more enduring than he had yet ex-

10 For full text of Helene von Dobeneck's letter, see Codignola, *op. cit.*, 314f.

perienced. So conscious of his own inner nature and sensible of his deficiencies, he may not have wished to impose a burden of this kind on a woman capable of such a feeling. He had known desire and passion, but he had no wish to know remorse.

It is clear that this charming, highly cultivated, unusually gifted and beautiful young woman, who had been forced by her dominating father to marry the vain and shallow Baron von Dobeneck, had, in her sudden wild infatuation, literally thrown herself into his arms. As his letter indicates, he was immensely flattered, and we may be sure that on her several visits to Frankfort and during the three days he spent with her in Ansbach, his golden courtesy did not stop with *un bacio in mezzo al palmo della mano*. Yet, ready though he always was to "mesh his soul within a woman's hair," he had now at forty-eight laid aside his youthful fervor so that there was no longer the old tendency, as in his younger days, to be swept off his feet by some sudden attachment. The old fires were already dying down, with the result that the snapping of any casual fetters left him with no abiding sense of loss. For as the perspicacious Harrys quickly noticed, he was essentially a lone wolf, with a genius for solitude—the fasting, the silence, the vigils were all inescapably inherent in his nature—everything in fact but discipline.

ii

Helene von Dobeneck, the most gifted and many sided of Feuerbach's exceptionally talented children, was also the most unfortunate. "Strange destiny! [wrote Anselm Feuerbach's mother]. This family, all so extraordinarily gifted and all of them unhappy; there is here no foothold, only a yawning abyss!" Although endowed far above the average as painter and portraitist, as linguist, writer, singer, and composer, Helene was coquettish and capricious by temperament, at times even hysterical, so that she never did full justice to her gifts. Falling madly—and as the future showed—irrevocably in love with Paganini, she obtained on November 14, 1830, a divorce from Baron von Dobeneck after a loveless marriage of four years, with the obvious expectation of becoming Paganini's wife. Did he encourage her in this? or did he use her marriage as an excuse for his reserve? It is, of course, possible that she did not attract him physically and that a *mariage de raison* with such an overwhelming passion frightened him. The point of view of the Italian peasant may also have influenced him. In other words, he may not have wanted to commit himself to marriage with a woman whose four years of childless marriage made it seem unlikely that she would bear children in the future. At all events, whatever lay behind his unresponsiveness, he seems to have made it plain to her before he left for Paris that her wish could never be fulfilled. Perhaps, too, religion played a certain role in his decision. Feuerbach was known as the "champion of the Bavarian Protestants" and the whole family was violently antipapist, so that they may have strenuously opposed Helene's conversion to the Roman Church, which created a religious gulf that Paganini could not overspan. Be that as it may, the abrupt shattering of all her hopes, together with Paganini's departure, brought on a severe attack of melancholia and since her brother Karl had twice tried to take his life in a short period of mental derangement (akin to melancholia), her father, after her recovery, sent her to a friend in Dresden, where she remained till the end of September (1831); then a few weeks later, accompanied by her brother Fritz, she too went to Paris, nominally to study singing with Manuel Garcia, who, according to the testimony of her contemporaries, "developed her beautiful and brilliant voice till, had she so desired, she could have been an ornament to any German stage." With the exception of a short period in Ireland as a governess in a private household, she lived for over a decade in Paris, where she and Béranger became fast friends and she set many of his songs to music. Nevertheless, despite her singing, her painting, and composing, Paganini was always uppermost in her thoughts and remained the great and only passion of her life. Indeed, she seems to have hoped up to the very end that she might win him after all, though we have no evidence that he ever saw her in Paris, or gave her any encouragement. When she learned of his death, she succumbed to another serious attack of melancholia and even had to spend some months in a sanitorium for the treatment of neurotics; then in 1847, while stopping at a Roman Catholic institution in Basel, "she slipped out unknown to anyone, threw herself into the arms of a monk, and became a Roman Catholic." She next declared her intention of taking the veil and, burning all Paganini's letters—which she carried with her everywhere—she entered the Benedictine convent Mariastein, near Basel, to serve her novitiate. Failing, however, to find in a religious life the peace of mind she sought, she abandoned the idea before taking her final vows, and from then on led a restless, unhappy existence, making religious pilgrimages to Rome and wandering from place to place like a lost spirit.

Henriette Feuerbach to Emma Herwegh, June 14, 1847.
For a long time we had no idea where Helene was; finally we got trace of her—she was living in a little village near Zürich. Her mother and brother have not yet heard about her conversion and I haven't the courage to tell my husband—with his excitable nature it might have serious consequences and I tremble every time her name is mentioned. . . . The only question is, how long is this wonder going to last?

Anselm Feuerbach to his mother, Rome, September 25, 1865.
Yesterday Morelli and I went to see Aunt Helene. The conversation was in Italian. She spoke very cleverly and was very kind, but it still made me very sad. She lives near St. Peter's in a very miserable little room, the simple bed festooned with rosaries. Every now and then in the evening I'll go to fetch her in the carriage and take her out to the Campagna.

Twenty-three years later she died at Treviso in her eighty-first year, after having lived there many years as a recluse.

Had Paganini really been searching all his "life for an ideal of womanhood that was a combination of beauty, grace, learning, taste, good family, etc," as his biographers would like us to believe, he had it here. But he did not choose to take it. Was the passionate Helene perhaps too brilliant for him? Was the atmosphere surrounding her too different from that in which he himself had been brought up and molded? Did the man with no detached intellectual resources within himself, one for whom quartet playing was his sole private recreation, fear her array of talents, her brilliant versatility? During the course of his career, his soul must often have cried out for understanding and affection, for someone to assist him in bearing the burden of life; but since he sought in woman only the satisfaction of his powerful sensual passions, he ultimately found the sympathy he craved in its three purest, ideal aspects: love for his mother, for his friend, and for his little son.

Meanwhile, summer was slipping into autumn and russet tints of every hue were already running up the hillsides as the Maestro, his mind saddened by his failing health and the realization that he "had worked only two months that year," strolled with Achilles up and down the flower-plotted alleys fringing Baden-Baden's little stream. Gloomy, self-absorbed and introspective, he went his lonely way, his face a little paler, the furrows a little deeper than they had been a year before. As Helene's picture flitted through his mind, he set over against her almost southern beauty—her dusky hair and languid eyes—the sparkling lustre of Achilles' future million, and at once banished all "thoughts of marriage" from his mind. For till this treasure was safe in Germi's capable hands, he would accept no permanent responsibilities that threatened to delay the attainment of this, his last, ambition.

iii

His stars, which in the past two years had swept him to the pinnacle of his fame, established the foundation of his fortune, and assured him his place among the Immortals, now on a sudden began to desert him, for his last four months in Frankfort can only be regarded as a personal *échec*. When he left on his spring tour, musical circles through sympathy for his late manager were anything but friendly and during his five months' absence Curiol's partisans had evidently not been idle. While his art had suffered no decline in popularity, in Frankfort as in Paris later, jealousy and maliciousness on the part of an envious clique, together with certain irritating traits in his own character, enabled those who were jealous of his earning power to prejudice the general public against him so that his erstwhile secretary was looked upon as the helpless victim of a foreigner's rapacity, he as an avaricious, ungrateful, perfidious churl.

Another circumstance that may also have contributed to his loss of drawing power was that he seems to have restricted his acquaintance (outside strictly professional circles) to the Italian and French colonies and the diplomatic corps—always a "touchy" matter in a relatively small town. Then, too, there were the inescapable effects of familiarity—the daily encounters in the streets, the cafés, and in the theatre had shorn him of his aureole of mystery, the most potent of magnets in that romantic age; so that outside a little band of devotees, the announcement of a concert, offering a program that by now all knew by heart, no longer exerted an appeal.[11]

Oblivious of these refrigerative processes going on around him, on November 8 he gave a concert with Carl Guhr in the salon of the Hotel Weidenbusch, which was seemingly intended as his formal farewell to Frankfort. Yet, despite this fact the response was less than lukewarm, as shown by his share of the receipts, which amounted to the paltry sum of 230 florins. After this "affront" it is quite possible that he would have shaken off the dust of this ungracious city and have left immediately, but Achilles suddenly came down with an attack of measles, which made it impossible for him to get away since the doctors advised against his taking the child on the long journey across the Vosges in the depth of winter till he had completely recovered. Weary and depressed from these buffetings of fate and perhaps emotionally upset by scenes with the overwrought Helene, who, as her nephew put it, was prone to "endless lamentations," it must have taken all his will power to prevent a total physical collapse. However, as the weeks passed and he recovered from his irritation at the inconsiderable response, he announced a farewell concert of his own on November 23, at which time "the entire receipts would go to charity." Moved no doubt with sympathy for his afflictions and touched also with remorse for having so ungratefully repaid the numerous hours of pleasure he had given them, Frankfort's music lovers now turned out en masse as in the good old days when even standing room was at a premium. Neither his notebooks nor the local papers reveal the amount of the receipts, but on this occasion he was probably not interested, his motive evidently being to show a thankless world that it was grossly misjudging him. As his vivid, darting eyes swept over the large assembly and his thoughts returned in memory to recent less flattering things, one can easily imagine the caustic smile that wreathed his gaunt and battered features. For to a person of his temperament it was surely sweet indeed to flourish his indifference like a bullfighter's cloak and reap the glory of one "who loved his fellow men." The satisfaction of such an aim achieved must have

11 The critics attributed the consumer resistance to the high prices. He was now a resident of Frankfort and should not charge more than the other local artists.

more than recompensed him for Frankfort's heartless raveling of his sorely stricken nerves.

To increase his wretchedness, he received about this time a letter from his friend telling of his brother Carlo's death on October 15 and of his mother's serious illness—a double blow that so unnerved him that it took him some weeks to recover. The inevitable reaction was to turn his thoughts to his own condition, and the melancholy that resulted alternated as usual with moods of arrogance, which engendered a far from fruitful soil for any enterprise.

Paganini to Germi, January 27, 1831.
The death of my poor brother, the obstinate illness of my mother, and the fact that I worked only two months last year have made me very sad. Moreover, my son's measles have delayed me but now that he has completely recovered, I shall leave on Tuesday, February 1, and after a concert in Karlsruhe and another in Strasbourg, shall go straight on to Paris, where I shall play during Lent, proceeding to London in the spring. This isn't the most favorable season, but since life is short, I shall try to lose no time, hoping to Heaven that I may have the pleasure of seeing you again before I die.

Karlsruhe threw a passing ray of sunshine on the gloomy picture, but the relief was only momentary.

Paganini to Germi, Karlsruhe, February 8, 1831.
I'm not going to tell you of the magic generated by my instrument at my concert here on the fifth. Today I'm leaving for Strasbourg and shall give a concert there. Then on to Paris, to meet their wishes and my own. At court yesterday, the Grand Duke, the Grand Duchess, and their four children entertained me for more than an hour in the most charming manner. I had promised them to pay my respects upon my return from my tour. . . . The room is full of people who have come to wish me a pleasant journey, and they bother me. *Addio*. With a tender kiss.

Leaving Karlsruhe on the eighth, he arrived in Strasbourg on the ninth and that evening was serenaded "by a large number of artists and musical amateurs." However, at his first concert he must still have been in such a highly emotional state that he could no longer control his nerves since he broke down twice and had to interrupt his performance till he had regained his self-control.[12] After a thorough rest his second concert six days later passed off without mishap, the orchestra in the meantime having been augmented by a number of "talented amateurs," which gave him more adequate support.

Paganini to Germi, February 19, 1831.
I can never give you an idea of the cordiality of these Strasbourg amateurs. In order not to be robbed at my two concerts in the theatre, a number of millionaire amateurs went to the box office to sell the tickets, and not only keep a sharp lookout but also check the exact receipts. . . . I'm leaving in half an hour for Paris, where they are impatiently awaiting me. I'll write you on arrival. . . . How's my mother? I forgot to tell you that not only at my first concert but at the second also I was crowned with garlands on the stage. I'm keeping one of my wreaths— very elegantly fashioned by two of the most charming young ladies here —amateur harpists—to place it on the head of my friend Germi when I'm fortunate enough to embrace you. . . . I was pleased with the remarks about me in the work of G. Imbert de Laphalèque. Read it.[13]

During his two years in Germany, his mind as usual was constantly racing down the highways of Europe and he was always on the point of taking off for Paris, for London, or elsewhere, with the result that the other European capitals were continually announcing his arrival, as they tried to keep pace with his movements. Although he had made a great deal of money since leaving Italy, he was quick to sense that Paris and London offered him more opulent opportunities, yet if his health were to continue to deteriorate, as it had recently done, there was no time to lose—he must first guarantee Achilles' patrimony, then, free from material cares, he could "return to southern skies to breathe once more the air of Dante and Petrarch" and enjoy himself in the *Delizia* that his friend was preparing for him. Home at last, his goal achieved, he would then be free to indulge the *farniente* that was one of the sweeter, suaver legacies of his hot Italian blood.

[12] His old friend Durand was evidently no longer in Strasbourg. The *Journal Politique et Littéraire du bas Rhin* of June 3, 1827, announced that the mayor of Strasbourg had appointed him conductor of the Municipal Theatre for the period 1827–28.

[13] Mompellio (Conestabile-Mompellio, *op. cit.*, 235) states that he was in Strasbourg twice, which is incorrect. Once he left Germany, he did not return.

It was therefore with high hopes and a sense of exhilaration that he set his horses across the Vosges,[14] prepared and ready to gain the last ruby in his diadem. As his carriage turned into the highroad, the portcullis fell once more on another stage of his career; but at this moment his mood was not prophetic. No inner voice warned him that he was on the threshold of the last decade of his eventful life; otherwise, he might perhaps have turned his horses southward with one of those quick impulsive decisions so characteristic of him, and have returned to a familiar shore. For the next nine years of life allotted to him were to bring him coronation—and crucifixion—a chronicle of triumphs and an intensity of suffering, spiritual and physical, that finds no counterpart in the entire history of music.

[14] On his journey to Paris he followed the route: Metz, Verdun, Chalons, Epernay, Meaux.